SPICE & WOLF

Lawrence
A merchant traveling with Holo, he plans to turn a huge profit by smuggling gold.

Holo
Lawrence's traveling companion, her true form is that of the wolf-god of the harvest.

Norah
The shepherdess of Ruvinheigen, she's aiding in the plan to smuggle gold.

Liebert
A man from the Remelio Company, he's been entrusted with funds from the company's master, Hans Remelio.

Introduction

Lawrence, having fallen into the Latparron Company's devious trap, has devised a scheme to reverse his fortunes by smuggling gold. Will he—along with Norah the shepherdess, who needs money to open her seamstress shop, and the Remelio Company, which itself is on the verge of total ruin—be able to succeed in their desperate gambit...?

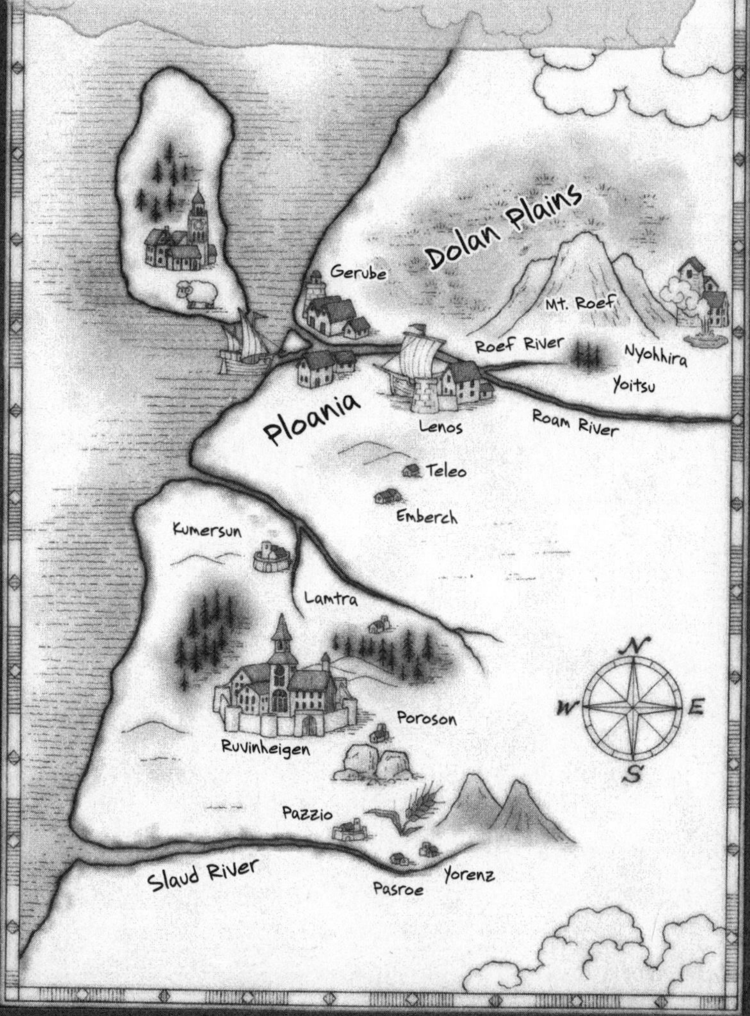
Dolan Plains
Gerube
Mt. Roef
Roef River
Nyohhira
Yoitsu
Ploania
Lenos
Roam River
Teleo
Emberch
Kumersun
Lamtra
N
W
E
S
Poroson
Ruvinheigen
Pazzio
Slaud River
Yorenz
Pasroe

Map illustration: Hidetada Idemitsu

SPICE & WOLF

CONTENTS

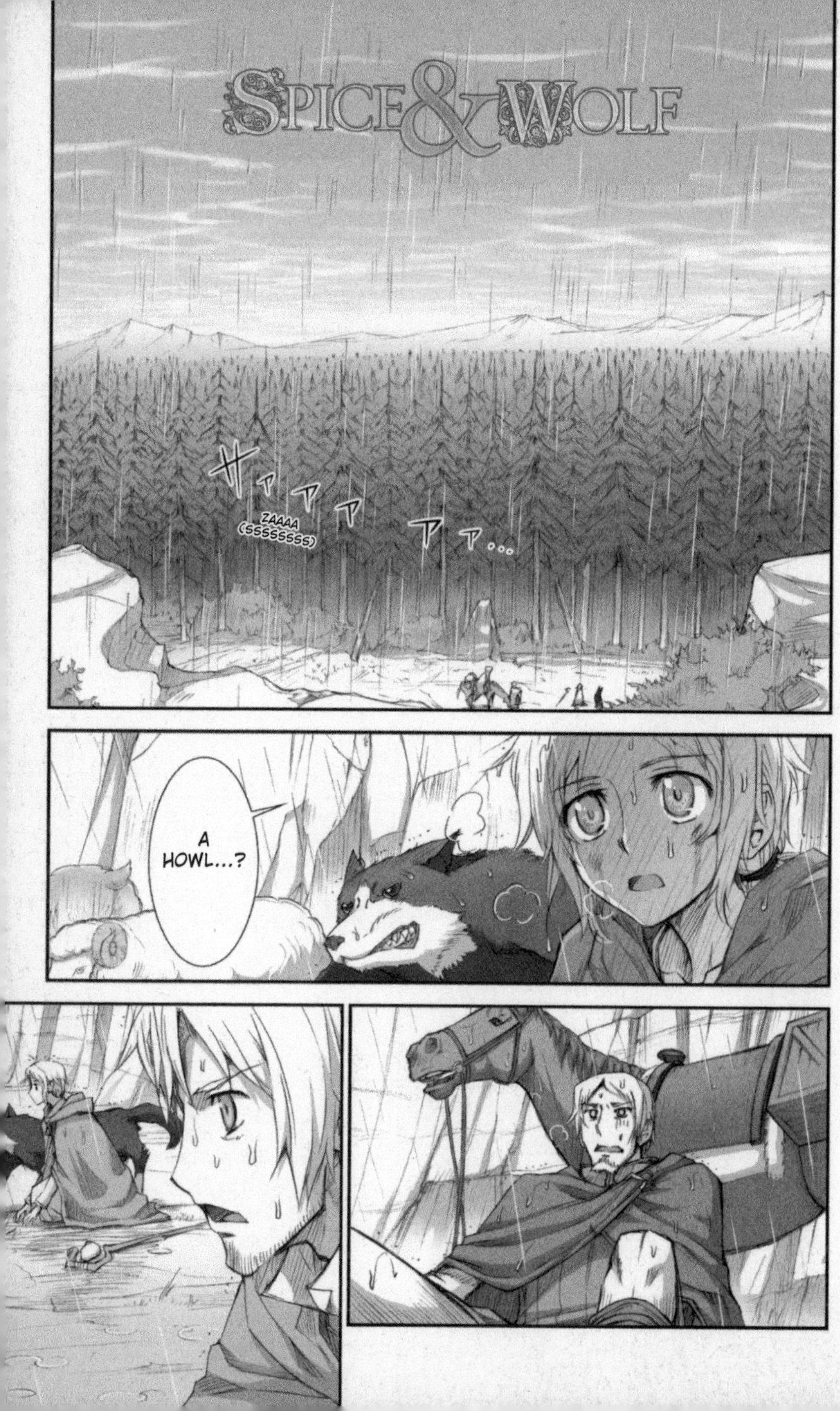
SPICE & WOLF
ザァァァァァ…
ZAAAA (SSSSSSSS)
A HOWL...?

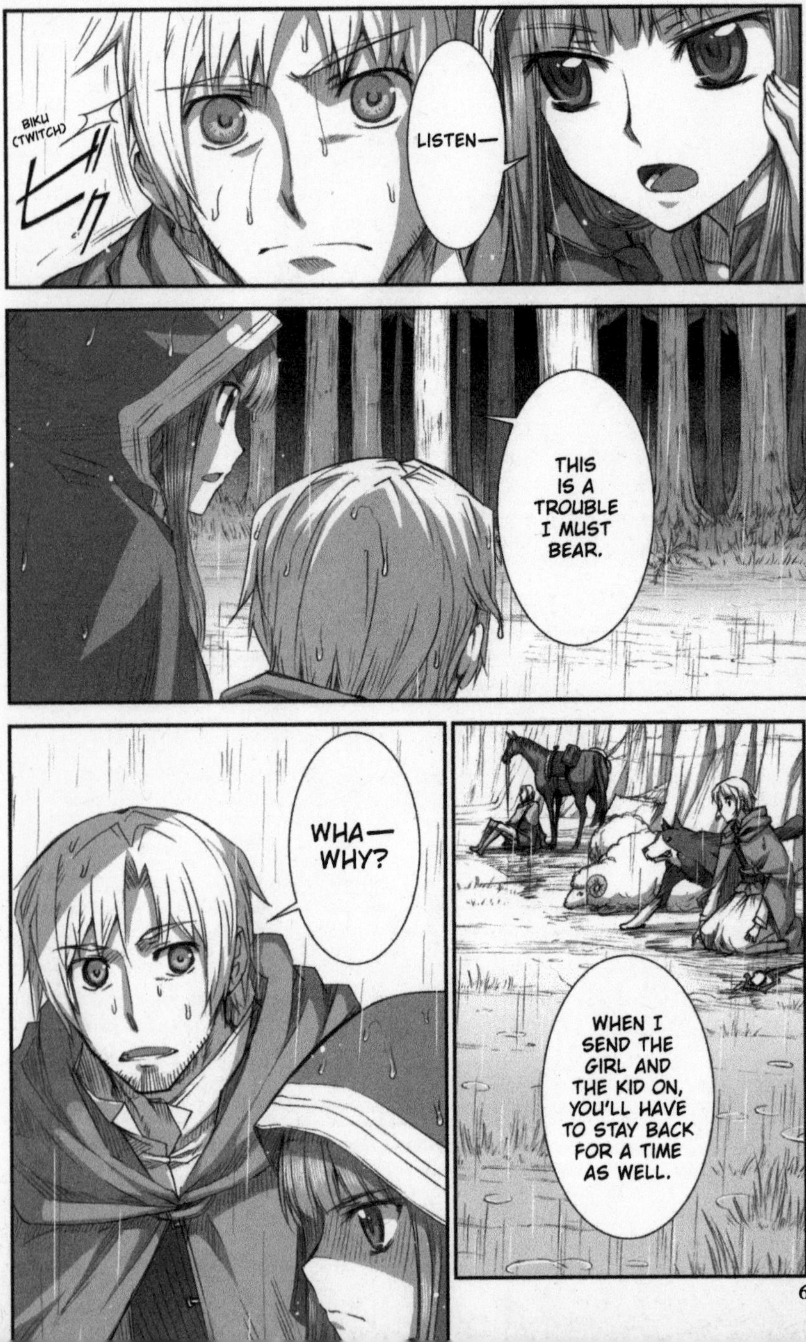
BIKU (TWITCH)
LISTEN—
THIS IS A TROUBLE I MUST BEAR.
WHEN I SEND THE GIRL AND THE KID ON, YOU'LL HAVE TO STAY BACK FOR A TIME AS WELL.
WHA— WHY?

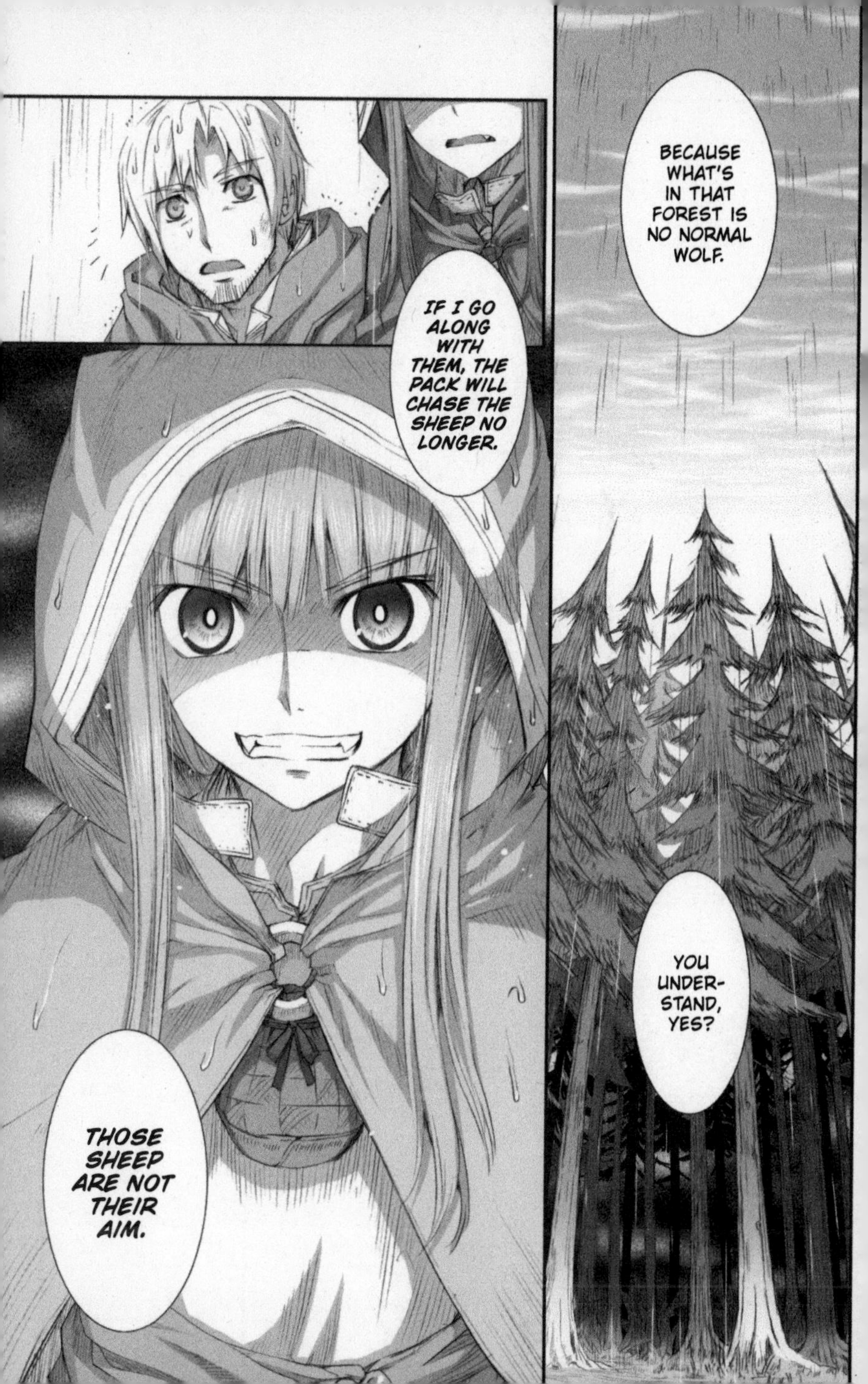
BECAUSE WHAT'S IN THAT FOREST IS NO NORMAL WOLF.
YOU UNDER-STAND, YES?
IF I GO ALONG WITH THEM, THE PACK WILL CHASE THE SHEEP NO LONGER.
THOSE SHEEP ARE NOT THEIR AIM.

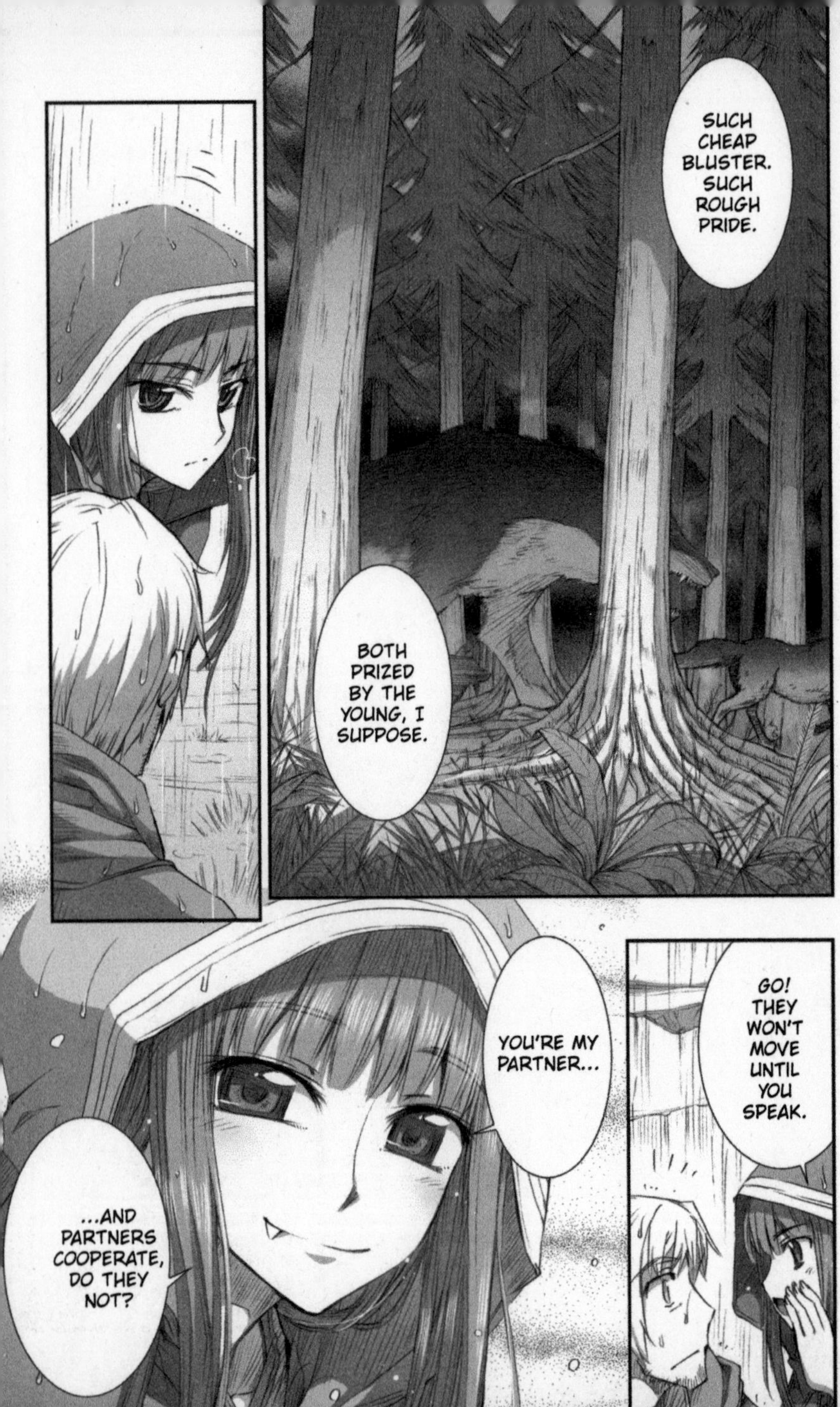
SUCH CHEAP BLUSTER. SUCH ROUGH PRIDE.
BOTH PRIZED BY THE YOUNG, I SUPPOSE.
GO! THEY WON'T MOVE UNTIL YOU SPEAK.
YOU'RE MY PARTNER...
...AND PARTNERS COOPERATE, DO THEY NOT?

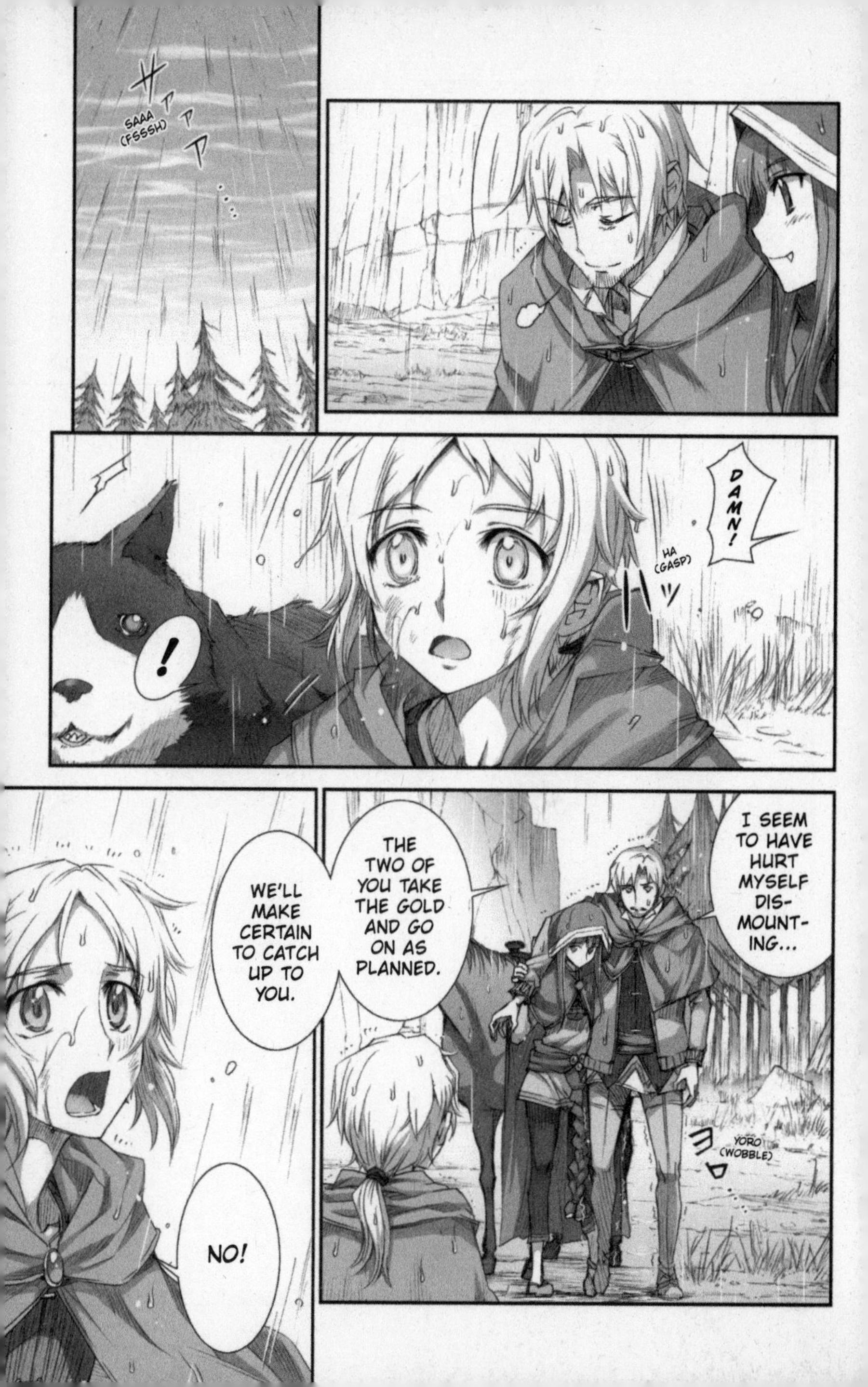
SAAA (FSSSH)
DAMN!
HA (GASP)
!
I SEEM TO HAVE HURT MYSELF DIS-MOUNT-ING...
THE TWO OF YOU TAKE THE GOLD AND GO ON AS PLANNED.
WE'LL MAKE CERTAIN TO CATCH UP TO YOU.
YORO (WOBBLE)
NO!

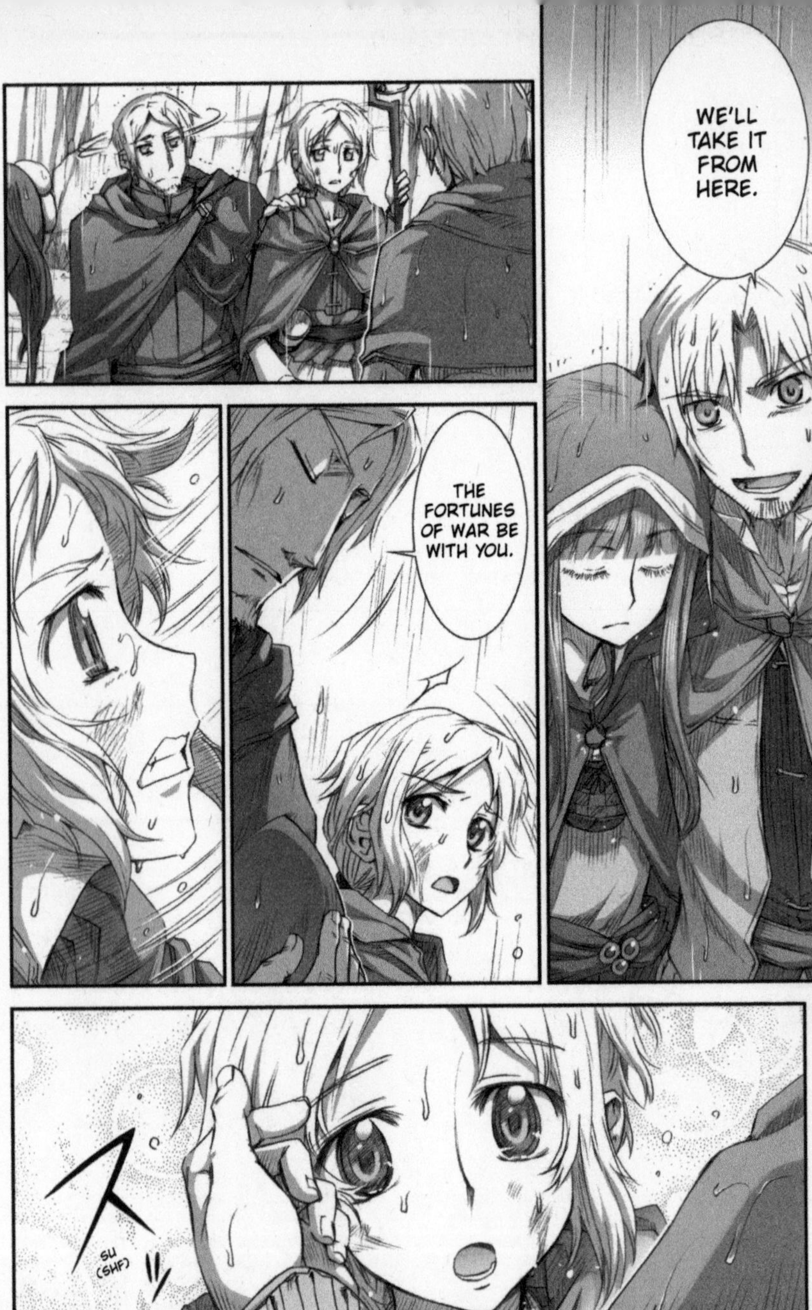
WE'LL TAKE IT FROM HERE.
THE FORTUNES OF WAR BE WITH YOU.
SU (SHF)

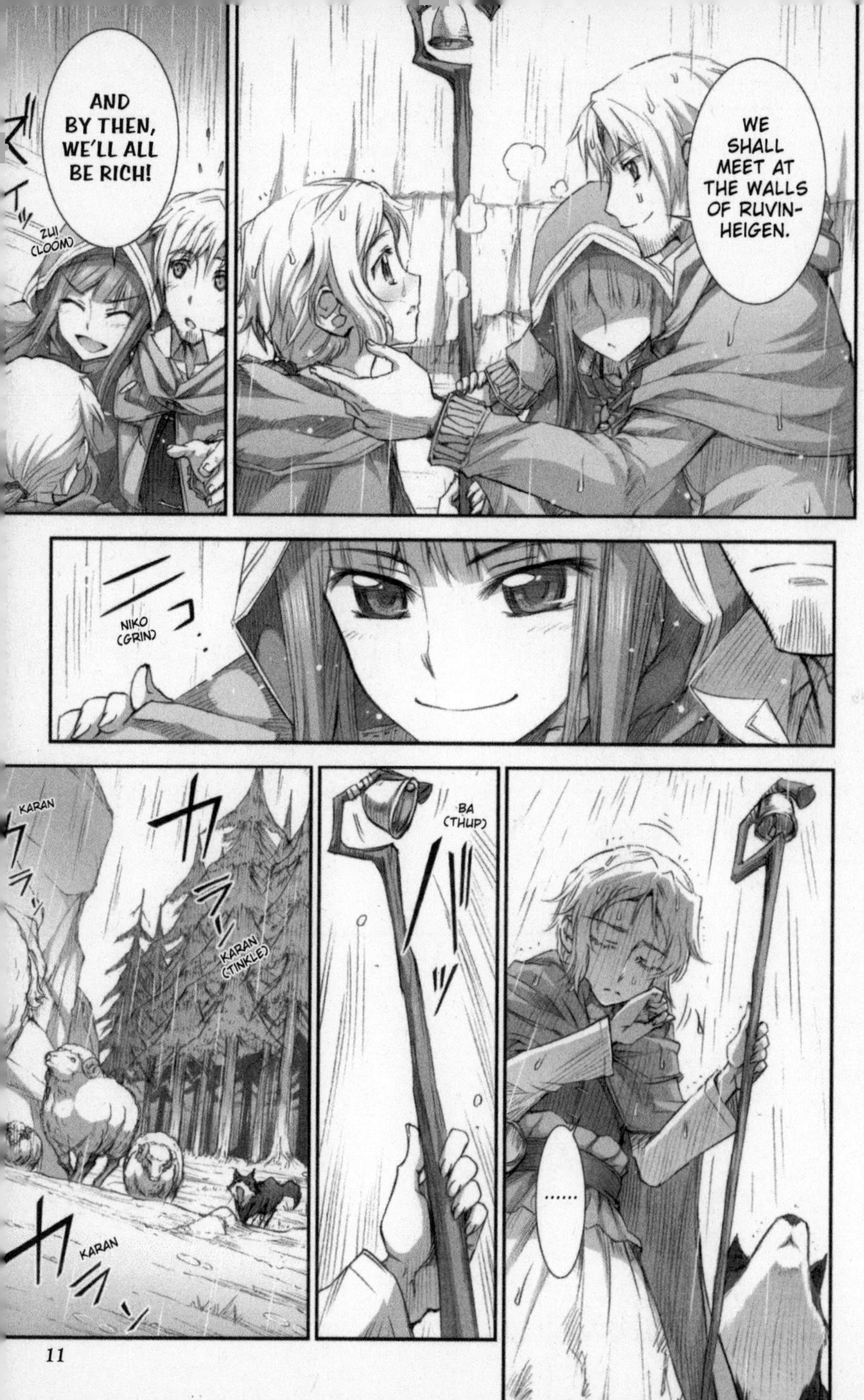
WE SHALL MEET AT THE WALLS OF RUVIN-HEIGEN.
AND BY THEN, WE'LL ALL BE RICH!
ZUI (LOOM)
NIKO (GRIN)
......
BA (THUP)
KARAN
KARAN (TINKLE)
KARAN

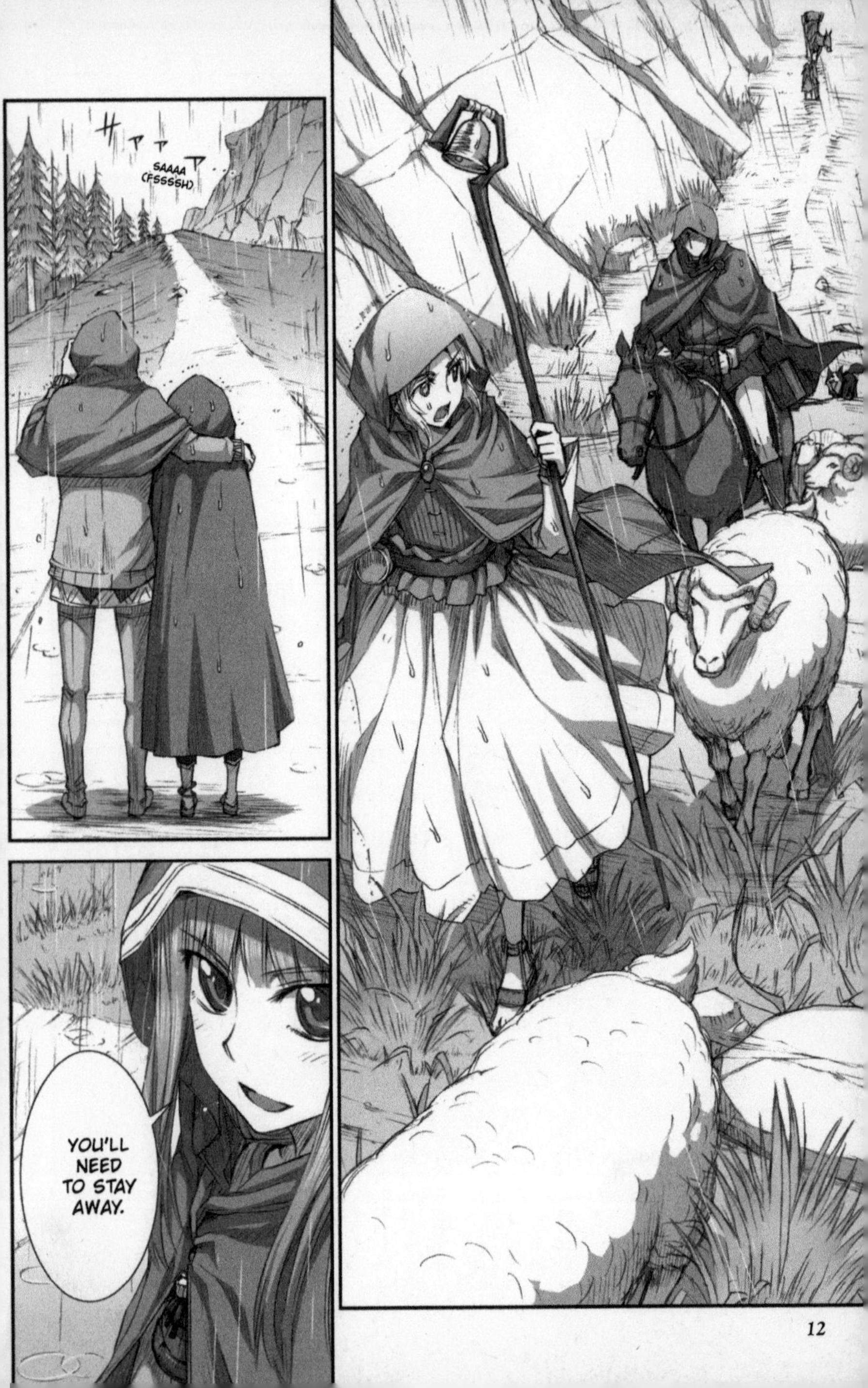
SAAAA (FSSSSH)
YOU'LL NEED TO STAY AWAY.

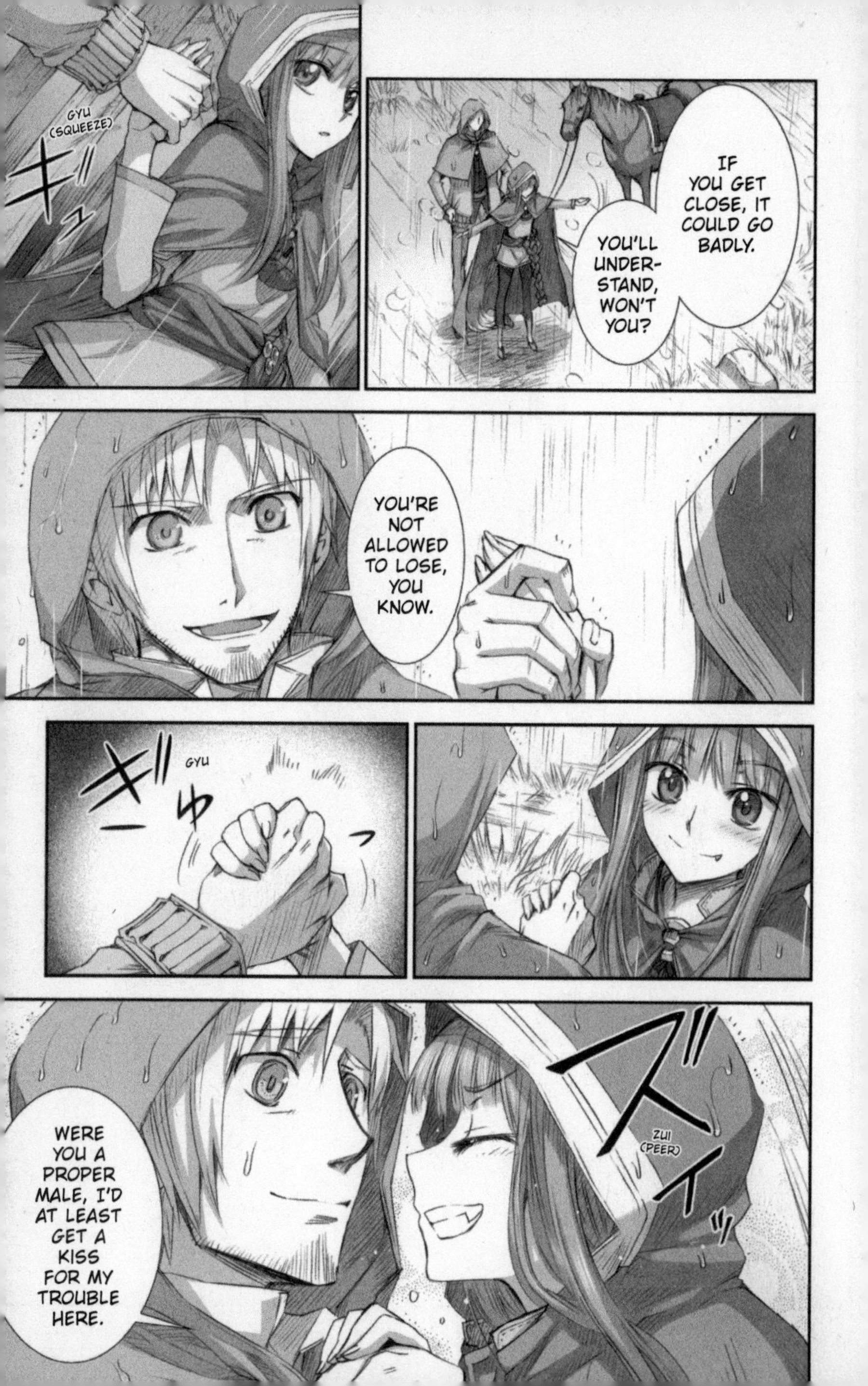
IF YOU GET CLOSE, IT COULD GO BADLY.
YOU'LL UNDER-STAND, WON'T YOU?
GYU (SQUEEZE)
YOU'RE NOT ALLOWED TO LOSE, YOU KNOW.
GYU
ZUI (PEER)
WERE YOU A PROPER MALE, I'D AT LEAST GET A KISS FOR MY TROUBLE HERE.

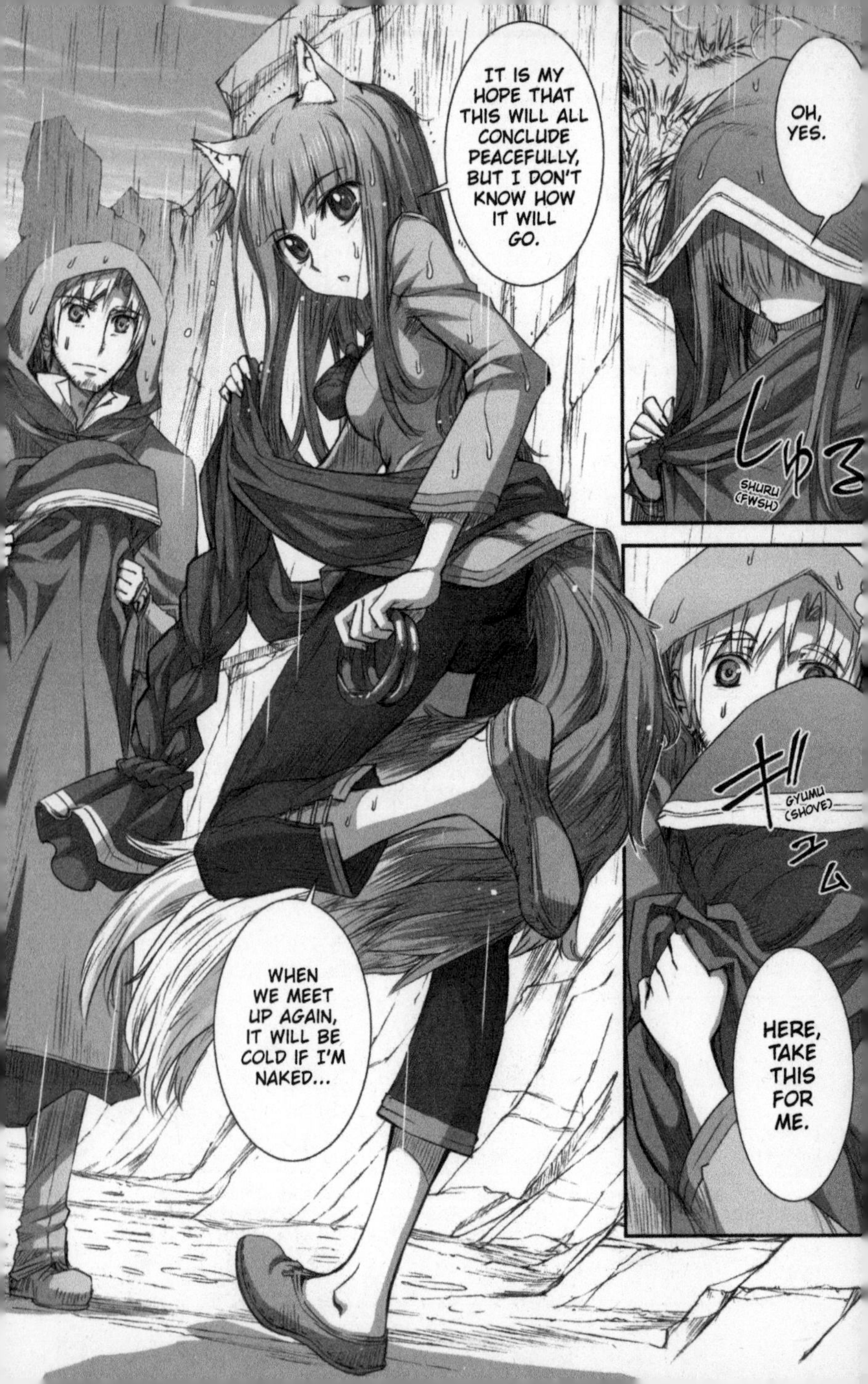

OH, YES.
しゅる
SHURU (FWSH)
HERE, TAKE THIS FOR ME.
ギュム
GYUMU (SHOVE)
IT IS MY HOPE THAT THIS WILL ALL CONCLUDE PEACEFULLY, BUT I DON'T KNOW HOW IT WILL GO.
WHEN WE MEET UP AGAIN, IT WILL BE COLD IF I'M NAKED...

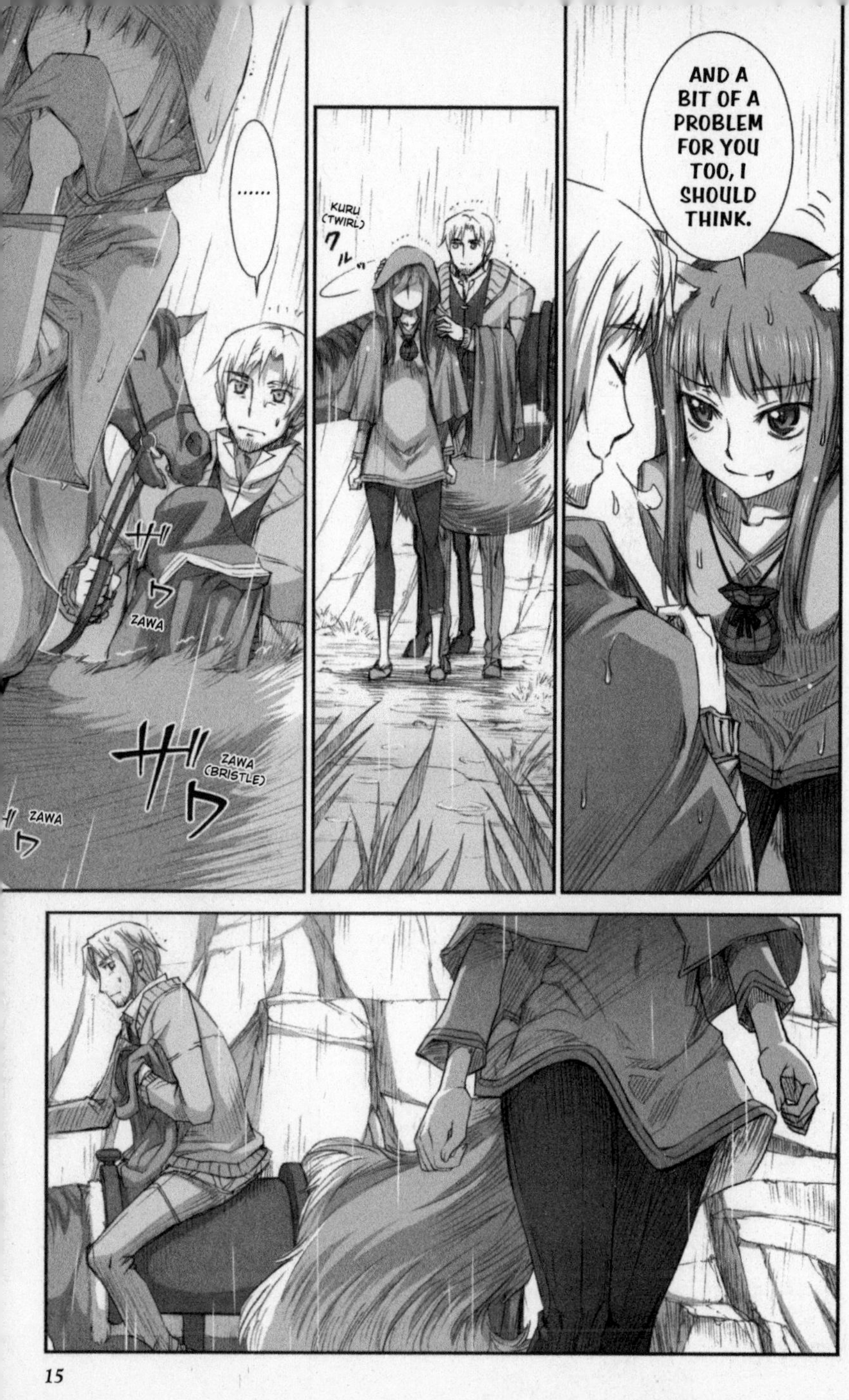
AND A BIT OF A PROBLEM FOR YOU TOO, I SHOULD THINK.
KURU (TWIRL)
クル
......
ZAWA
ZAWA (BRISTLE)
ZAWA

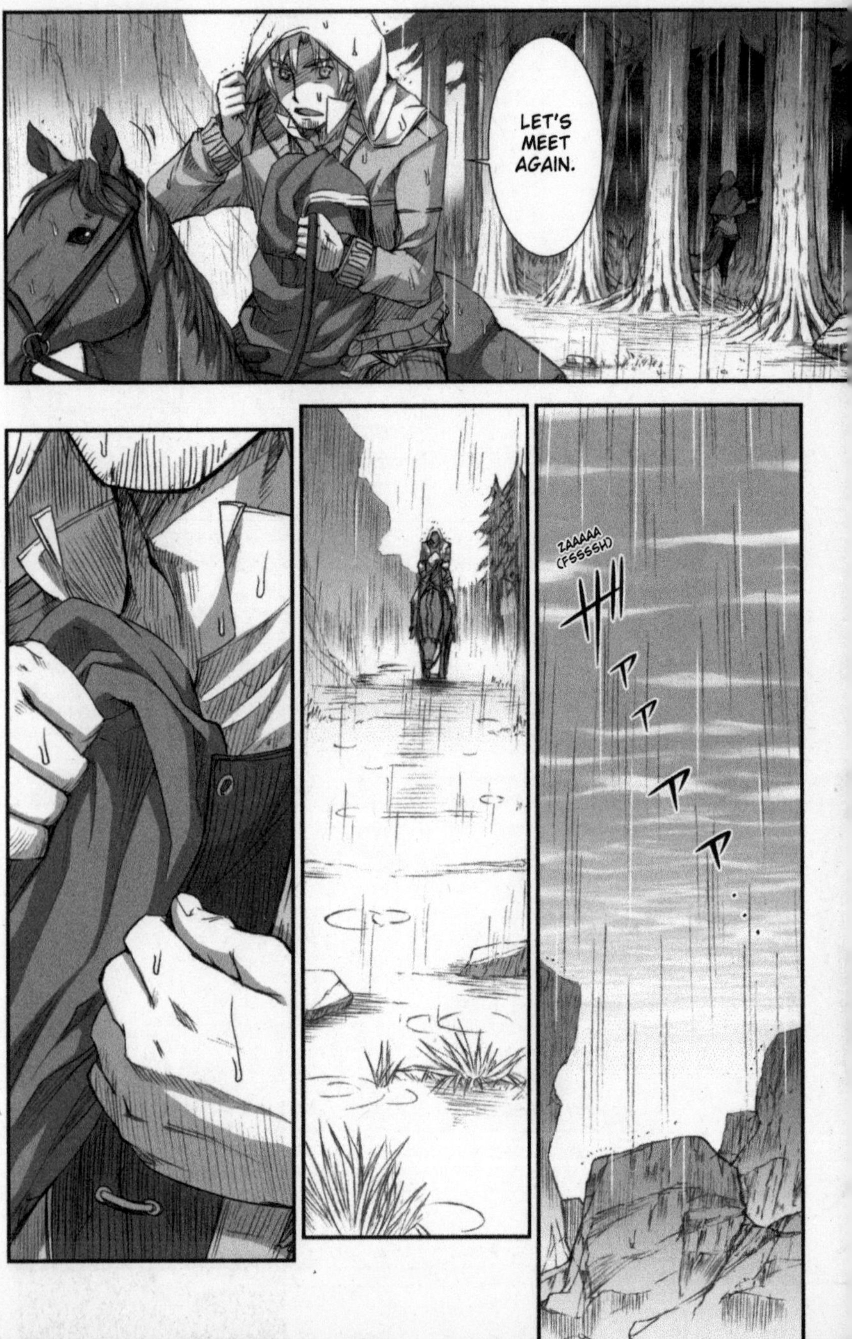
LET'S MEET AGAIN.
ZAAAAA (FSSSSH)

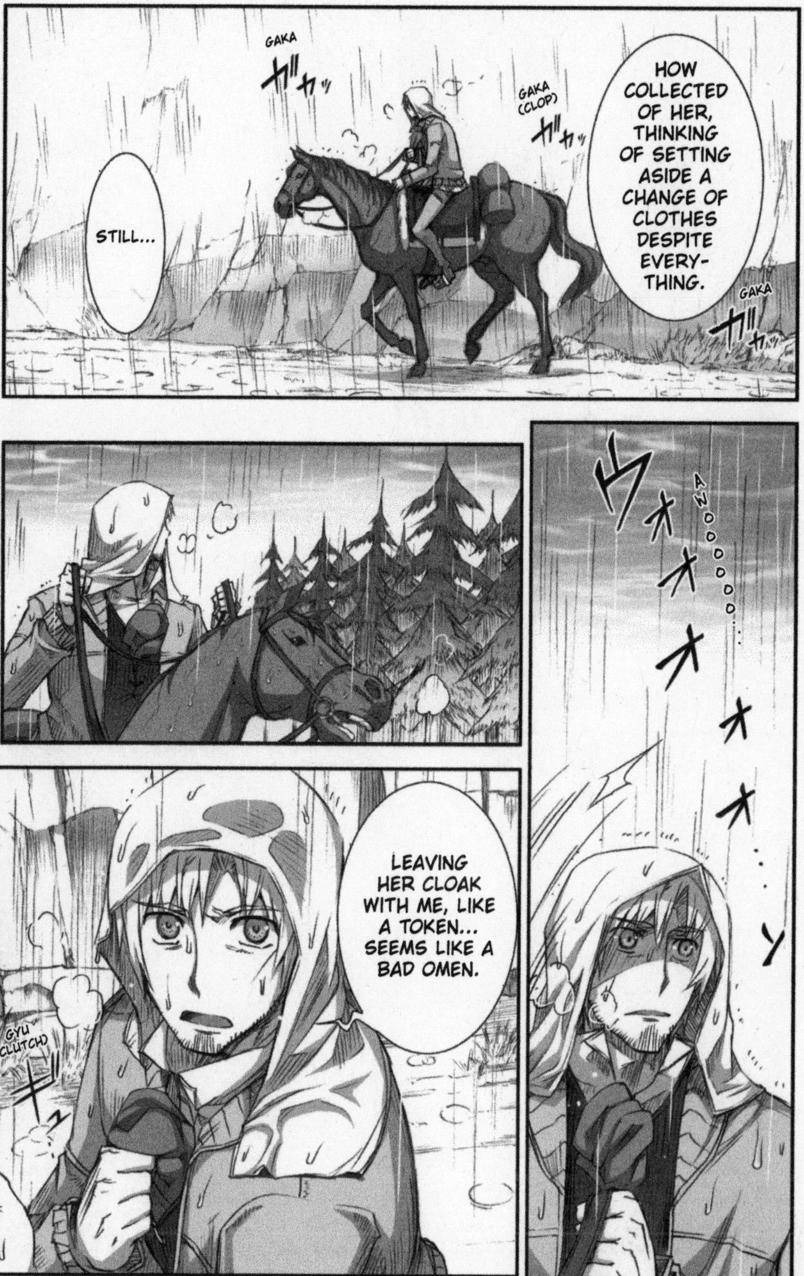
HOW COLLECTED OF HER, THINKING OF SETTING ASIDE A CHANGE OF CLOTHES DESPITE EVERY-THING.
GAKA
GAKA (CLOP)
GAKA
STILL...
AWOOOOOOO...
LEAVING HER CLOAK WITH ME, LIKE A TOKEN... SEEMS LIKE A BAD OMEN.
GYU (CLUTCH)

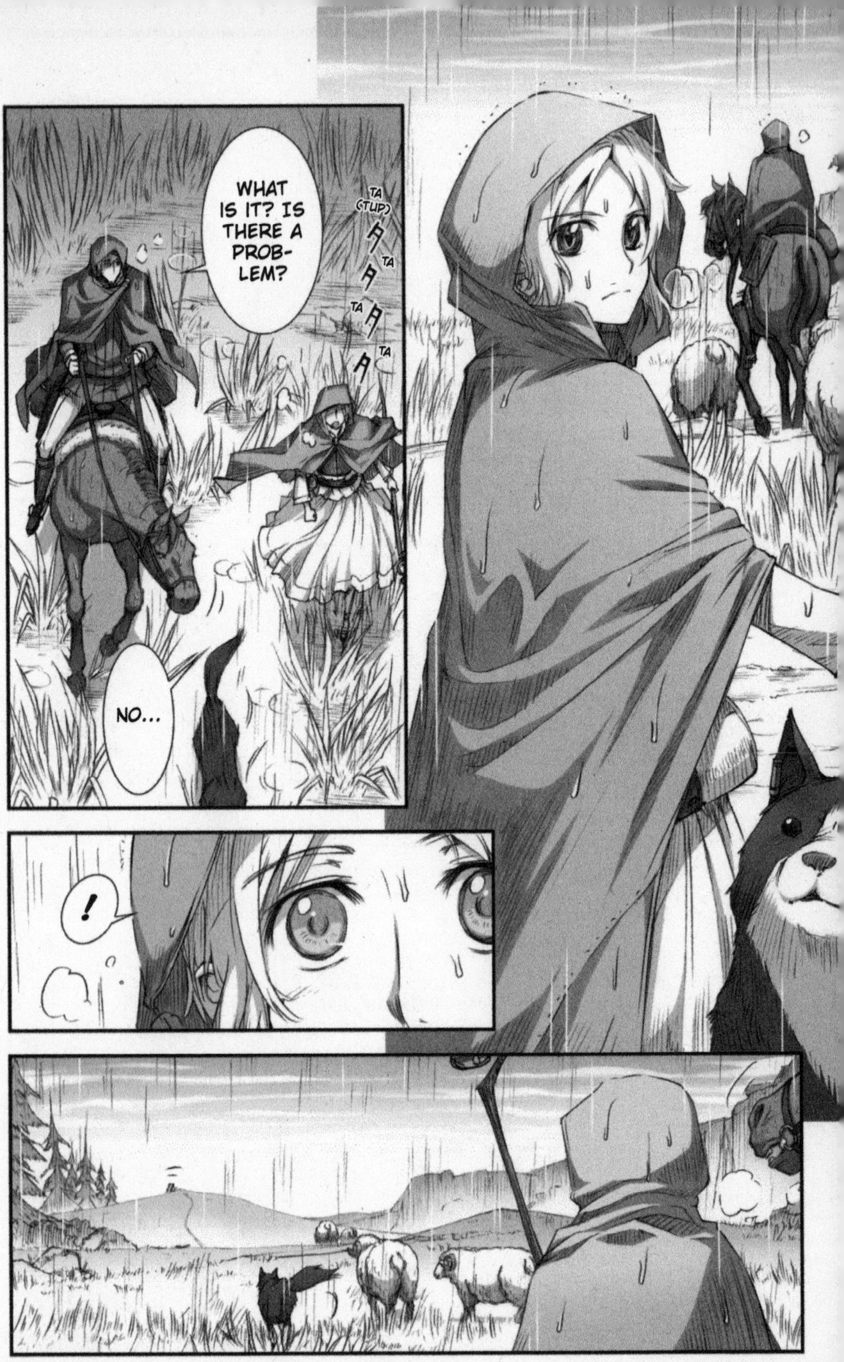
WHAT IS IT? IS THERE A PROB-LEM?
TA (TUP)
TA
TA
TA
NO...
!

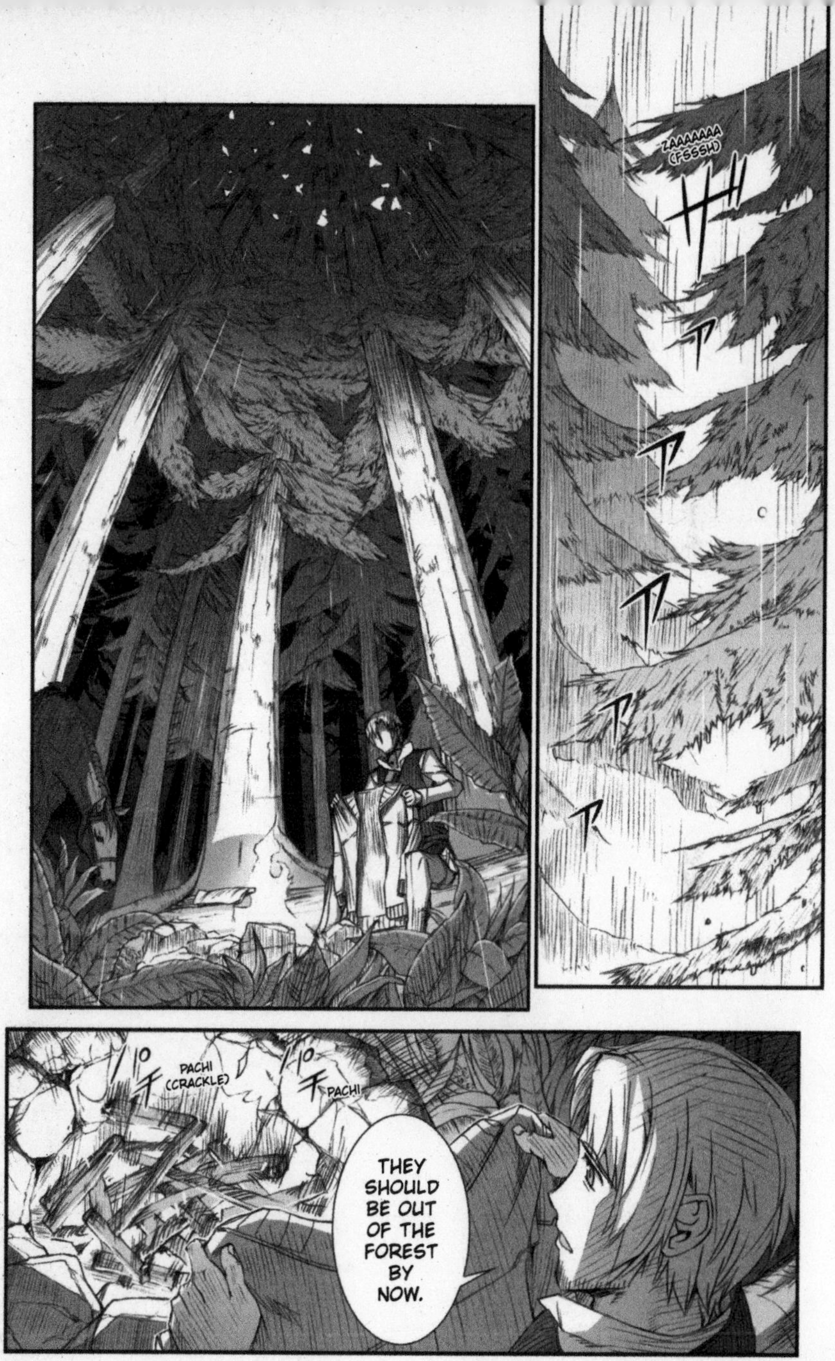
ZAAAAAAA (FSSSH)
PACHI!
PACHI (CRACKLE)
THEY SHOULD BE OUT OF THE FOREST BY NOW.

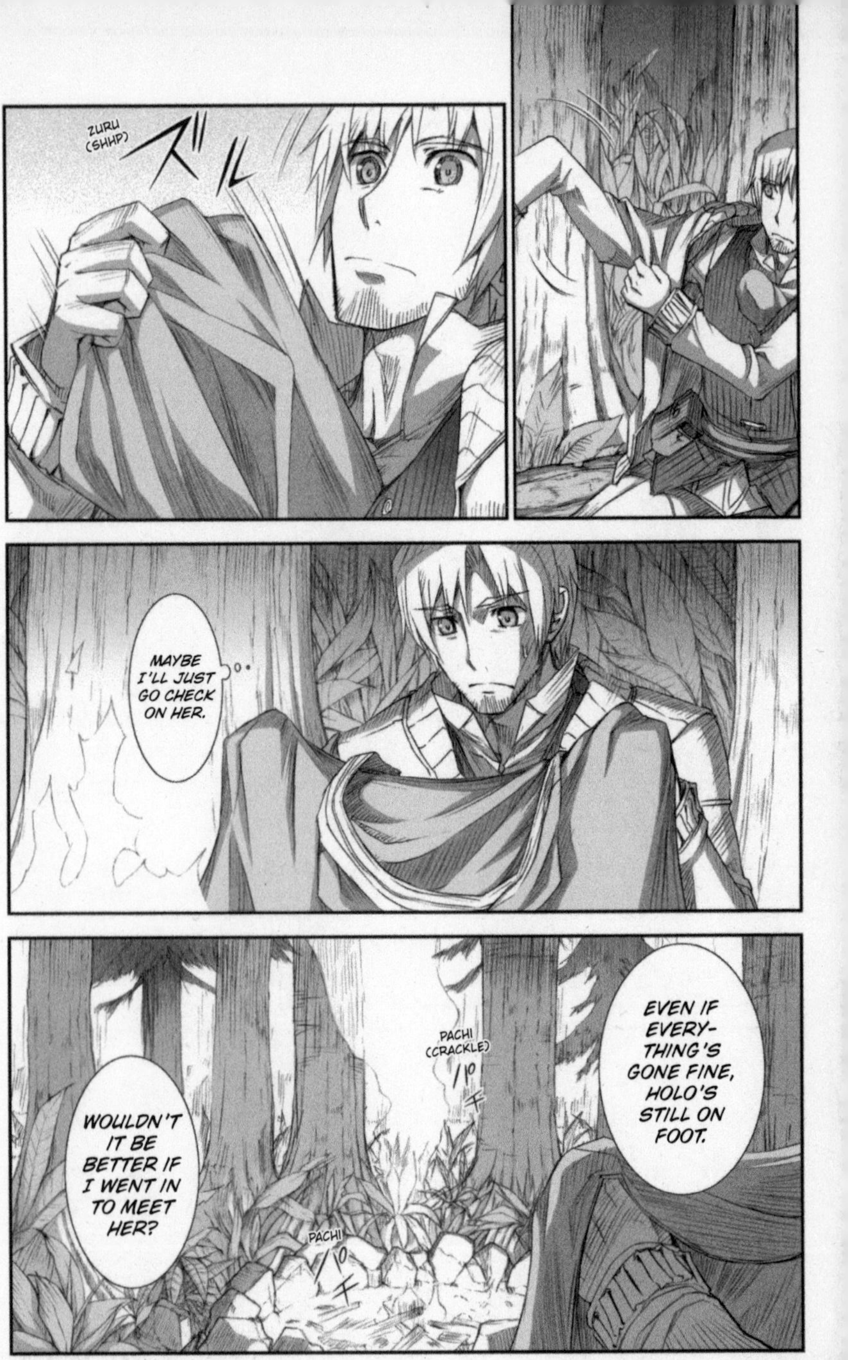
ZURU (SHHP)
ズル
MAYBE I'LL JUST GO CHECK ON HER.
EVEN IF EVERY-THING'S GONE FINE, HOLO'S STILL ON FOOT.
PACHI (CRACKLE)
パチ
WOULDN'T IT BE BETTER IF I WENT IN TO MEET HER?
PACHI
パチ

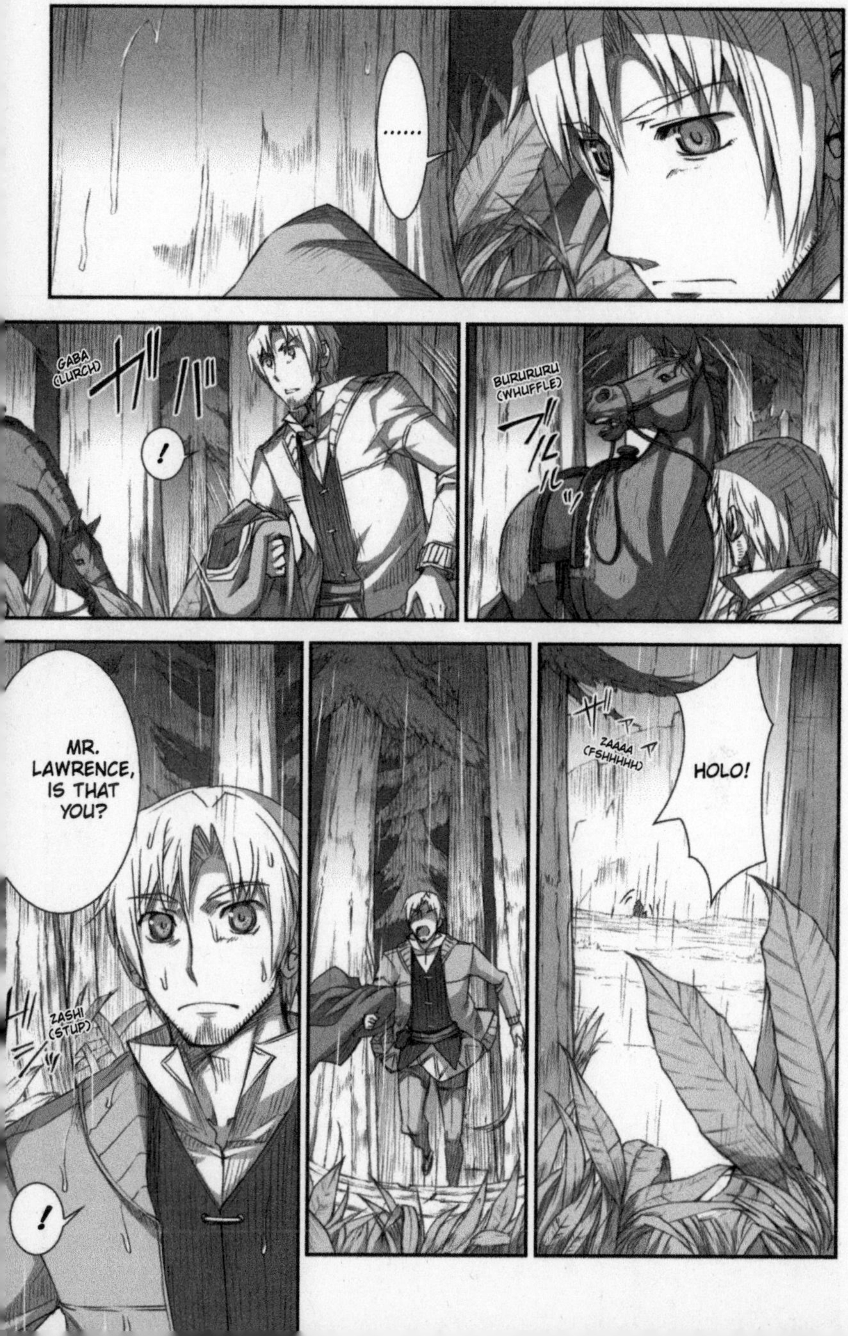
......
BURURURU (WHUFFLE)
GABA (LURCH)
!
ZAAAA (FSHHHHH)
HOLO!
MR. LAWRENCE, IS THAT YOU?
ZASHI (STUP)
!

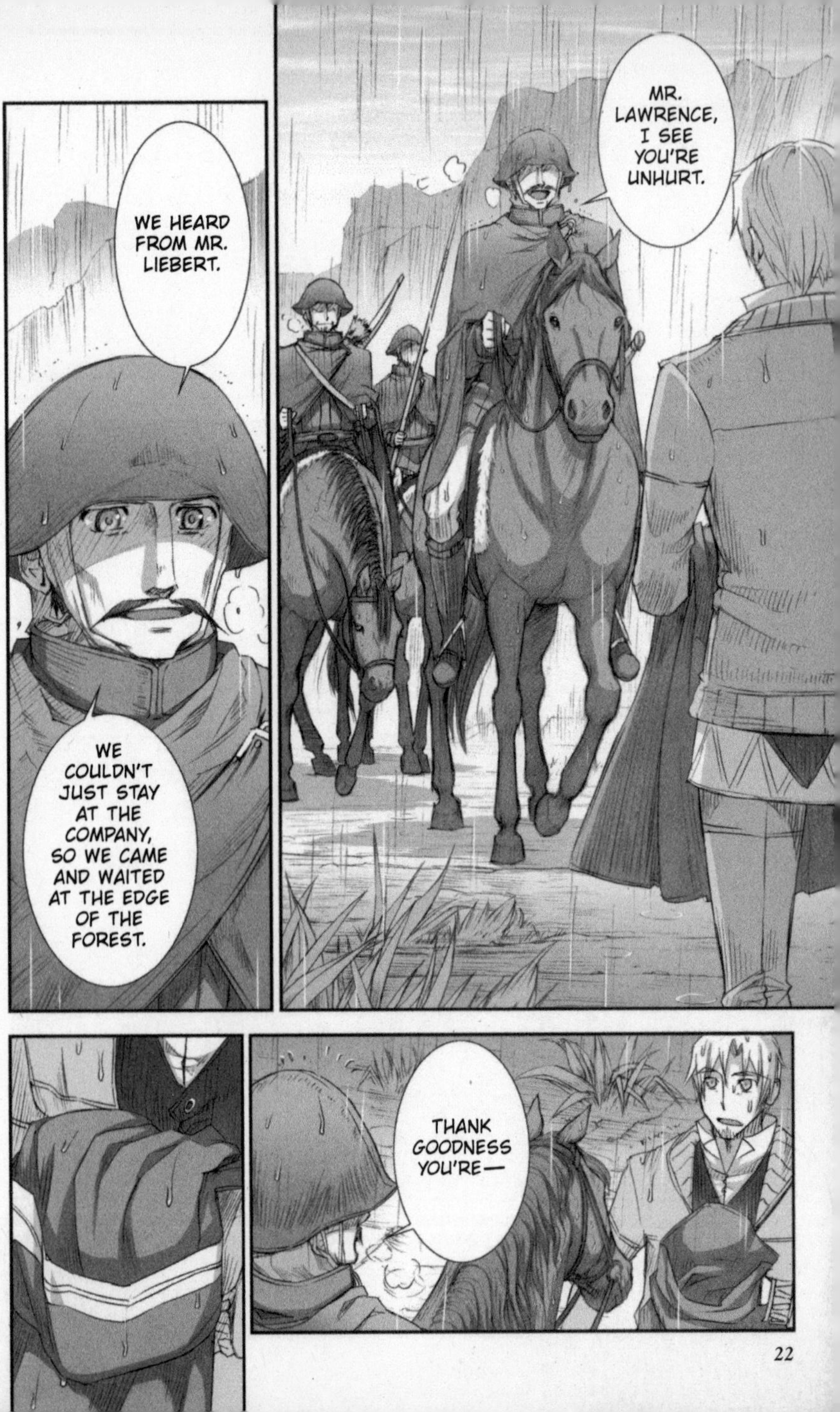
MR. LAWRENCE, I SEE YOU'RE UNHURT.
WE HEARD FROM MR. LIEBERT.
WE COULDN'T JUST STAY AT THE COMPANY, SO WE CAME AND WAITED AT THE EDGE OF THE FOREST.
THANK GOODNESS YOU'RE—

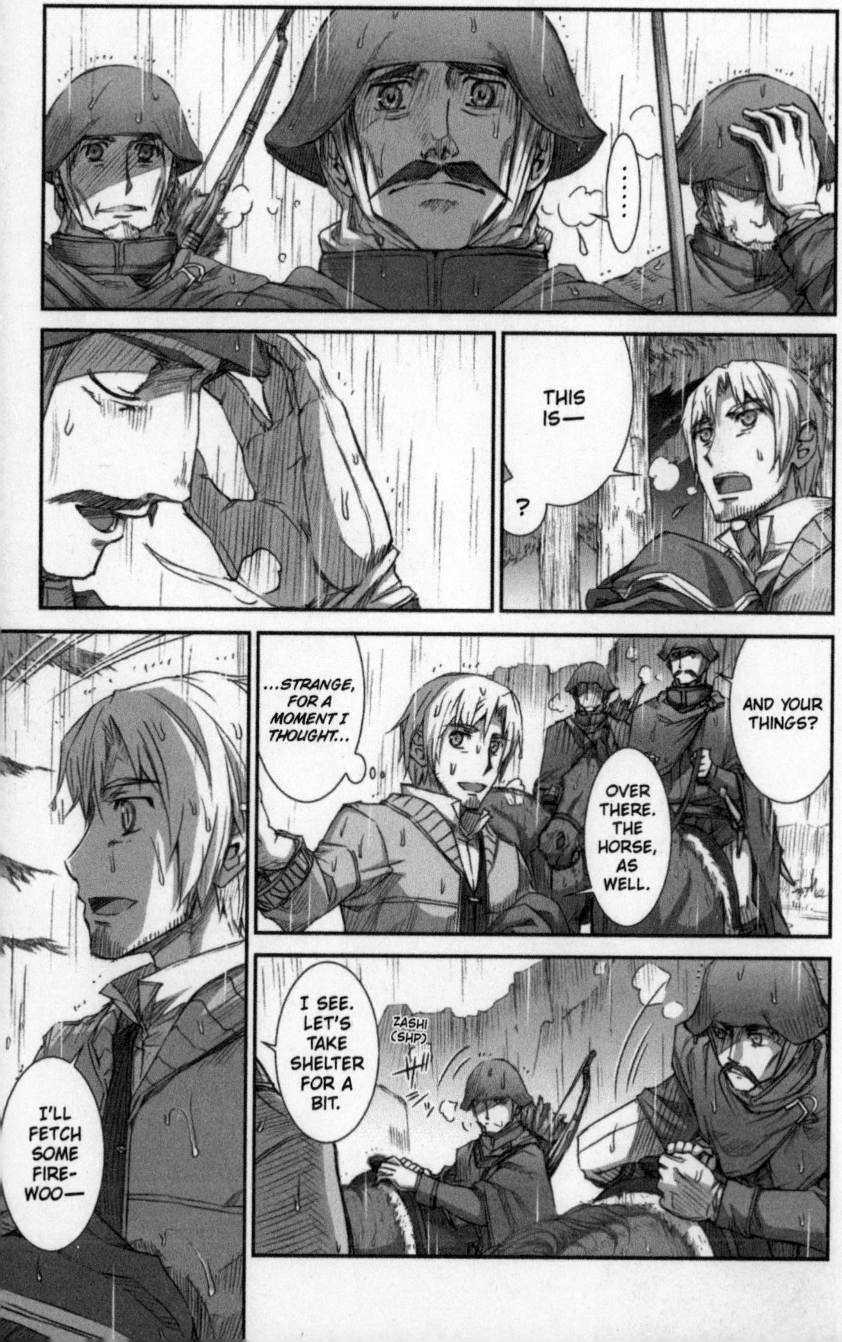
......
THIS IS—
?
AND YOUR THINGS?
...STRANGE, FOR A MOMENT I THOUGHT...
OVER THERE. THE HORSE, AS WELL.
I SEE. LET'S TAKE SHELTER FOR A BIT.
ZASHI (SHP)
I'LL FETCH SOME FIRE-WOO—

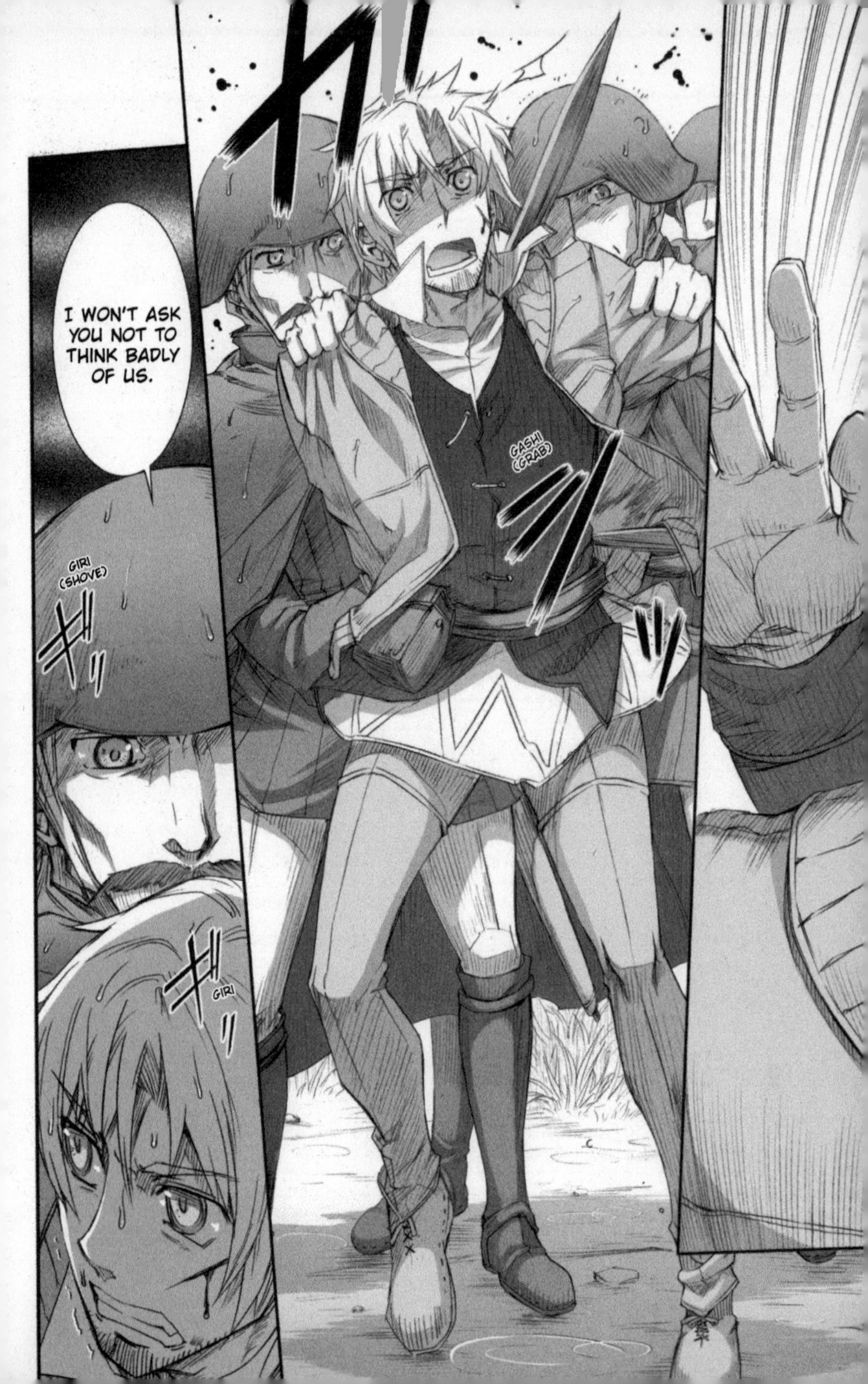
GASHI (GRAB)
I WON'T ASK YOU NOT TO THINK BADLY OF US.
GIRI (SHOVE)
GIRI

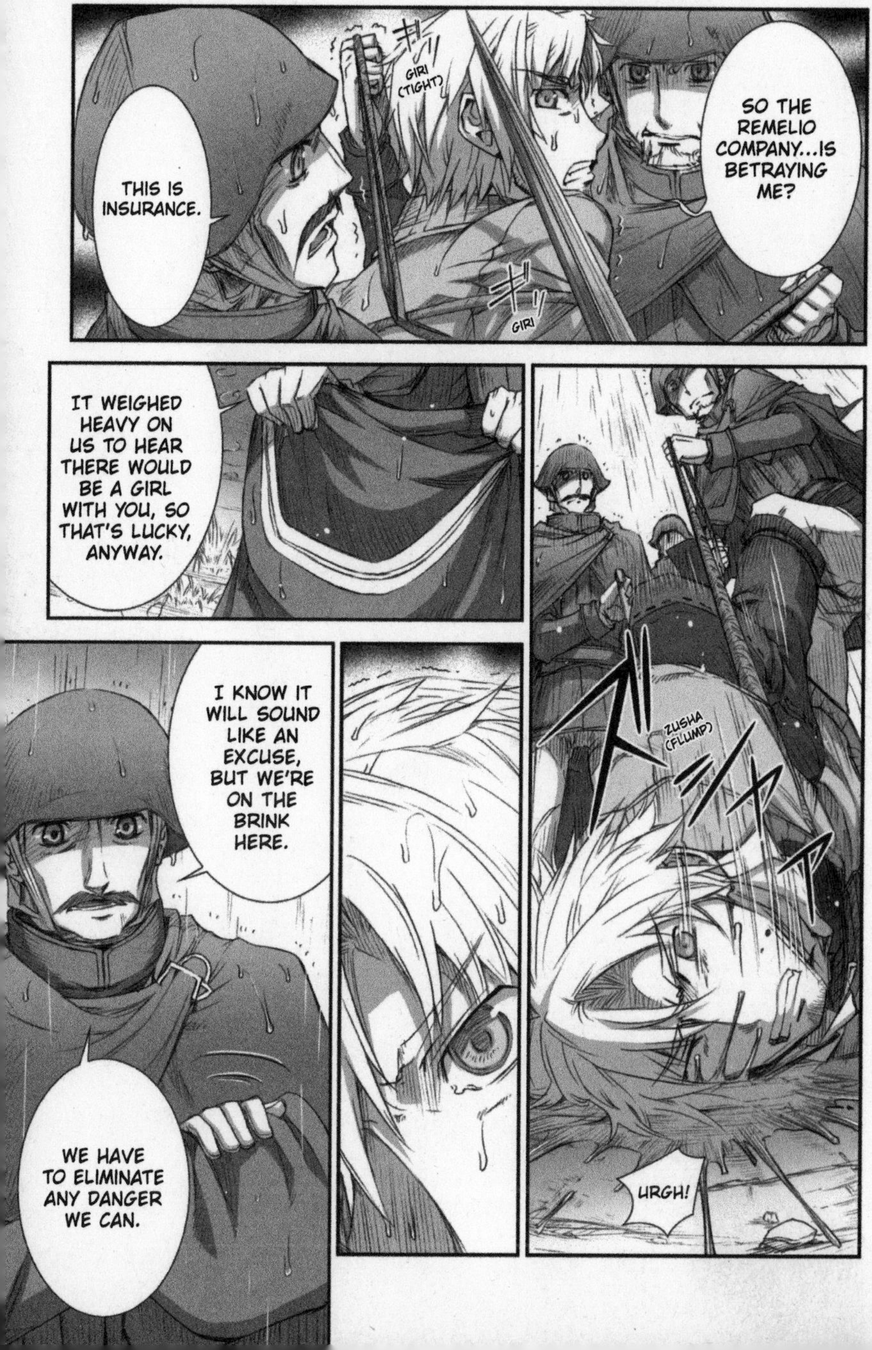
SO THE REMELIO COMPANY...IS BETRAYING ME?
GIRI (TIGHT)
THIS IS INSURANCE.
GIRI
ZUSHA (FLUMP)
URGH!
IT WEIGHED HEAVY ON US TO HEAR THERE WOULD BE A GIRL WITH YOU, SO THAT'S LUCKY, ANYWAY.
I KNOW IT WILL SOUND LIKE AN EXCUSE, BUT WE'RE ON THE BRINK HERE.
WE HAVE TO ELIMINATE ANY DANGER WE CAN.

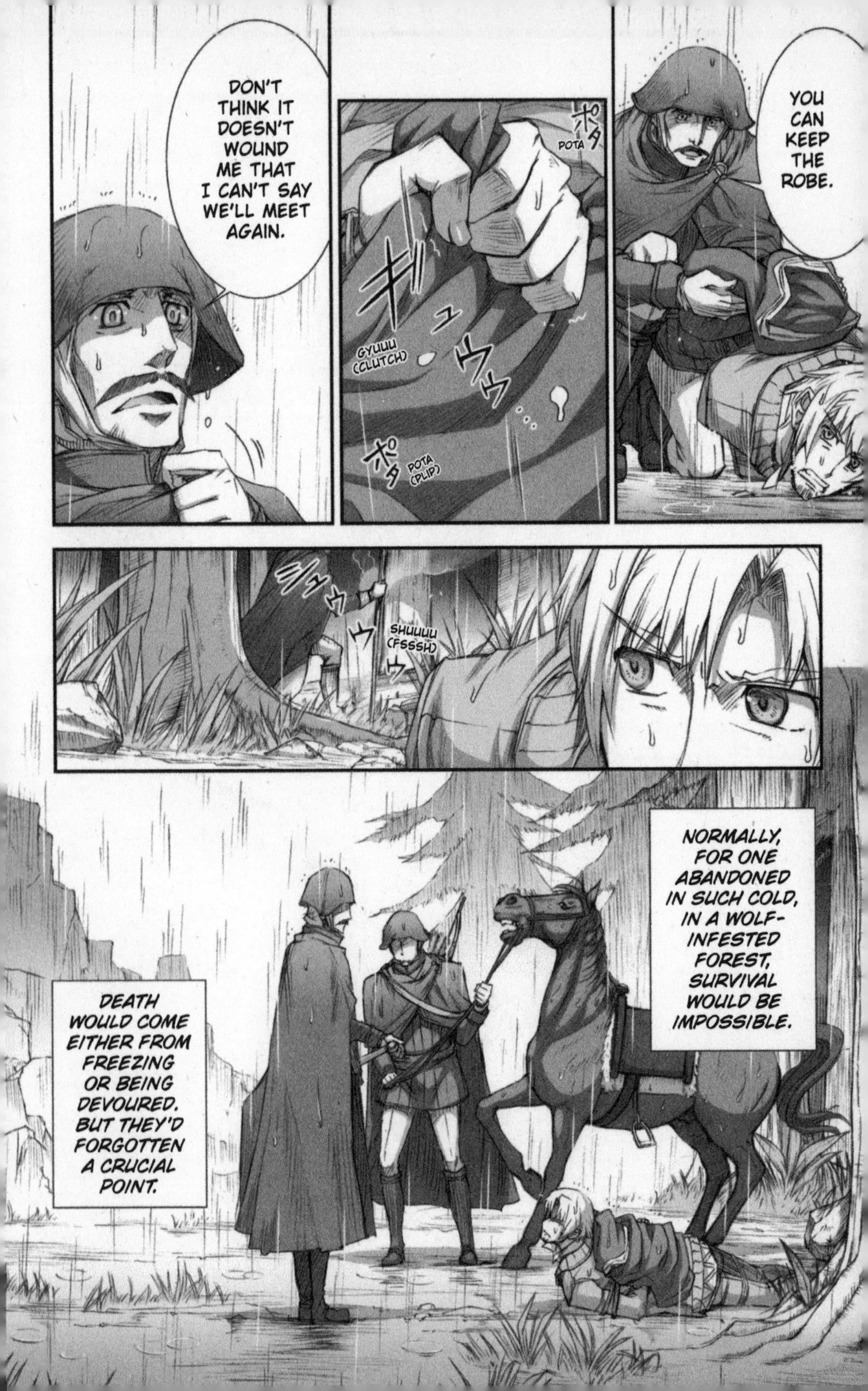
YOU CAN KEEP THE ROBE.
ポタ
POTA
ギュウウ
GYUUU (CLUTCH)
ポタ
POTA (PLIP)
DON'T THINK IT DOESN'T WOUND ME THAT I CAN'T SAY WE'LL MEET AGAIN.
シュウウウ
SHUUUU (FSSSH)
NORMALLY, FOR ONE ABANDONED IN SUCH COLD, IN A WOLF-INFESTED FOREST, SURVIVAL WOULD BE IMPOSSIBLE.
DEATH WOULD COME EITHER FROM FREEZING OR BEING DEVOURED. BUT THEY'D FORGOTTEN A CRUCIAL POINT.

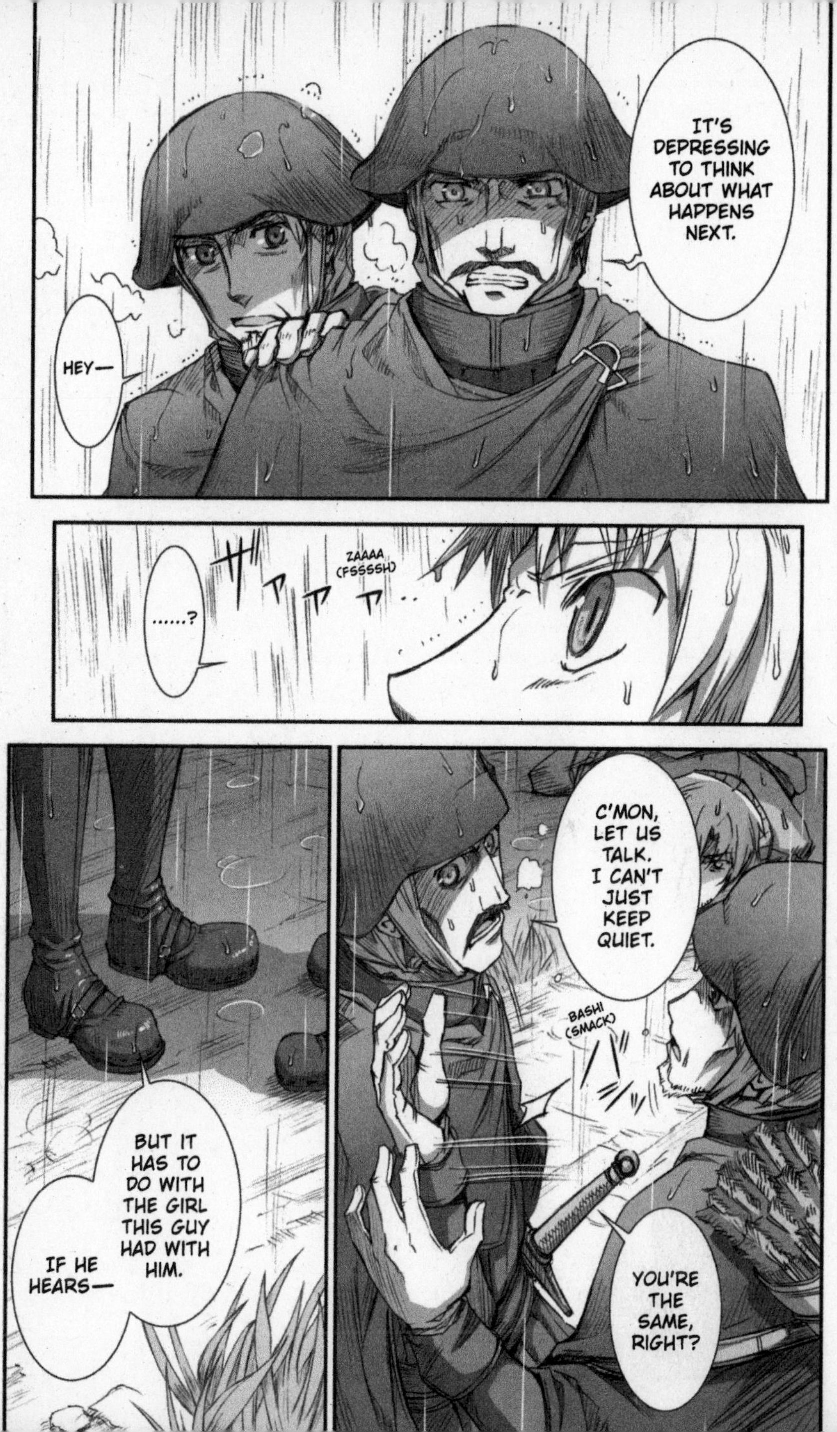
IT'S DEPRESSING TO THINK ABOUT WHAT HAPPENS NEXT.
HEY—
ZAAAA (FSSSSH)
......?
C'MON, LET US TALK. I CAN'T JUST KEEP QUIET.
BASHI (SMACK)
YOU'RE THE SAME, RIGHT?
BUT IT HAS TO DO WITH THE GIRL THIS GUY HAD WITH HIM.
IF HE HEARS—

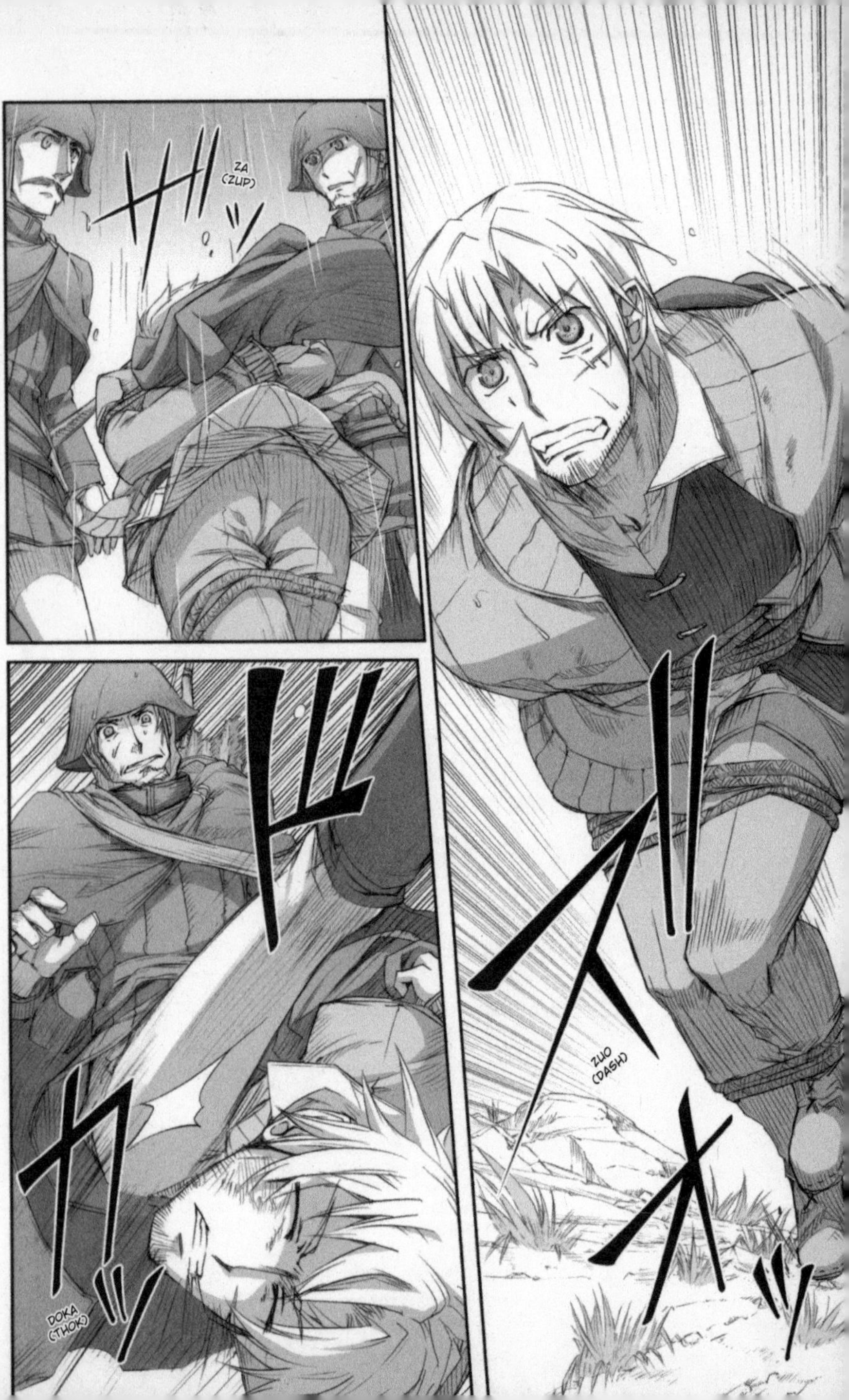
ZUO
(DASH)
ZA
(ZUP)
DOKA
(THOK)

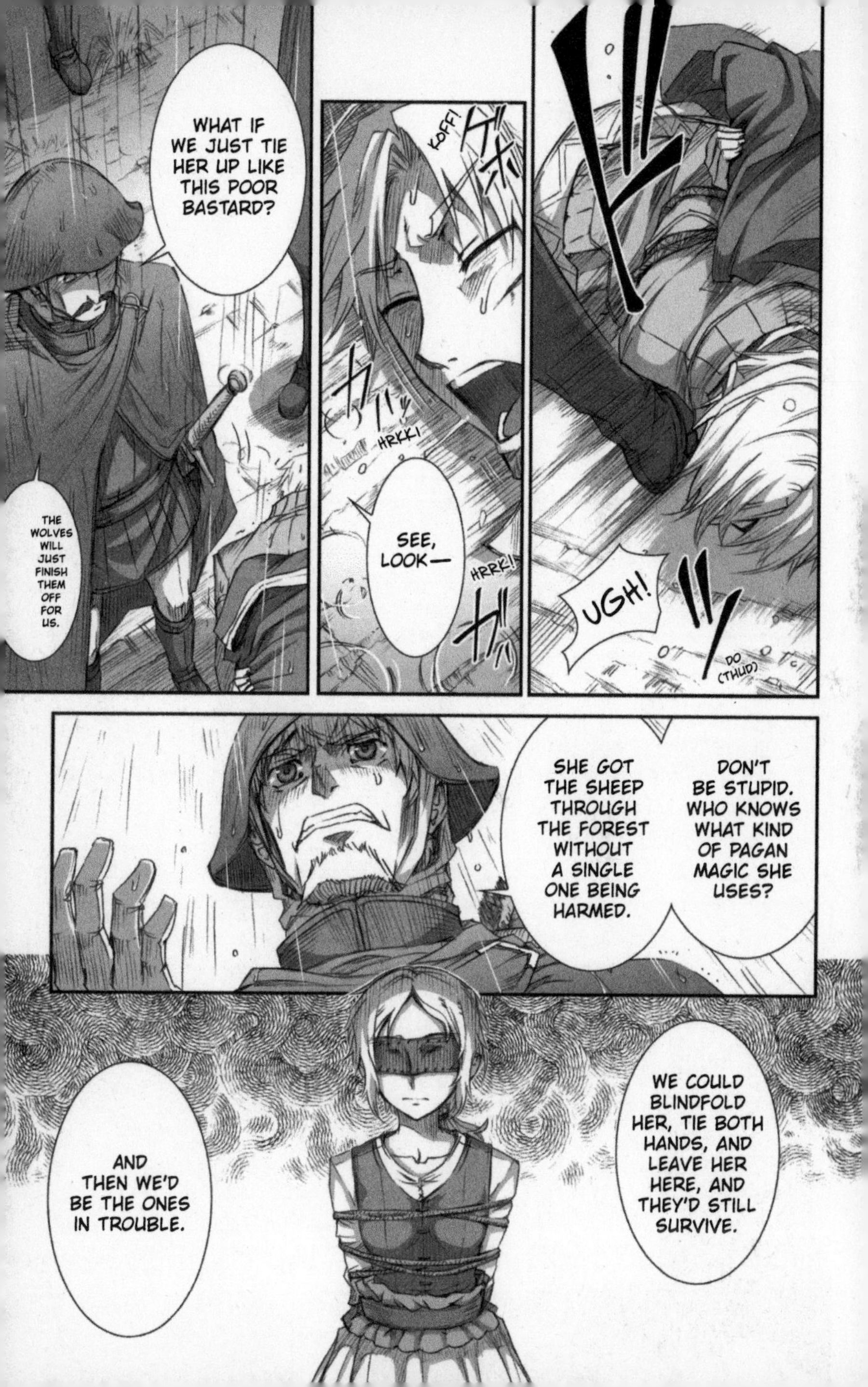
UGH!
DO (THUD)
KOFF!
HRKK!
SEE, LOOK—
HRRK!
WHAT IF WE JUST TIE HER UP LIKE THIS POOR BASTARD?
THE WOLVES WILL JUST FINISH THEM OFF FOR US.
DON'T BE STUPID. WHO KNOWS WHAT KIND OF PAGAN MAGIC SHE USES?
SHE GOT THE SHEEP THROUGH THE FOREST WITHOUT A SINGLE ONE BEING HARMED.
WE COULD BLINDFOLD HER, TIE BOTH HANDS, AND LEAVE HER HERE, AND THEY'D STILL SURVIVE.
AND THEN WE'D BE THE ONES IN TROUBLE.

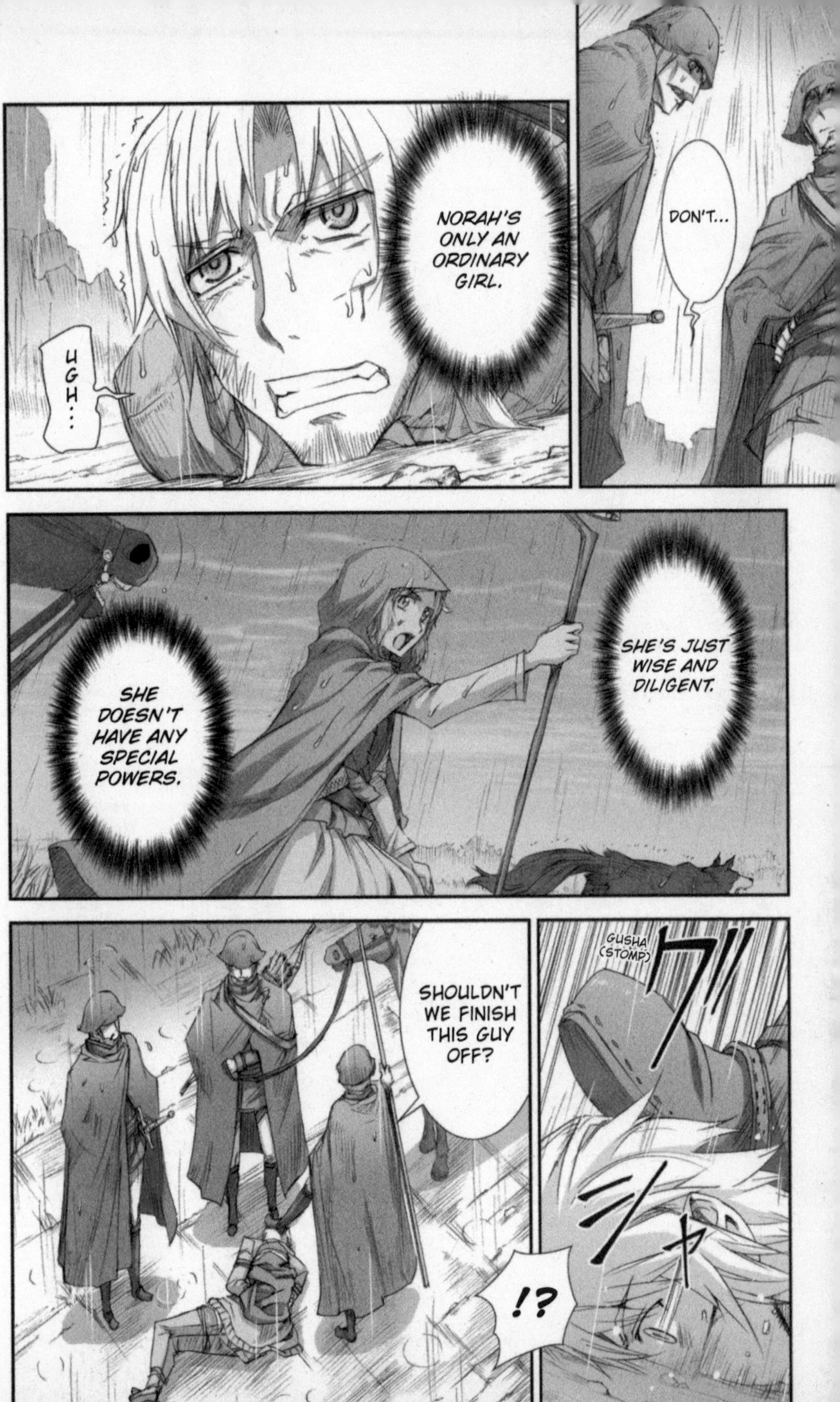
DON'T...
NORAH'S ONLY AN ORDINARY GIRL.
UGH...
SHE'S JUST WISE AND DILIGENT.
SHE DOESN'T HAVE ANY SPECIAL POWERS.
GUSHA (STOMP)
!?
SHOULDN'T WE FINISH THIS GUY OFF?

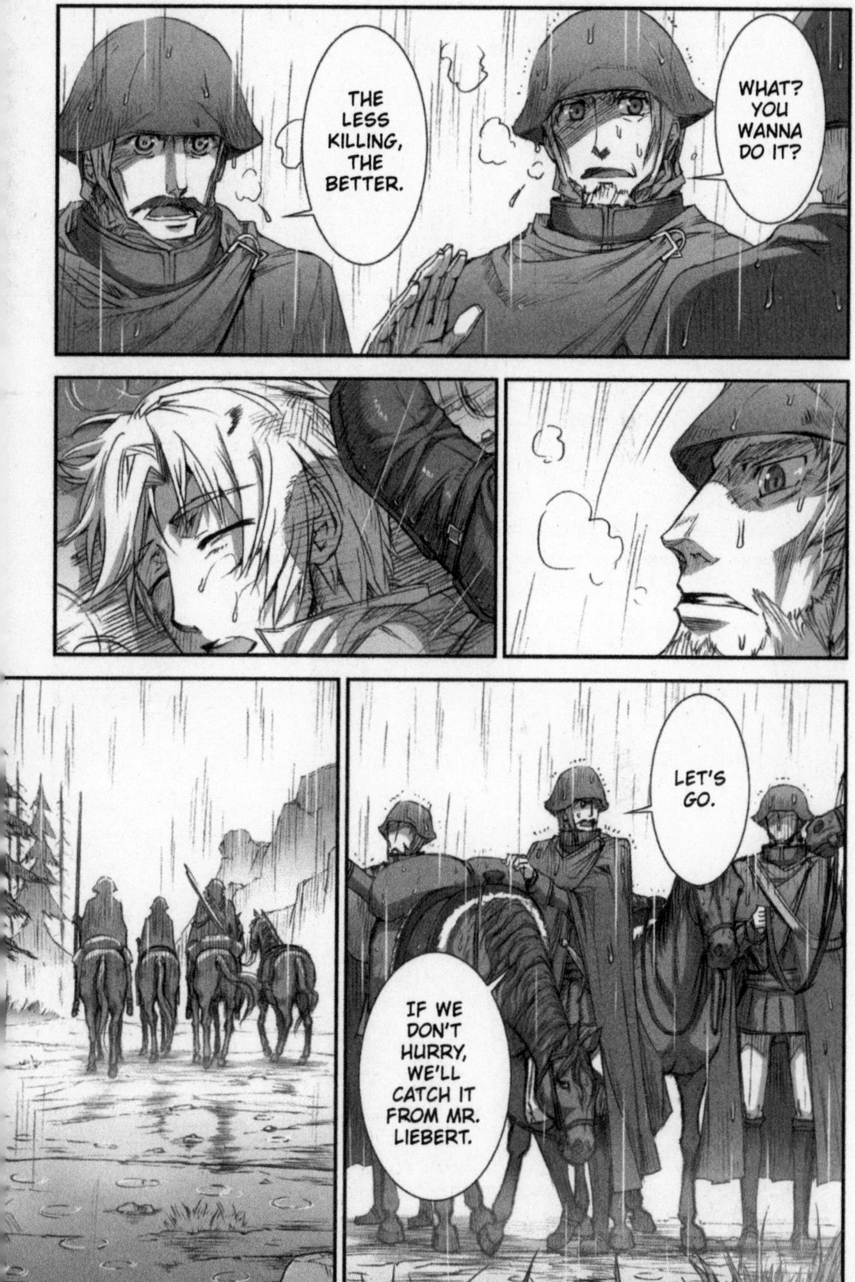
WHAT? YOU WANNA DO IT?
THE LESS KILLING, THE BETTER.
LET'S GO.
IF WE DON'T HURRY, WE'LL CATCH IT FROM MR. LIEBERT.

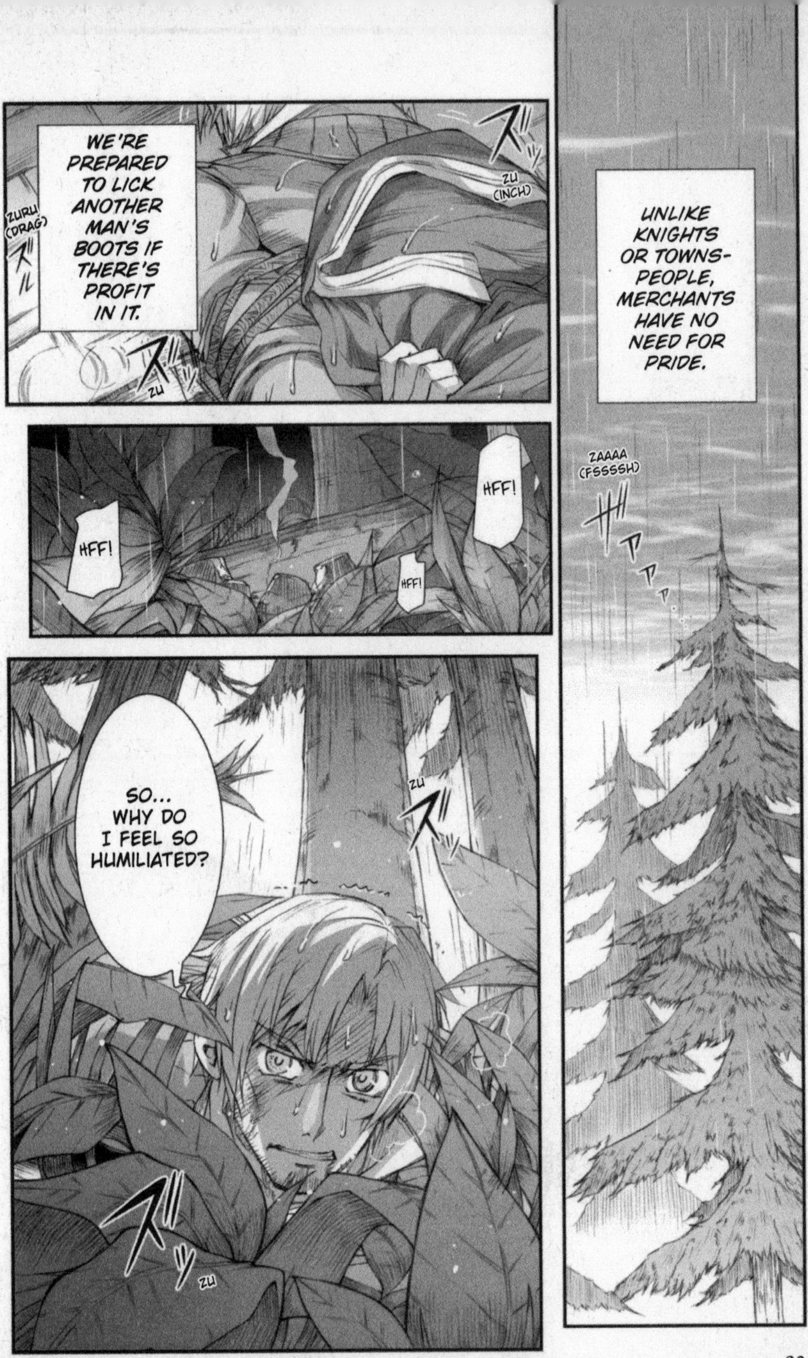
UNLIKE KNIGHTS OR TOWNS-PEOPLE, MERCHANTS HAVE NO NEED FOR PRIDE.
ZAAAA (FSSSSH)
ZU (INCH)
WE'RE PREPARED TO LICK ANOTHER MAN'S BOOTS IF THERE'S PROFIT IN IT.
ZURU (DRAG)
ZU
HFF!
HFF!
HFF!
ZU
SO... WHY DO I FEEL SO HUMILIATED?
ZU

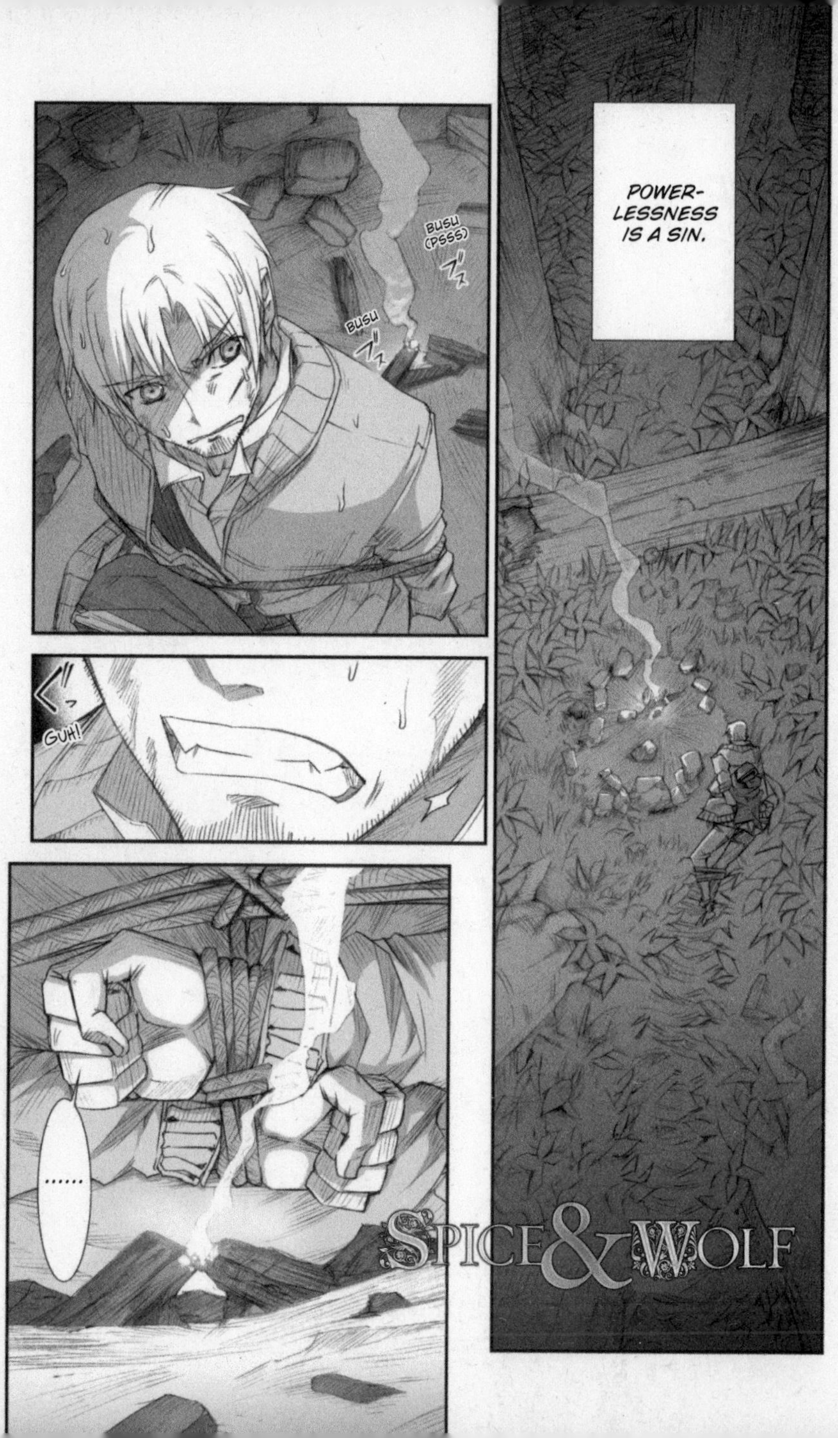
POWER-LESSNESS IS A SIN.
SPICE & WOLF
BUSU (PSSS)
BUSU
GUH!
......

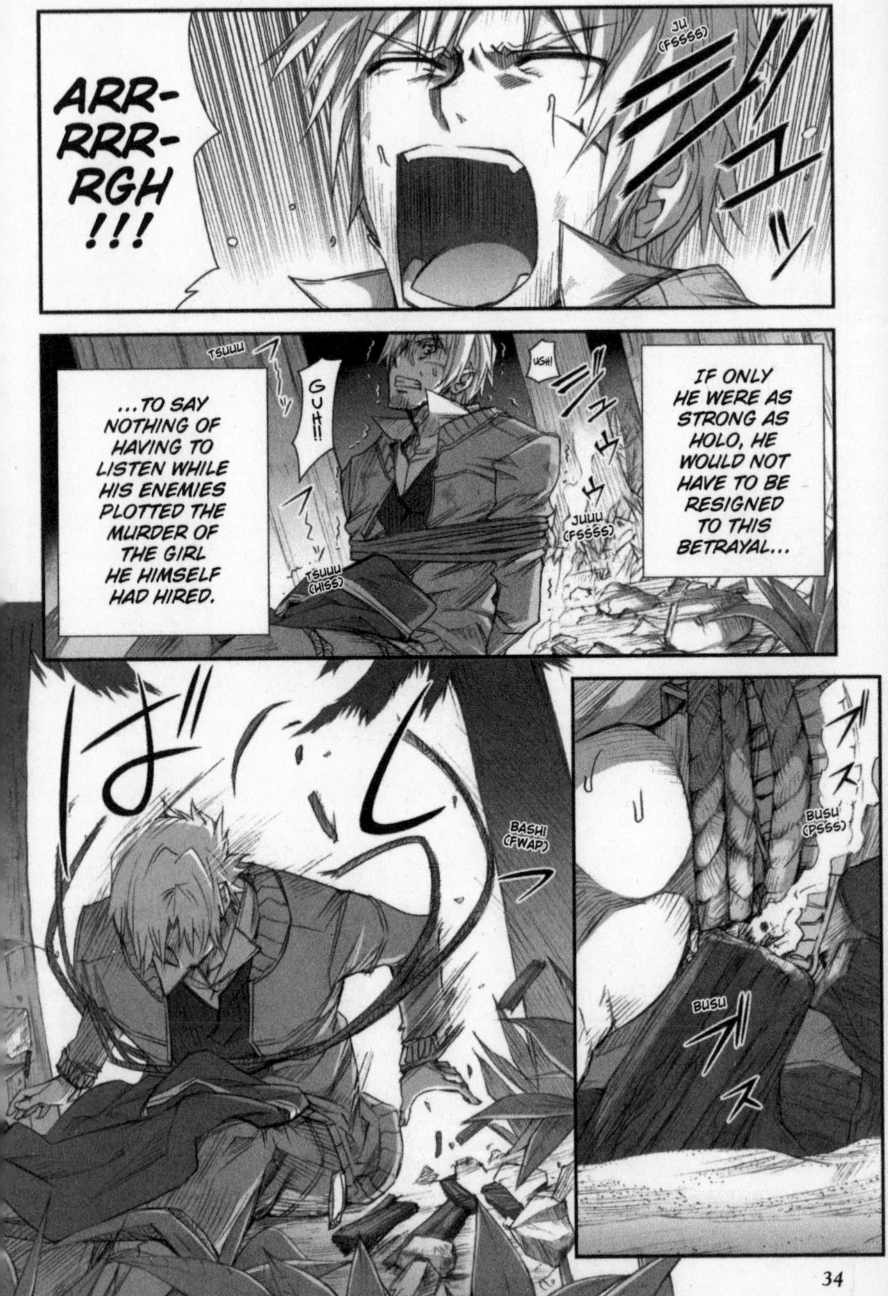
JU (FSSSS)
ARR-RRR-RGH!!!
IF ONLY HE WERE AS STRONG AS HOLO, HE WOULD NOT HAVE TO BE RESIGNED TO THIS BETRAYAL...
UGH!
JUUU (FSSSS)
GUH!!
TSUUU
TSUUU (HISS)
...TO SAY NOTHING OF HAVING TO LISTEN WHILE HIS ENEMIES PLOTTED THE MURDER OF THE GIRL HE HIMSELF HAD HIRED.
BUSU (PSSSS)
BUSU
BASHI (FWAP)

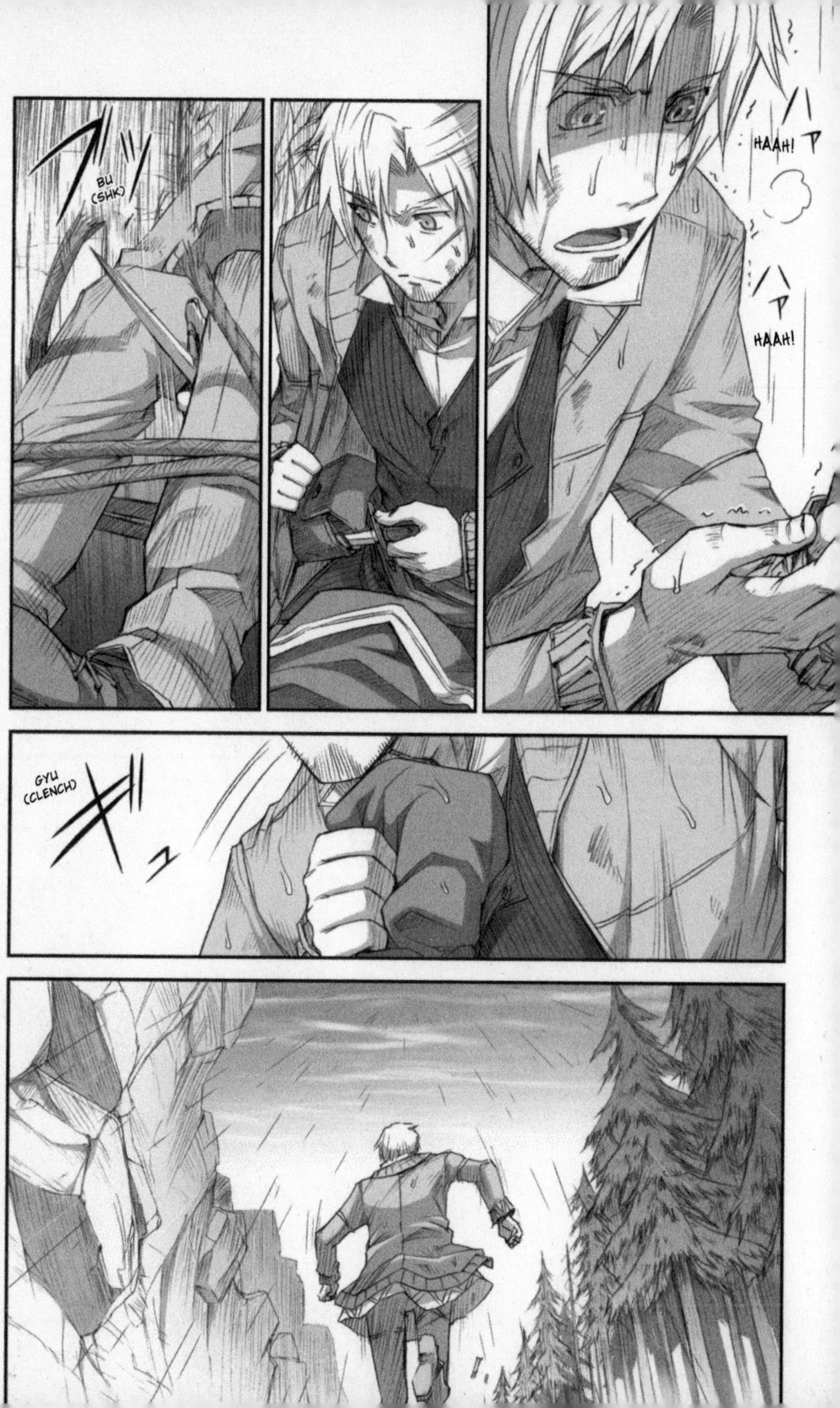
HAAH!
HAAH!
BU (SHK)
GYU (CLENCH)

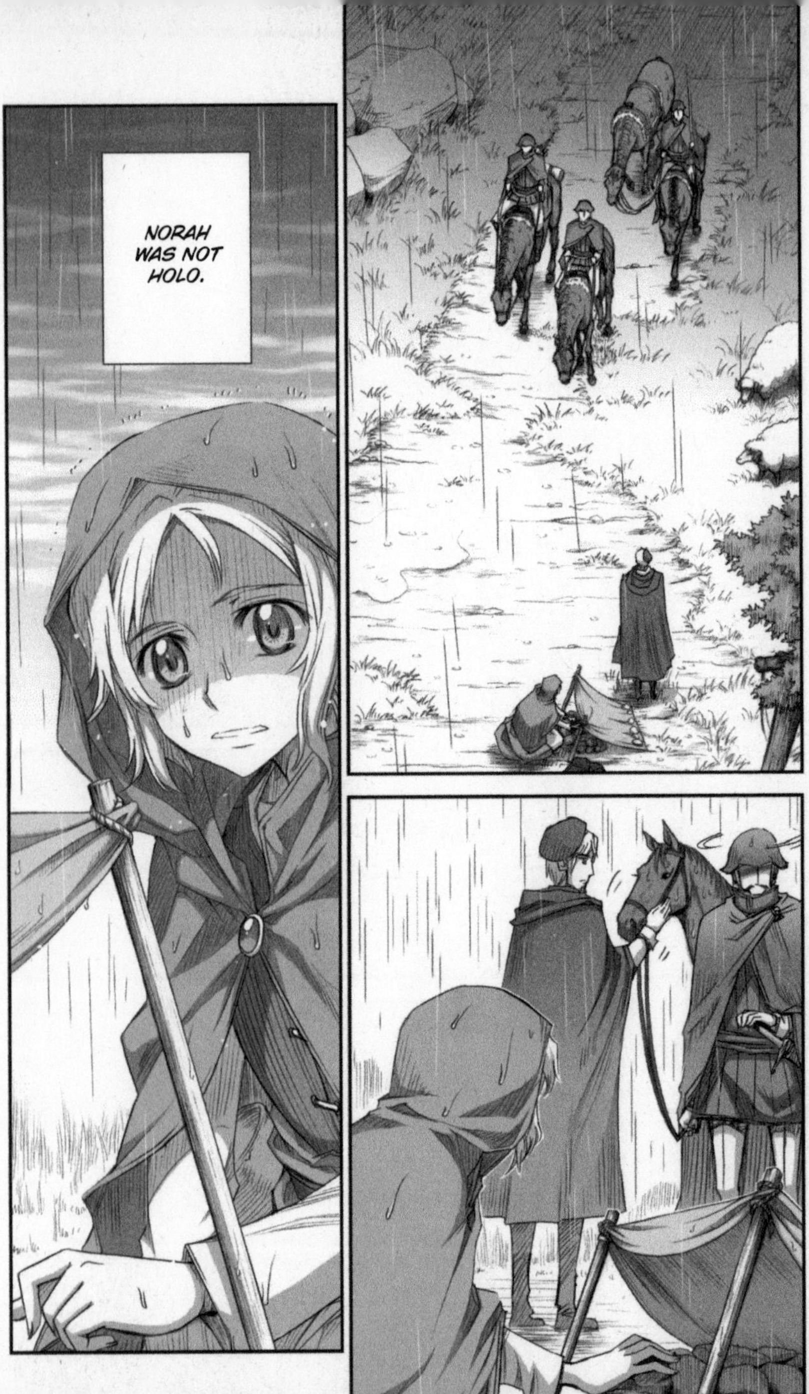
NORAH WAS NOT HOLO.

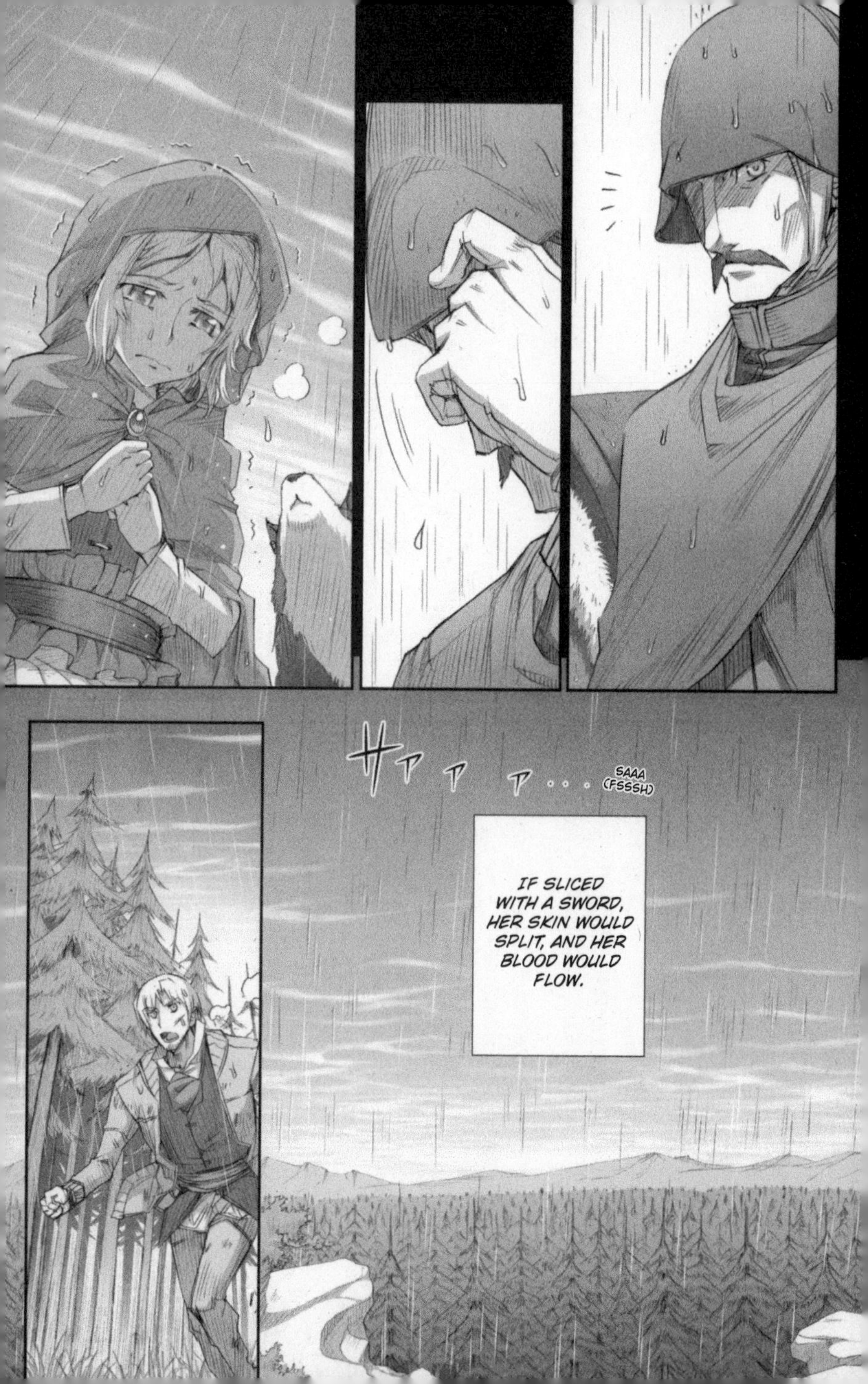
SAAA (FSSSH)
IF SLICED WITH A SWORD, HER SKIN WOULD SPLIT, AND HER BLOOD WOULD FLOW.

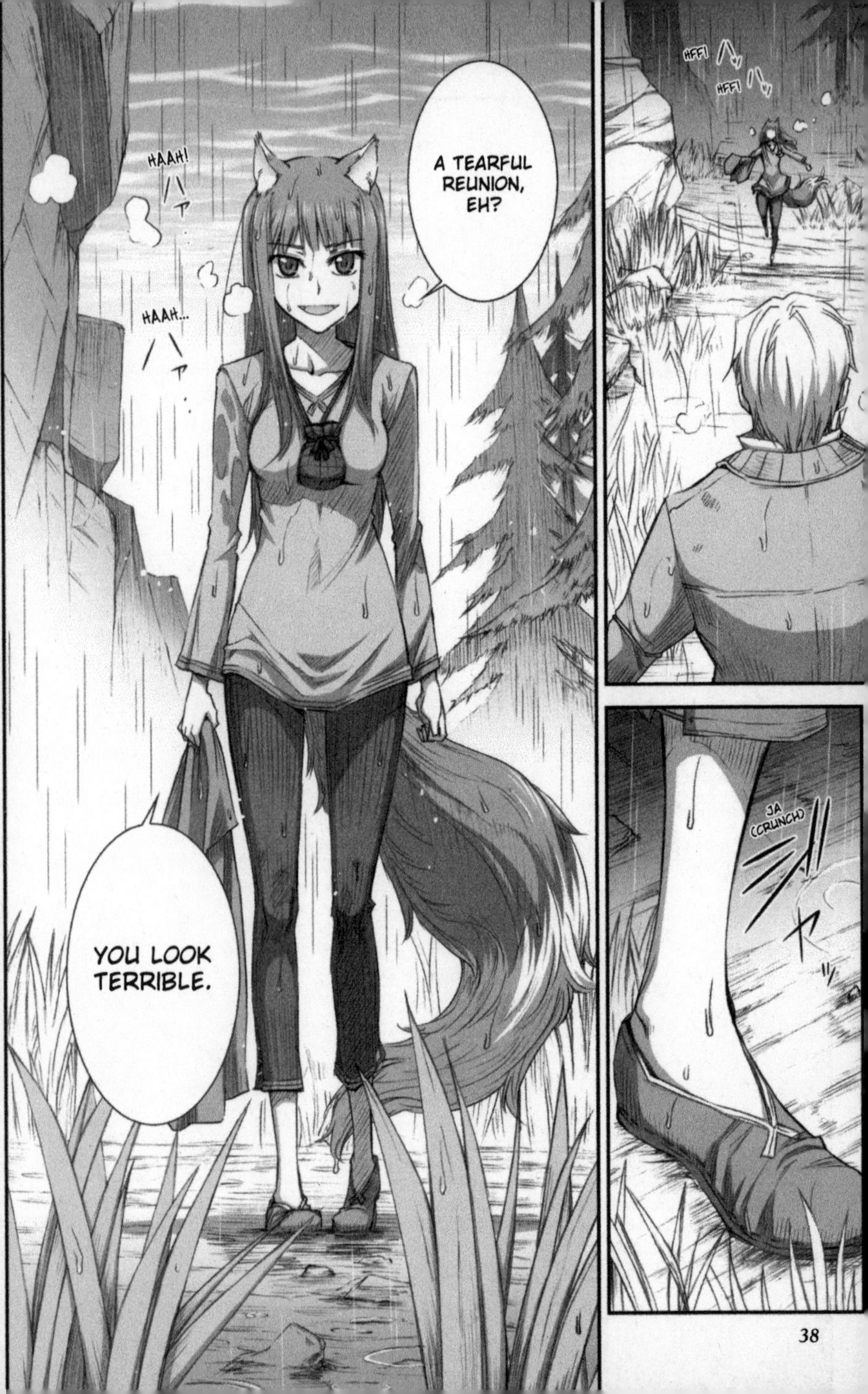
HFF!
HFF!
JA (CRUNCH)
HAAH!
HAAH...
A TEARFUL REUNION, EH?
YOU LOOK TERRIBLE.

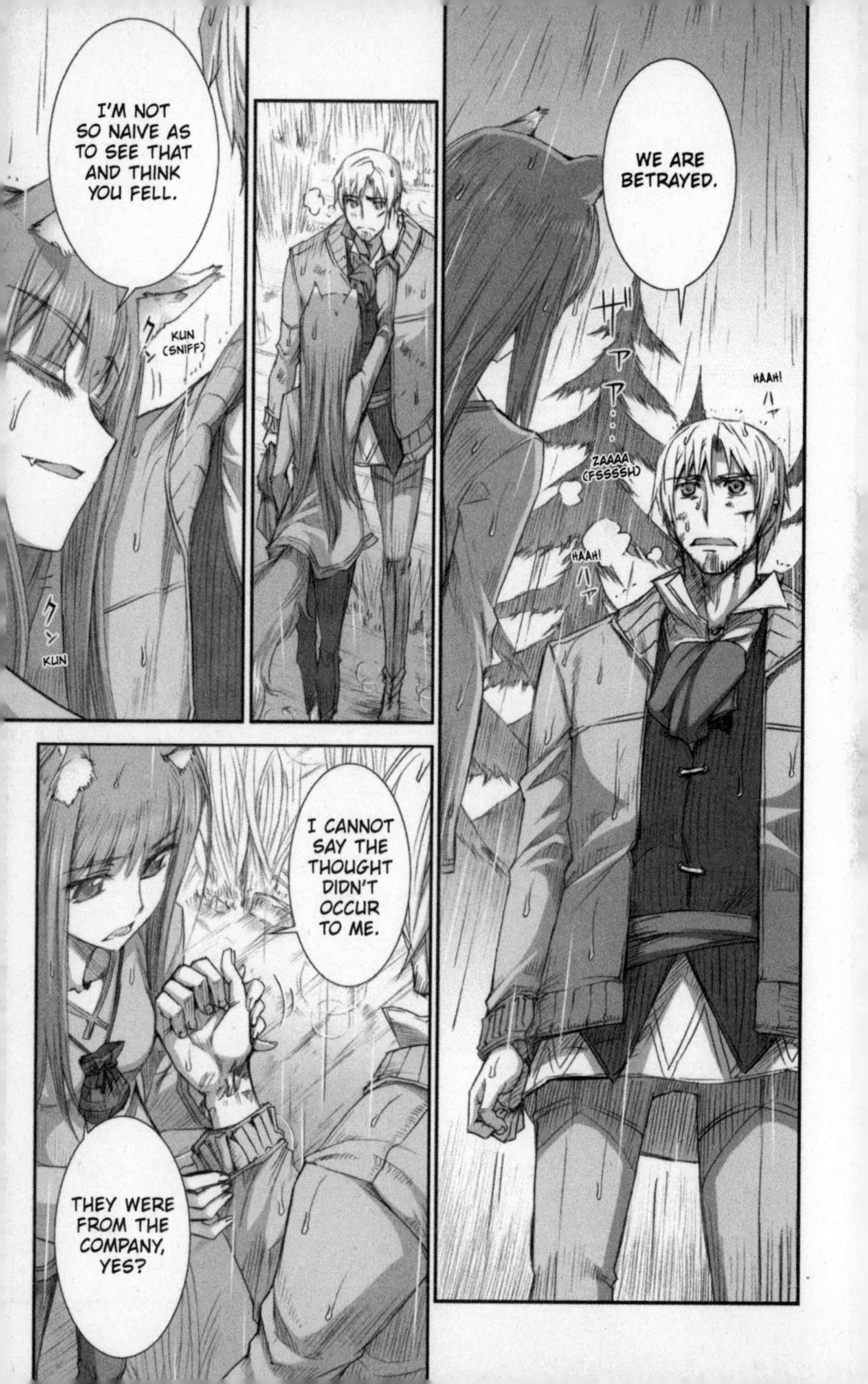
WE ARE BETRAYED.
HAAH!
ZAAAA (FSSSSH)
HAAH!
I'M NOT SO NAIVE AS TO SEE THAT AND THINK YOU FELL.
KUN (SNIFF)
KUN
I CANNOT SAY THE THOUGHT DIDN'T OCCUR TO ME.
THEY WERE FROM THE COMPANY, YES?

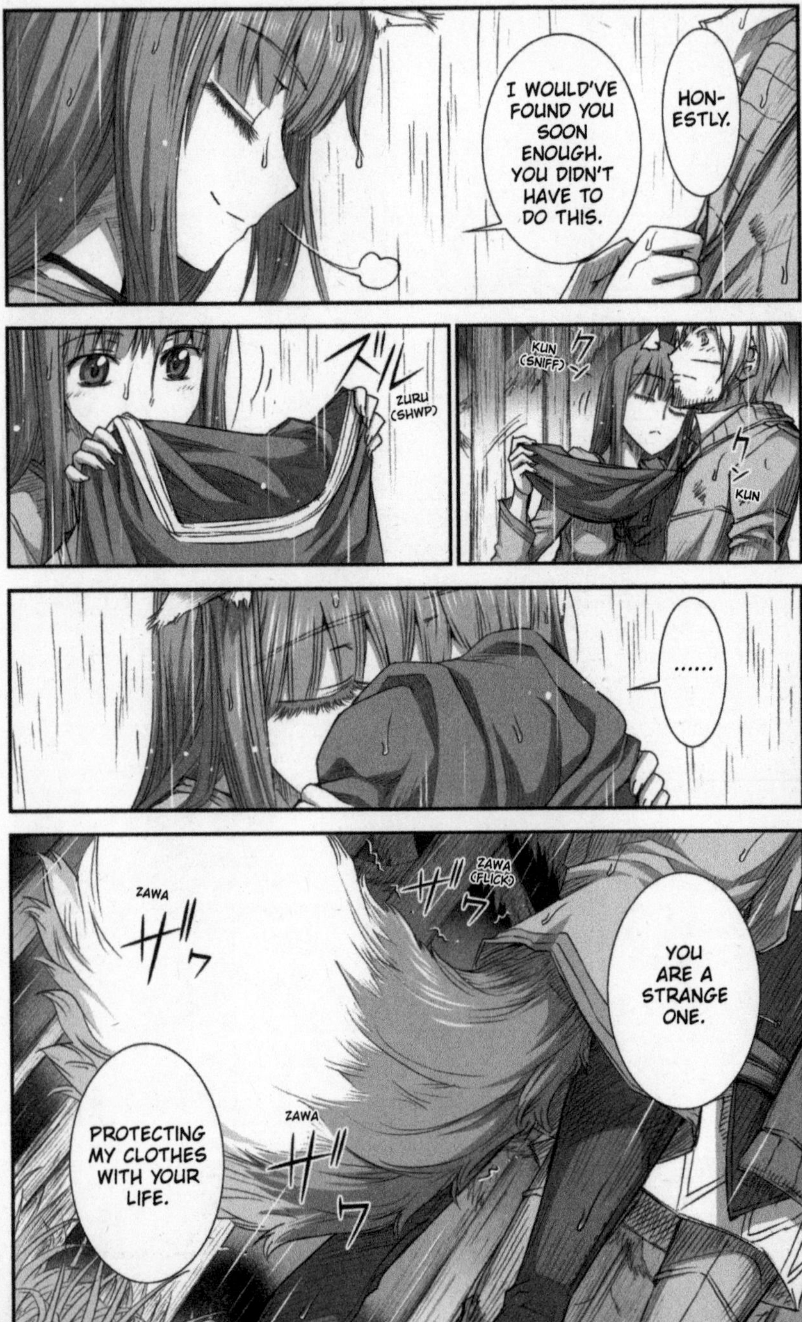
HON-ESTLY.
I WOULD'VE FOUND YOU SOON ENOUGH. YOU DIDN'T HAVE TO DO THIS.
クン
KUN (SNIFF)
クン
KUN
ズル
ZURU (SHWP)
......
ザワ
ZAWA (FLICK)
YOU ARE A STRANGE ONE.
ザワ
ZAWA
ザワ
ZAWA
PROTECTING MY CLOTHES WITH YOUR LIFE.

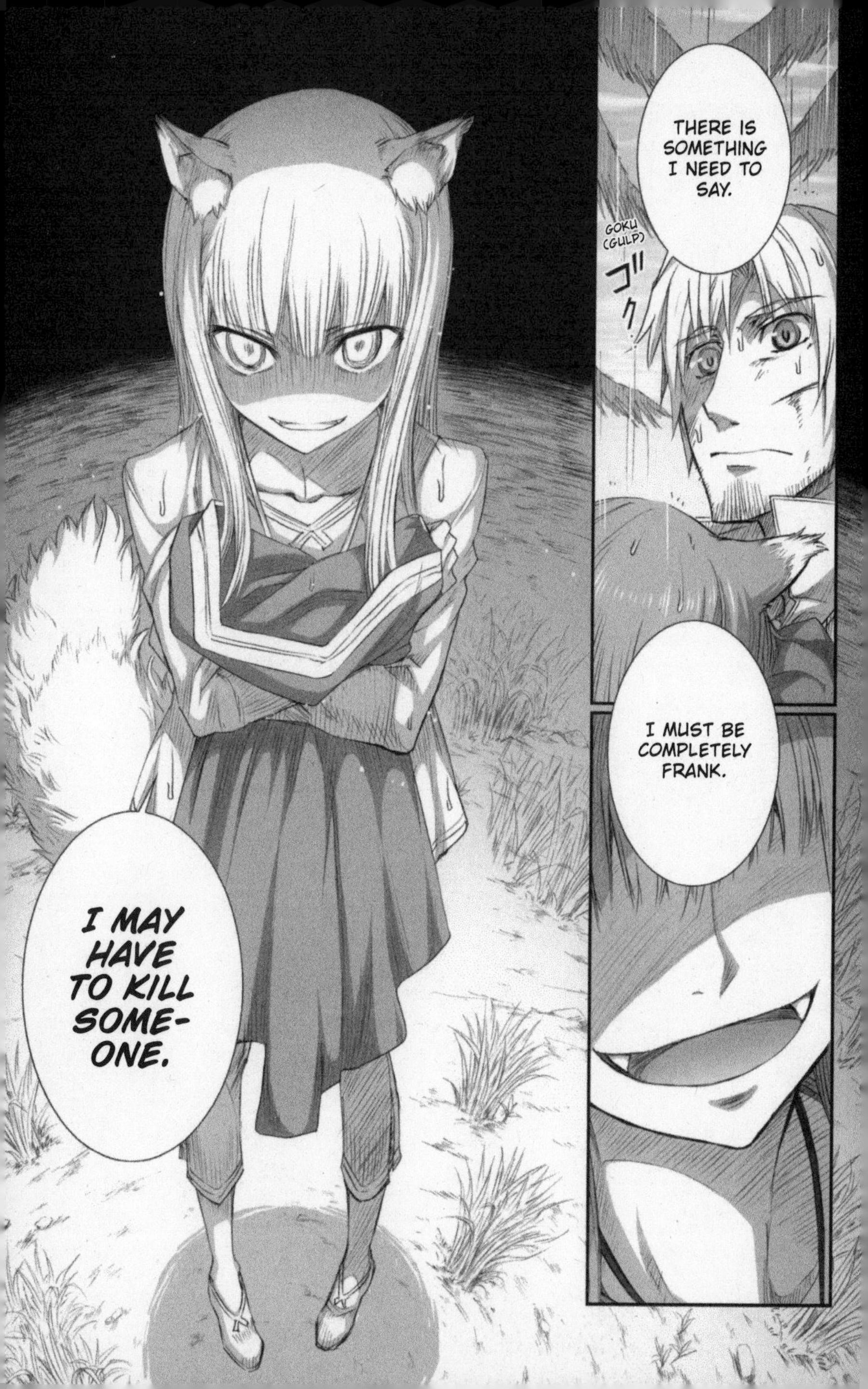
THERE IS SOMETHING I NEED TO SAY.
GOKU (GULP)
ゴク
I MUST BE COMPLETELY FRANK.
I MAY HAVE TO KILL SOME-ONE.

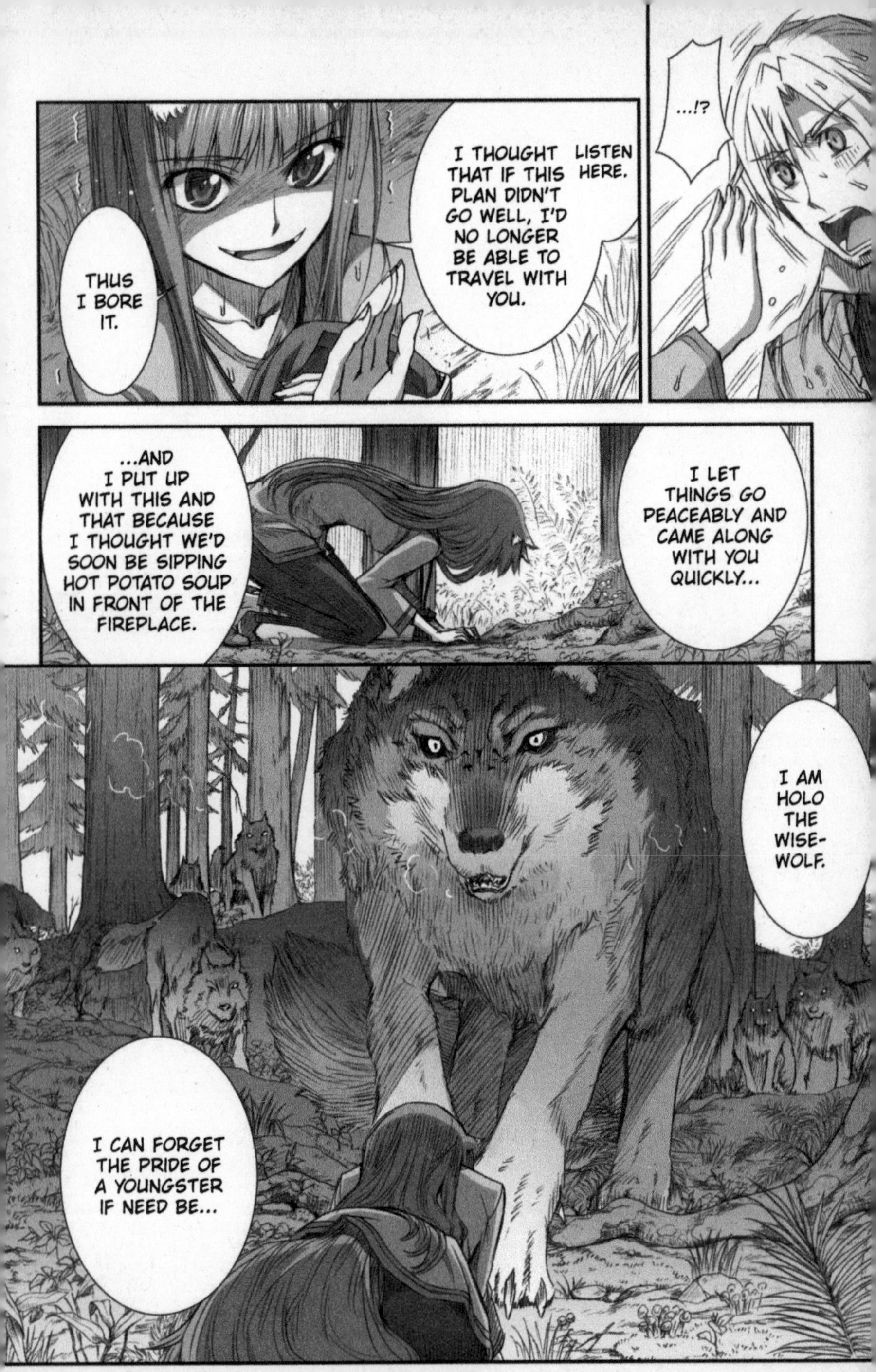
...!?
LISTEN HERE.
I THOUGHT THAT IF THIS PLAN DIDN'T GO WELL, I'D NO LONGER BE ABLE TO TRAVEL WITH YOU.
THUS I BORE IT.
I LET THINGS GO PEACEABLY AND CAME ALONG WITH YOU QUICKLY...
...AND I PUT UP WITH THIS AND THAT BECAUSE I THOUGHT WE'D SOON BE SIPPING HOT POTATO SOUP IN FRONT OF THE FIREPLACE.
I AM HOLO THE WISE-WOLF.
I CAN FORGET THE PRIDE OF A YOUNGSTER IF NEED BE...

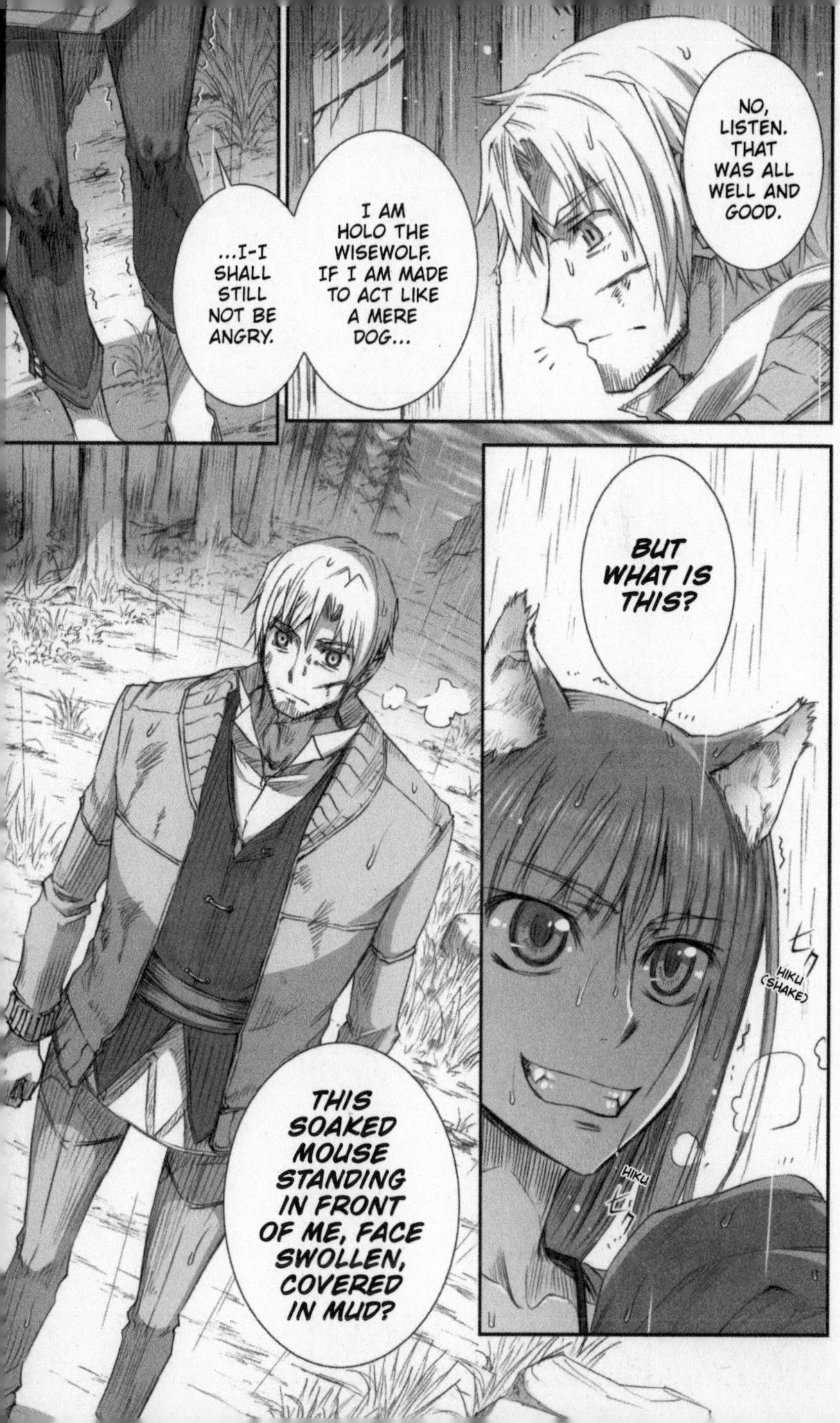
NO, LISTEN. THAT WAS ALL WELL AND GOOD.
I AM HOLO THE WISEWOLF. IF I AM MADE TO ACT LIKE A MERE DOG...
...I-I SHALL STILL NOT BE ANGRY.
BUT WHAT IS THIS?
HIKU (SHAKE)
HIKU
THIS SOAKED MOUSE STANDING IN FRONT OF ME, FACE SWOLLEN, COVERED IN MUD?

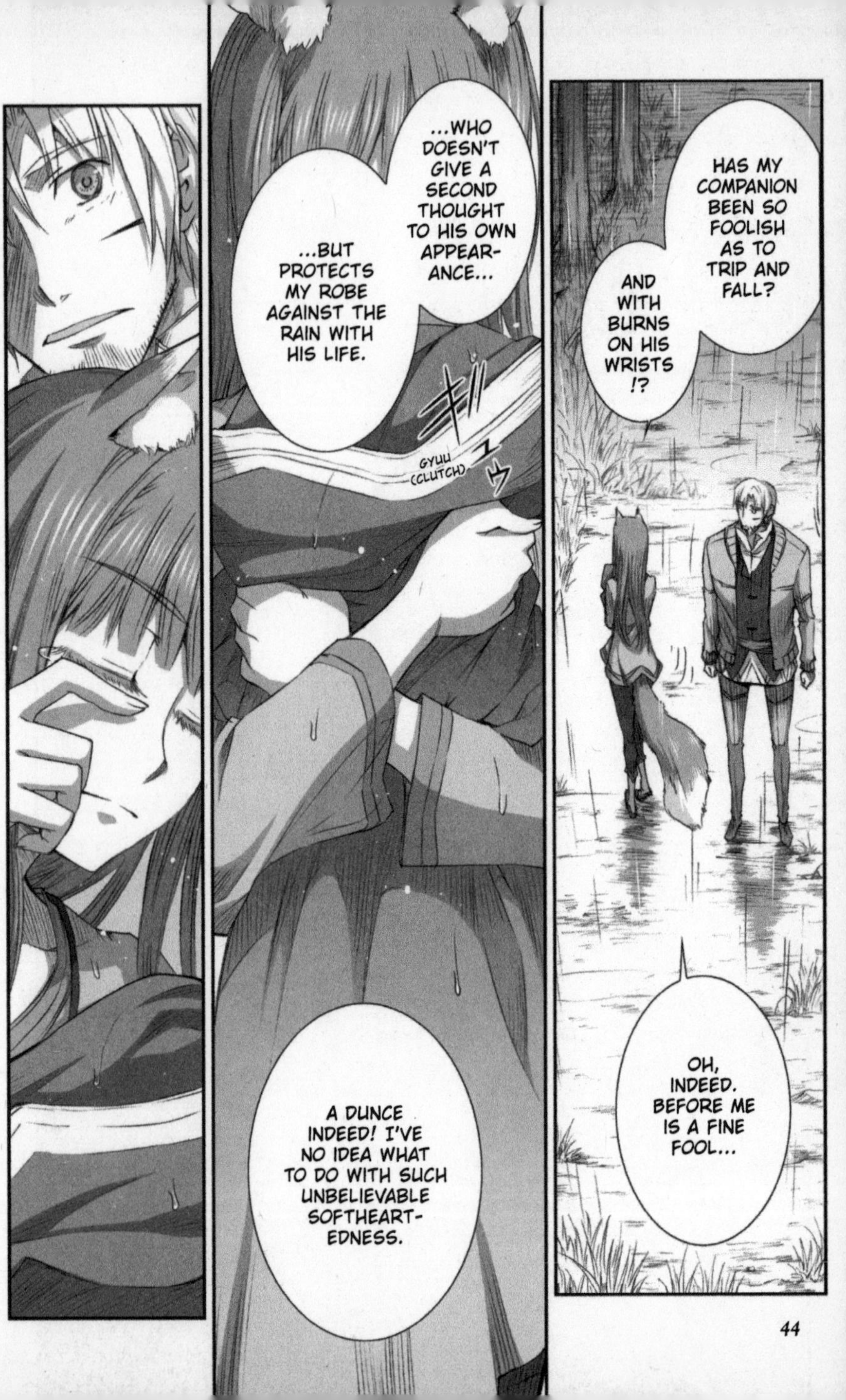
HAS MY COMPANION BEEN SO FOOLISH AS TO TRIP AND FALL?
AND WITH BURNS ON HIS WRISTS !?
OH, INDEED. BEFORE ME IS A FINE FOOL...
...WHO DOESN'T GIVE A SECOND THOUGHT TO HIS OWN APPEAR-ANCE...
...BUT PROTECTS MY ROBE AGAINST THE RAIN WITH HIS LIFE.
GYUU (CLUTCH)
A DUNCE INDEED! I'VE NO IDEA WHAT TO DO WITH SUCH UNBELIEVABLE SOFTHEART-EDNESS.

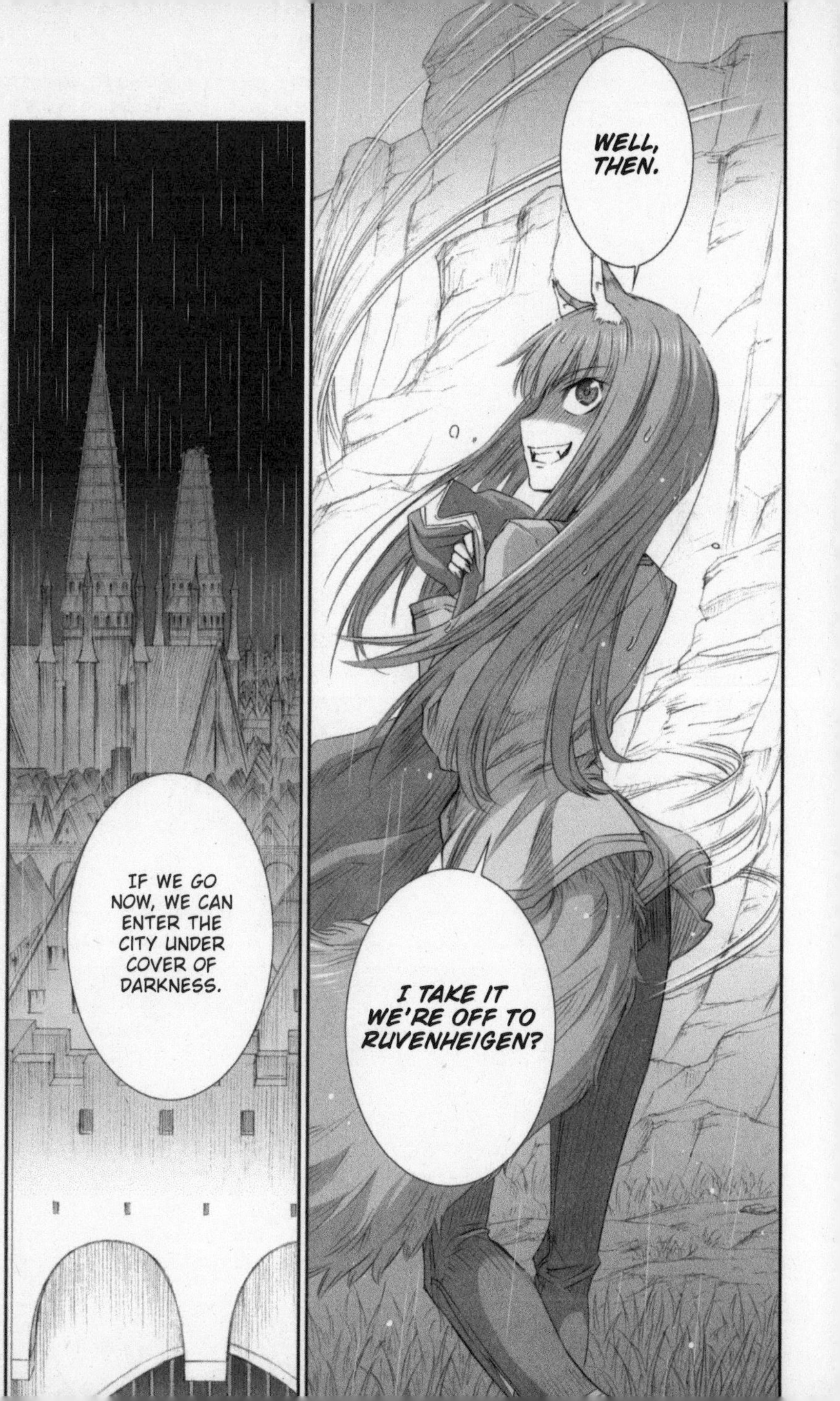
WELL, THEN.
I TAKE IT WE'RE OFF TO RUVENHEIGEN?
IF WE GO NOW, WE CAN ENTER THE CITY UNDER COVER OF DARKNESS.

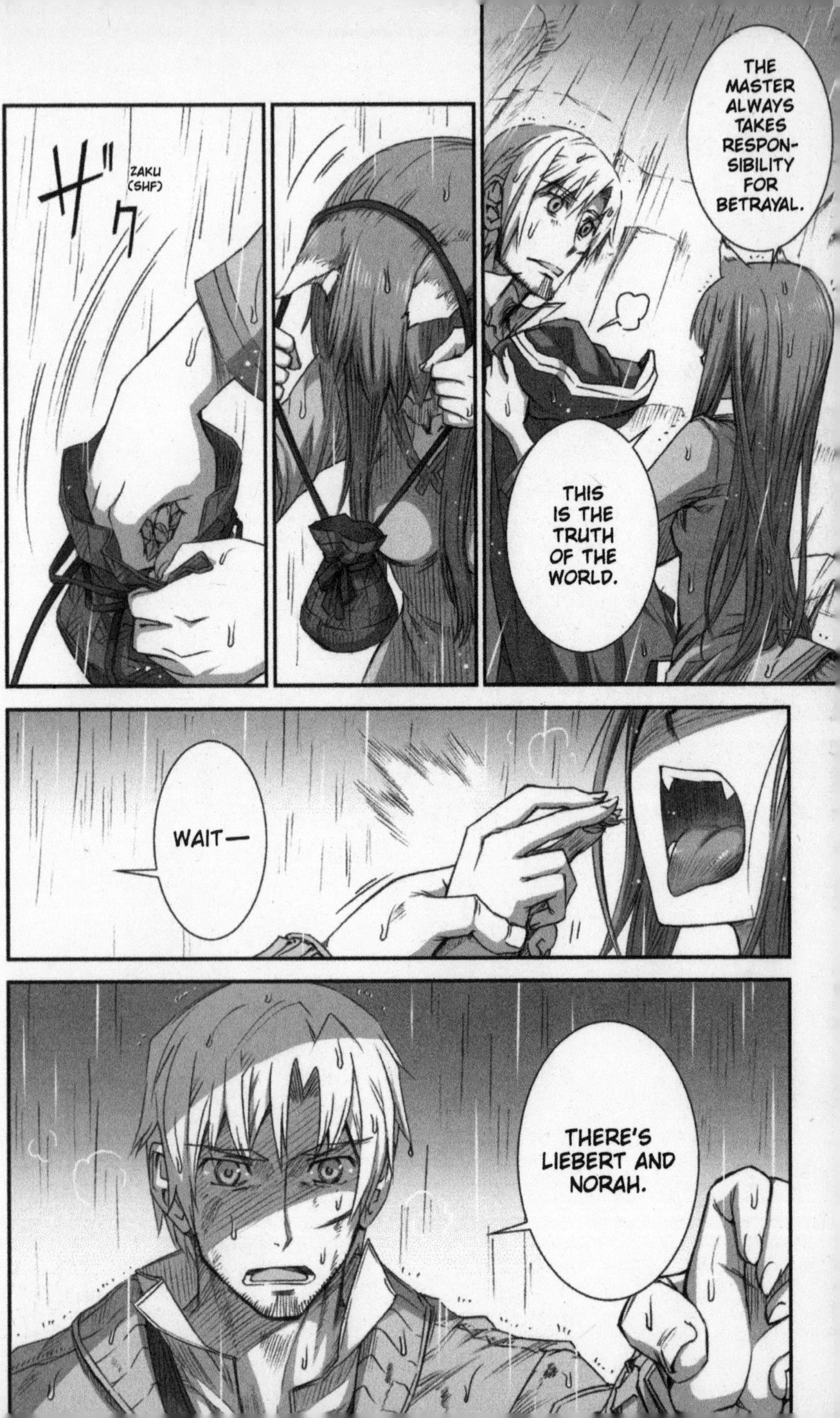
THE MASTER ALWAYS TAKES RESPON-SIBILITY FOR BETRAYAL.
THIS IS THE TRUTH OF THE WORLD.
ザク
ZAKU (SHF)
WAIT—
THERE'S LIEBERT AND NORAH.

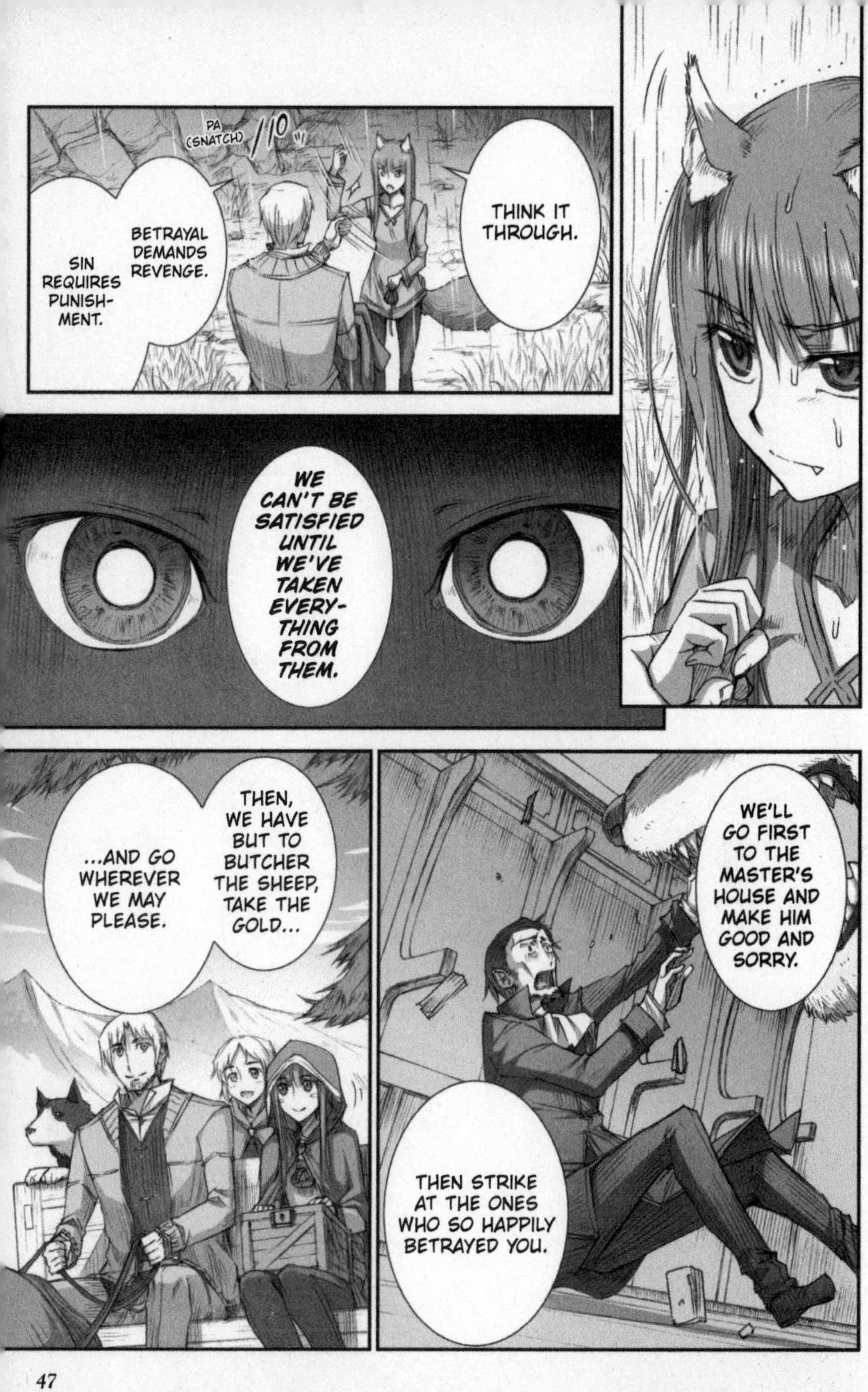
THINK IT THROUGH.
PA (SNATCH)
BETRAYAL DEMANDS REVENGE.
SIN REQUIRES PUNISHMENT.
WE CAN'T BE SATISFIED UNTIL WE'VE TAKEN EVERYTHING FROM THEM.
WE'LL GO FIRST TO THE MASTER'S HOUSE AND MAKE HIM GOOD AND SORRY.
THEN STRIKE AT THE ONES WHO SO HAPPILY BETRAYED YOU.
THEN, WE HAVE BUT TO BUTCHER THE SHEEP, TAKE THE GOLD...
...AND GO WHEREVER WE MAY PLEASE.

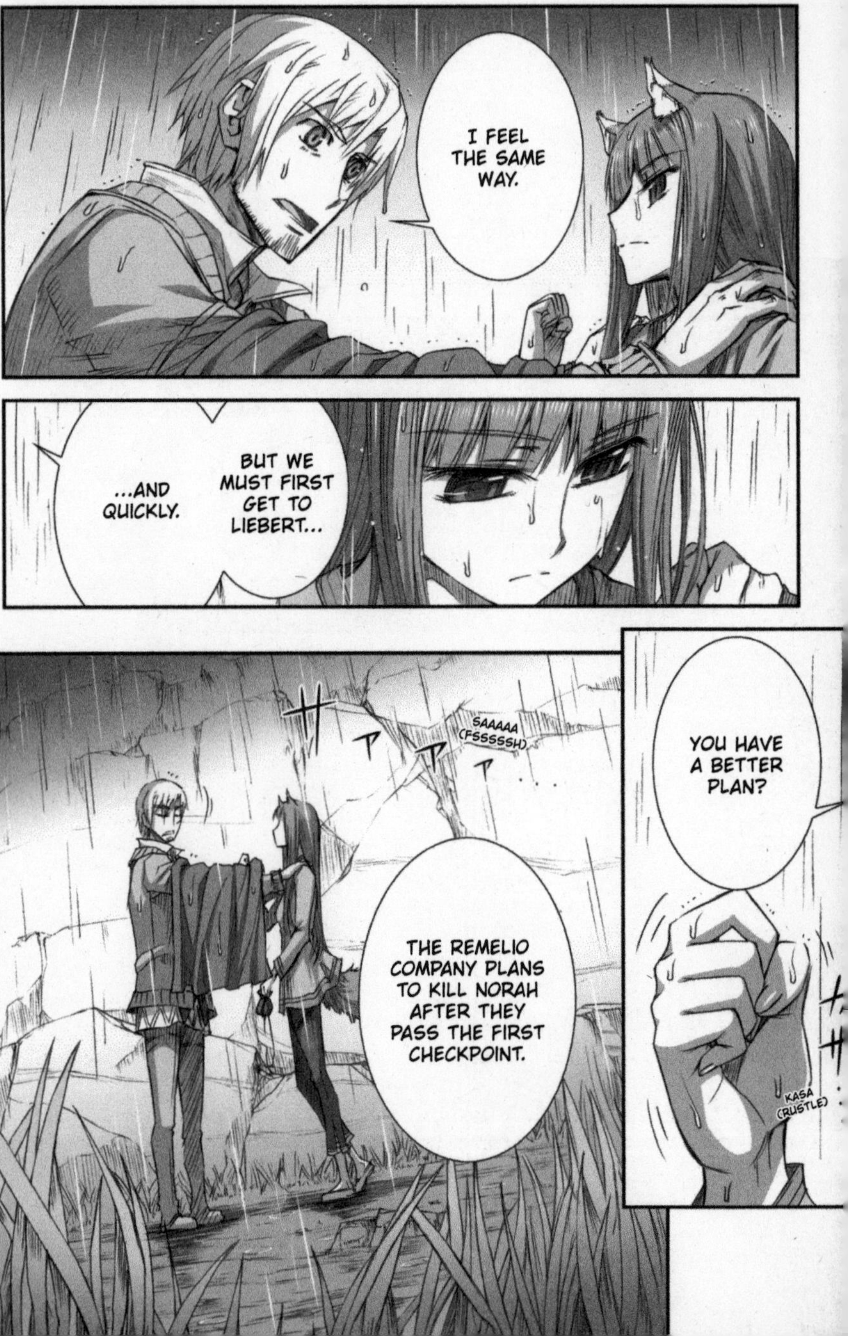
I FEEL THE SAME WAY.
BUT WE MUST FIRST GET TO LIEBERT...
...AND QUICKLY.
YOU HAVE A BETTER PLAN?
KASA (RUSTLE)
SAAAAA (FSSSSSH)
THE REMELIO COMPANY PLANS TO KILL NORAH AFTER THEY PASS THE FIRST CHECKPOINT.

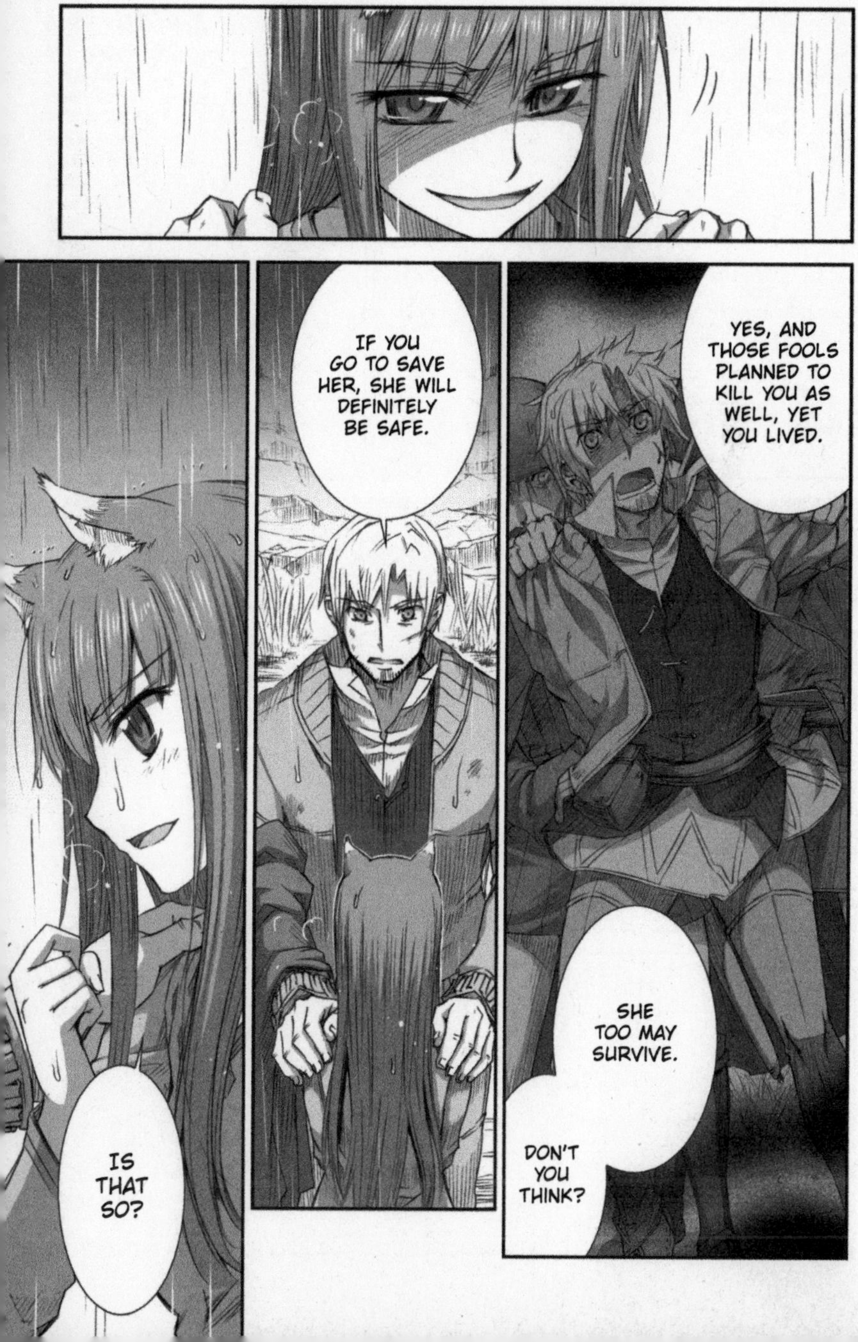
YES, AND THOSE FOOLS PLANNED TO KILL YOU AS WELL, YET YOU LIVED.
SHE TOO MAY SURVIVE.
DON'T YOU THINK?
IF YOU GO TO SAVE HER, SHE WILL DEFINITELY BE SAFE.
IS THAT SO?

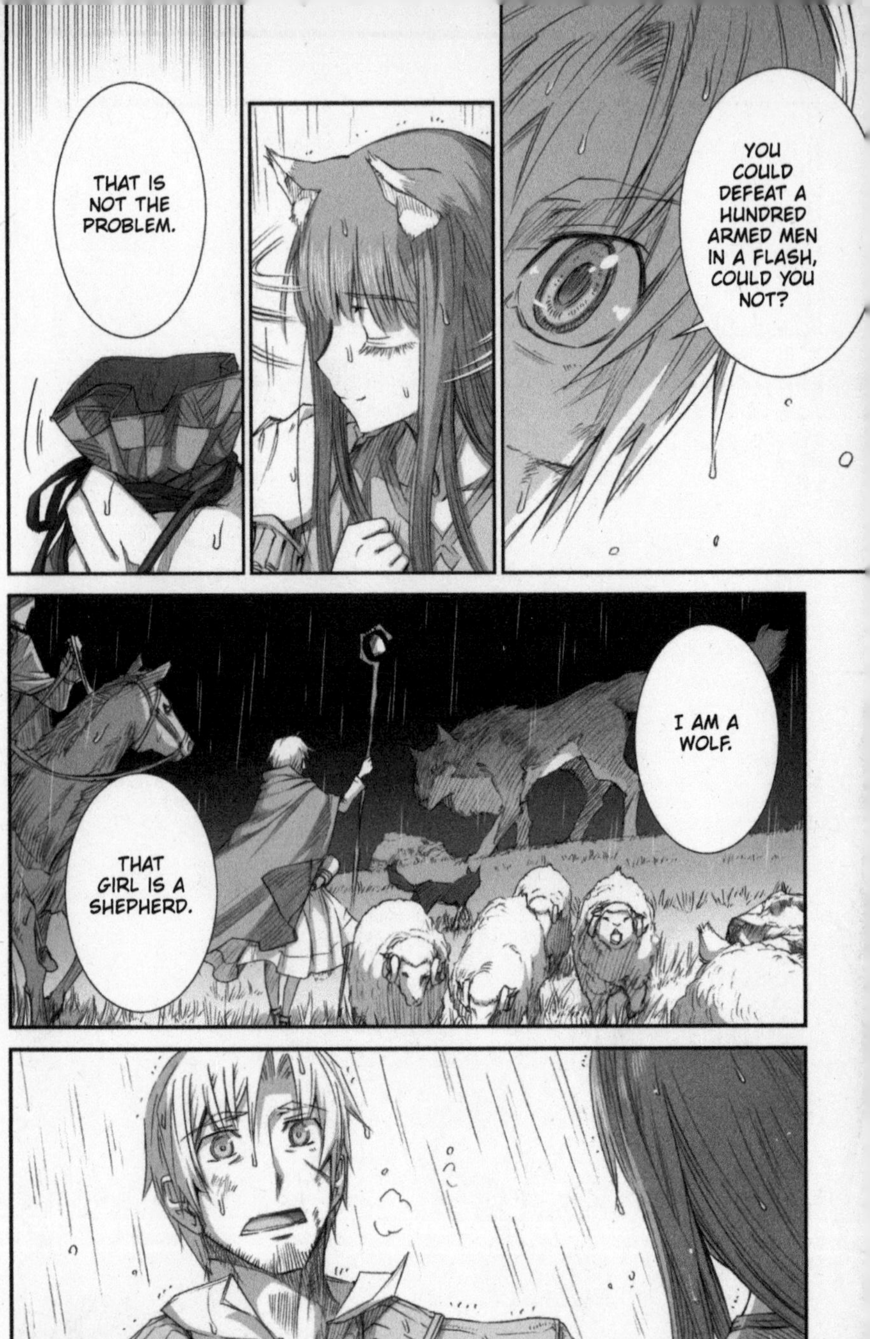
YOU COULD DEFEAT A HUNDRED ARMED MEN IN A FLASH, COULD YOU NOT?
THAT IS NOT THE PROBLEM.
I AM A WOLF.
THAT GIRL IS A SHEPHERD.

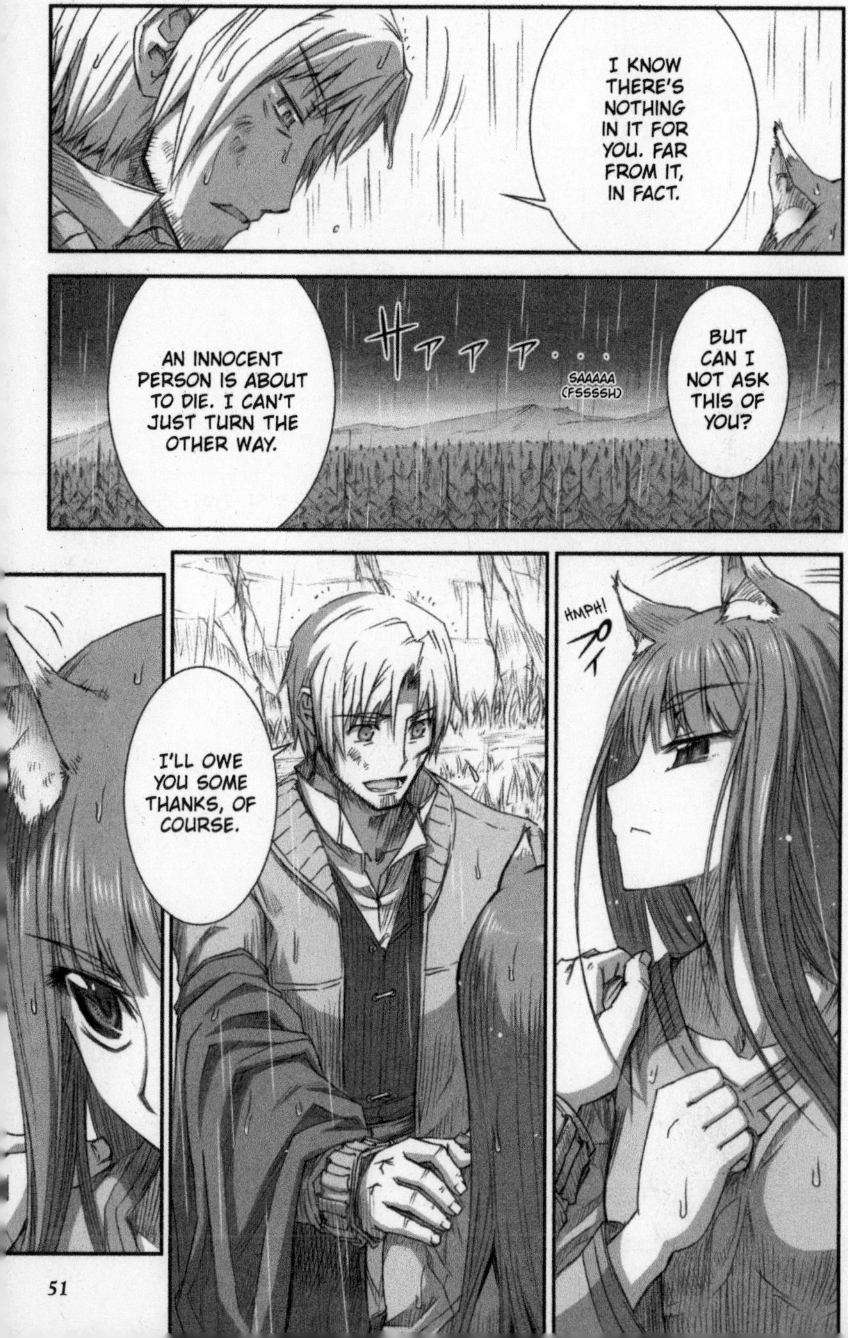
I KNOW THERE'S NOTHING IN IT FOR YOU. FAR FROM IT, IN FACT.
BUT CAN I NOT ASK THIS OF YOU?
SAAAAA (FSSSSH)
AN INNOCENT PERSON IS ABOUT TO DIE. I CAN'T JUST TURN THE OTHER WAY.
HMPH!
I'LL OWE YOU SOME THANKS, OF COURSE.

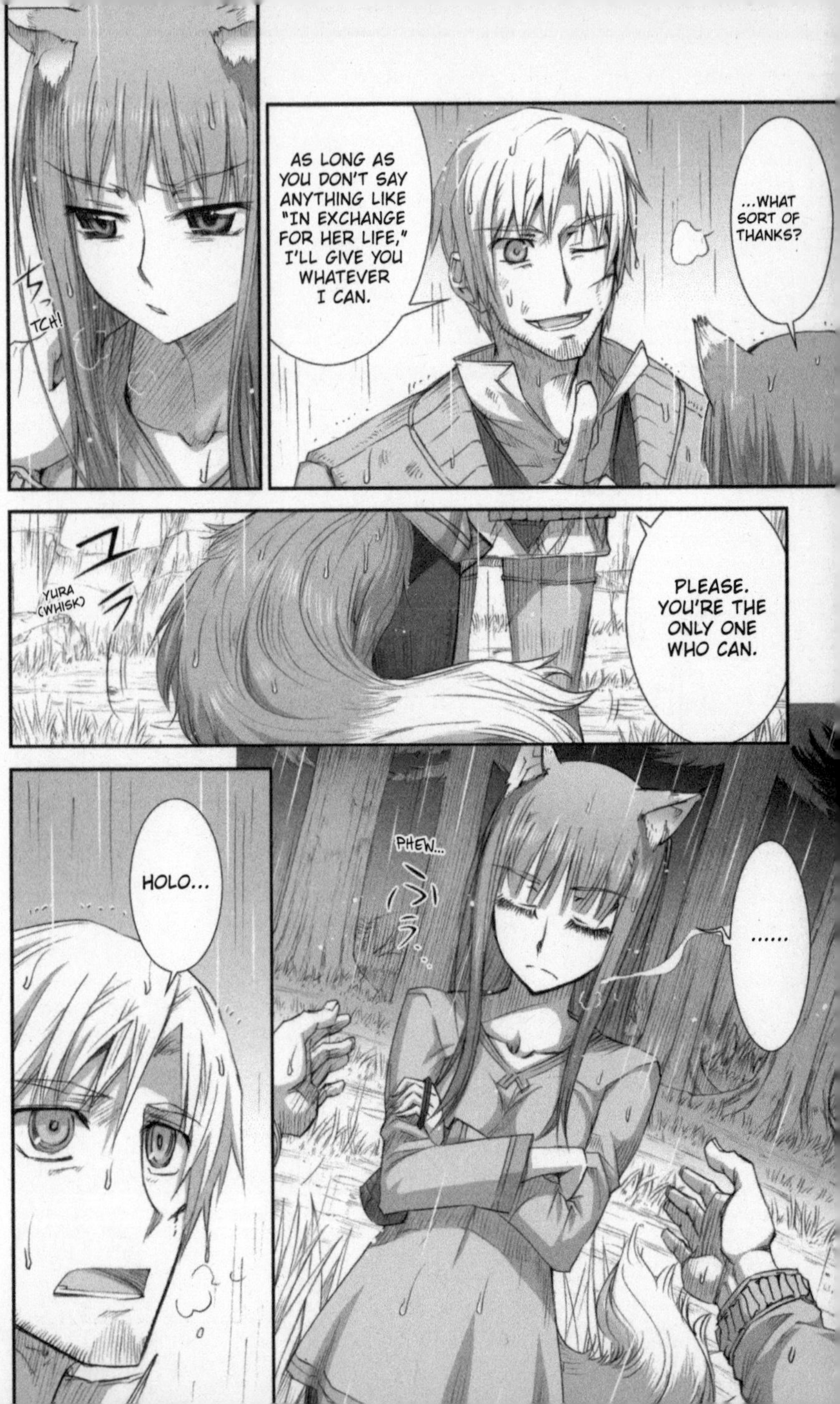
...WHAT SORT OF THANKS?
AS LONG AS YOU DON'T SAY ANYTHING LIKE "IN EXCHANGE FOR HER LIFE," I'LL GIVE YOU WHATEVER I CAN.
TCH!
PLEASE. YOU'RE THE ONLY ONE WHO CAN.
YURA (WHISK)
......
PHEW...
HOLO...

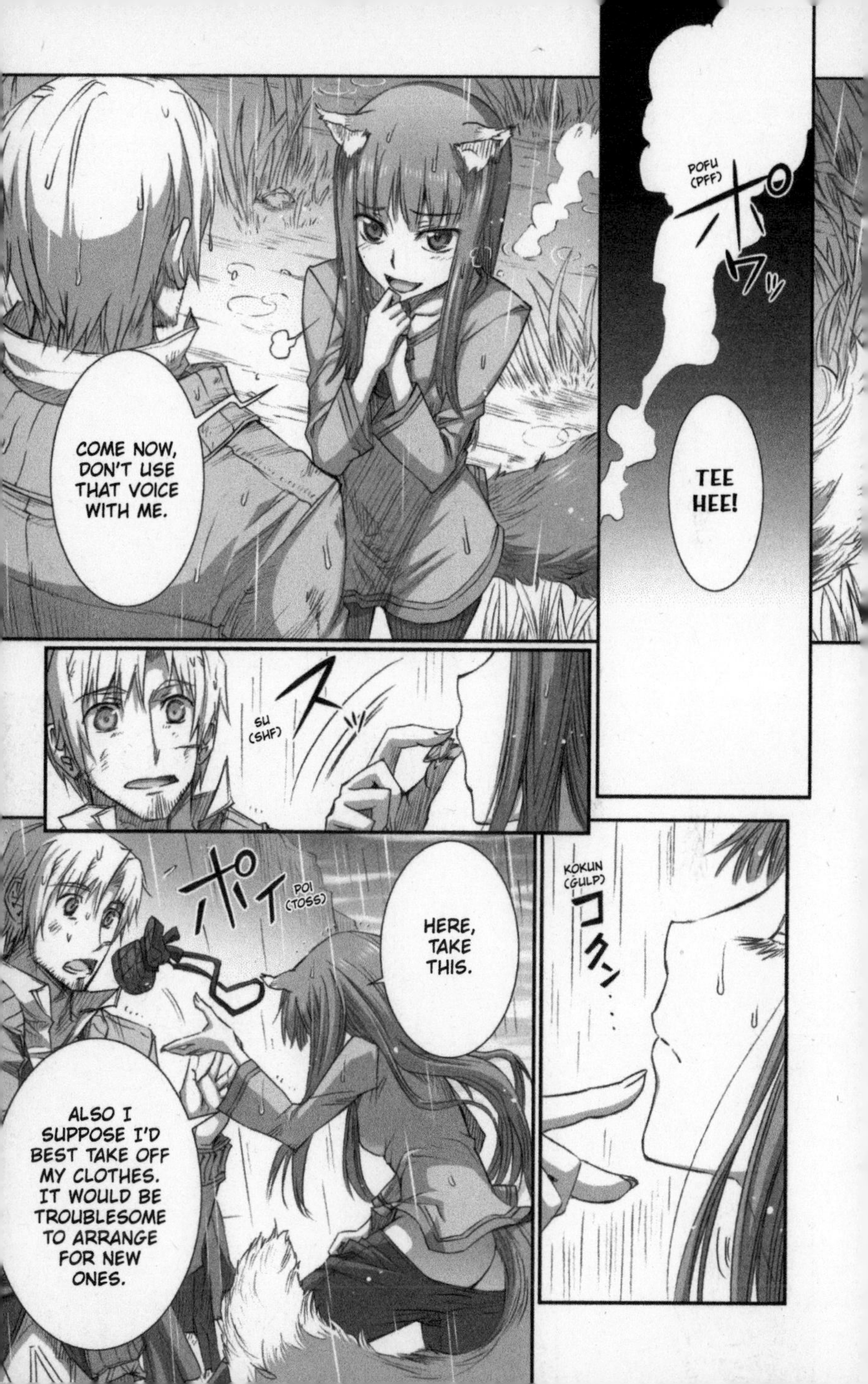
POFU (PFF)
ポフッ
TEE HEE!
COME NOW, DON'T USE THAT VOICE WITH ME.
SU (SHF)
スッ
KOKUN (GULP)
コクン…
ポイ
POI (TOSS)
HERE, TAKE THIS.
ALSO I SUPPOSE I'D BEST TAKE OFF MY CLOTHES. IT WOULD BE TROUBLESOME TO ARRANGE FOR NEW ONES.

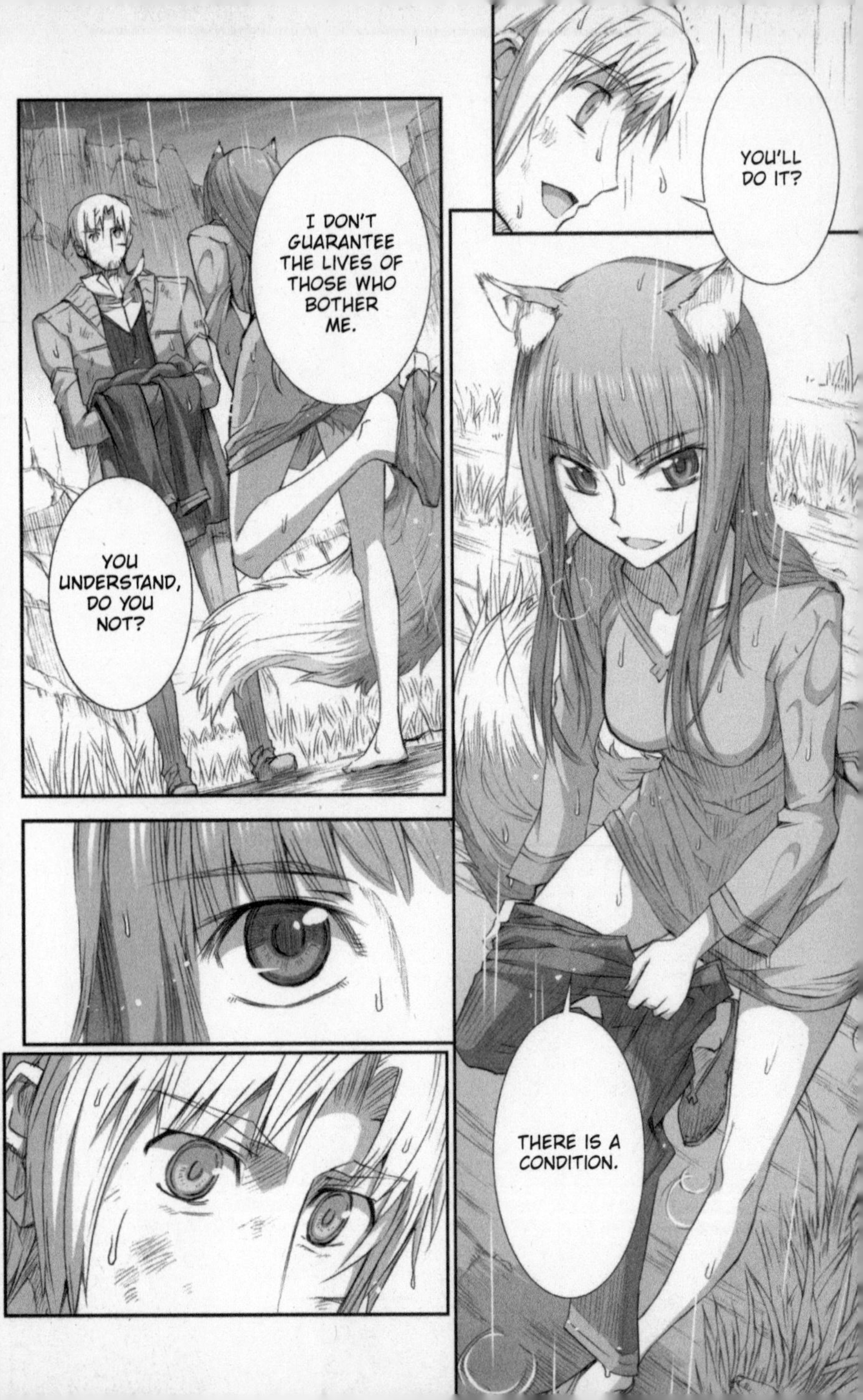
YOU'LL DO IT?
I DON'T GUARANTEE THE LIVES OF THOSE WHO BOTHER ME.
YOU UNDERSTAND, DO YOU NOT?
THERE IS A CONDITION.

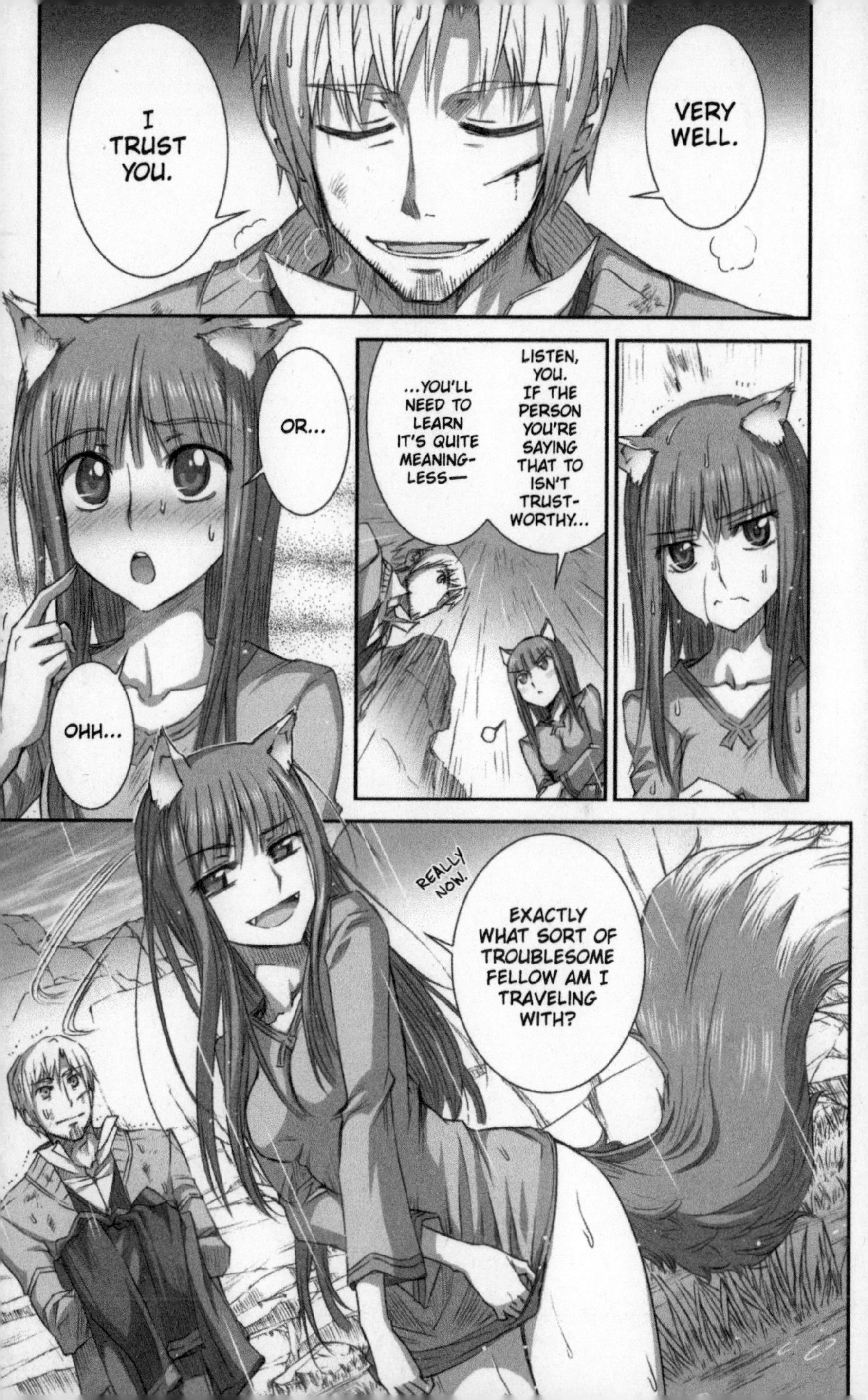
VERY WELL.
I TRUST YOU.
LISTEN, YOU. IF THE PERSON YOU'RE SAYING THAT TO ISN'T TRUST-WORTHY...
...YOU'LL NEED TO LEARN IT'S QUITE MEANING-LESS—
OR...
OHH...
REALLY NOW.
EXACTLY WHAT SORT OF TROUBLESOME FELLOW AM I TRAVELING WITH?

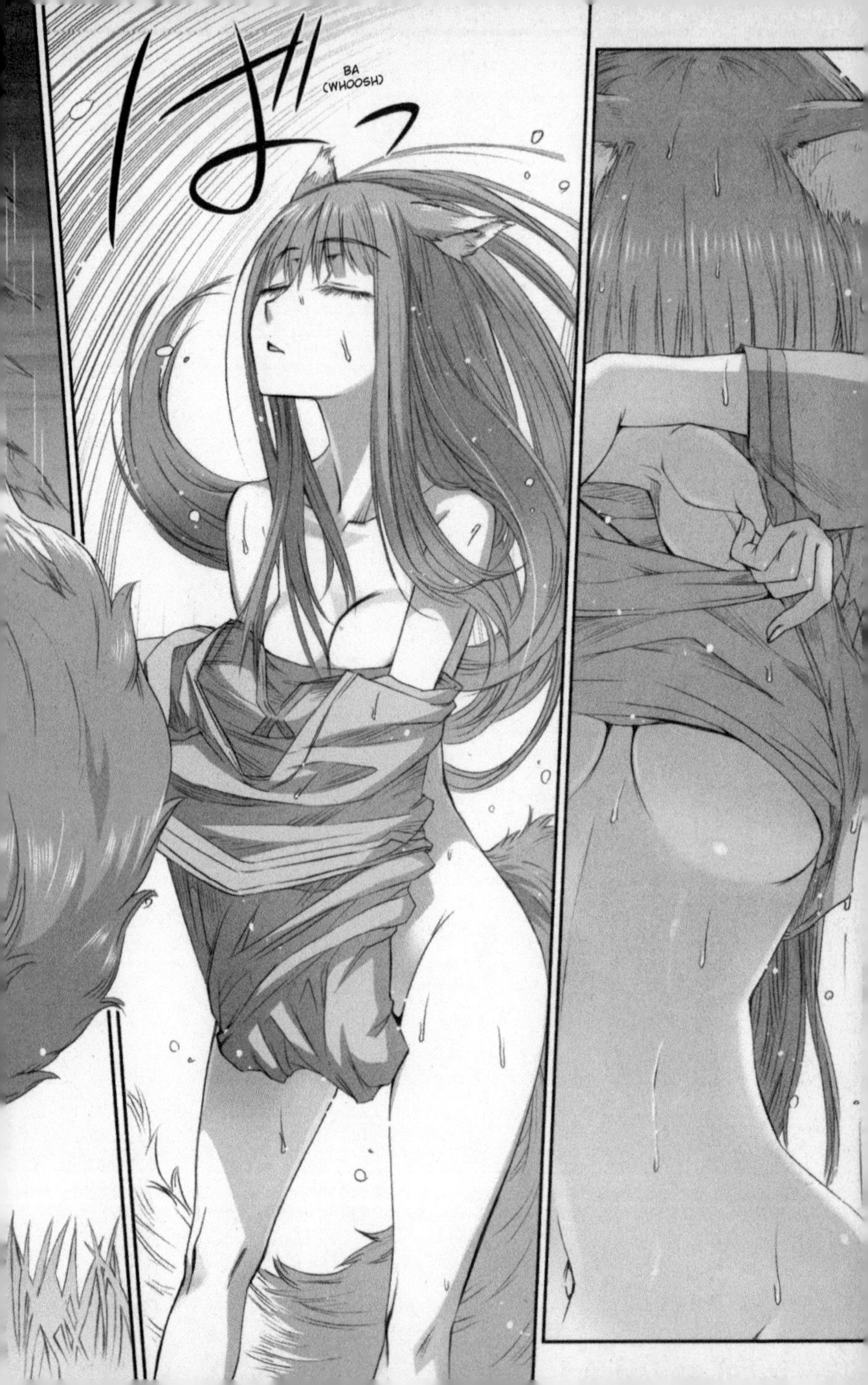
ばっ
BA (WHOOSH)

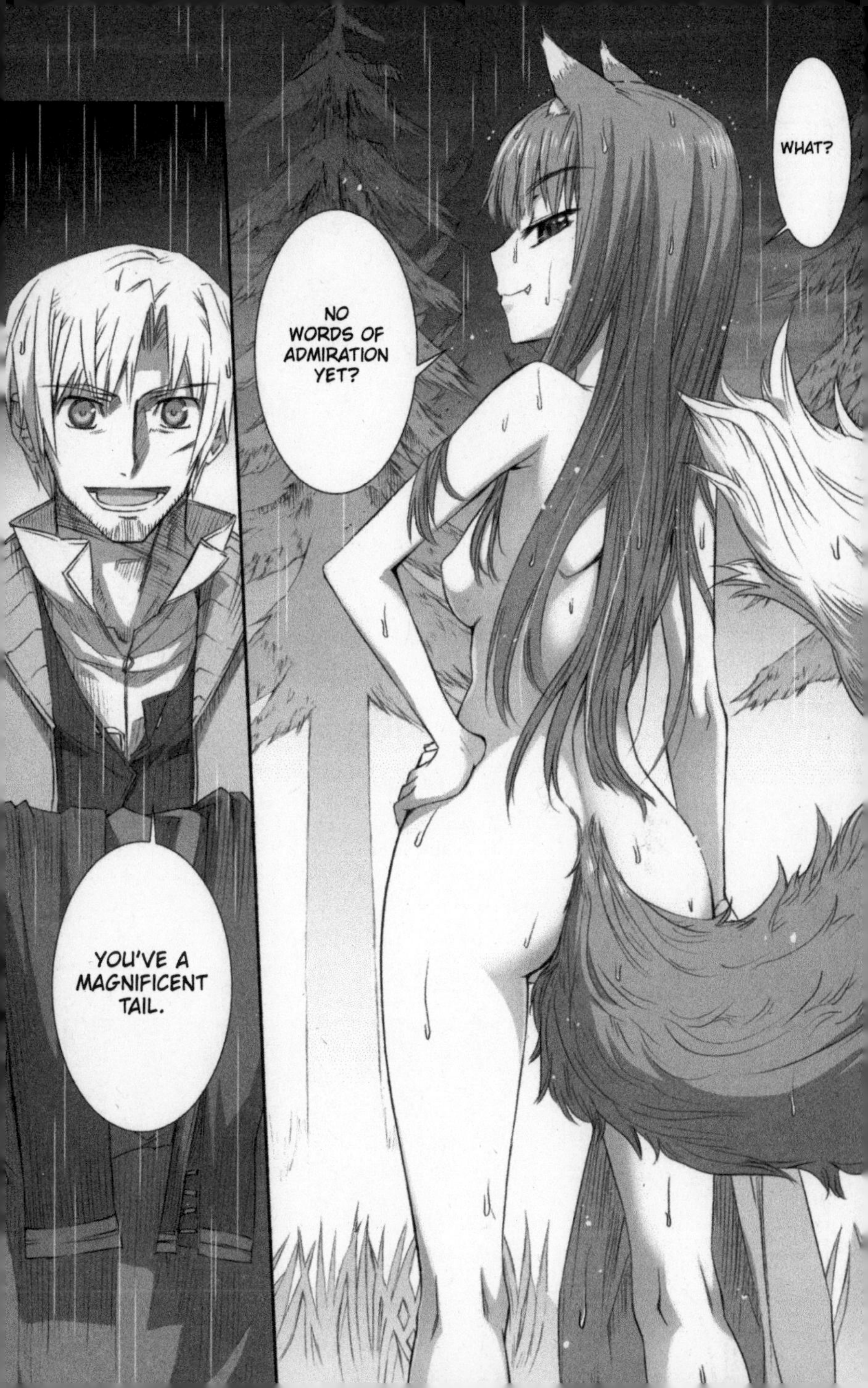
WHAT?
NO WORDS OF ADMIRATION YET?
YOU'VE A MAGNIFICENT TAIL.

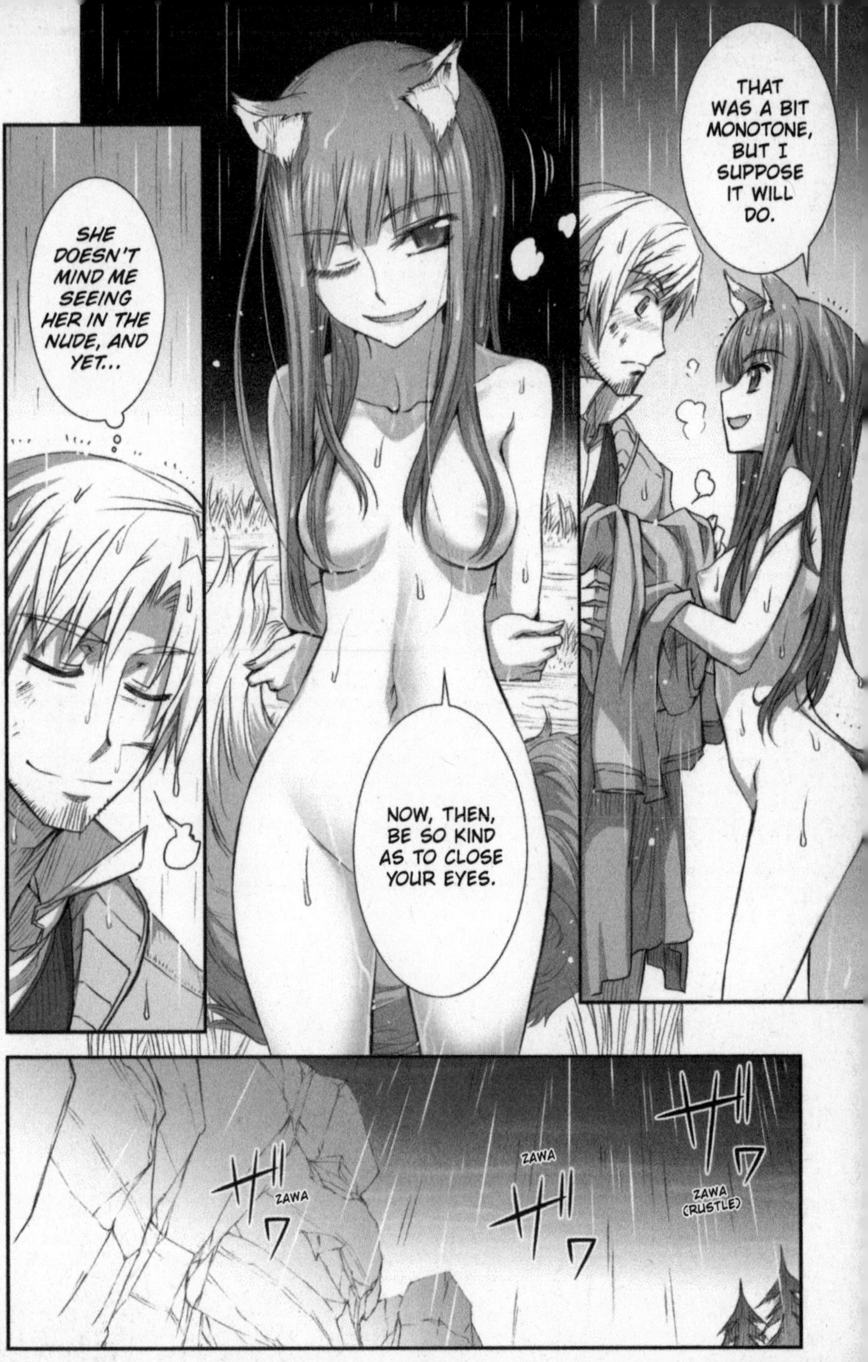
THAT WAS A BIT MONOTONE, BUT I SUPPOSE IT WILL DO.
NOW, THEN, BE SO KIND AS TO CLOSE YOUR EYES.
SHE DOESN'T MIND ME SEEING HER IN THE NUDE, AND YET...
ZAWA (RUSTLE)
ZAWA
ZAWA

SPICE & WOLF

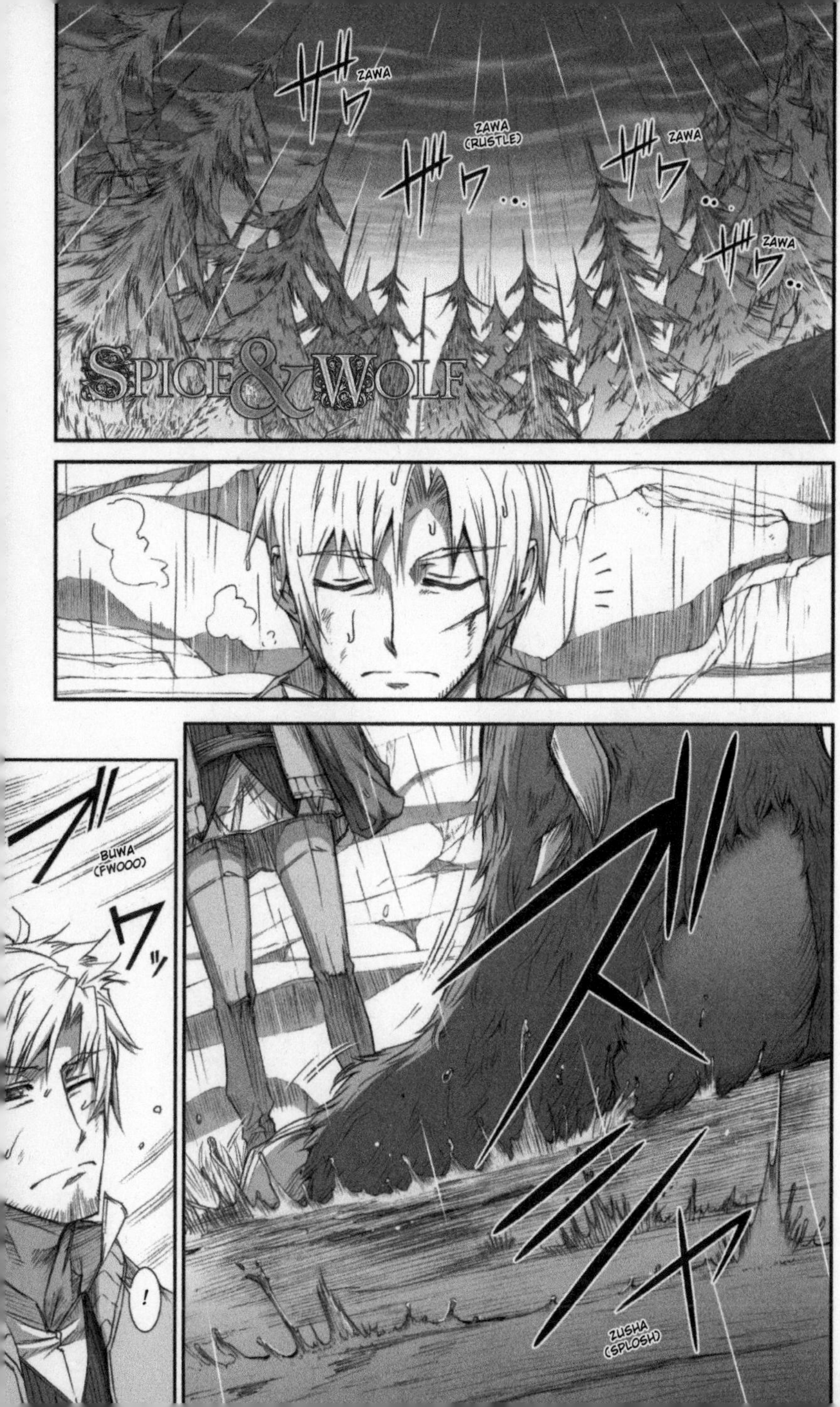

ZAWA
ZAWA
ZAWA (RUSTLE)
ZAWA
SPICE & WOLF
ZUSHA (SPLOSH)
BUWA (FWOOO)
!

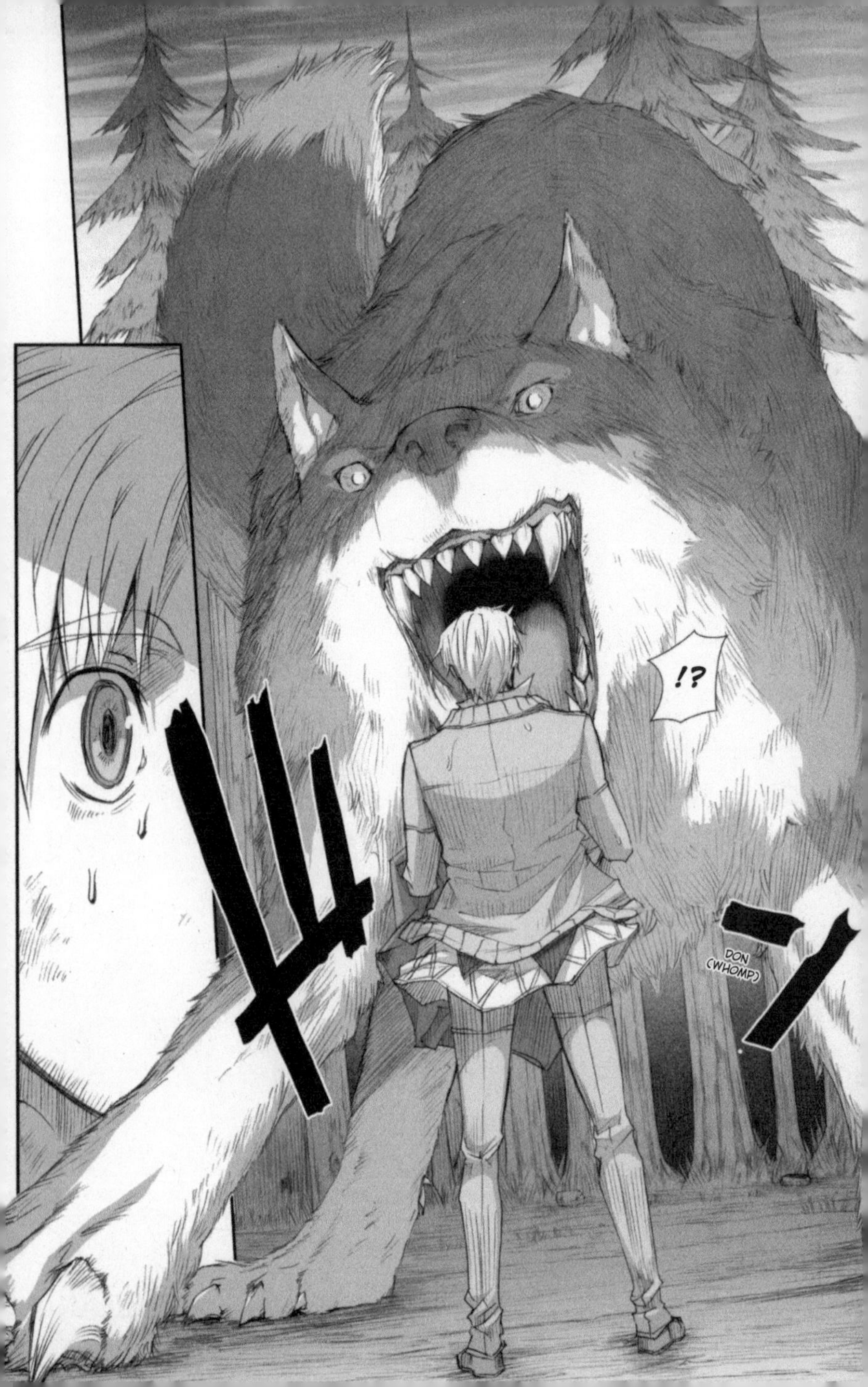
!?
ドン
DON
(WHOMP)

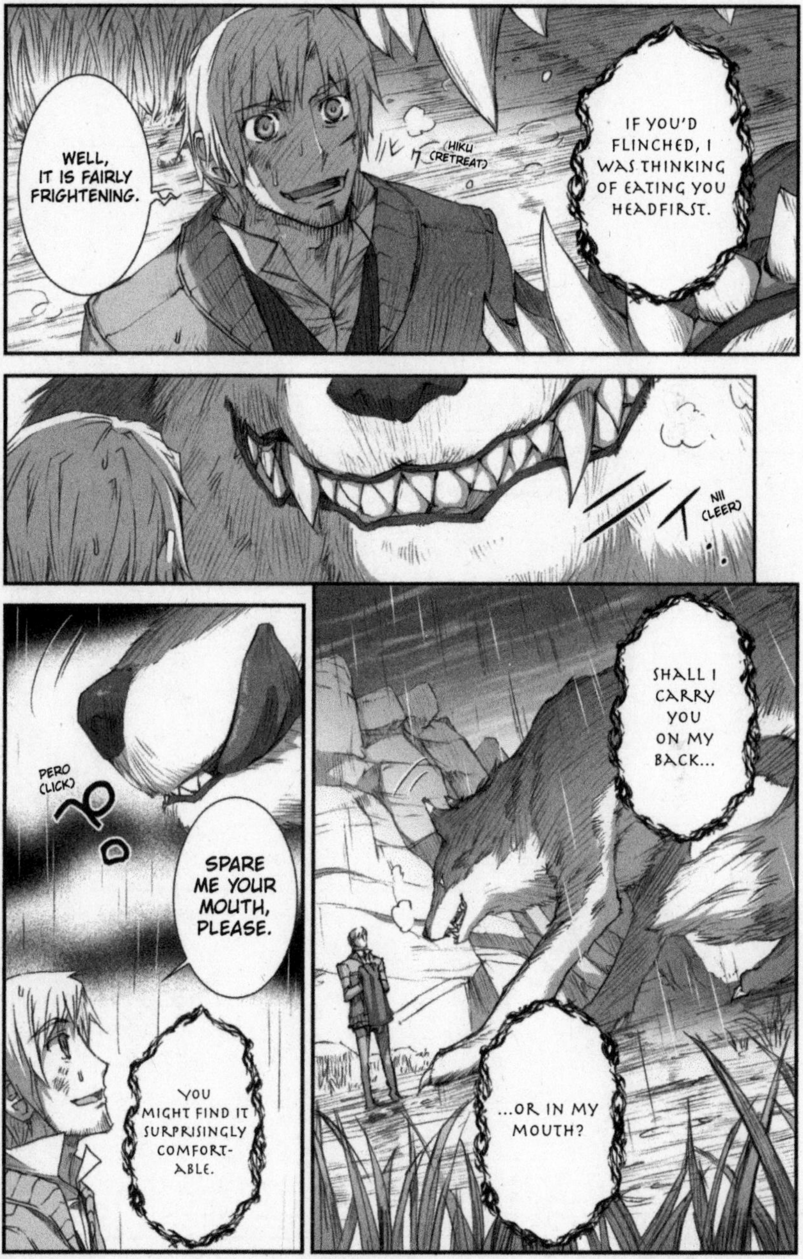
IF YOU'D FLINCHED, I WAS THINKING OF EATING YOU HEADFIRST.
HIKU (RETREAT)
WELL, IT IS FAIRLY FRIGHTENING.
NII (LEER)
SHALL I CARRY YOU ON MY BACK...
...OR IN MY MOUTH?
PERO (LICK)
SPARE ME YOUR MOUTH, PLEASE.
YOU MIGHT FIND IT SURPRISINGLY COMFORT-ABLE.

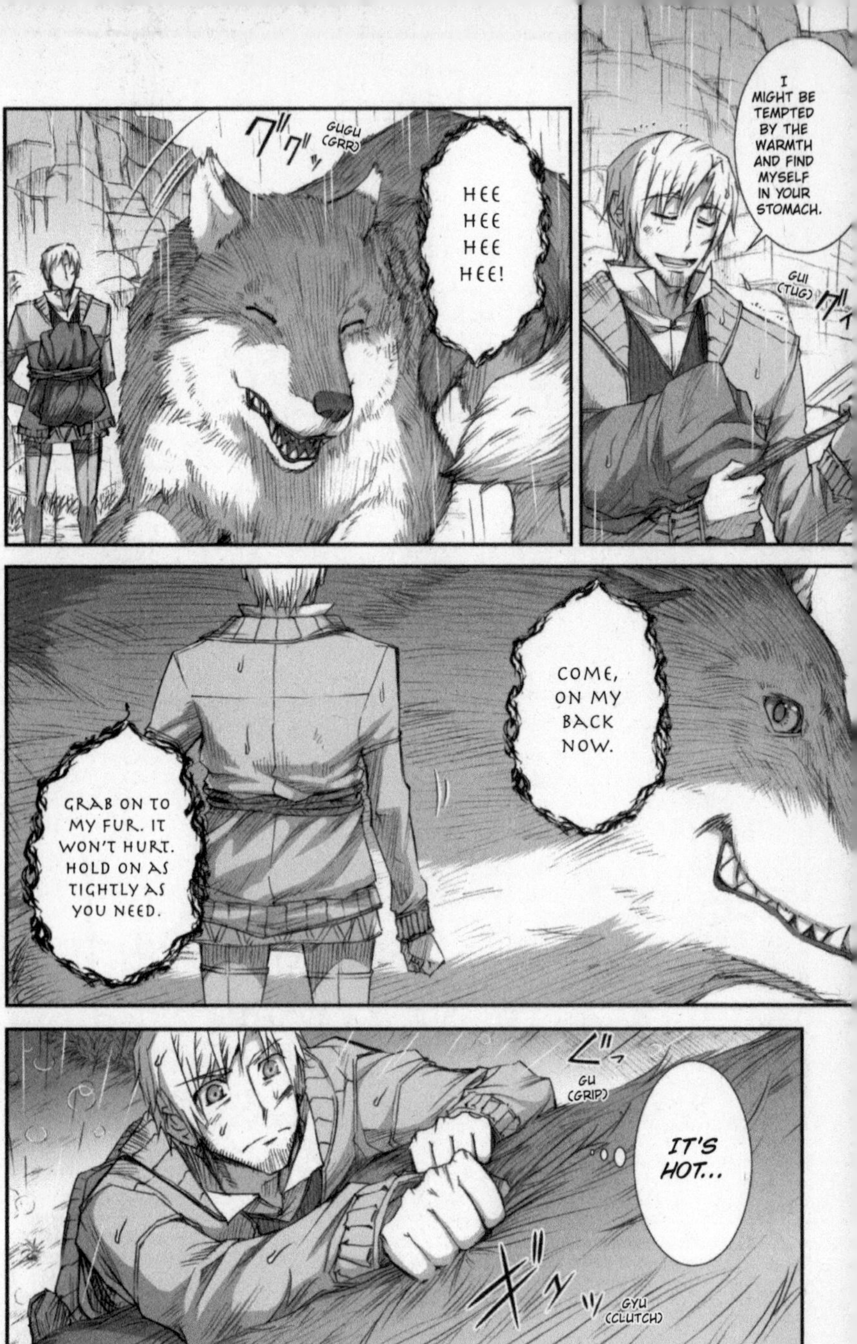
I MIGHT BE TEMPTED BY THE WARMTH AND FIND MYSELF IN YOUR STOMACH.
GUI (TUG)
GUGU (GRR)
HEE HEE HEE HEE!
COME, ON MY BACK NOW.
GRAB ON TO MY FUR. IT WON'T HURT. HOLD ON AS TIGHTLY AS YOU NEED.
GU (GRIP)
IT'S HOT...
GYU (CLUTCH)

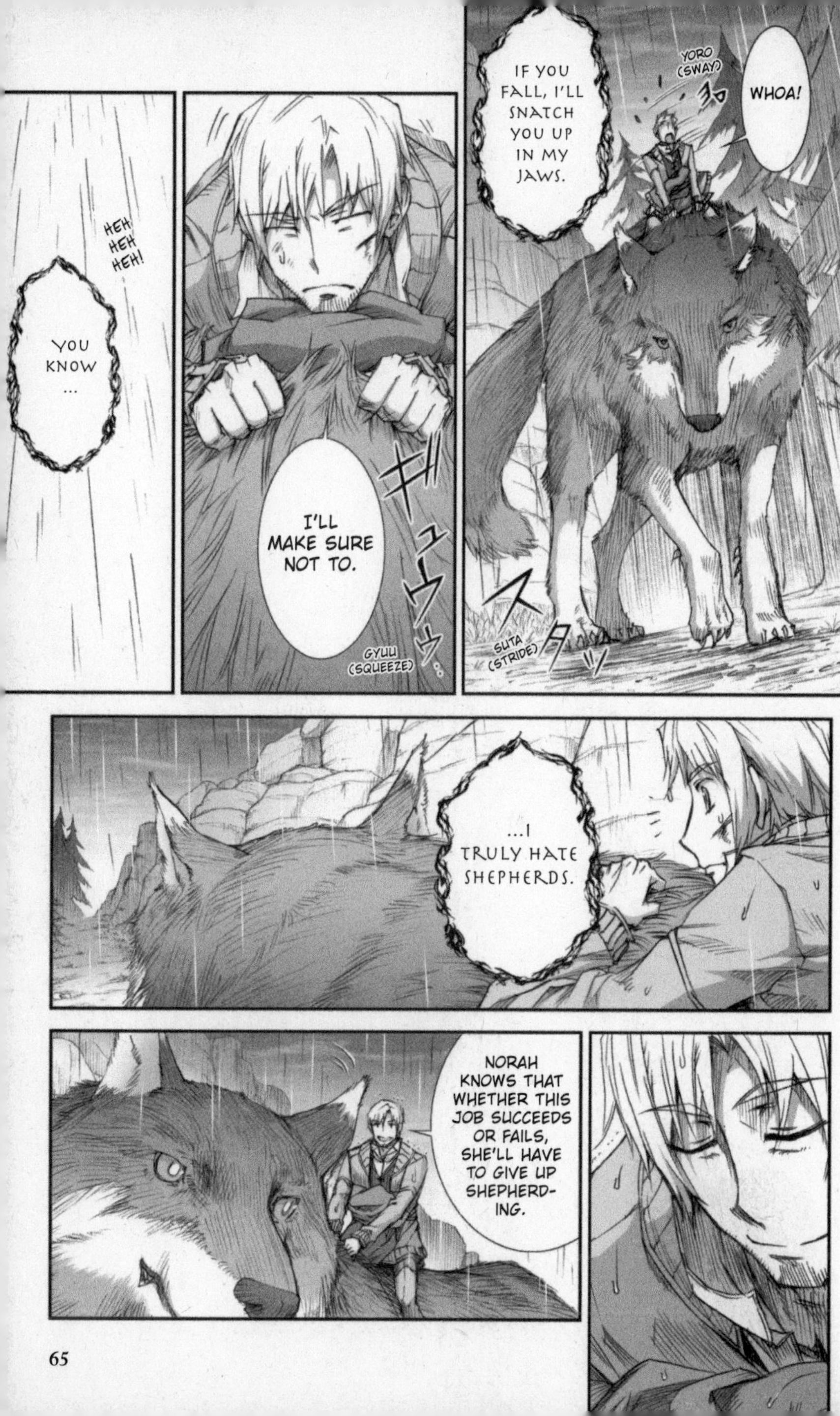
WHOA!
YORO (SWAY)
IF YOU FALL, I'LL SNATCH YOU UP IN MY JAWS.
SUTA (STRIDE)
I'LL MAKE SURE NOT TO.
GYUU (SQUEEZE)
HEH HEH HEH!
YOU KNOW ...
...I TRULY HATE SHEPHERDS.
NORAH KNOWS THAT WHETHER THIS JOB SUCCEEDS OR FAILS, SHE'LL HAVE TO GIVE UP SHEPHERD-ING.

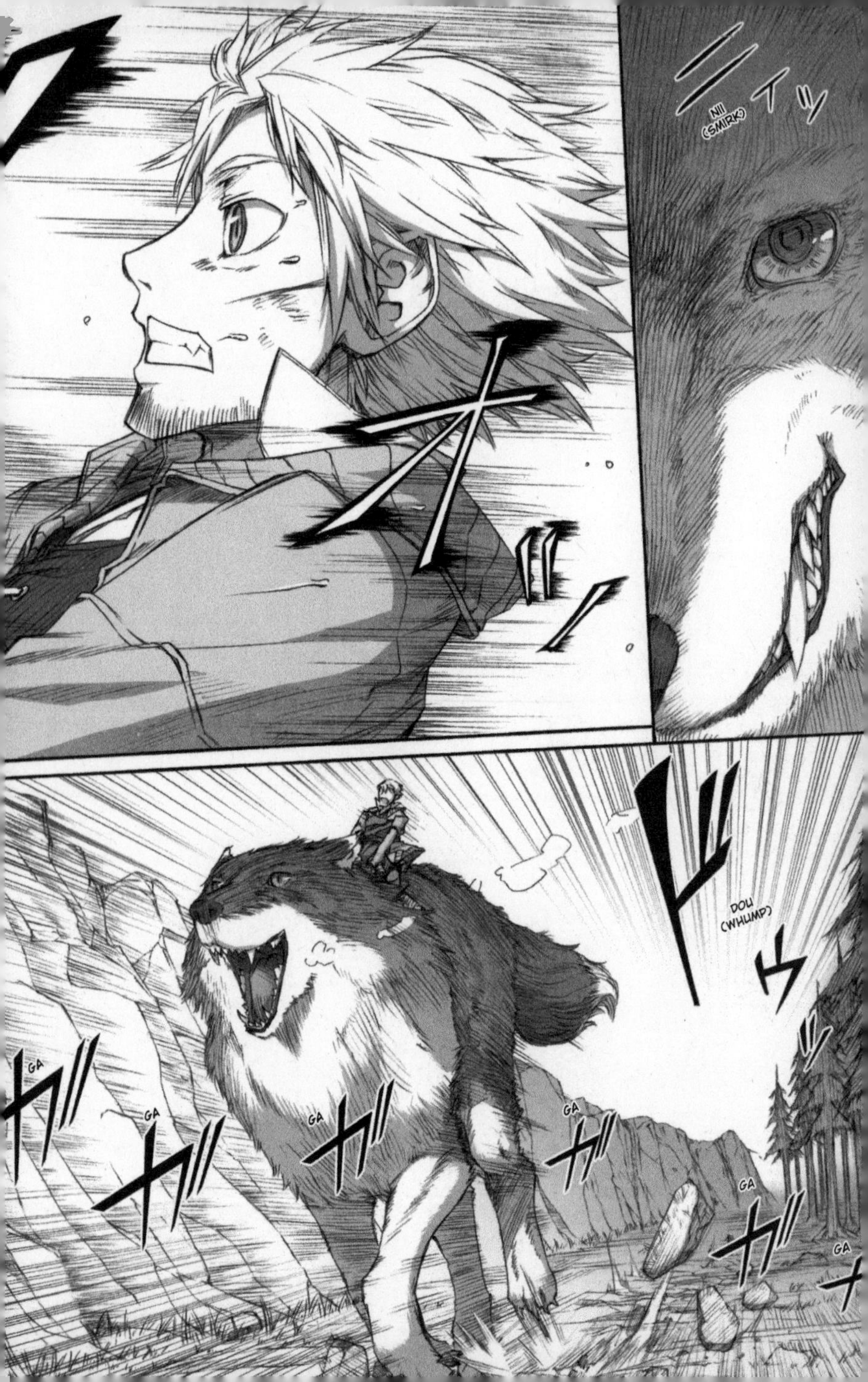
NII (SMIRK)
DOU (WHUMP)
GA
GA
GA
GA
GA
GA

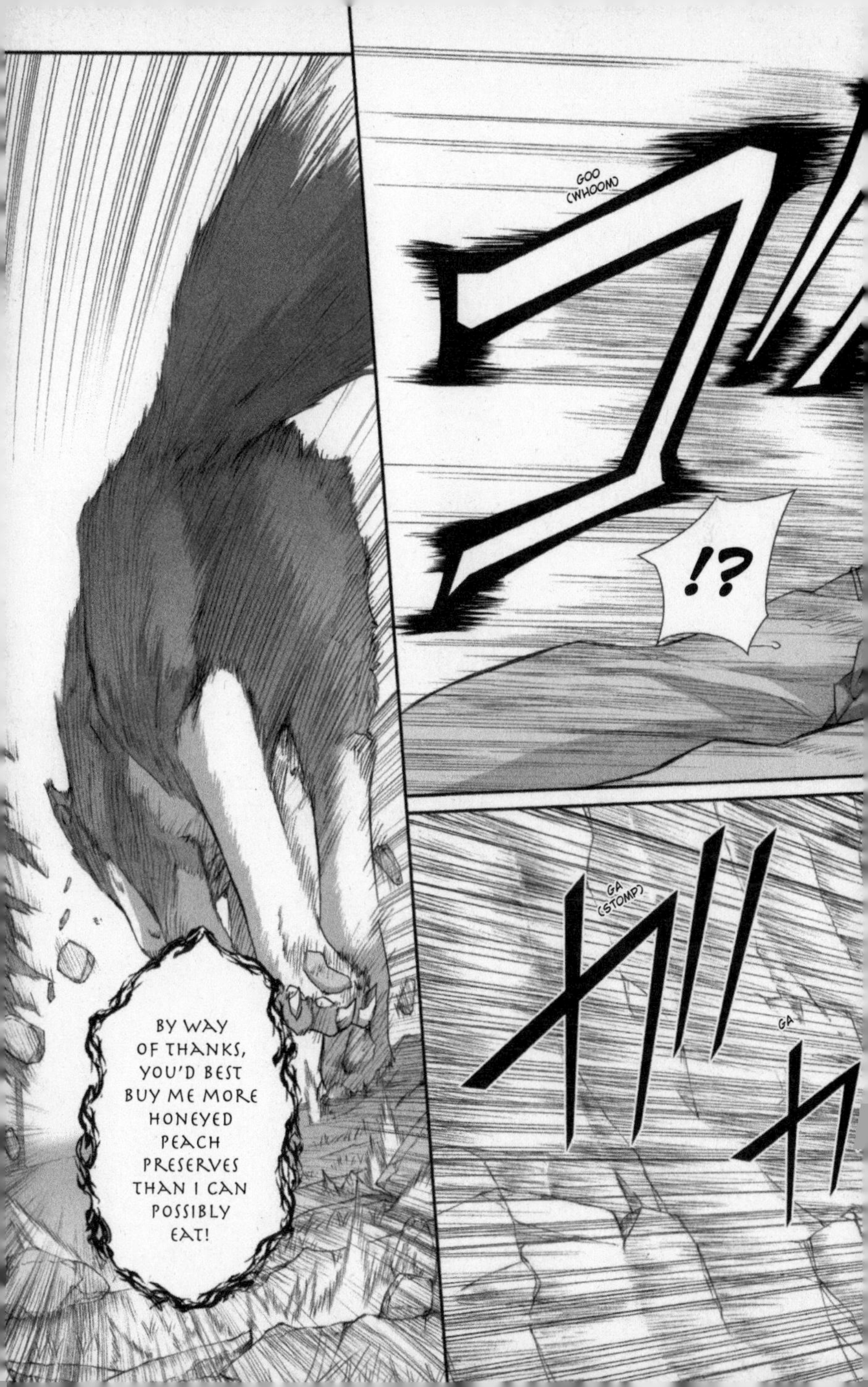
GOO
(WHOOM)
!?
GA
(STOMP)
GA
BY WAY OF THANKS, YOU'D BEST BUY ME MORE HONEYED PEACH PRESERVES THAN I CAN POSSIBLY EAT!

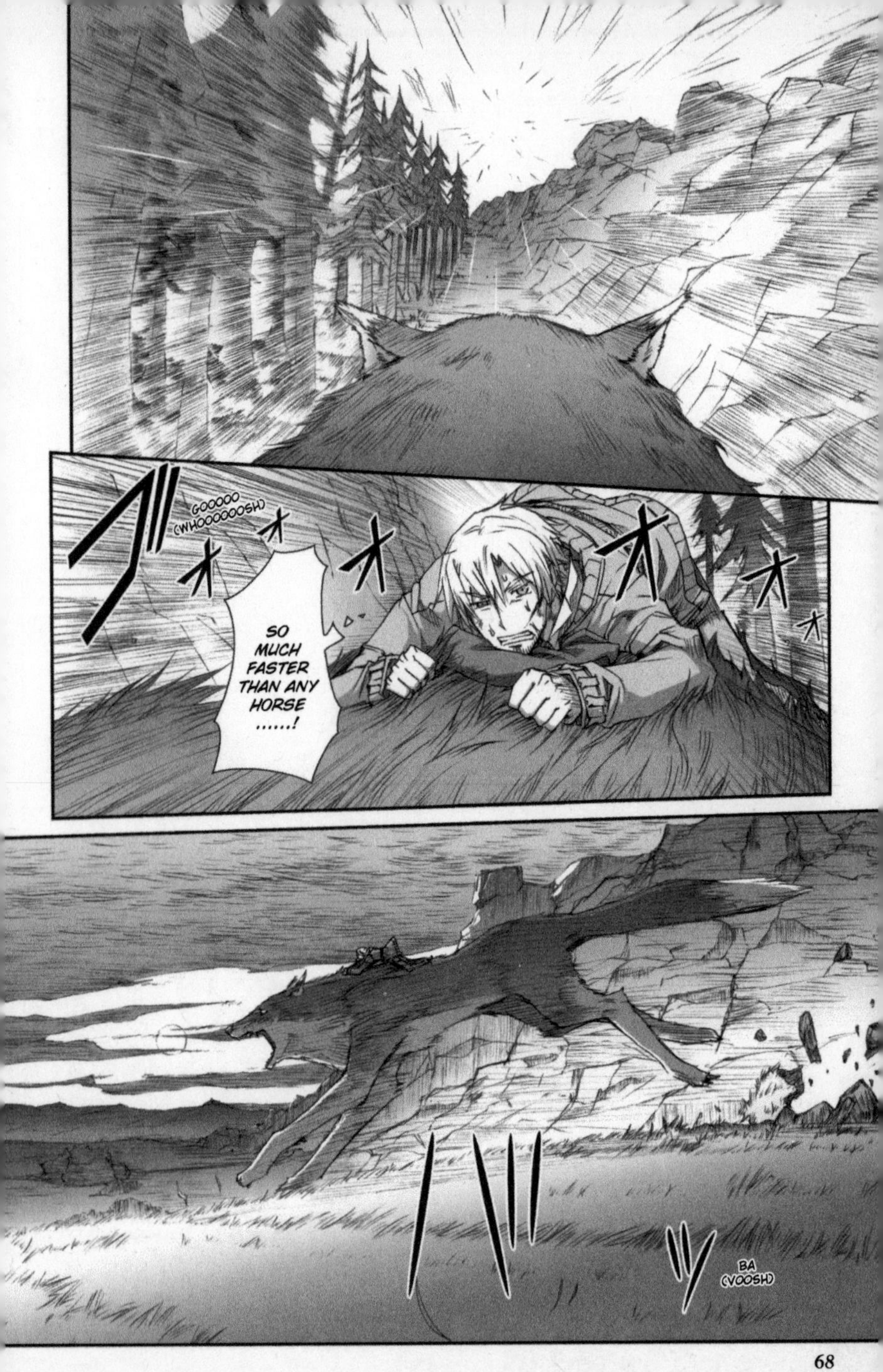
GOOOOO
(WHOOOOOOSH)
SO MUCH FASTER THAN ANY HORSE ......!
BA
(VOOSH)

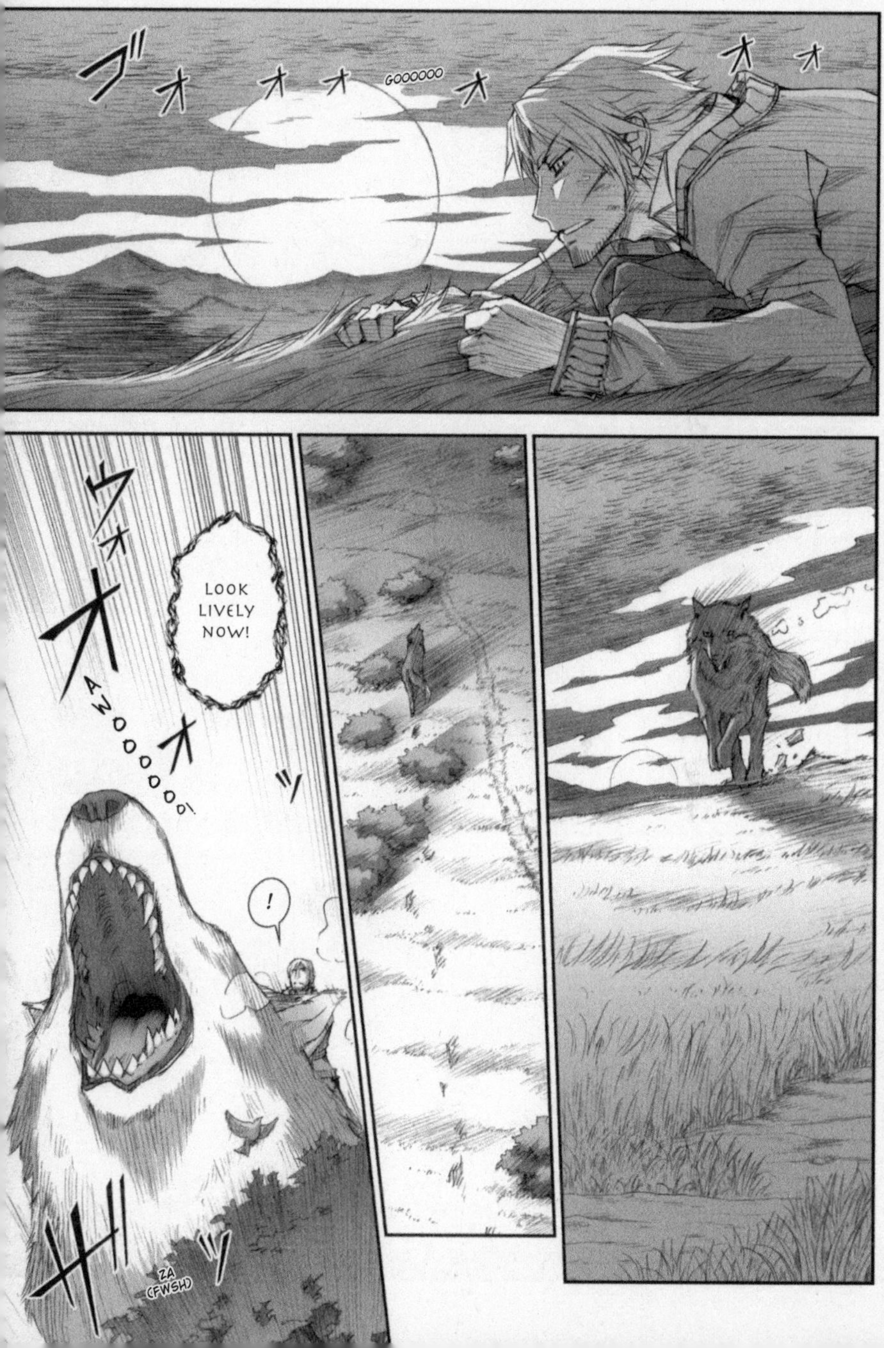
ゴオオオオオオ
GOOOOOO
ウォオオッ
LOOK LIVELY NOW!
AWOOOOOOO!
!
ザッ
ZA (FWSH)

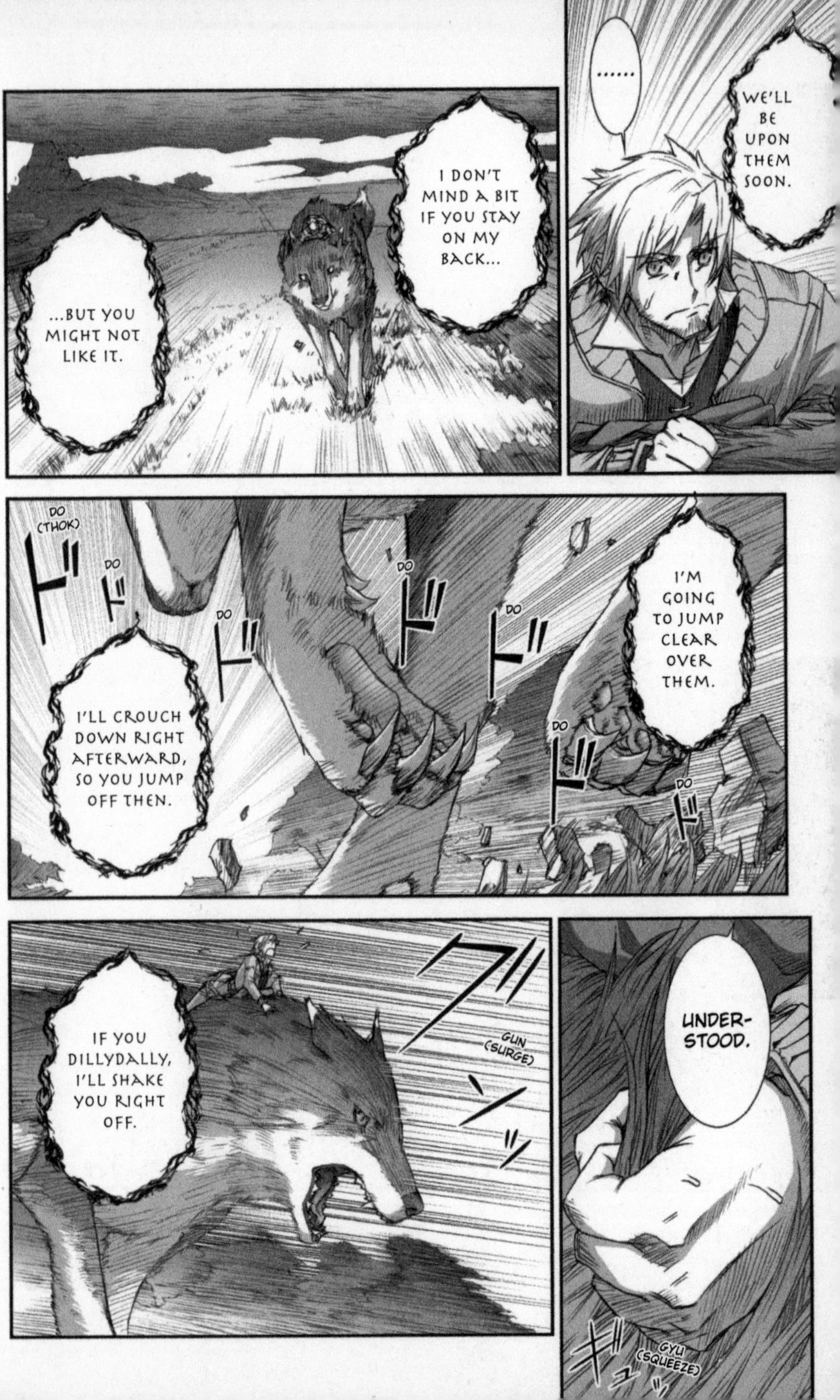
......
WE'LL BE UPON THEM SOON.
I DON'T MIND A BIT IF YOU STAY ON MY BACK...
...BUT YOU MIGHT NOT LIKE IT.
I'M GOING TO JUMP CLEAR OVER THEM.
DO DO DO DO DO DO DO (THOK)
I'LL CROUCH DOWN RIGHT AFTERWARD, SO YOU JUMP OFF THEN.
UNDER-STOOD.
GYU (SQUEEZE)
GUN (SURGE)
IF YOU DILLYDALLY, I'LL SHAKE YOU RIGHT OFF.

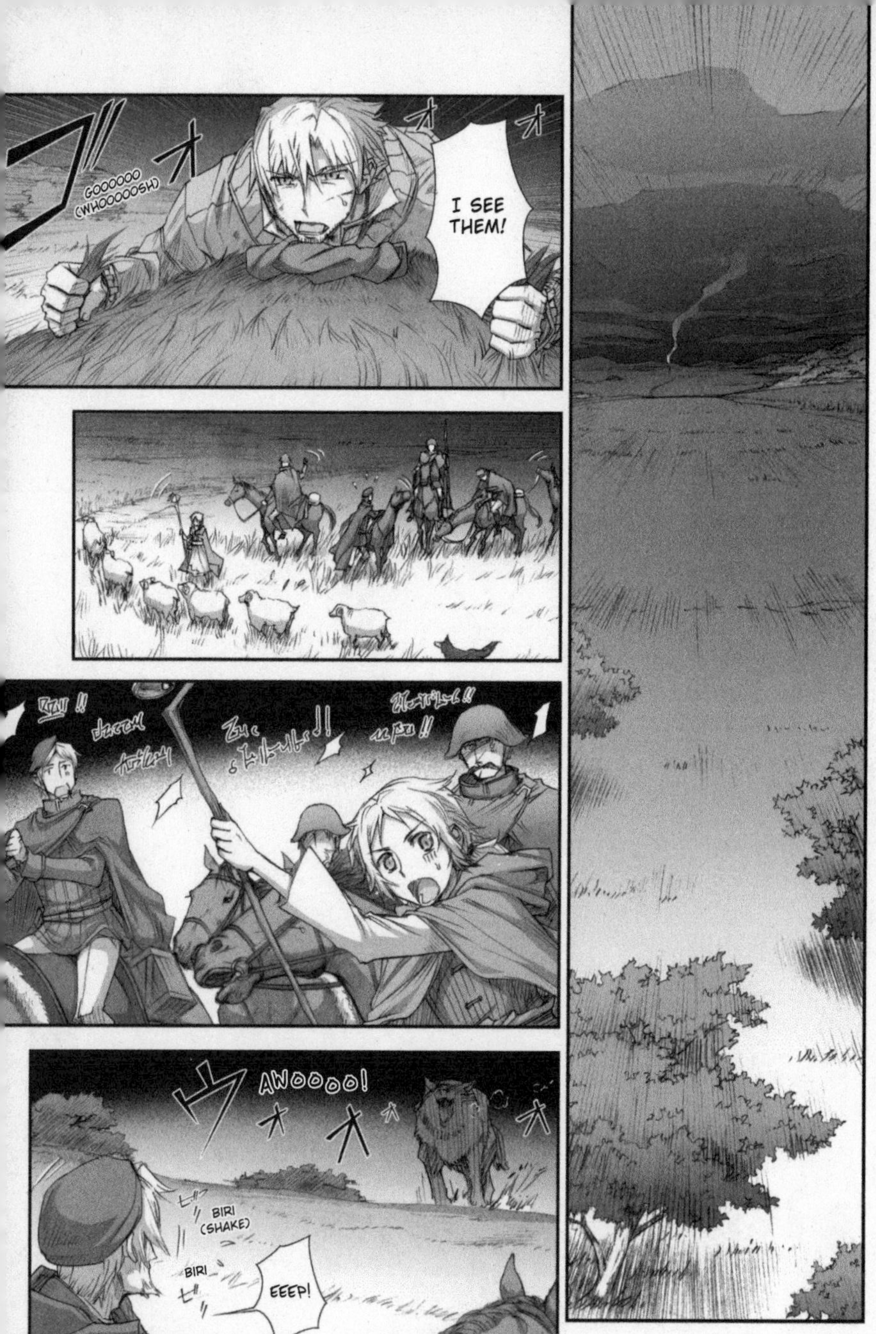
I SEE THEM!
GOOOOOO (WHOOOOOSH)
AWOOOOO!
BIRI (SHAKE)
EEEP!
BIRI

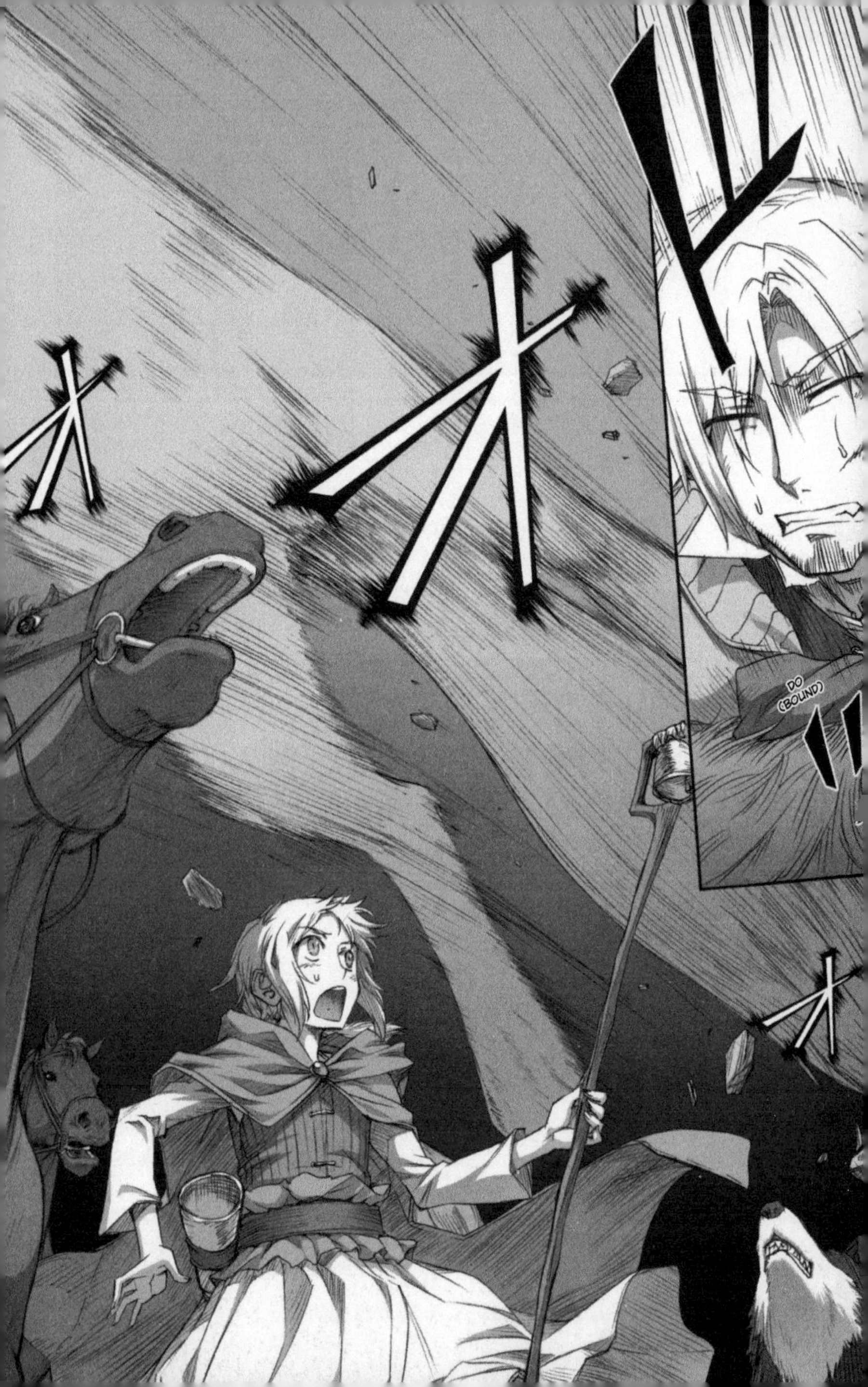
DO
(BOUND)

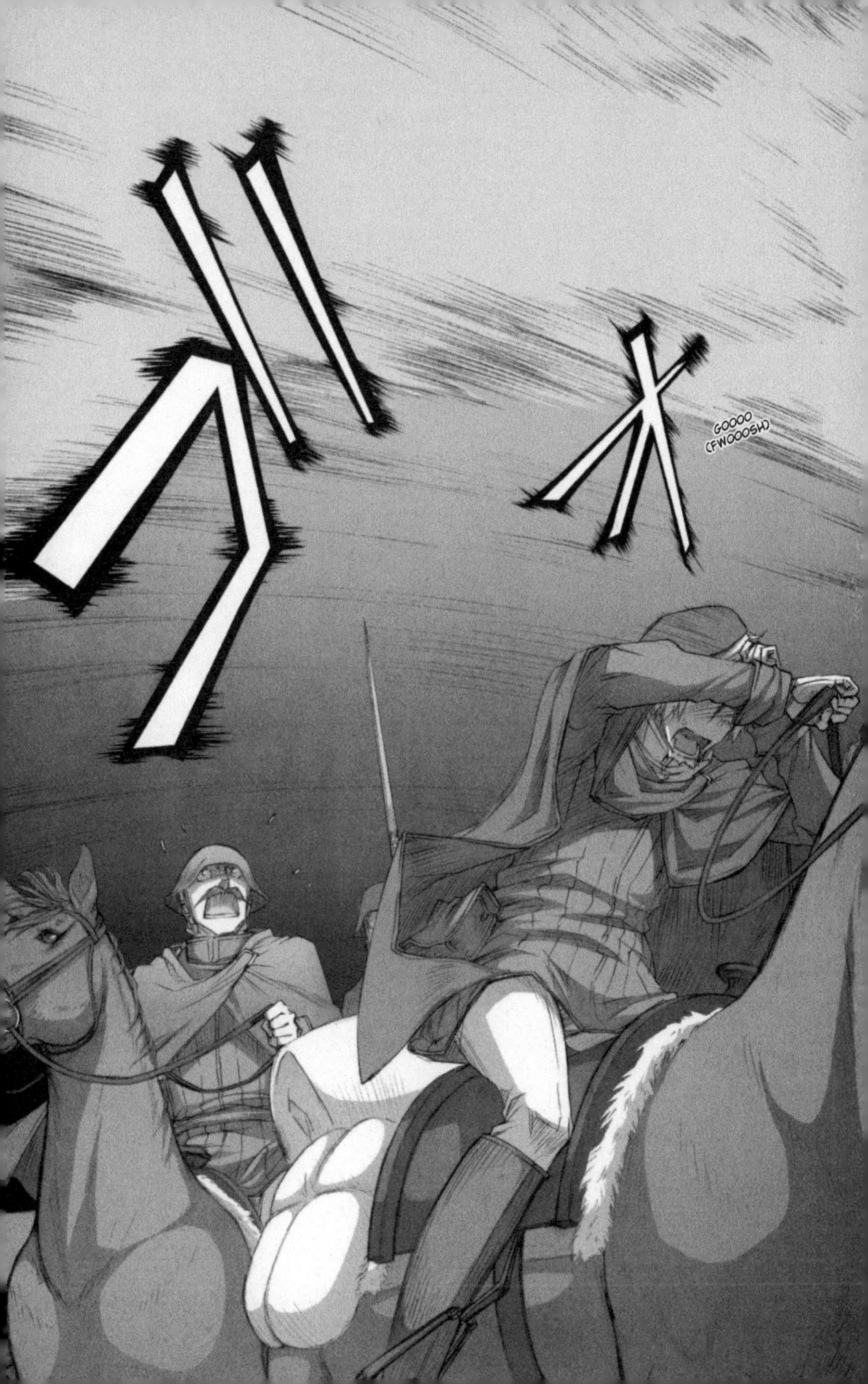
ゴォォ
GOOOO
(FWOOOSH)

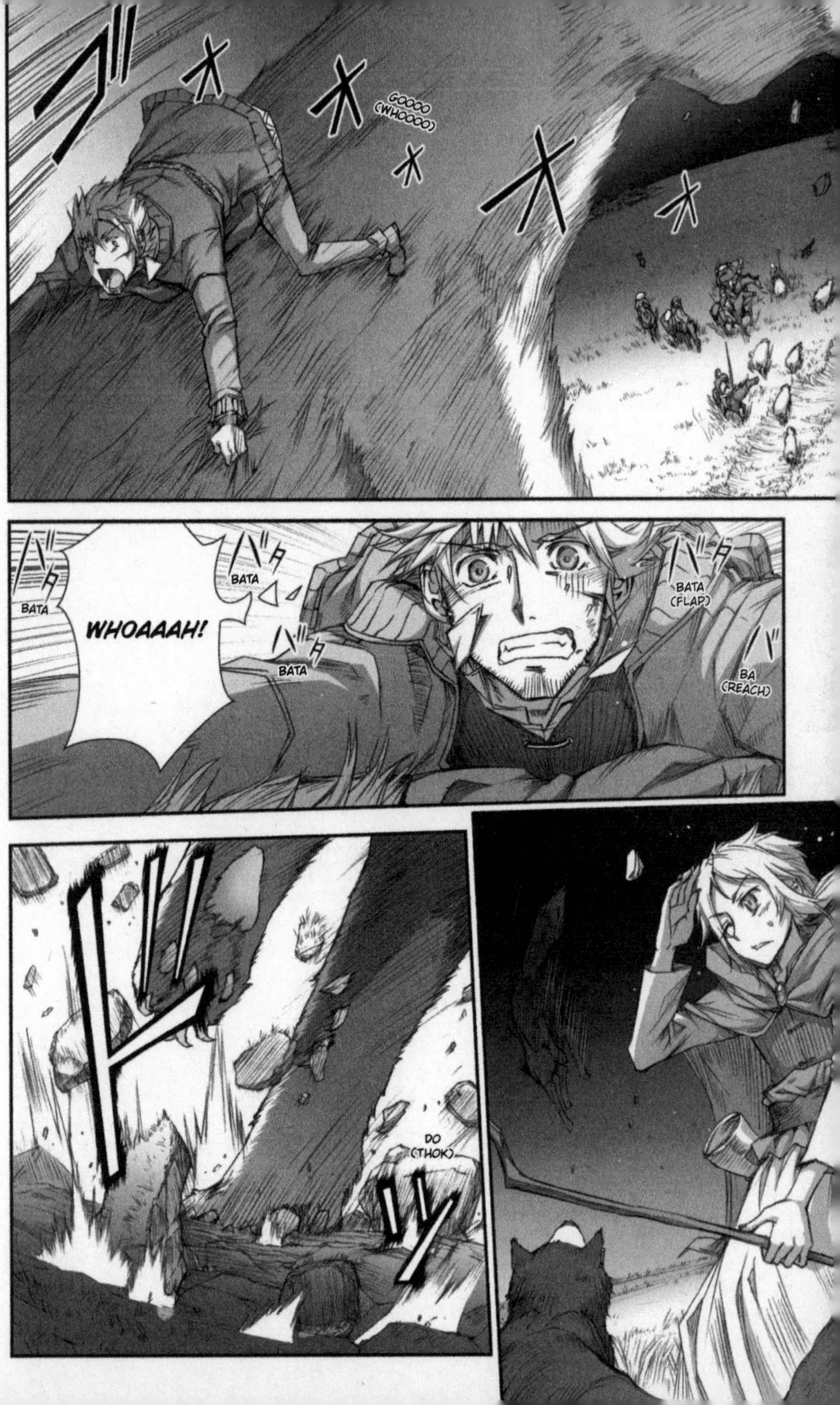
GOOOO
(WHOOOO)
BATA
(FLAP)
BA
(REACH)
BATA
BATA
WHOAAAH!
BATA
DO
(THOK)

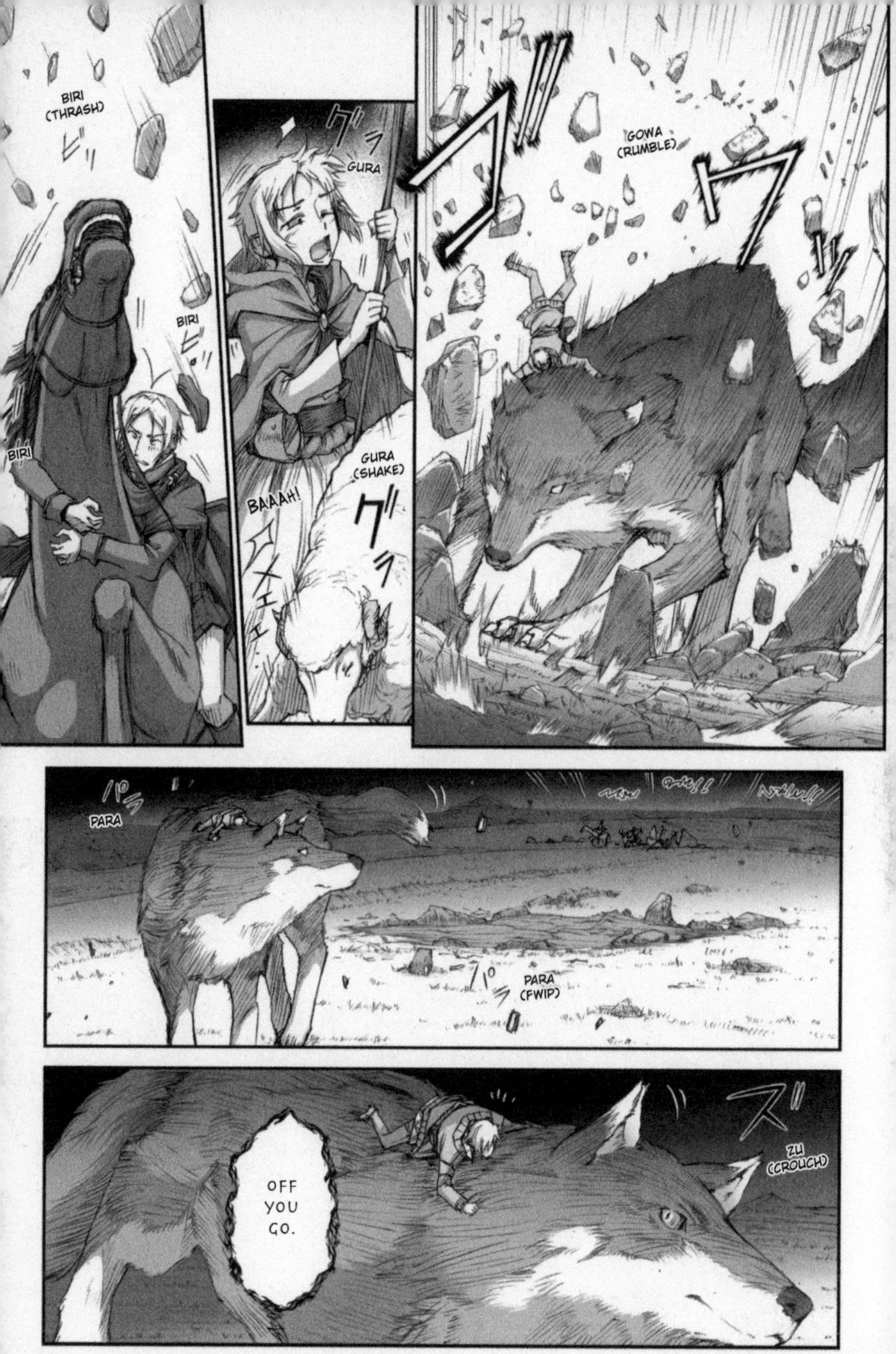
GOWA (RUMBLE)
GURA
GURA (SHAKE)
BAAAH!
BIRI (THRASH)
BIRI
BIRI
PARA
PARA (FWIP)
ZU (CROUCH)
OFF YOU GO.

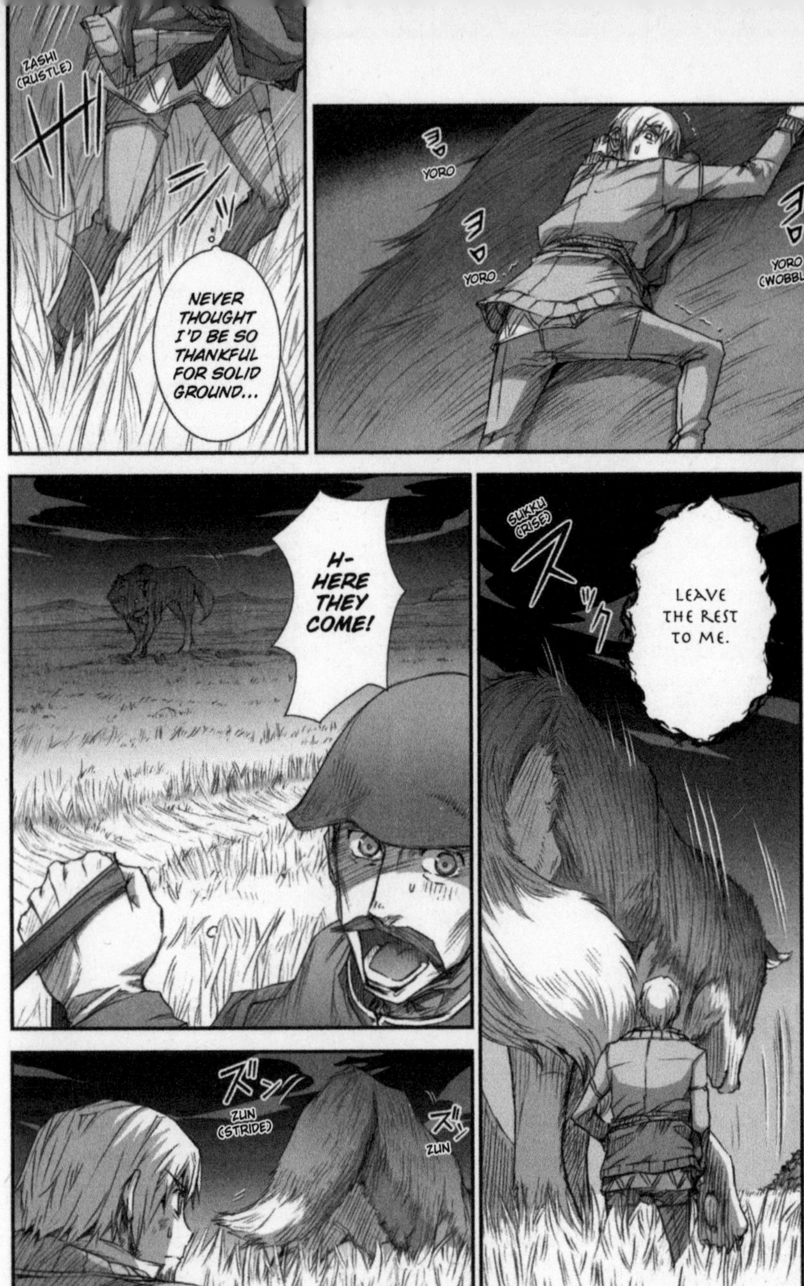
ヨロ
YORO
ヨロ
YORO
ヨロ
YORO (WOBBLE)
ZASHI (RUSTLE)
NEVER THOUGHT I'D BE SO THANKFUL FOR SOLID GROUND...
SUKKU (RISE)
スック
LEAVE THE REST TO ME.
H- HERE THEY COME!
ズンッ
ZUN (STRIDE)
ズンッ
ZUN

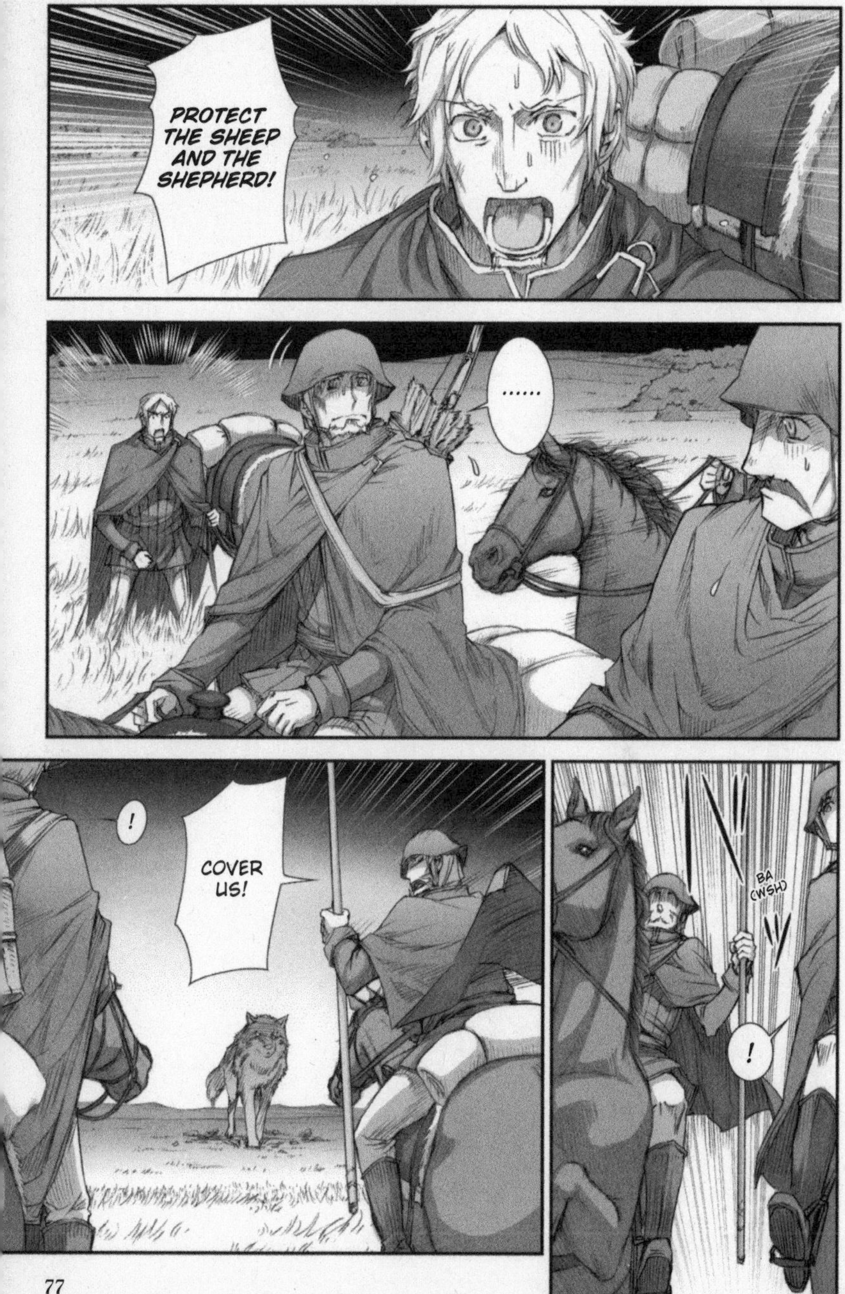
PROTECT THE SHEEP AND THE SHEPHERD!
......
BA (WSH)
!
!
COVER US!

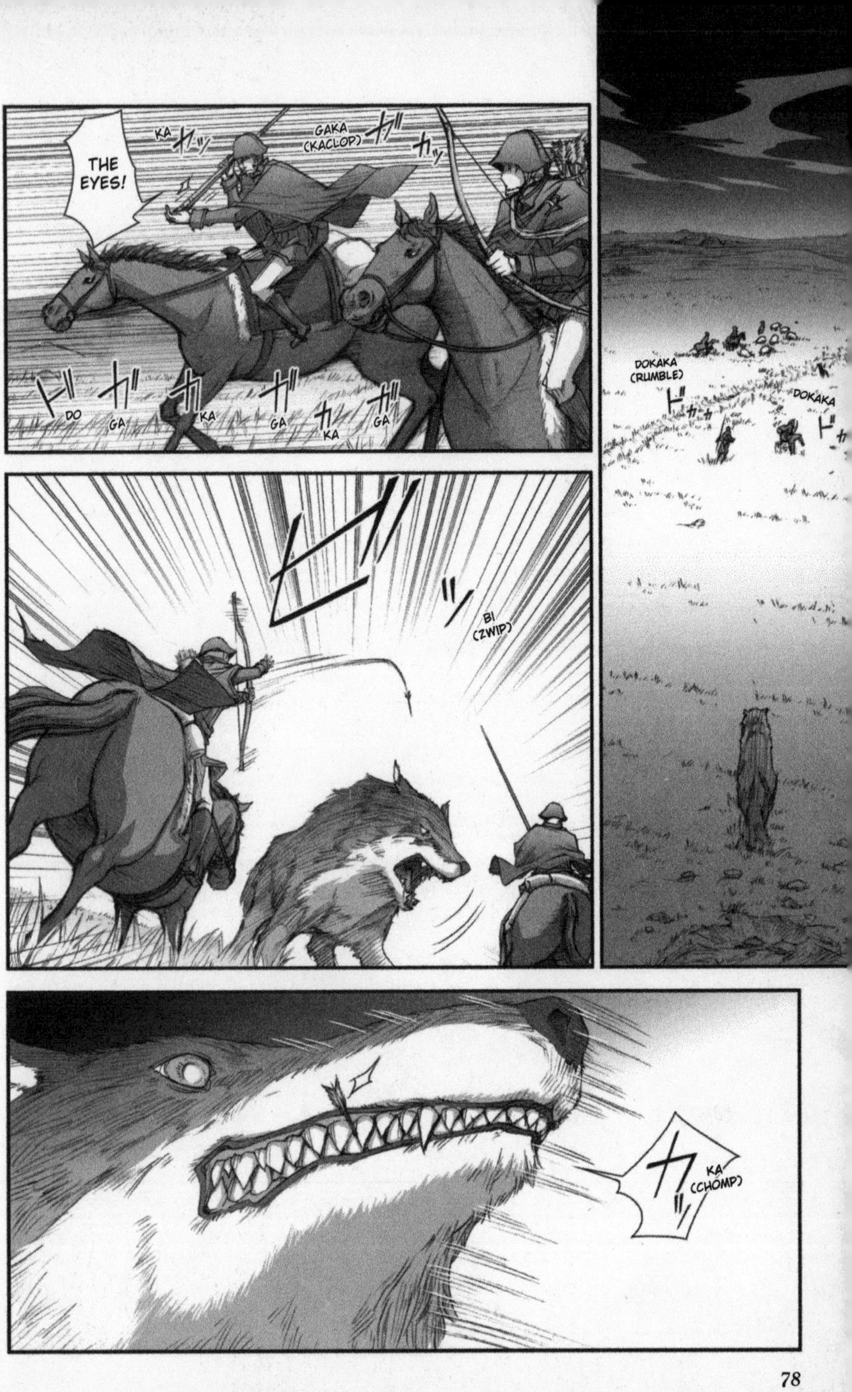

DOKAKA (RUMBLE)
DOKAKA
GAKA (KACLOP)
KA
THE EYES!
DO
GA
KA
GA
KA
GA
BI (ZWIP)
KA (CHOMP)

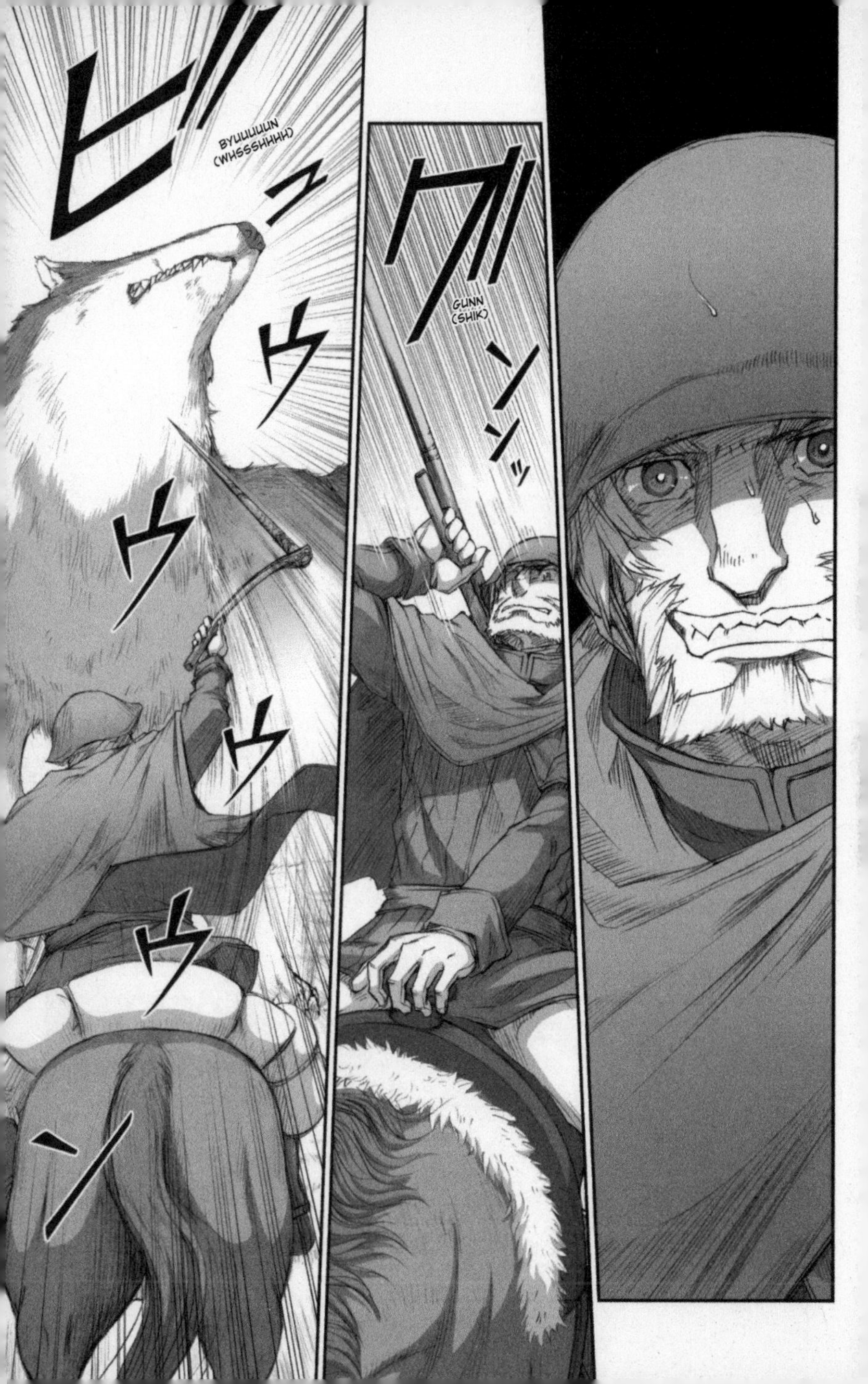
GUNN
(SHIK)
BYUUUUUN
(WHSSSHHHH)

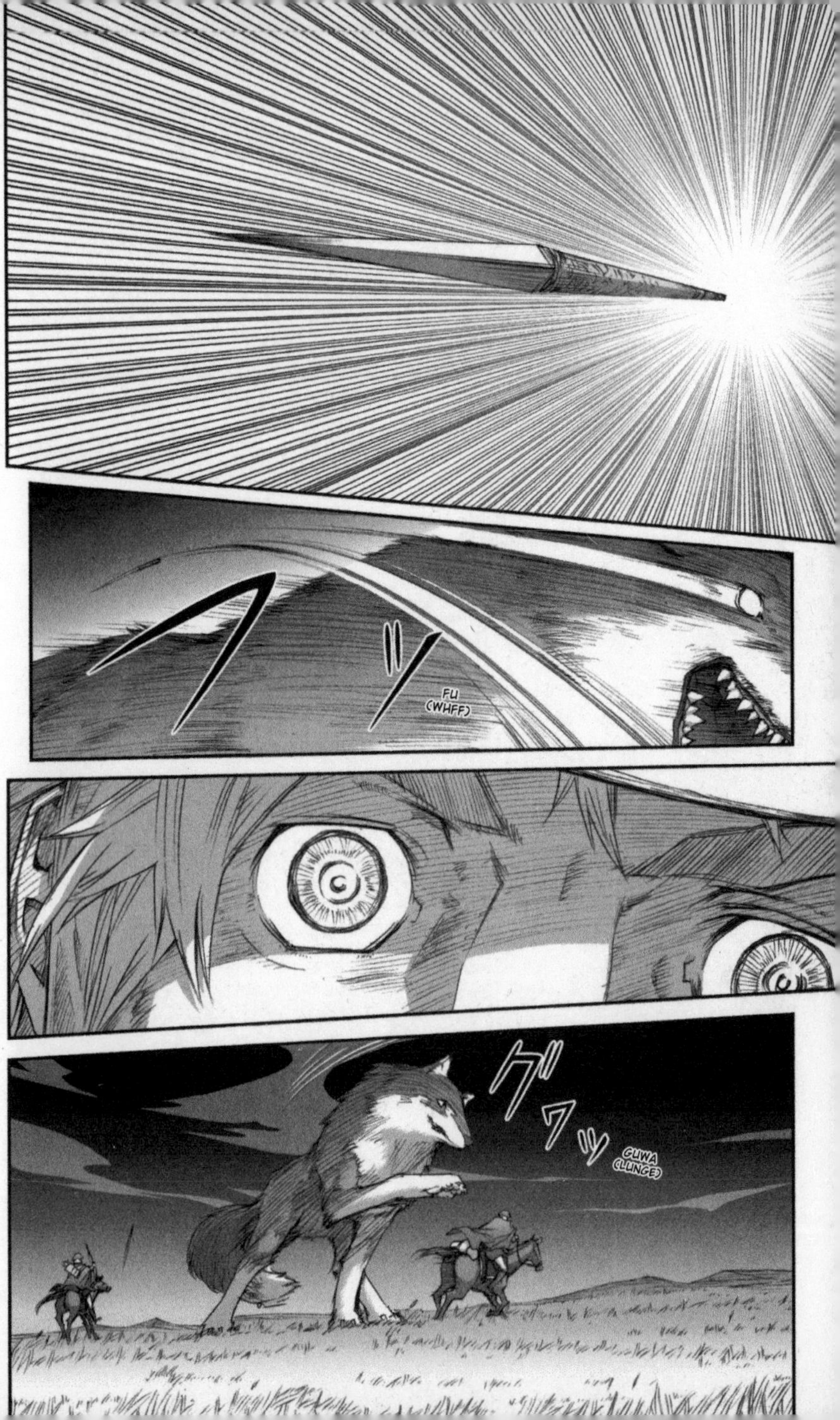
フッ
FU
(WHFF)
グワッ
GUWA
(LUNGE)

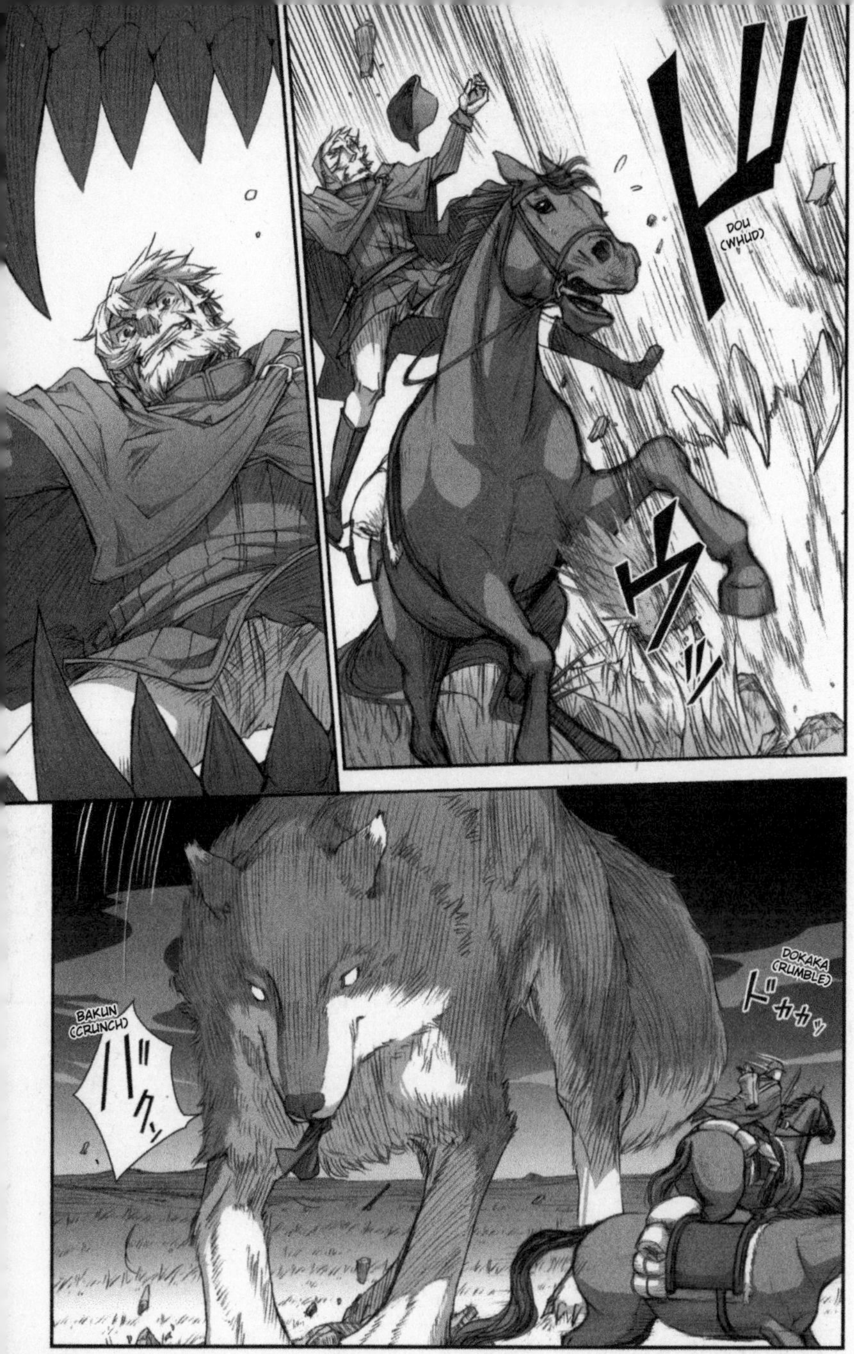
DOU (WHUD)
DOKAKA (RUMBLE)
BAKUN (CRUNCH)

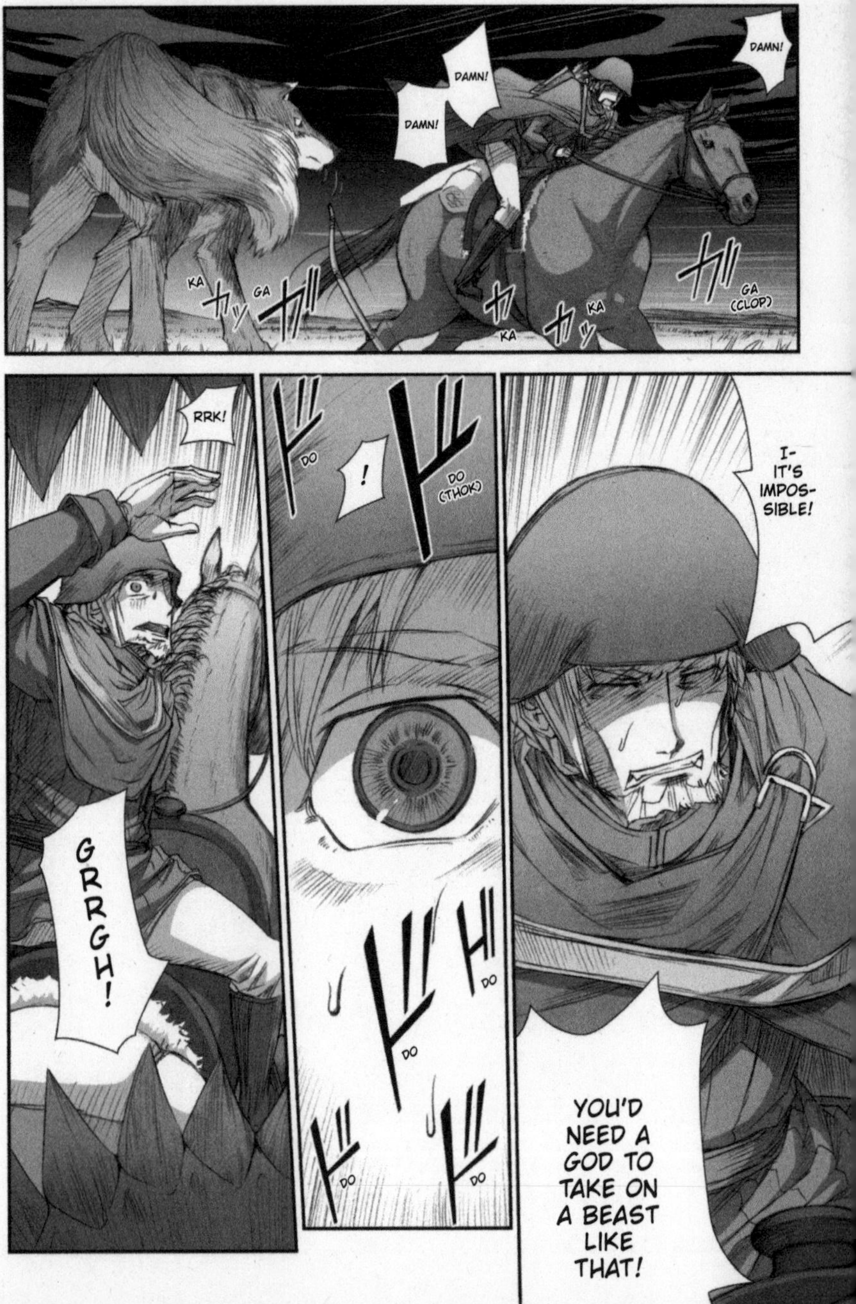
DAMN!
DAMN!
DAMN!
GA (CLOP)
KA
KA
GA
KA
I- IT'S IMPOSSIBLE!
YOU'D NEED A GOD TO TAKE ON A BEAST LIKE THAT!
DO (THOK)
DO
!
DO
DO
DO
DO
RRK!
GRRGH!

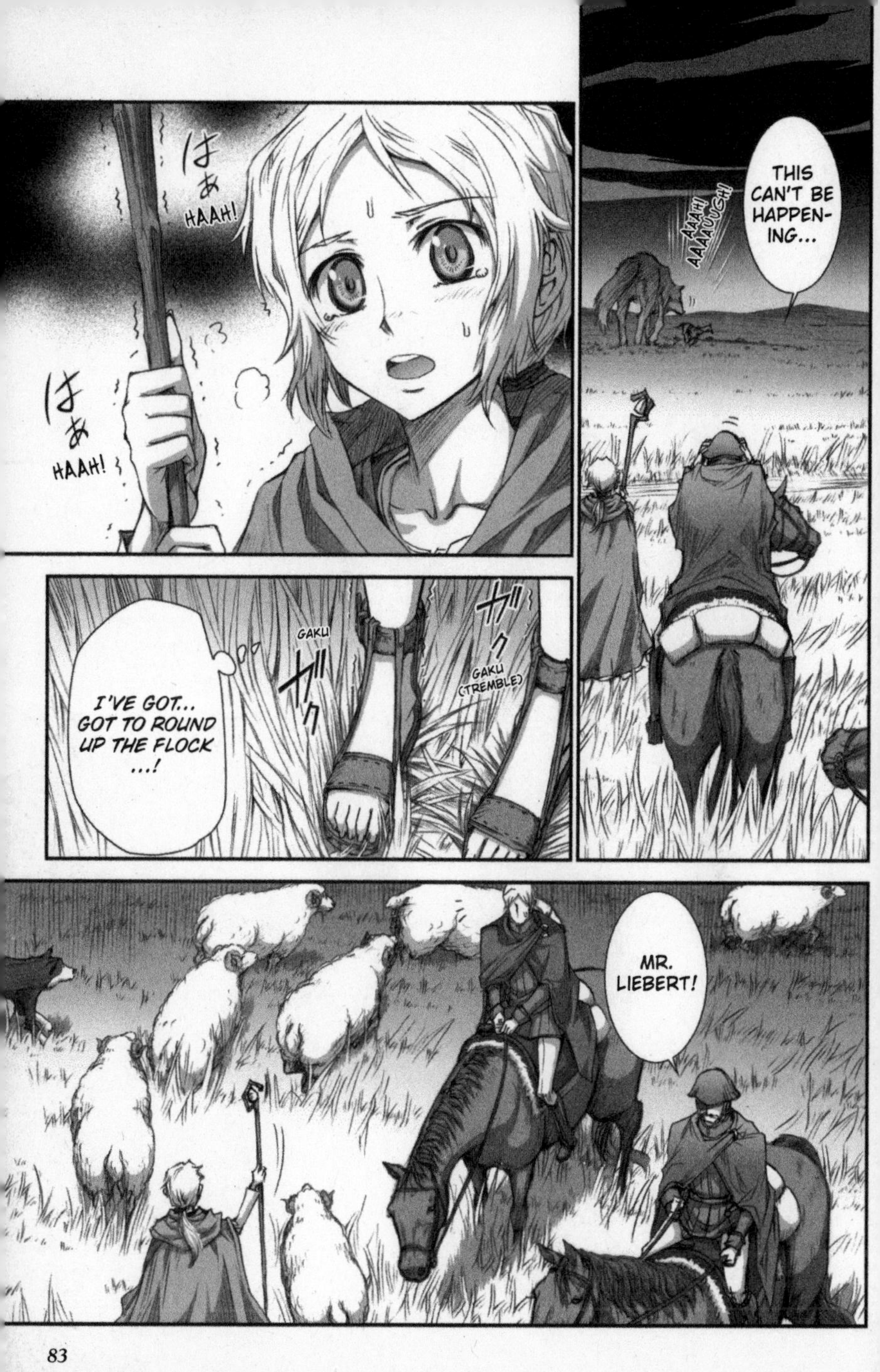

THIS CAN'T BE HAPPEN-ING...
AAAH! AAAAUUGH!
はぁ
HAAH!
はぁ
HAAH!
ガク
GAKU
ガク
GAKU (TREMBLE)
I'VE GOT... GOT TO ROUND UP THE FLOCK ...!
MR. LIEBERT!

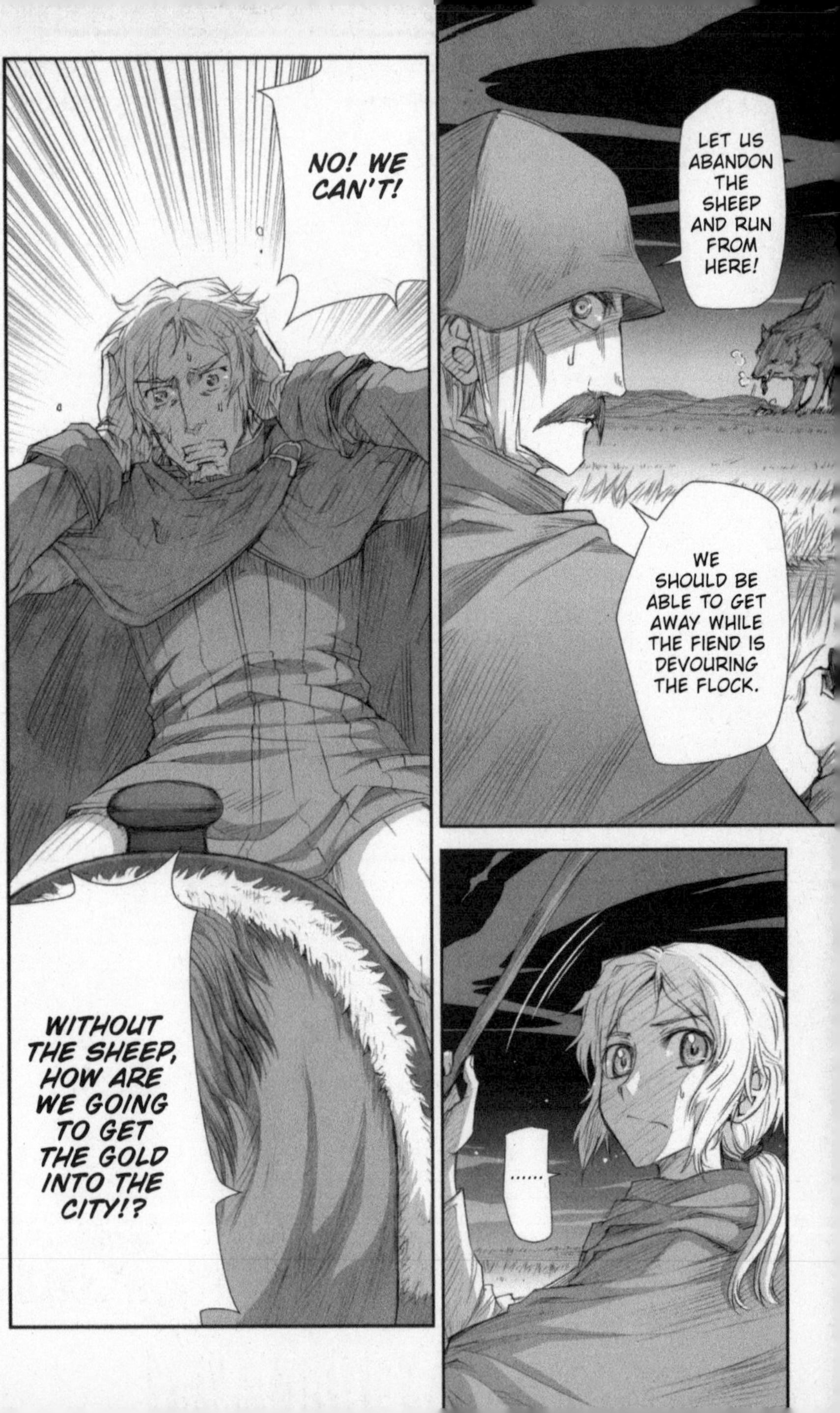
LET US ABANDON THE SHEEP AND RUN FROM HERE!
WE SHOULD BE ABLE TO GET AWAY WHILE THE FIEND IS DEVOURING THE FLOCK.
......
NO! WE CAN'T!
WITHOUT THE SHEEP, HOW ARE WE GOING TO GET THE GOLD INTO THE CITY!?

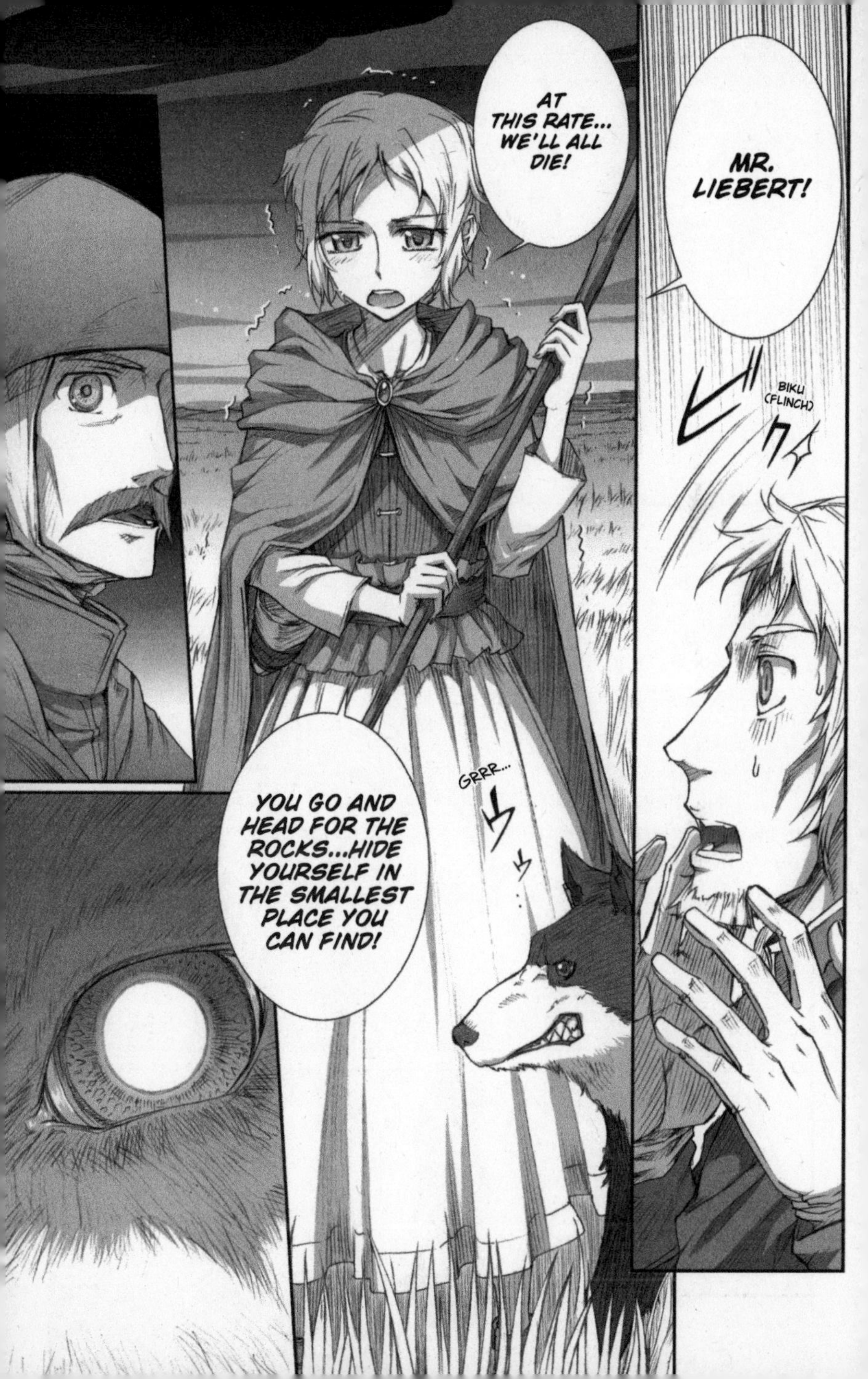
MR. LIEBERT!
BIKU (FLINCH)
AT THIS RATE... WE'LL ALL DIE!
GRRR...
YOU GO AND HEAD FOR THE ROCKS...HIDE YOURSELF IN THE SMALLEST PLACE YOU CAN FIND!

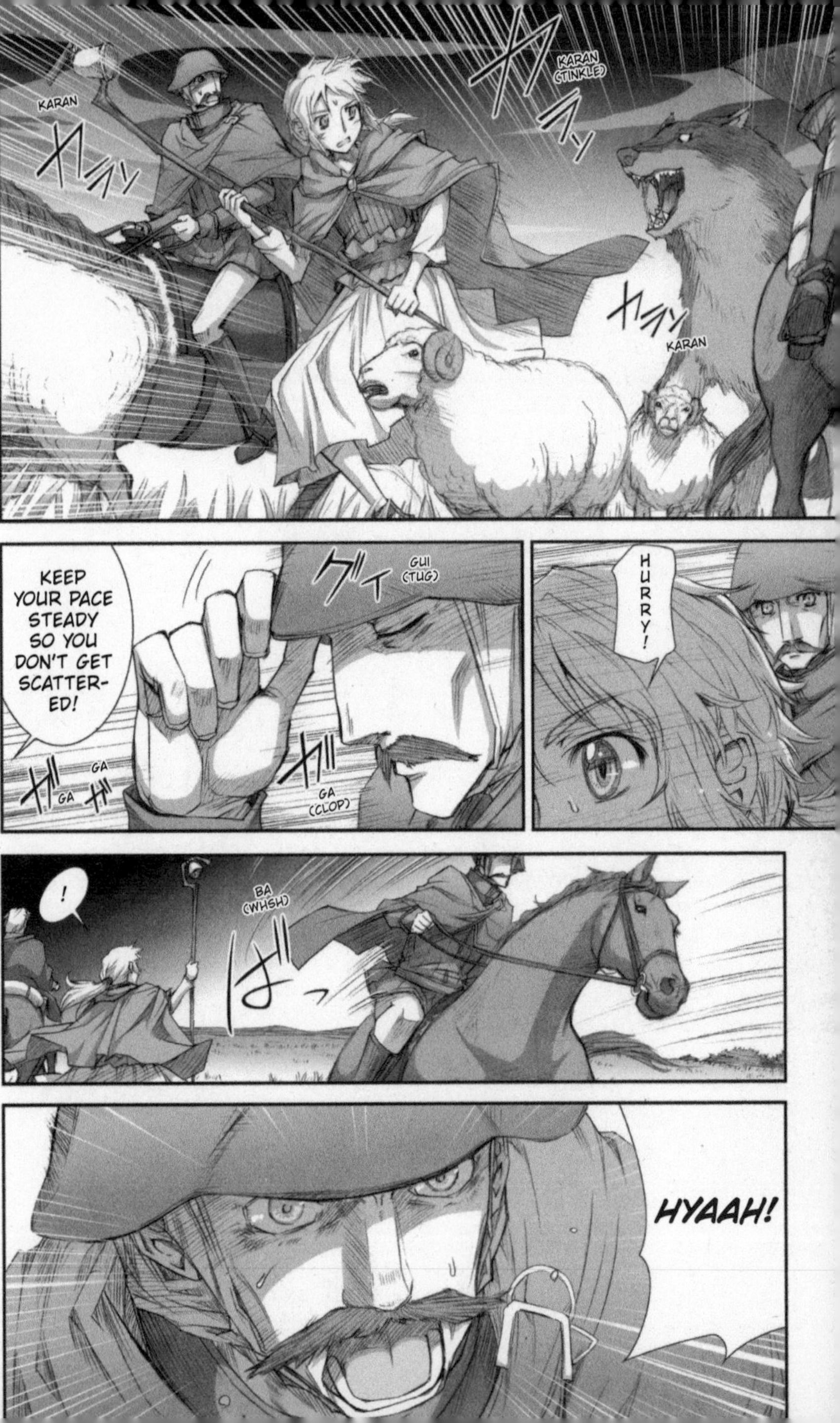
KARAN (TINKLE)
KARAN
KARAN
HURRY!
GUI (TUG)
KEEP YOUR PACE STEADY SO YOU DON'T GET SCATTER-ED!
GA (CLOP)
GA
GA
BA (WHSH)
!
HYAAH!

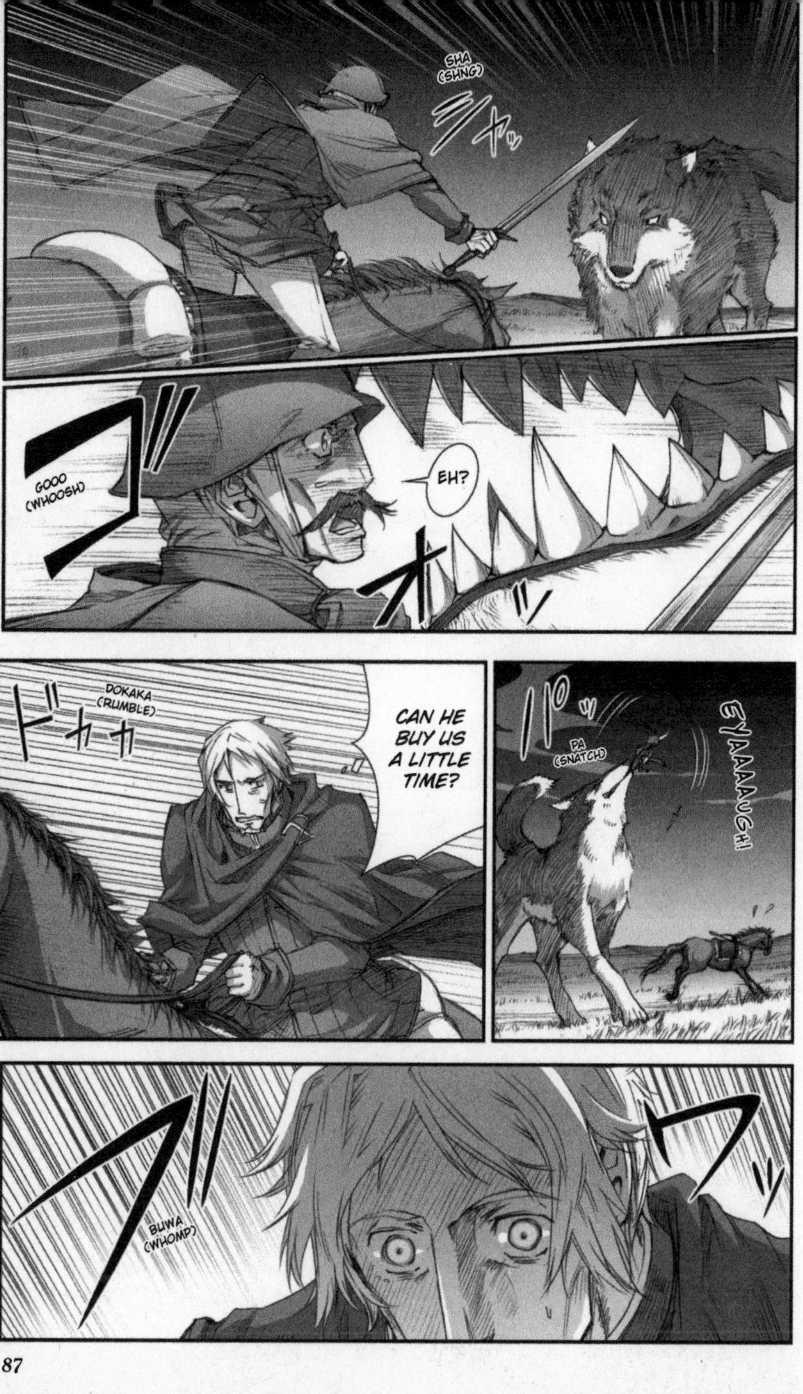
SHA (SHNG)
GOOO (WHOOSH)
EH?
PA (SNATCH)
EYAAAAAUGH!
DOKAKA (RUMBLE)
CAN HE BUY US A LITTLE TIME?
BUWA (WHOMP)

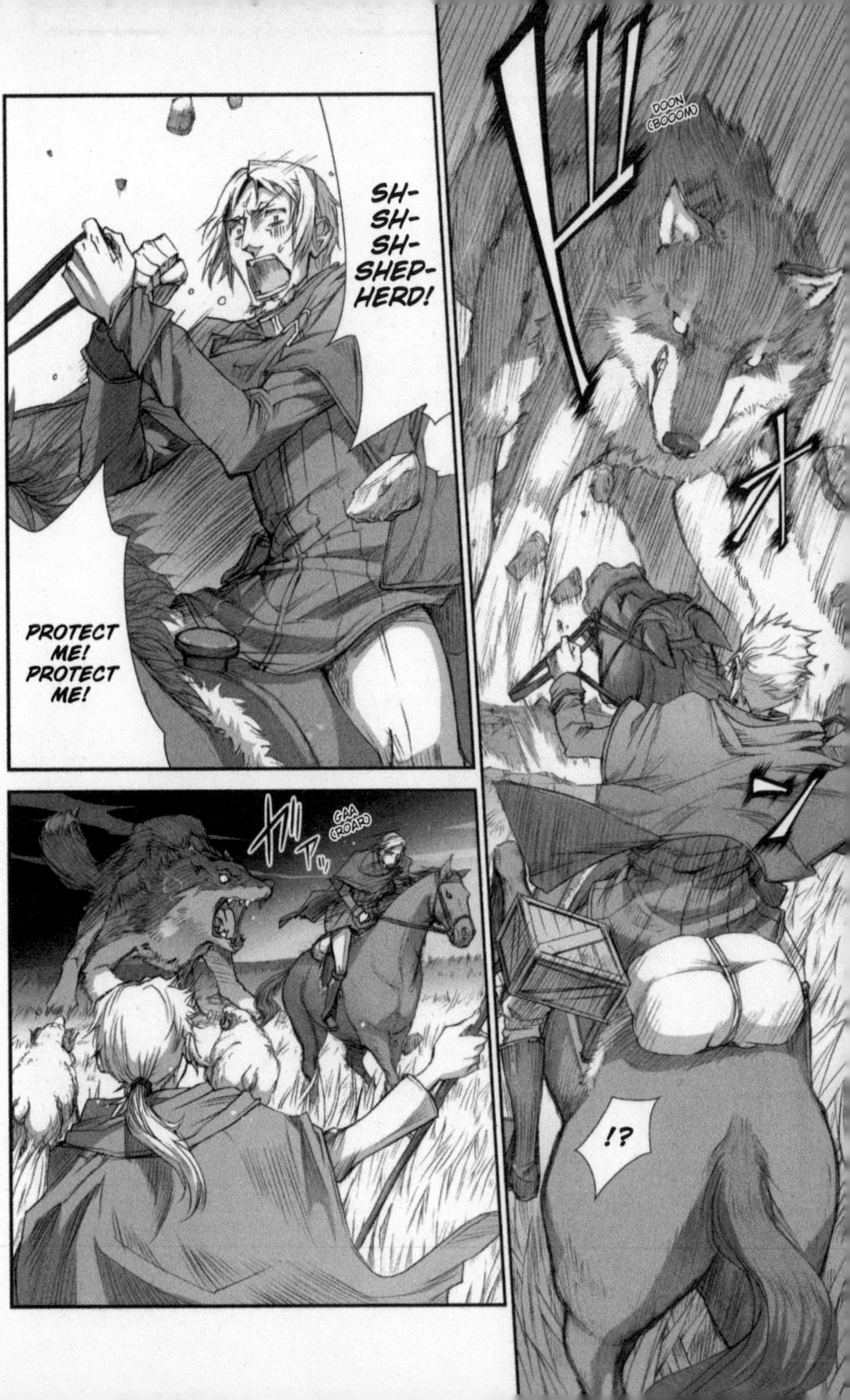
DOON (BOOOM)
!?
SH-SH-SH-SHEPHERD!
PROTECT ME! PROTECT ME!
GAA (ROAR)

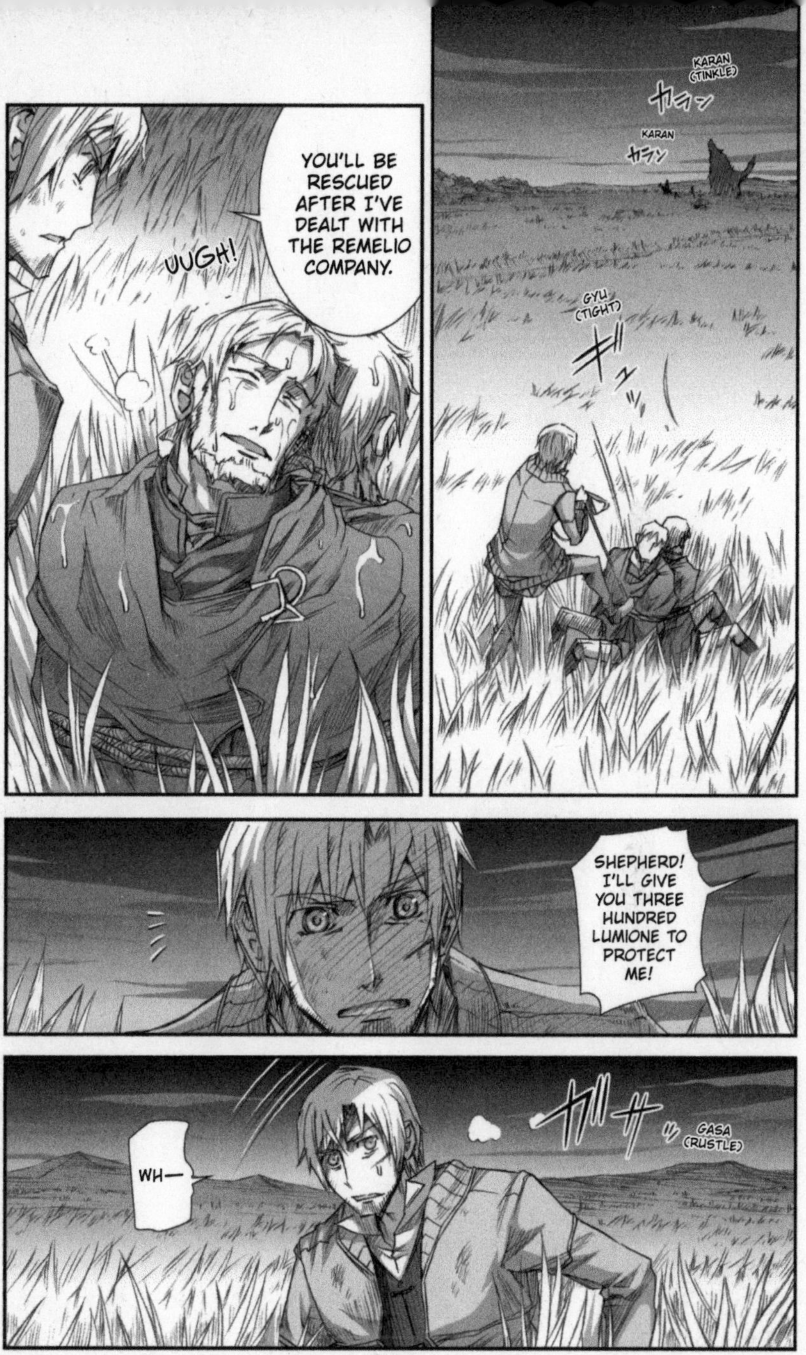
KARAN (TINKLE)
KARAN
GYU (TIGHT)
YOU'LL BE RESCUED AFTER I'VE DEALT WITH THE REMELIO COMPANY.
UUGH!
SHEPHERD! I'LL GIVE YOU THREE HUNDRED LUMIONE TO PROTECT ME!
GASA (RUSTLE)
WH—

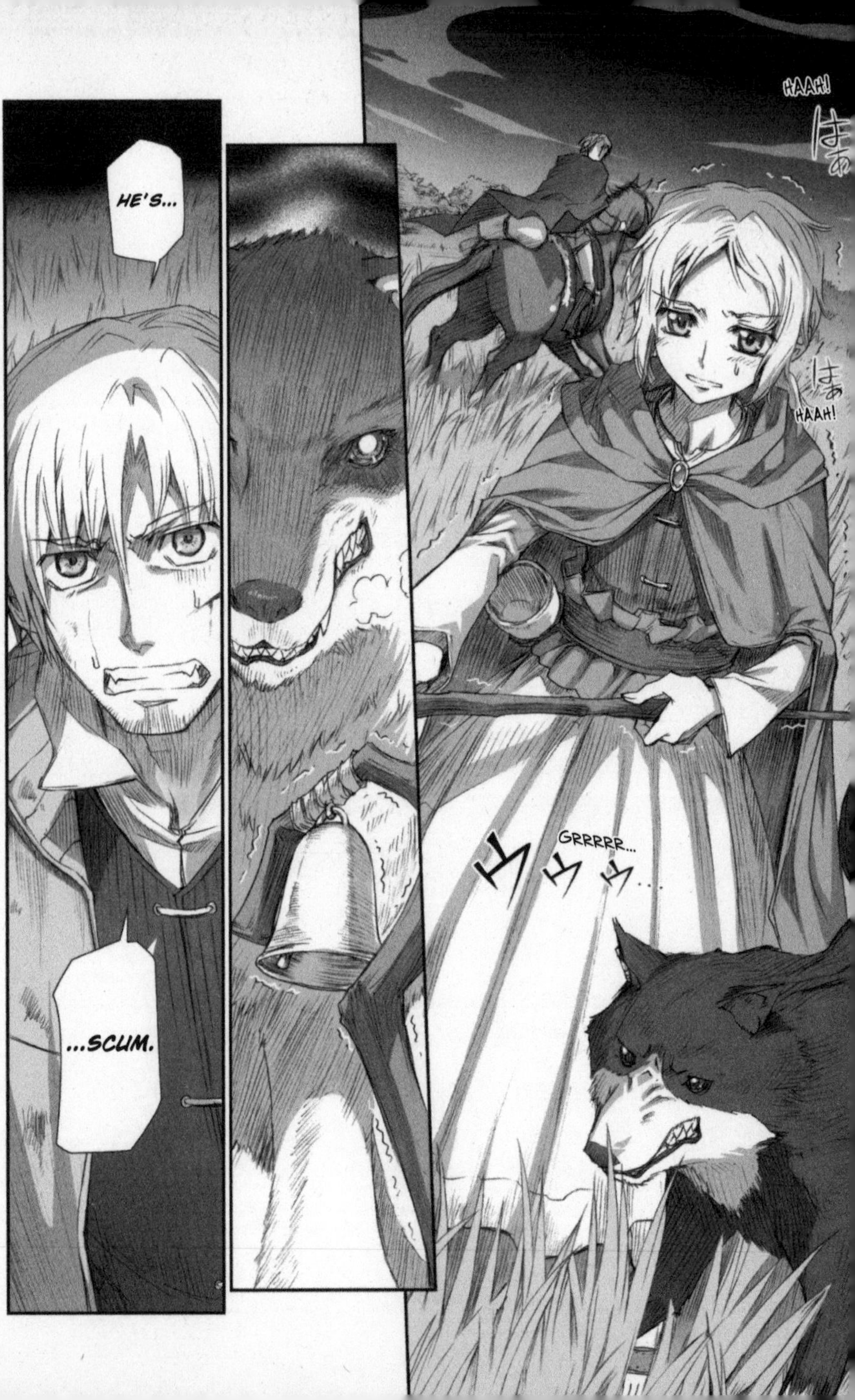
HAAH!
はぁ
はぁ
HAAH!
GRRRRR...
HE'S...
...SCUM.

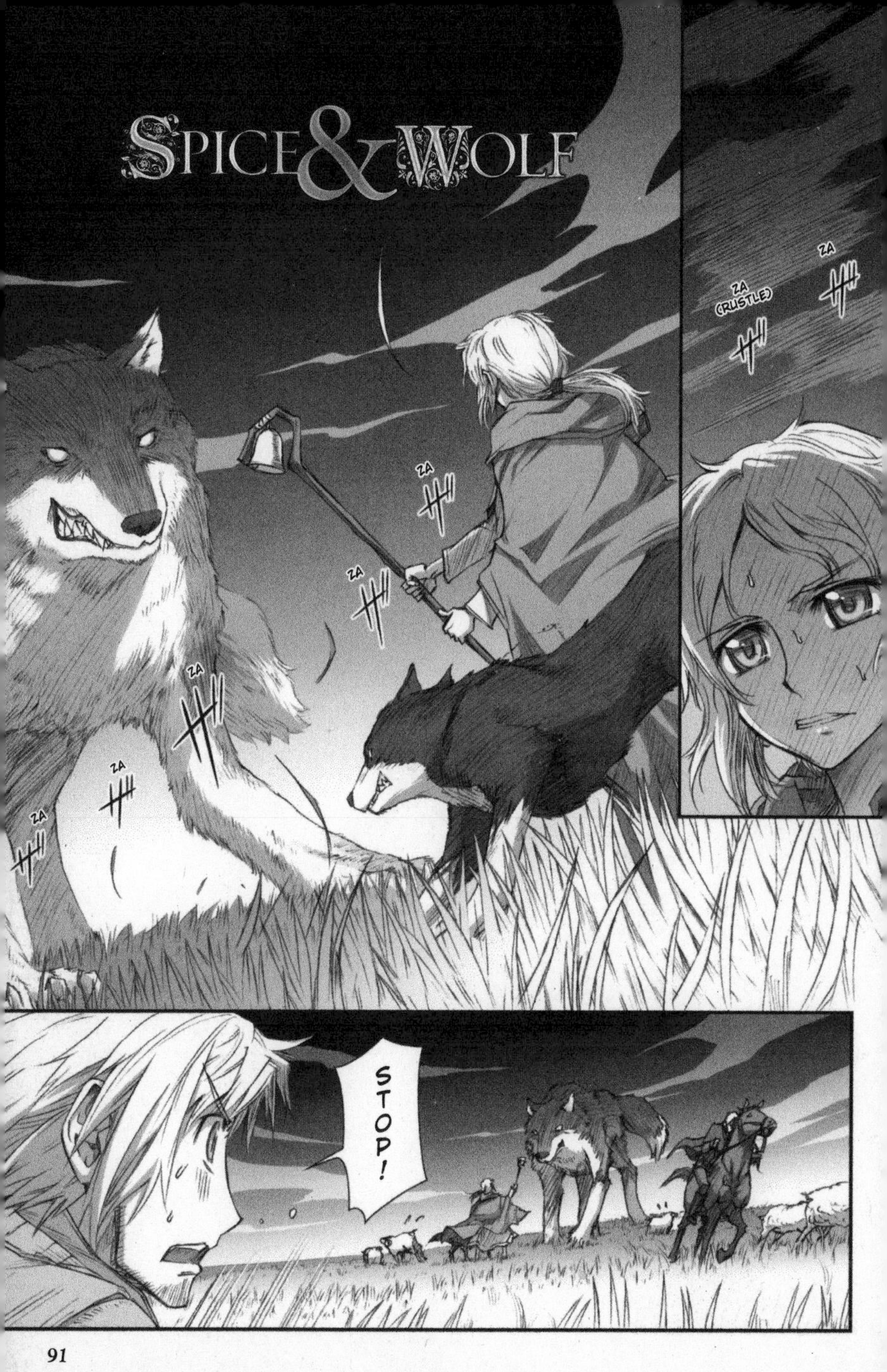
SPICE & WOLF
ZA
ZA (RUSTLE)
ZA
ZA
ZA
ZA
ZA
STOP!

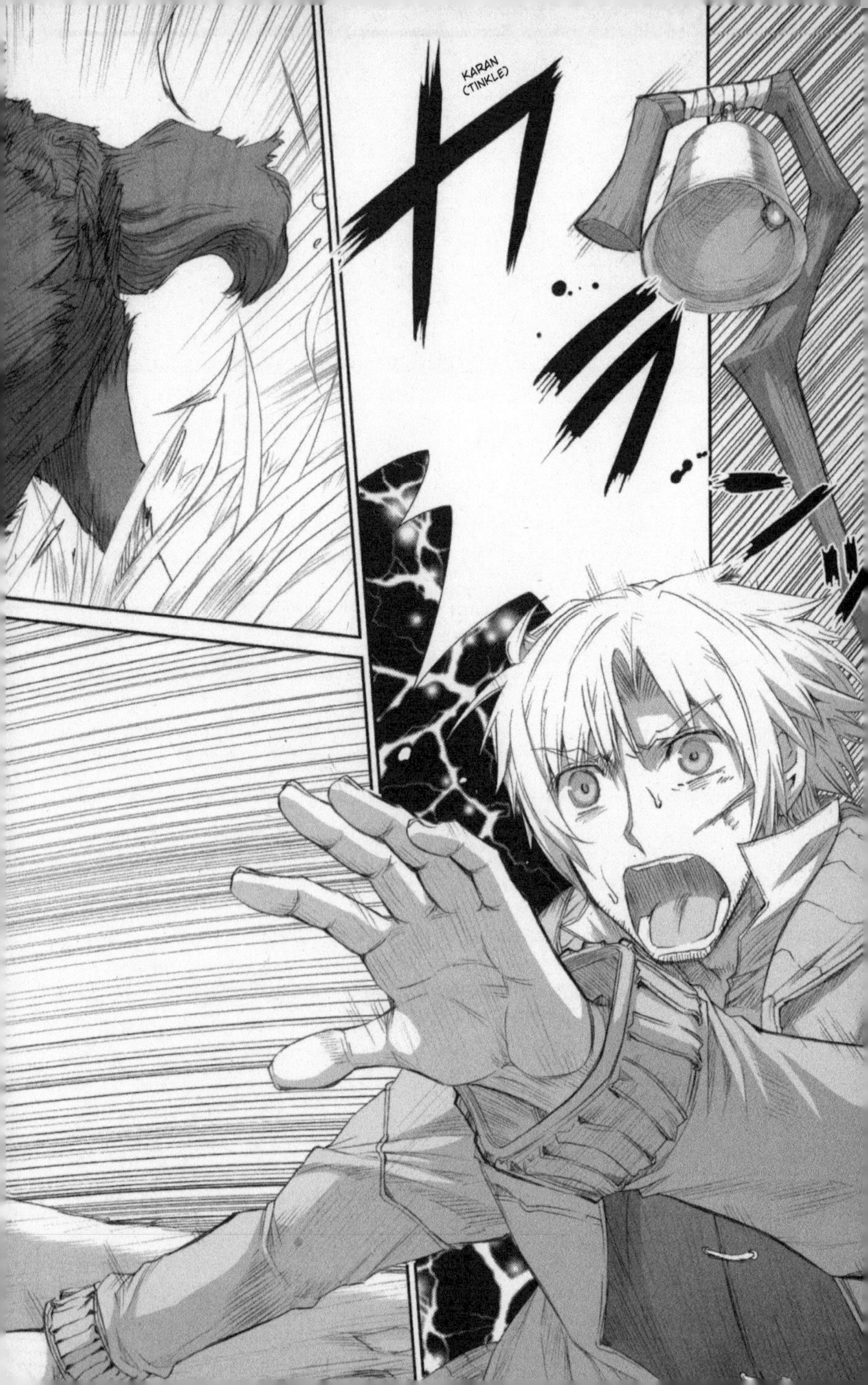
KARAN
(TINKLE)

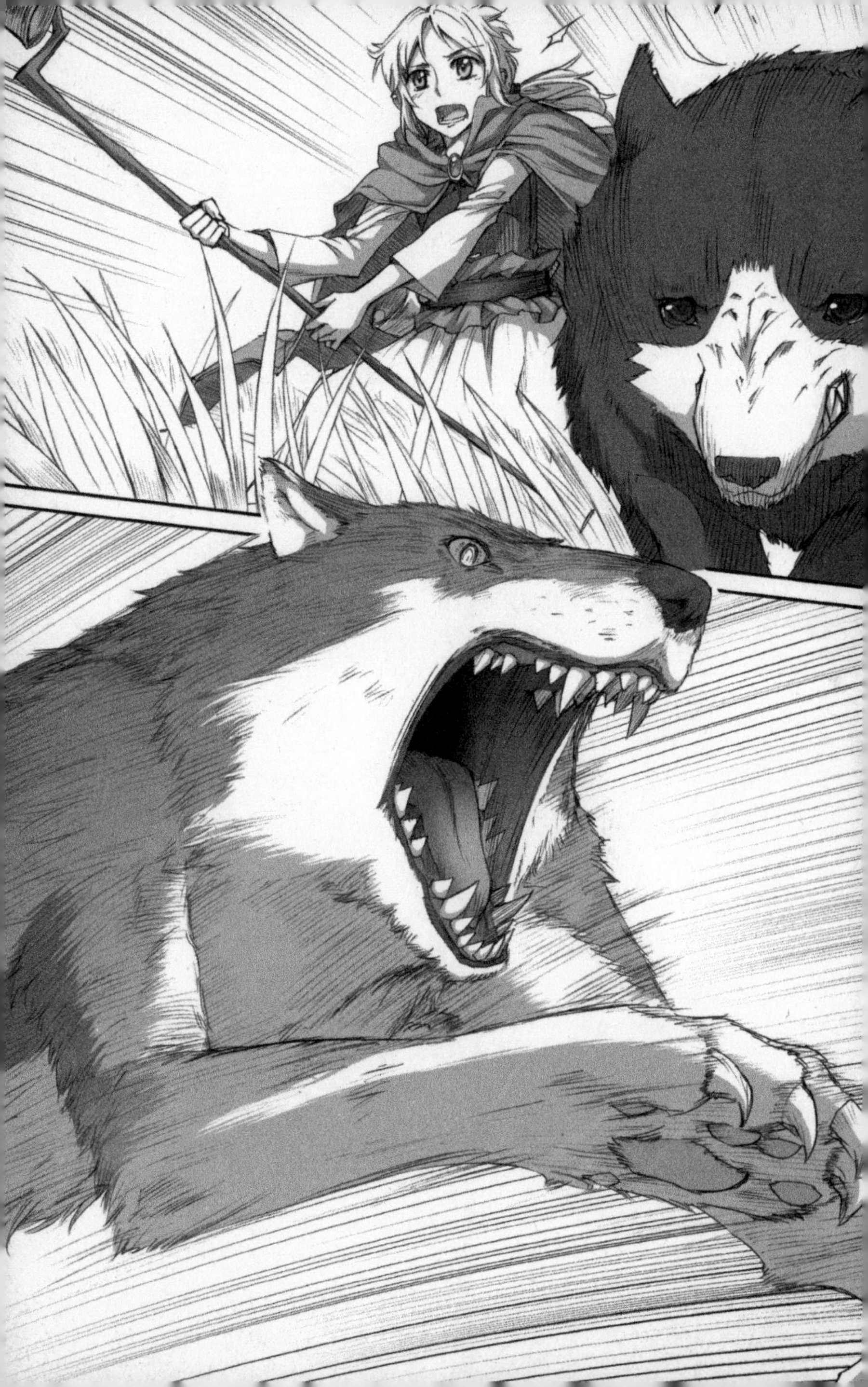

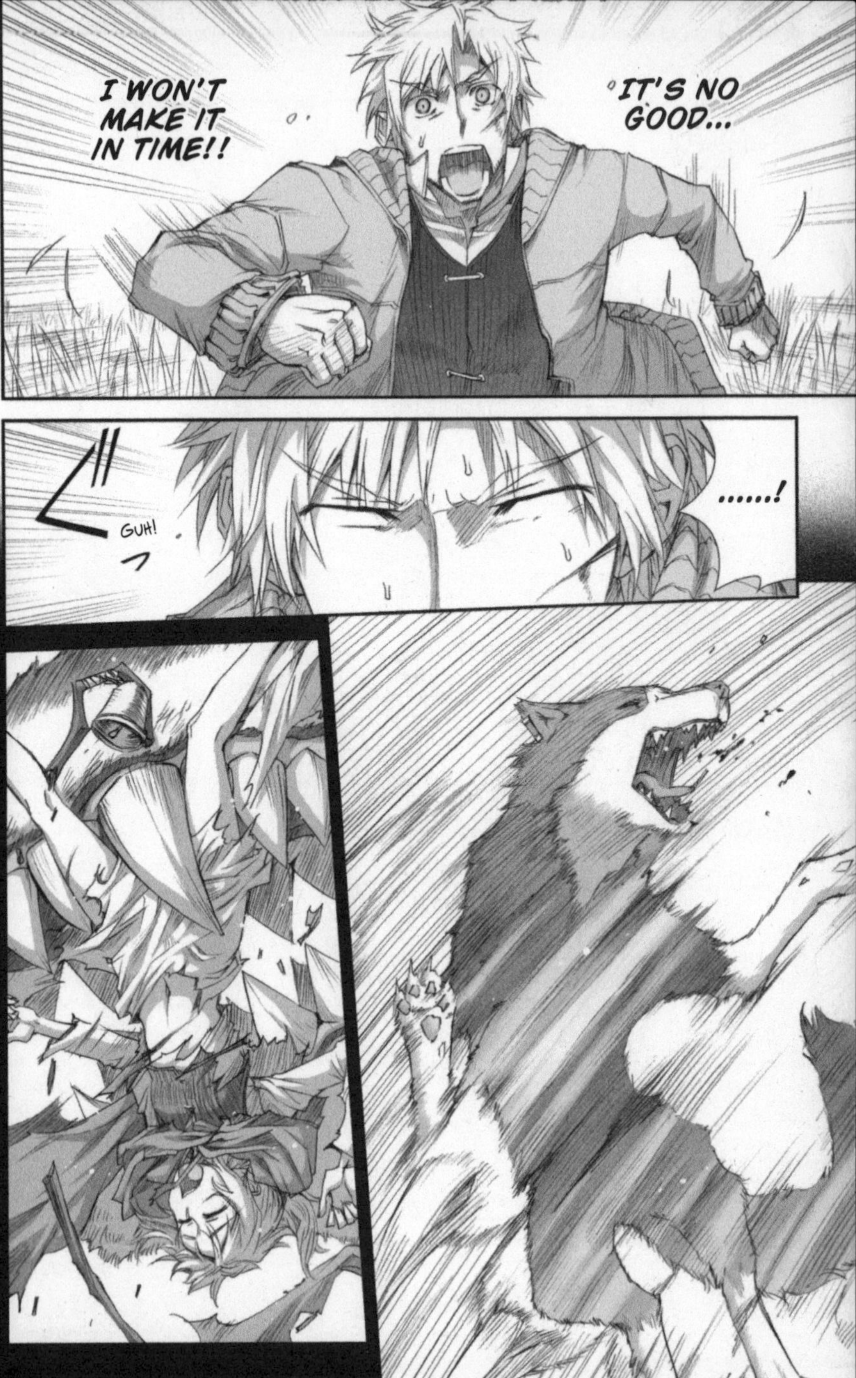
IT'S NO GOOD...
I WON'T MAKE IT IN TIME!!
......!
GUH!

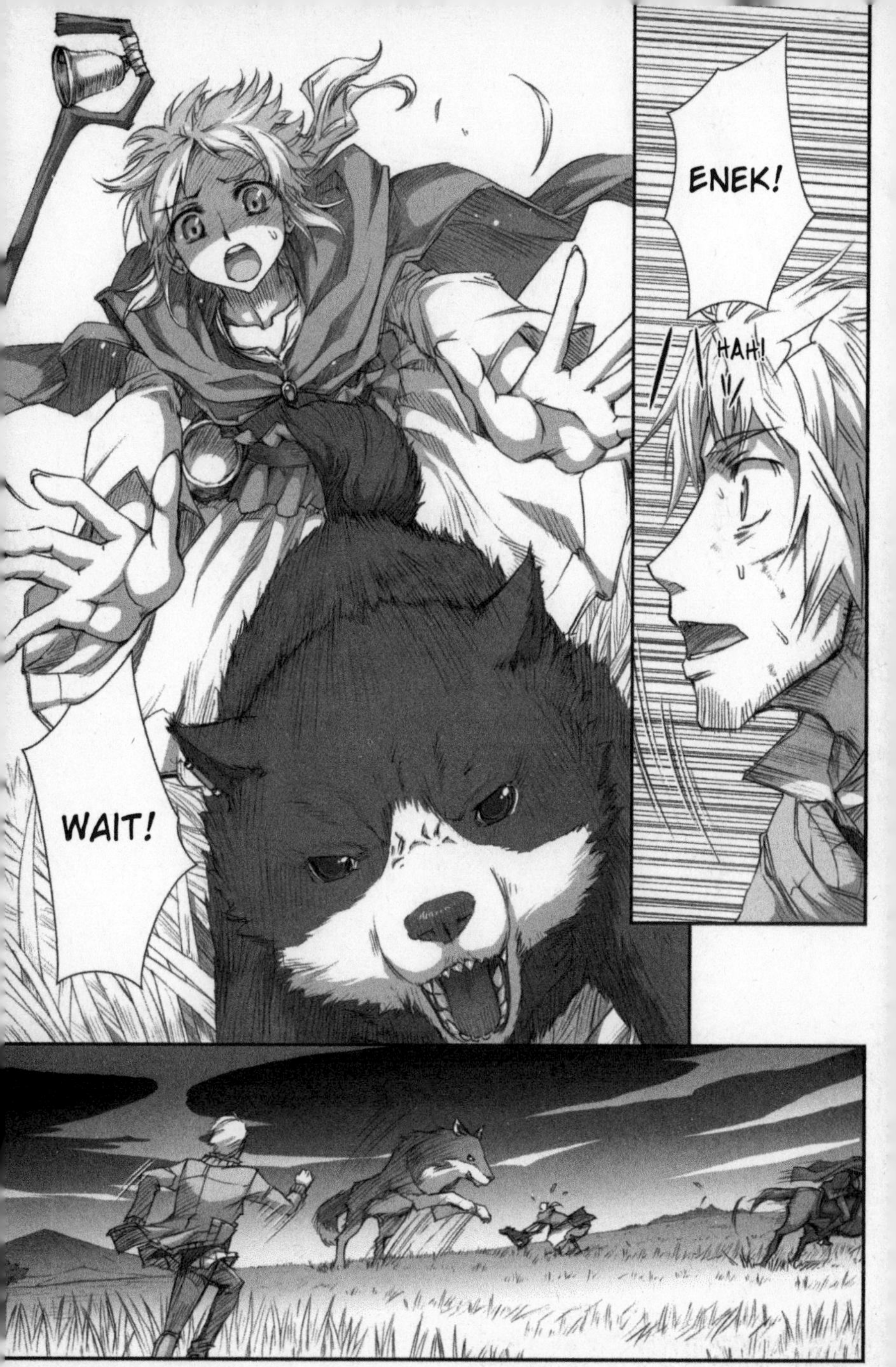

ENEK!
HAH!
WAIT!

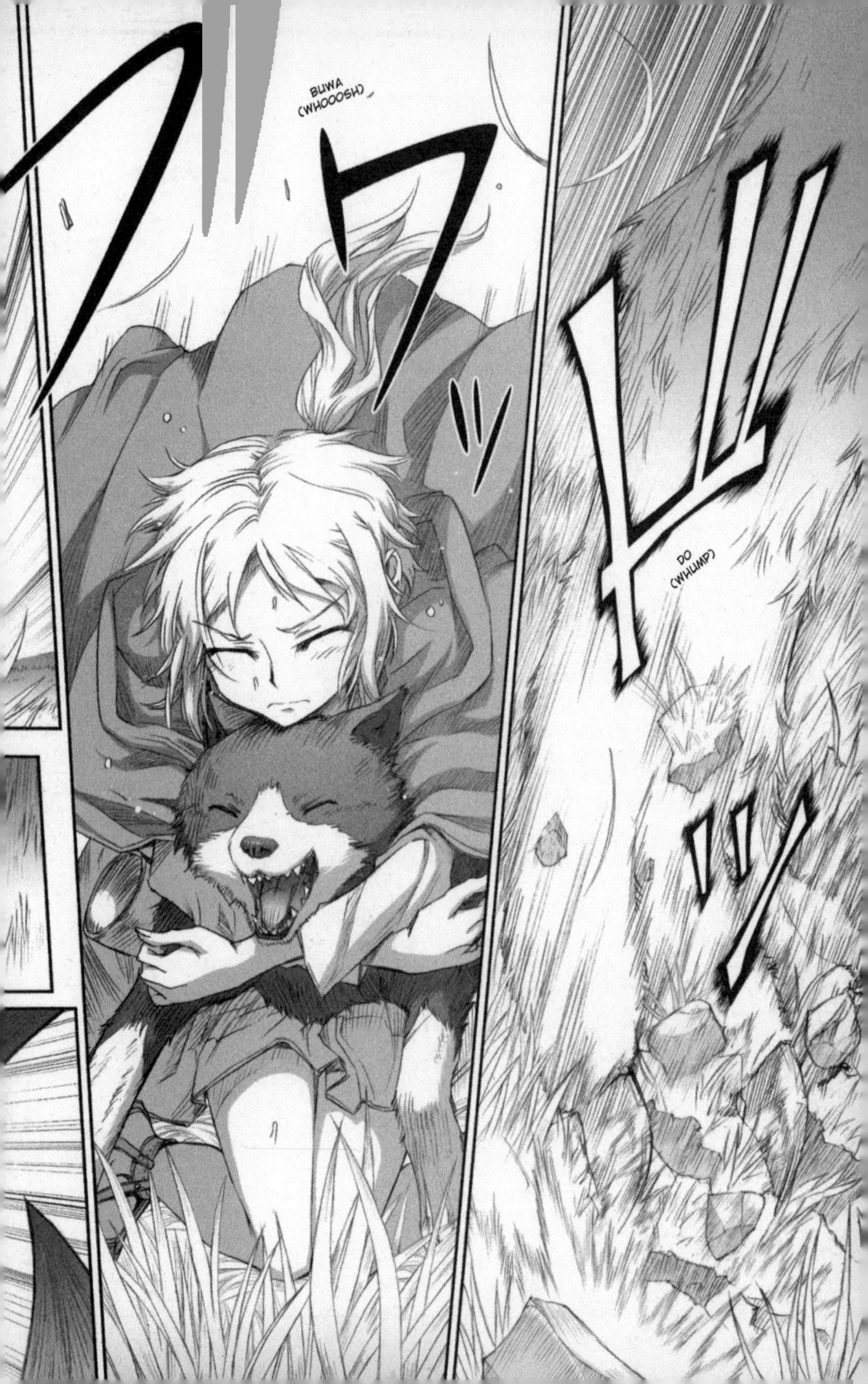
DO
(WHUMP)
BUWA
(WHOOOSH)

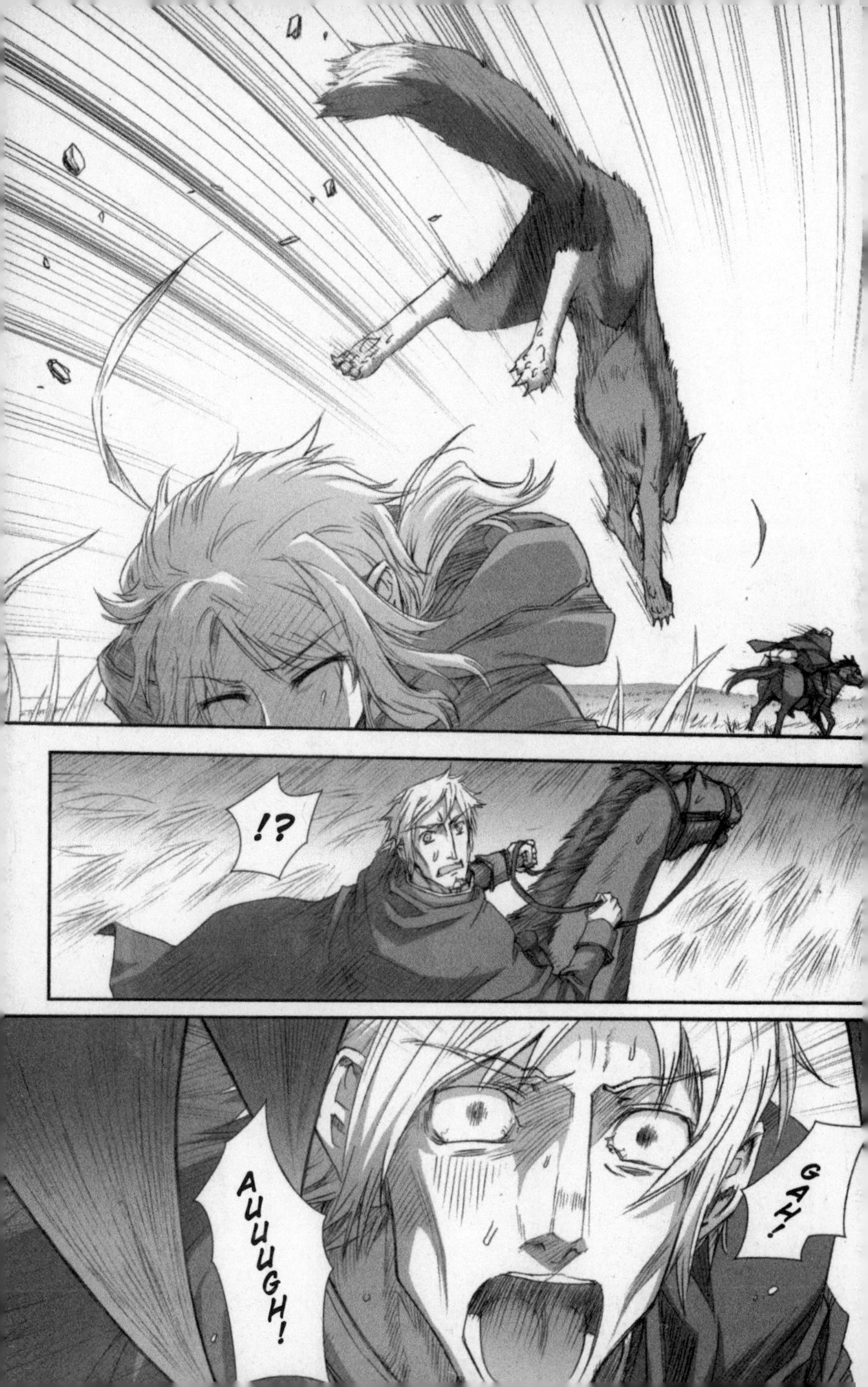
!?
GAH!
AUUUGH!

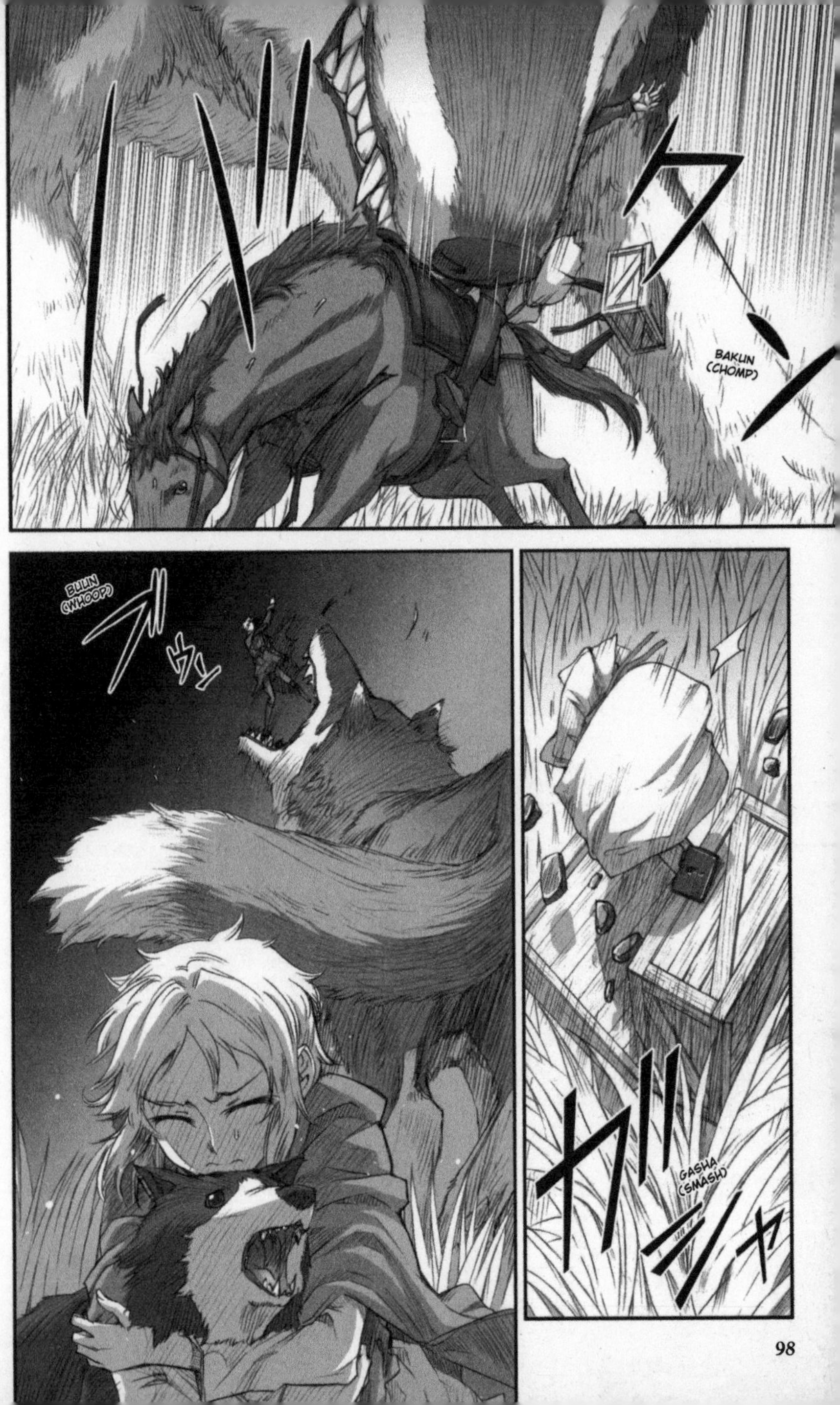
BAKUN
(CHOMP)
GASHA
(SMASH)
BUUN
(WHOOP)

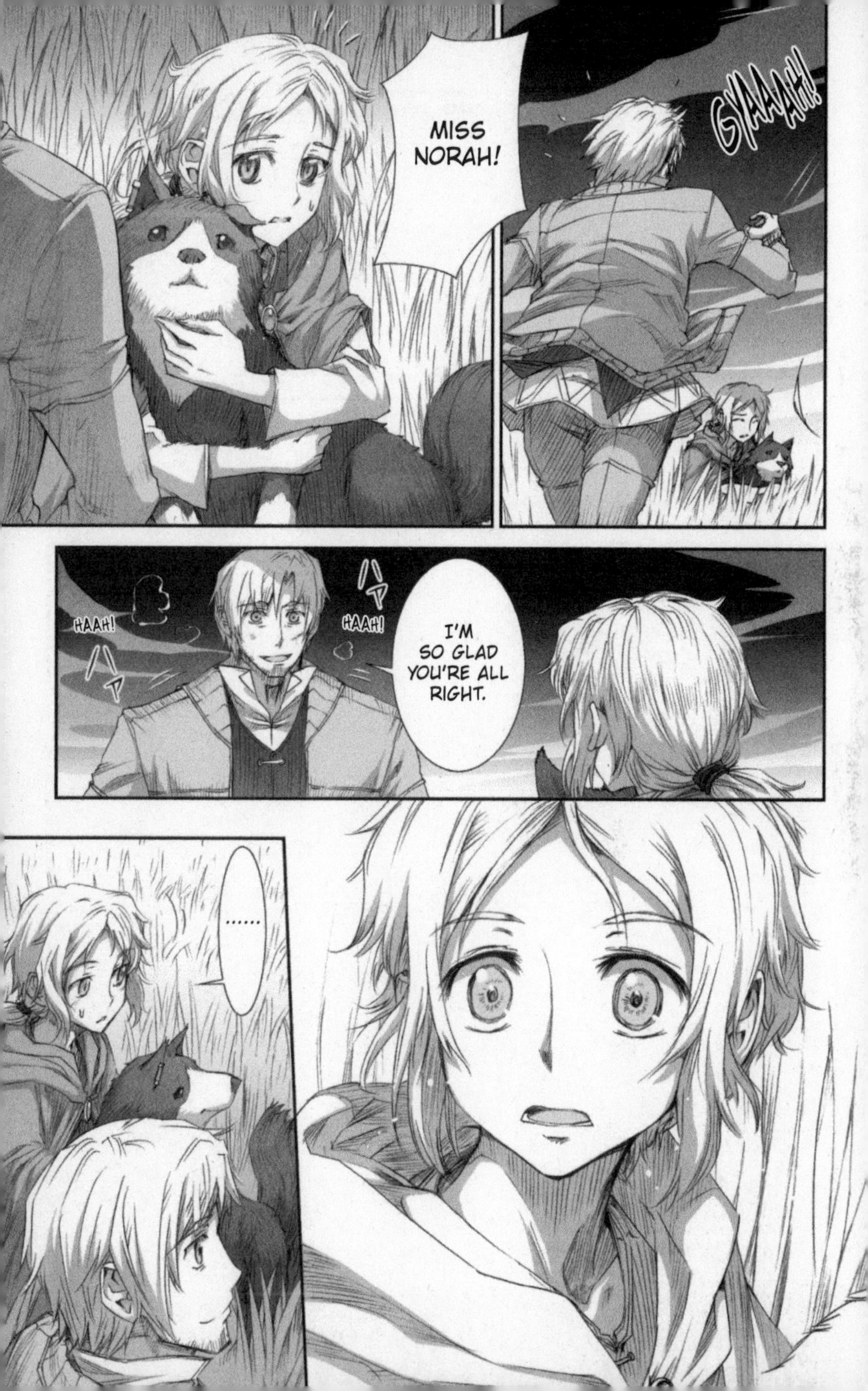
GYAAAH!
MISS NORAH!
I'M SO GLAD YOU'RE ALL RIGHT.
ハァ
HAAAH!
HAAAH!
ハァ
......

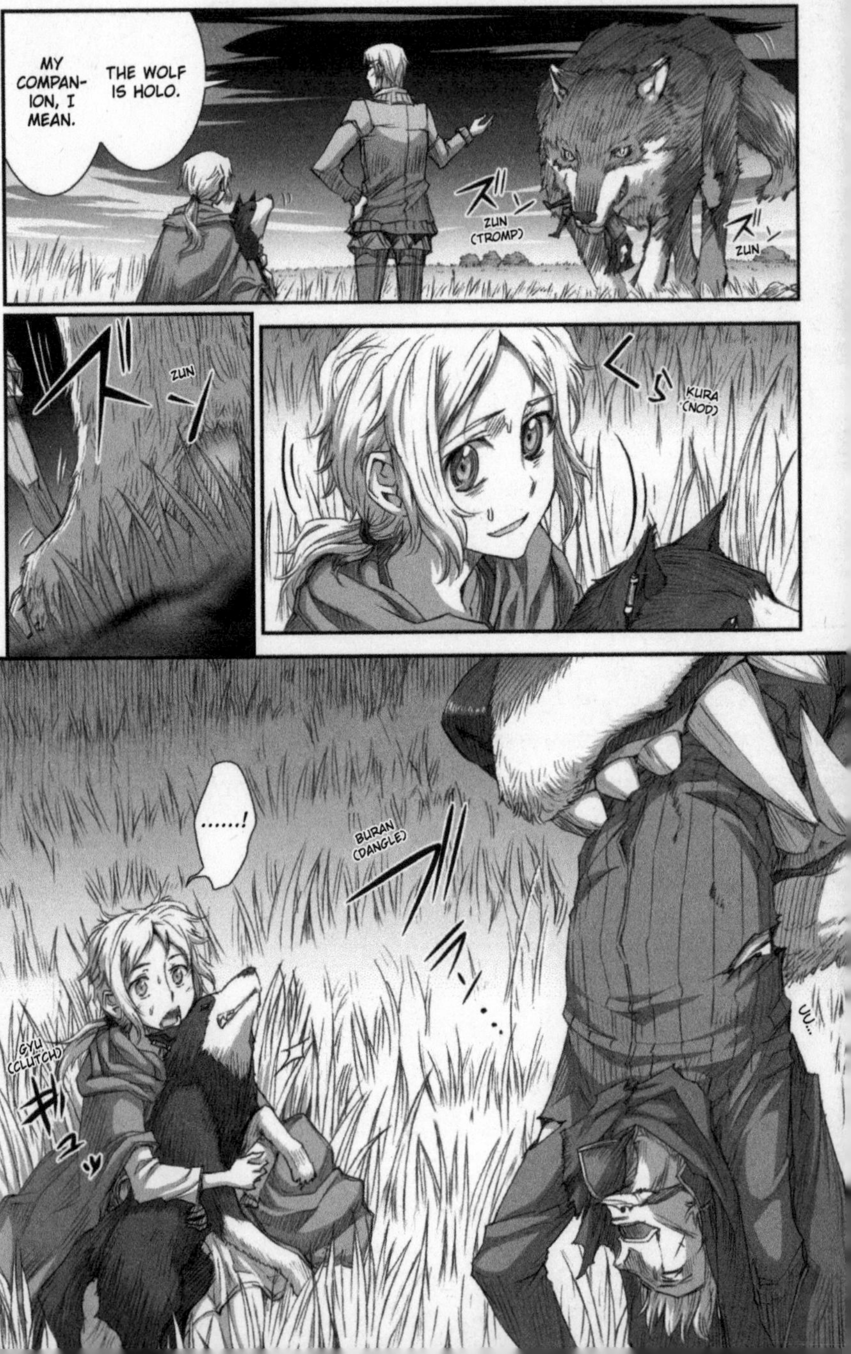
THE WOLF IS HOLO.
MY COMPANION, I MEAN.
ZUN
ZUN (TROMP)
KURA (NOD)
ZUN
UU...
BURAN (DANGLE)
......!
GYU (CLUTCH)

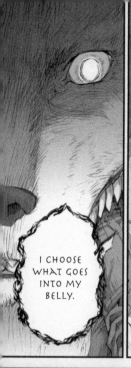

IF IT HAD BEEN ME, I WOULD'VE EATEN HIM IN ONE BITE.

!

I CHOOSE WHAT GOES INTO MY BELLY.

UGH...

THERE IT IS.

ガサ
GASA

ガサ
GASA
(RUSTLE)

ゾゾ
ZOO
(CHILL)

THE GOLD.

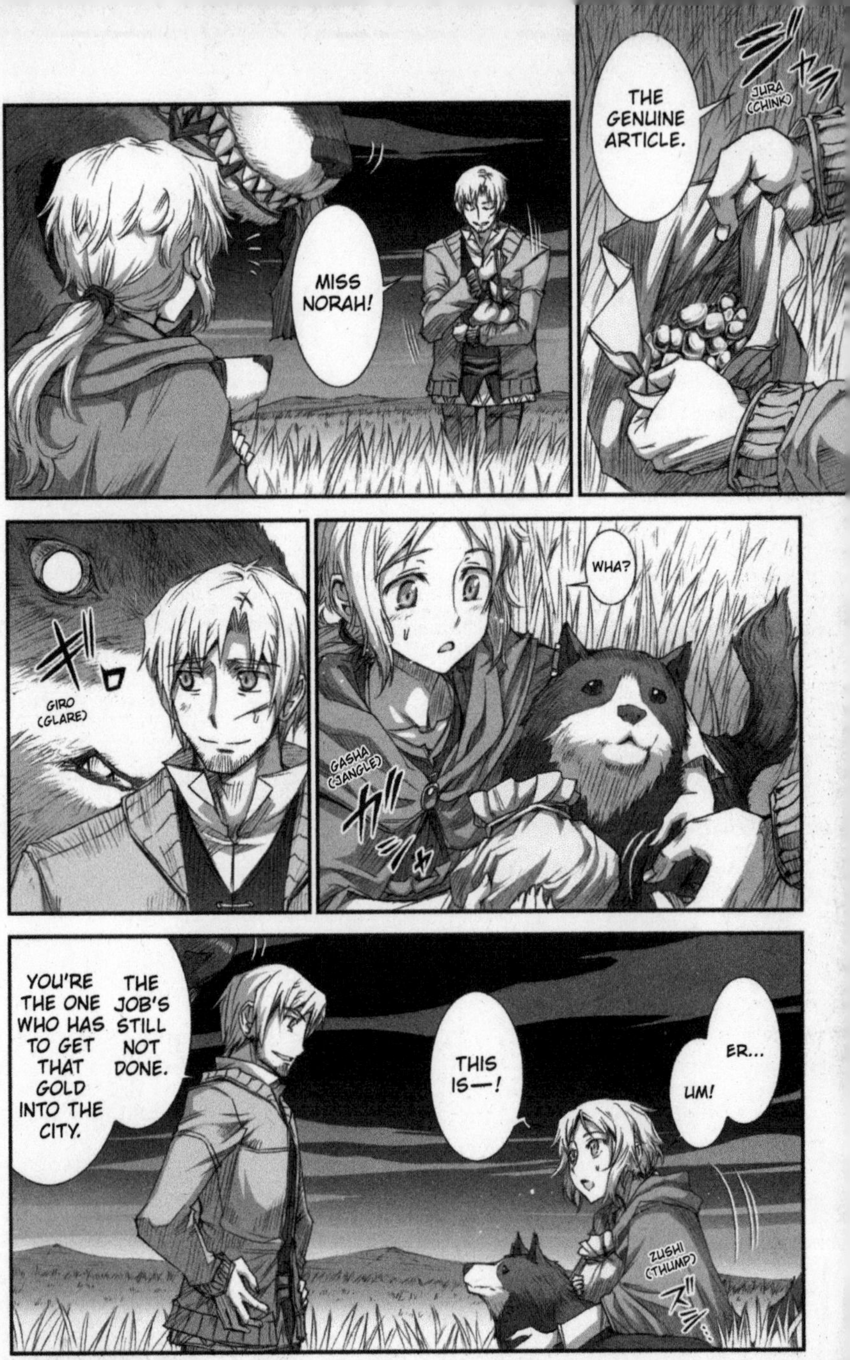
JURA (CHINK)
THE GENUINE ARTICLE.
MISS NORAH!
WHA?
GASHA (JANGLE)
GIRO (GLARE)
ER... UM!
ZUSHI (THUMP)
THIS IS—!
THE JOB'S STILL NOT DONE.
YOU'RE THE ONE WHO HAS TO GET THAT GOLD INTO THE CITY.

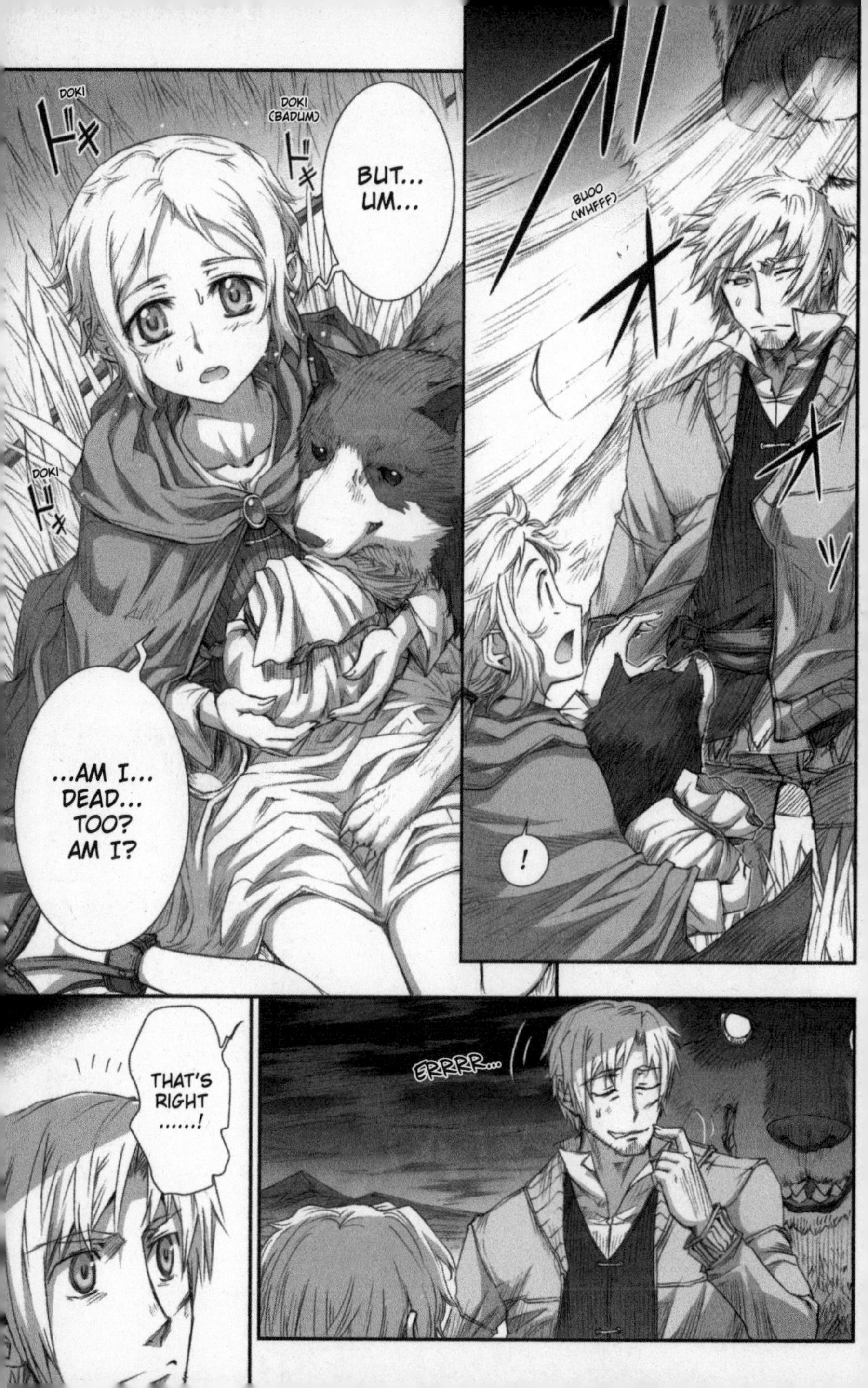
BUOO (WHFFF)
!
DOKI
DOKI (BADUM)
BUT... UM...
DOKI
...AM I... DEAD... TOO? AM I?
ERRRR...
THAT'S RIGHT ......!

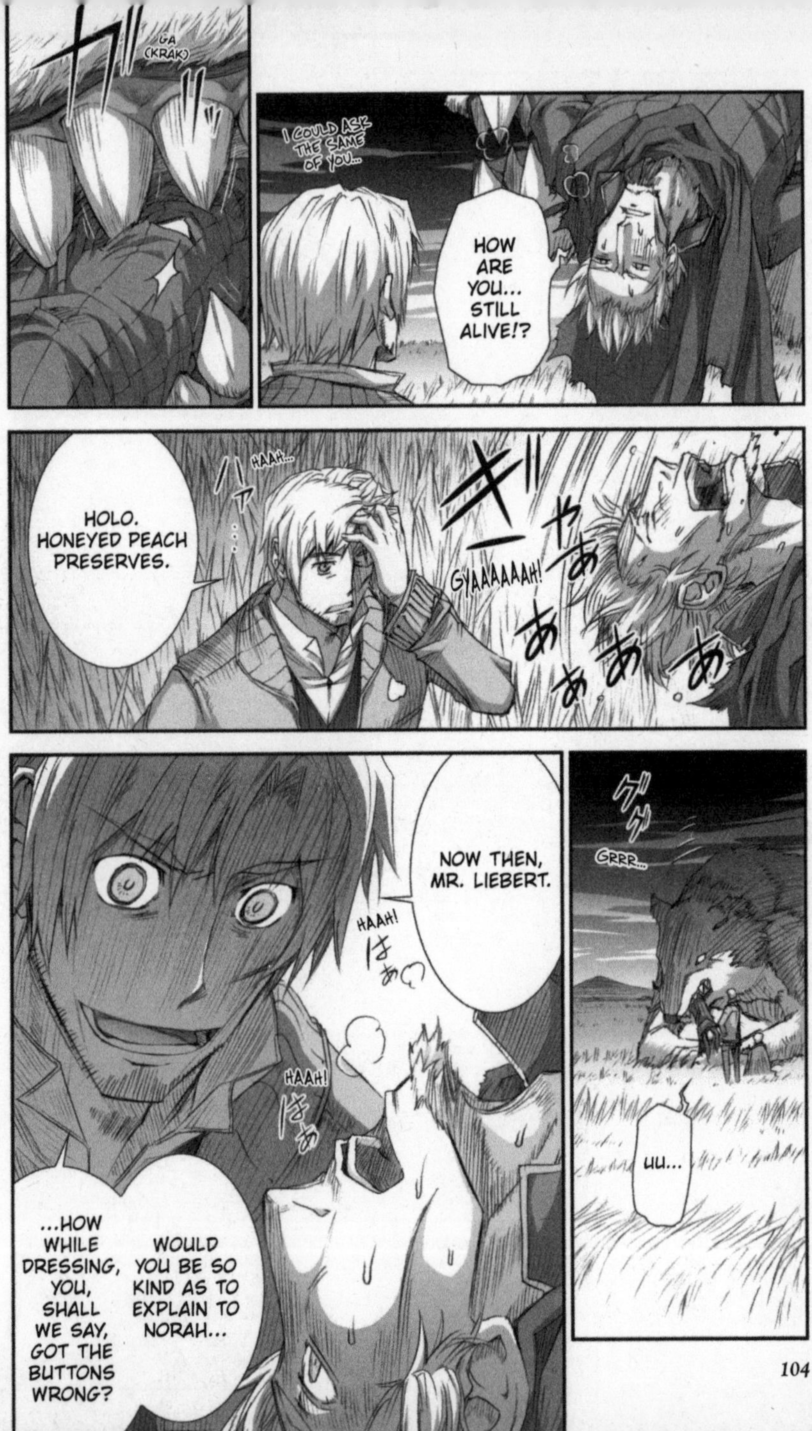
HOW ARE YOU... STILL ALIVE!?
I COULD ASK THE SAME OF YOU...
GA (KRAK)
GYAAAAAAH!
HAAH...
HOLO. HONEYED PEACH PRESERVES.
GRRR...
UU...
NOW THEN, MR. LIEBERT.
HAAH!
HAAH!
WOULD YOU BE SO KIND AS TO EXPLAIN TO NORAH... ...HOW WHILE DRESSING, YOU, SHALL WE SAY, GOT THE BUTTONS WRONG?

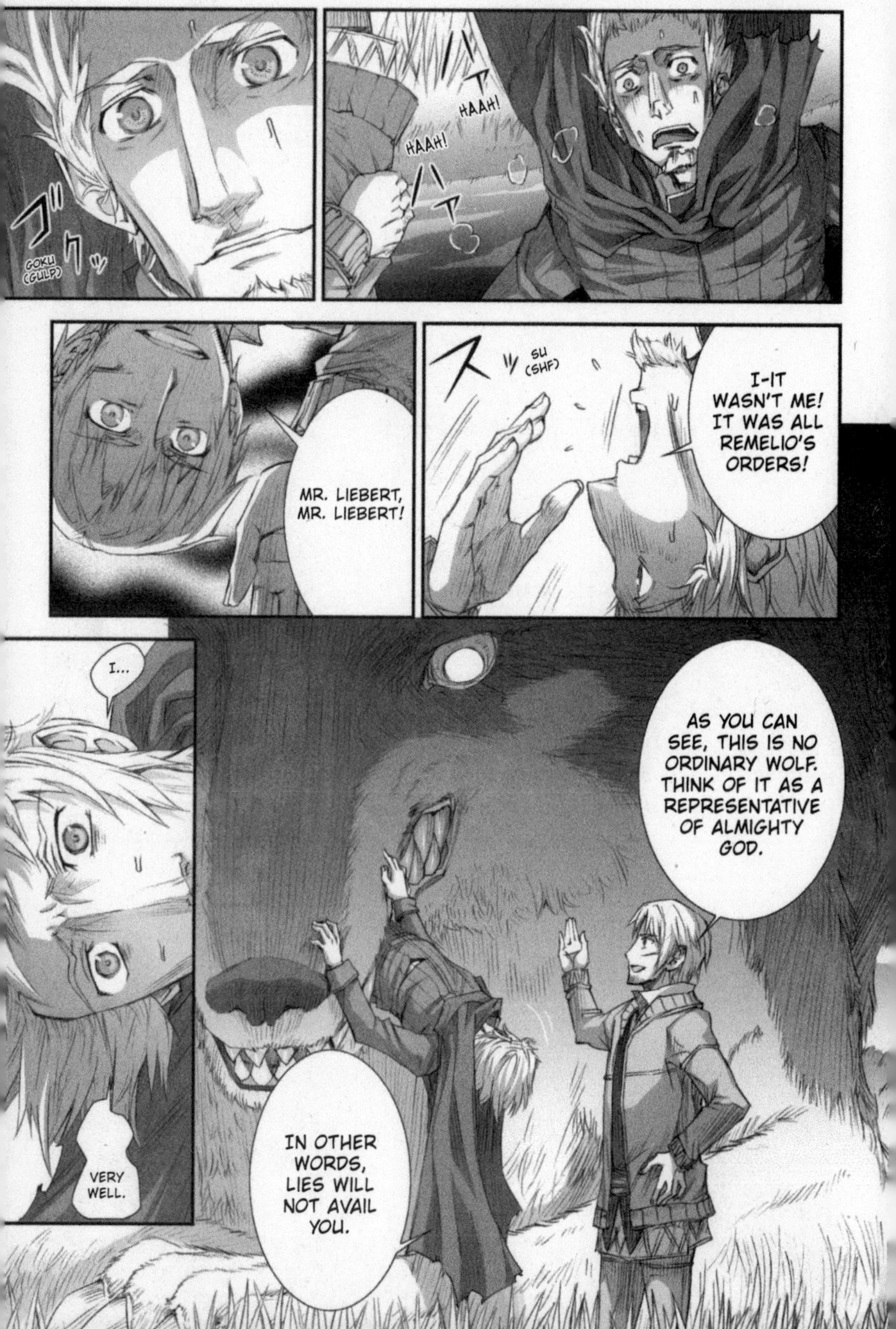
HAAH!
HAAH!
GOKU (GULP)
I-IT WASN'T ME! IT WAS ALL REMELIO'S ORDERS!
SU (SHF)
MR. LIEBERT, MR. LIEBERT!
AS YOU CAN SEE, THIS IS NO ORDINARY WOLF. THINK OF IT AS A REPRESENTATIVE OF ALMIGHTY GOD.
IN OTHER WORDS, LIES WILL NOT AVAIL YOU.
I...
VERY WELL.

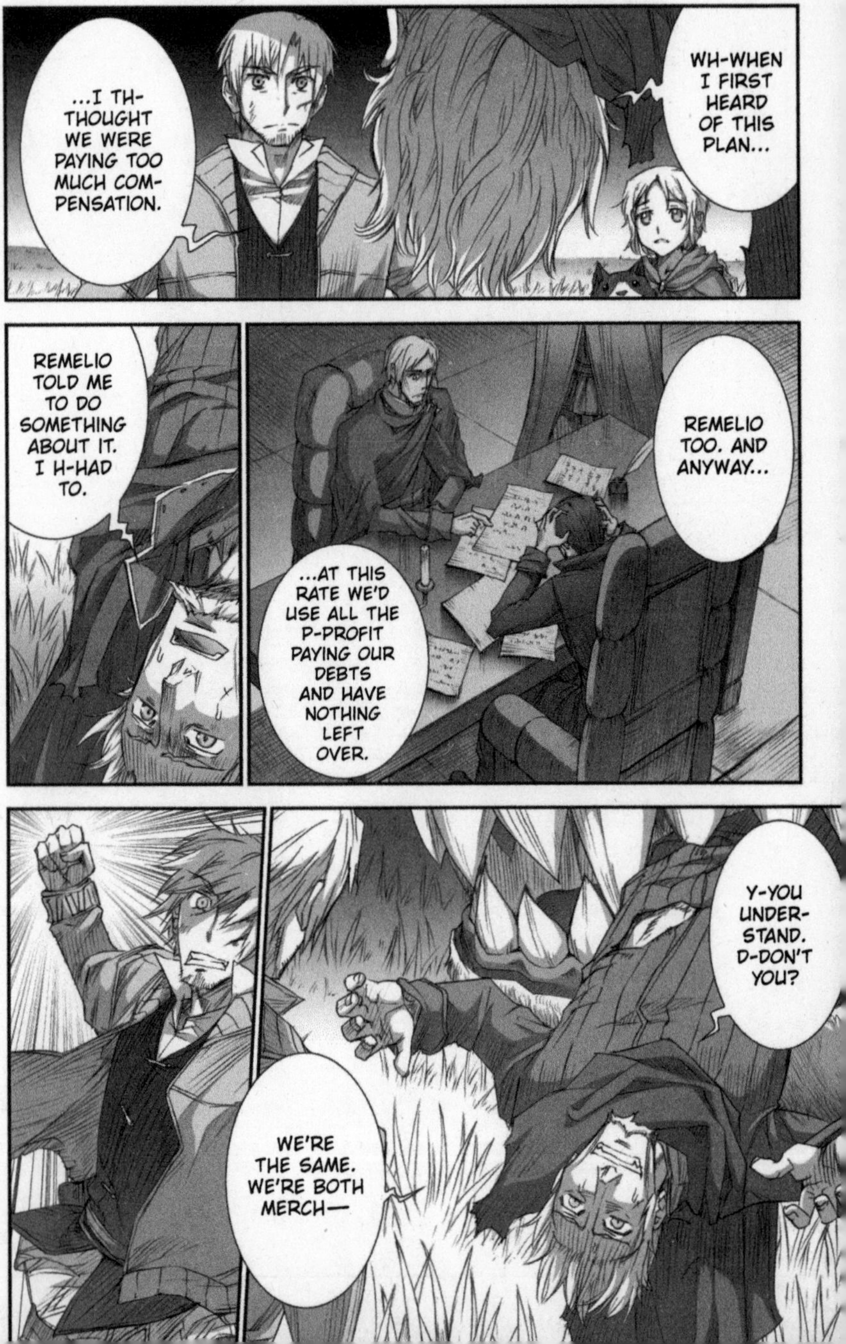
WH-WHEN I FIRST HEARD OF THIS PLAN...
...I TH-THOUGHT WE WERE PAYING TOO MUCH COMPENSATION.
REMELIO TOO. AND ANYWAY...
...AT THIS RATE WE'D USE ALL THE P-PROFIT PAYING OUR DEBTS AND HAVE NOTHING LEFT OVER.
REMELIO TOLD ME TO DO SOMETHING ABOUT IT. I H-HAD TO.
Y-YOU UNDERSTAND. D-DON'T YOU?
WE'RE THE SAME. WE'RE BOTH MERCH—

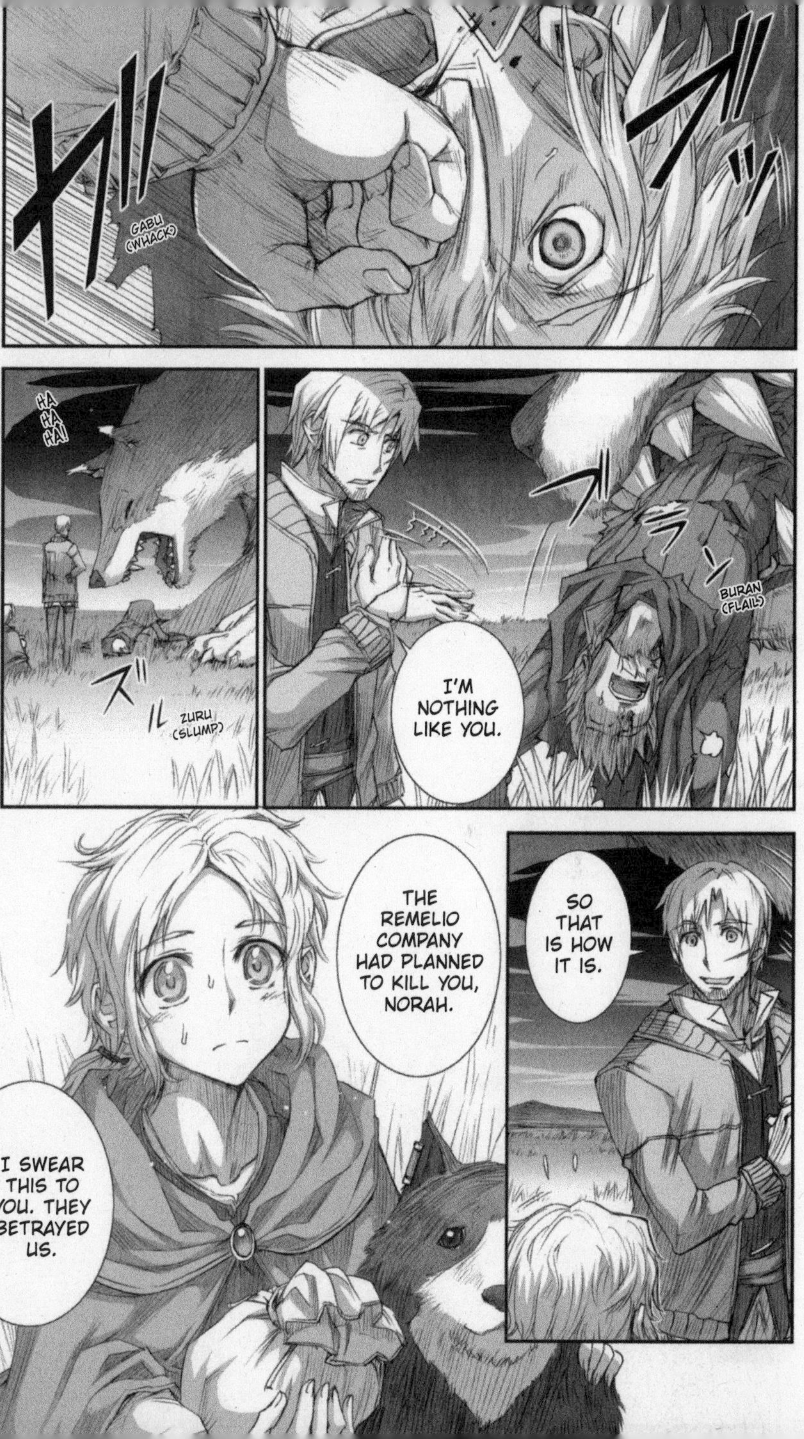
GABU (WHACK)
BURAN (FLAIL)
I'M NOTHING LIKE YOU.
HA HA HA!
ZURU (SLUMP)
SO THAT IS HOW IT IS.
THE REMELIO COMPANY HAD PLANNED TO KILL YOU, NORAH.
I SWEAR THIS TO YOU. THEY BETRAYED US.

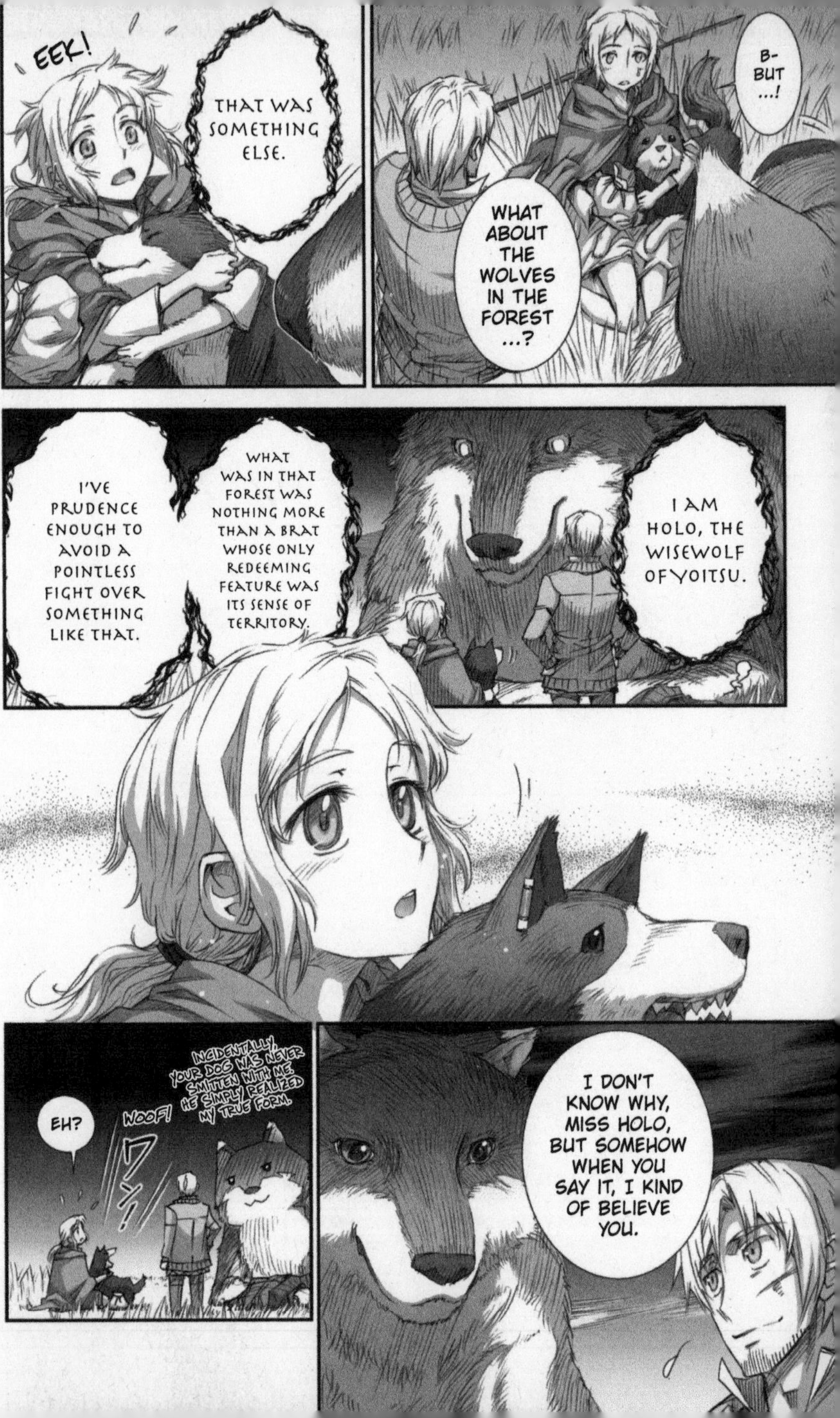
B-BUT...!
WHAT ABOUT THE WOLVES IN THE FOREST...?
EEK!
THAT WAS SOMETHING ELSE.
I AM HOLO, THE WISEWOLF OF YOITSU.
WHAT WAS IN THAT FOREST WAS NOTHING MORE THAN A BRAT WHOSE ONLY REDEEMING FEATURE WAS ITS SENSE OF TERRITORY.
I'VE PRUDENCE ENOUGH TO AVOID A POINTLESS FIGHT OVER SOMETHING LIKE THAT.
I DON'T KNOW WHY, MISS HOLO, BUT SOMEHOW WHEN YOU SAY IT, I KIND OF BELIEVE YOU.
INCIDENTALLY, YOUR DOG WAS NEVER SMITTEN WITH ME. HE SIMPLY REALIZED MY TRUE FORM.
WOOF!
EH?

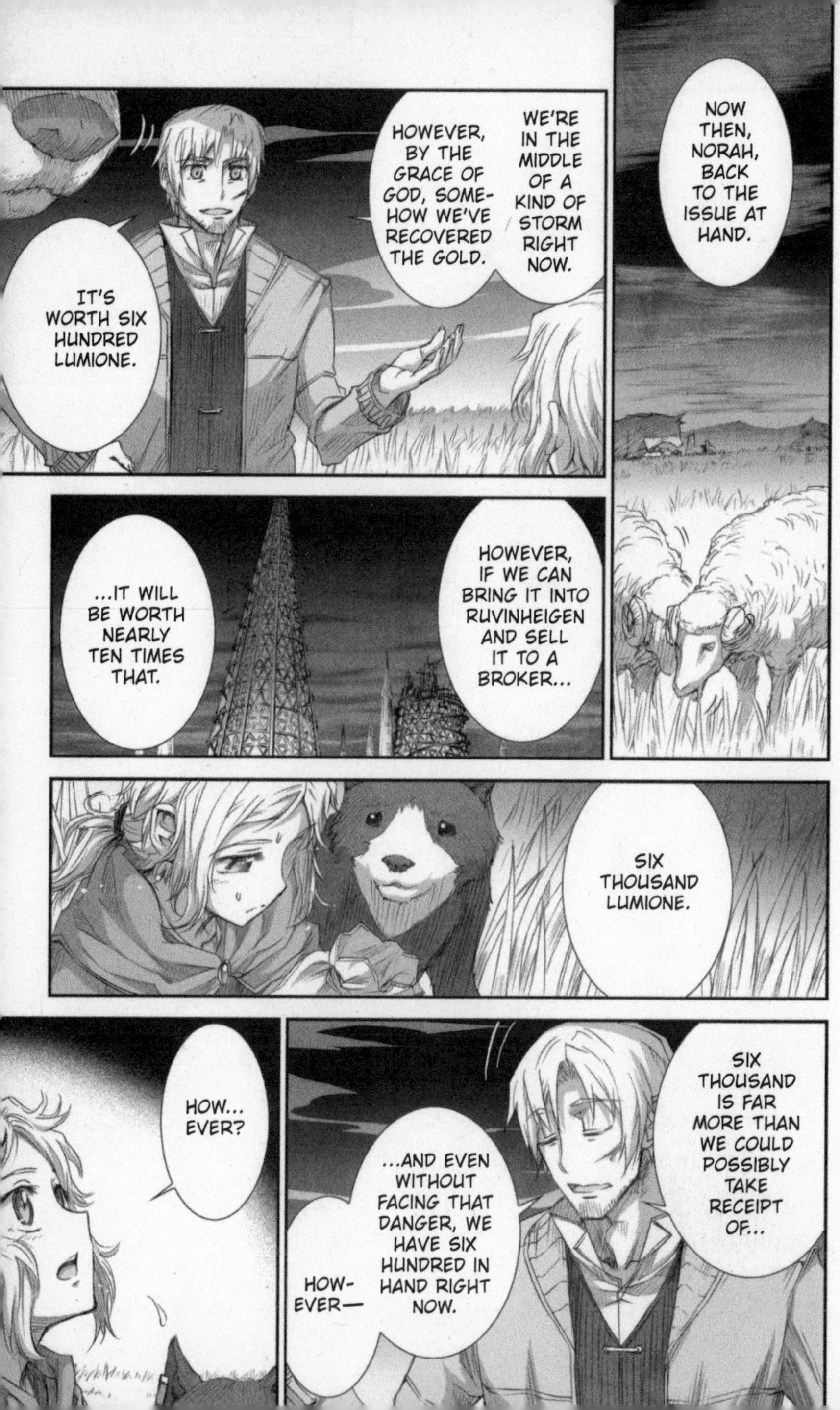
NOW THEN, NORAH, BACK TO THE ISSUE AT HAND.
WE'RE IN THE MIDDLE OF A KIND OF STORM RIGHT NOW.
HOWEVER, BY THE GRACE OF GOD, SOME-HOW WE'VE RECOVERED THE GOLD.
IT'S WORTH SIX HUNDRED LUMIONE.
HOWEVER, IF WE CAN BRING IT INTO RUVINHEIGEN AND SELL IT TO A BROKER...
...IT WILL BE WORTH NEARLY TEN TIMES THAT.
SIX THOUSAND LUMIONE.
SIX THOUSAND IS FAR MORE THAN WE COULD POSSIBLY TAKE RECEIPT OF...
...AND EVEN WITHOUT FACING THAT DANGER, WE HAVE SIX HUNDRED IN HAND RIGHT NOW.
HOW-EVER—
HOW... EVER?

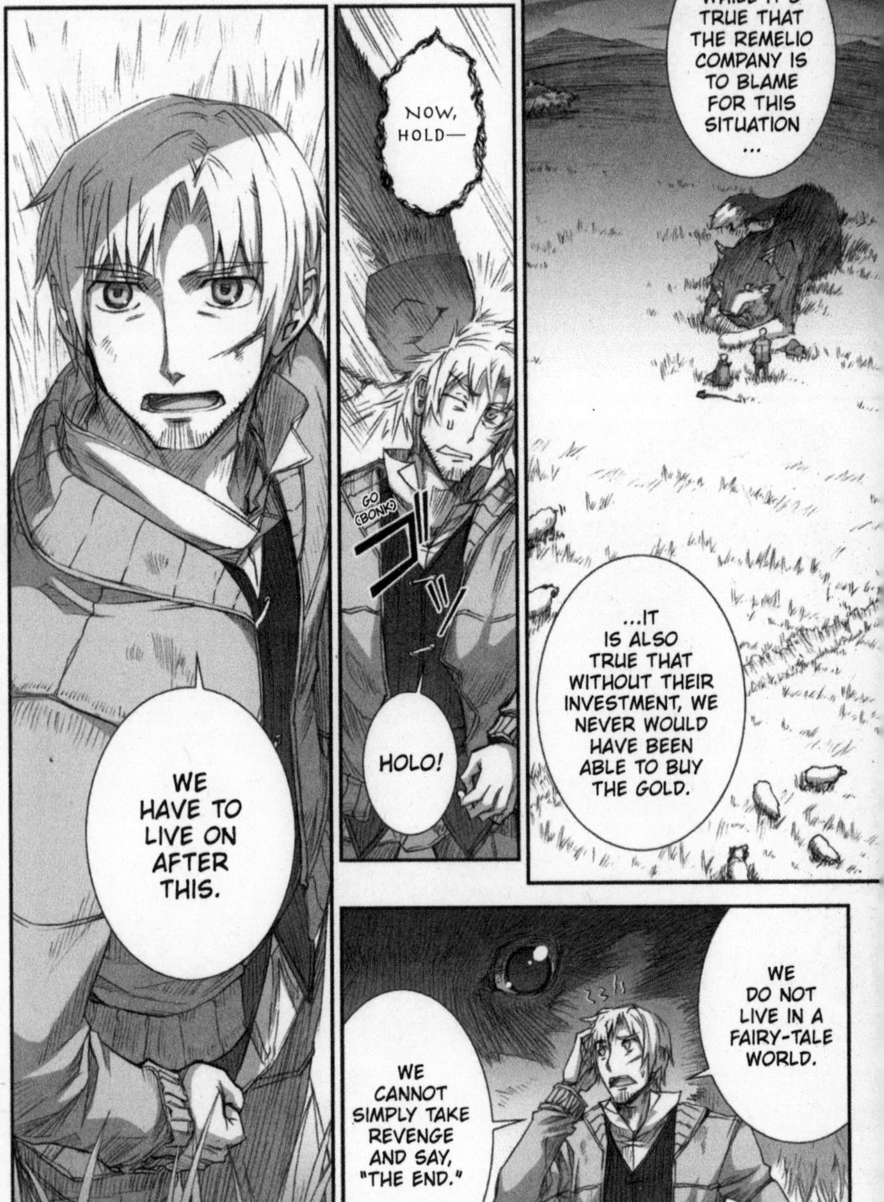
HOWEVER, WHILE IT'S TRUE THAT THE REMELIO COMPANY IS TO BLAME FOR THIS SITUATION ...
...IT IS ALSO TRUE THAT WITHOUT THEIR INVESTMENT, WE NEVER WOULD HAVE BEEN ABLE TO BUY THE GOLD.
NOW, HOLD—
GO (BONK)
HOLO!
WE DO NOT LIVE IN A FAIRY-TALE WORLD.
WE CANNOT SIMPLY TAKE REVENGE AND SAY, "THE END."
WE HAVE TO LIVE ON AFTER THIS.

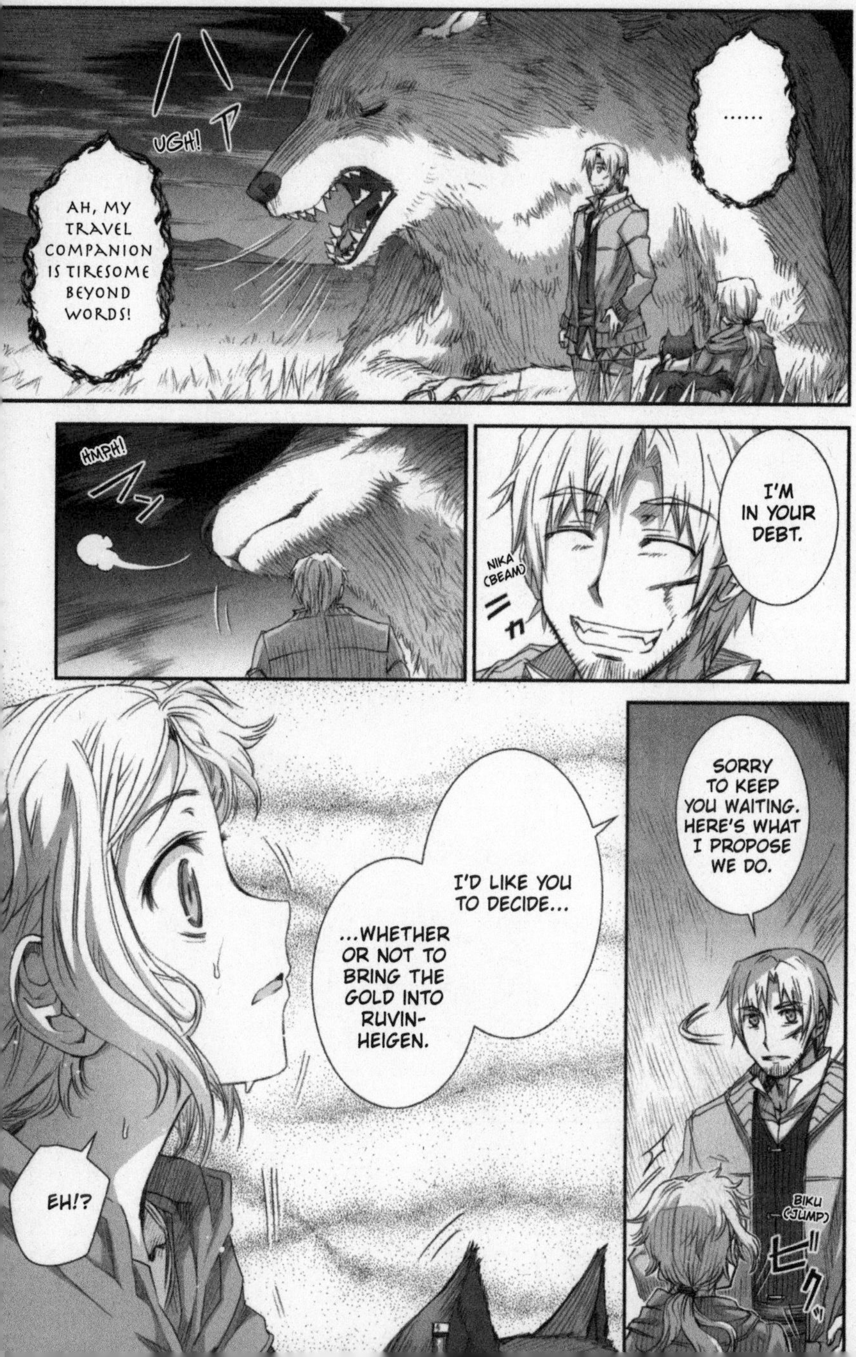
......
UGH!
AH, MY TRAVEL COMPANION IS TIRESOME BEYOND WORDS!
I'M IN YOUR DEBT.
NIKA (BEAM)
HMPH!
SORRY TO KEEP YOU WAITING. HERE'S WHAT I PROPOSE WE DO.
BIKU (JUMP)
I'D LIKE YOU TO DECIDE...
...WHETHER OR NOT TO BRING THE GOLD INTO RUVIN-HEIGEN.
EH!?

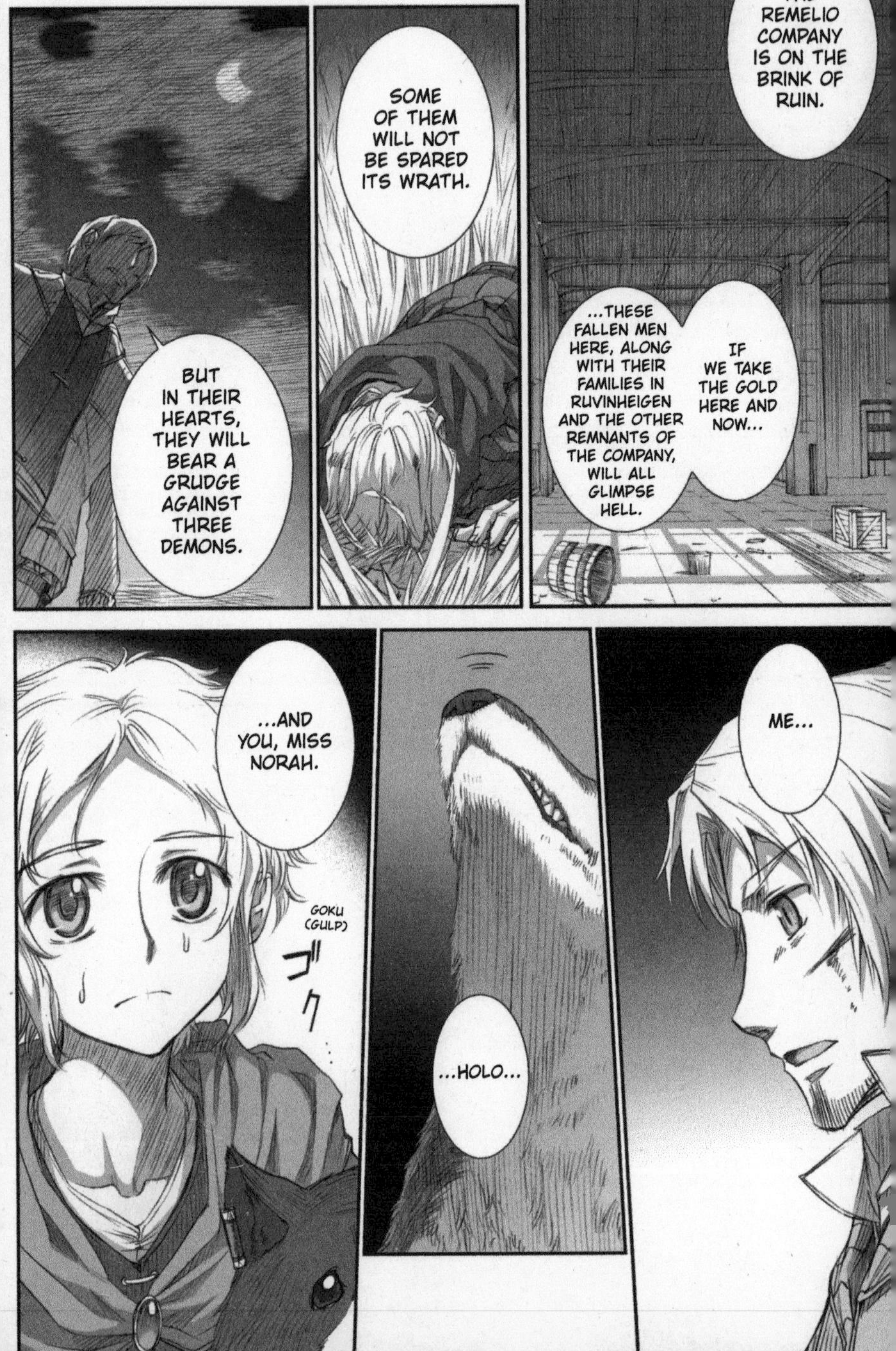
THE REMELIO COMPANY IS ON THE BRINK OF RUIN.
IF WE TAKE THE GOLD HERE AND NOW...
...THESE FALLEN MEN HERE, ALONG WITH THEIR FAMILIES IN RUVINHEIGEN AND THE OTHER REMNANTS OF THE COMPANY, WILL ALL GLIMPSE HELL.
SOME OF THEM WILL NOT BE SPARED ITS WRATH.
BUT IN THEIR HEARTS, THEY WILL BEAR A GRUDGE AGAINST THREE DEMONS.
ME...
...HOLO...
...AND YOU, MISS NORAH.
GOKU (GULP)
ゴク

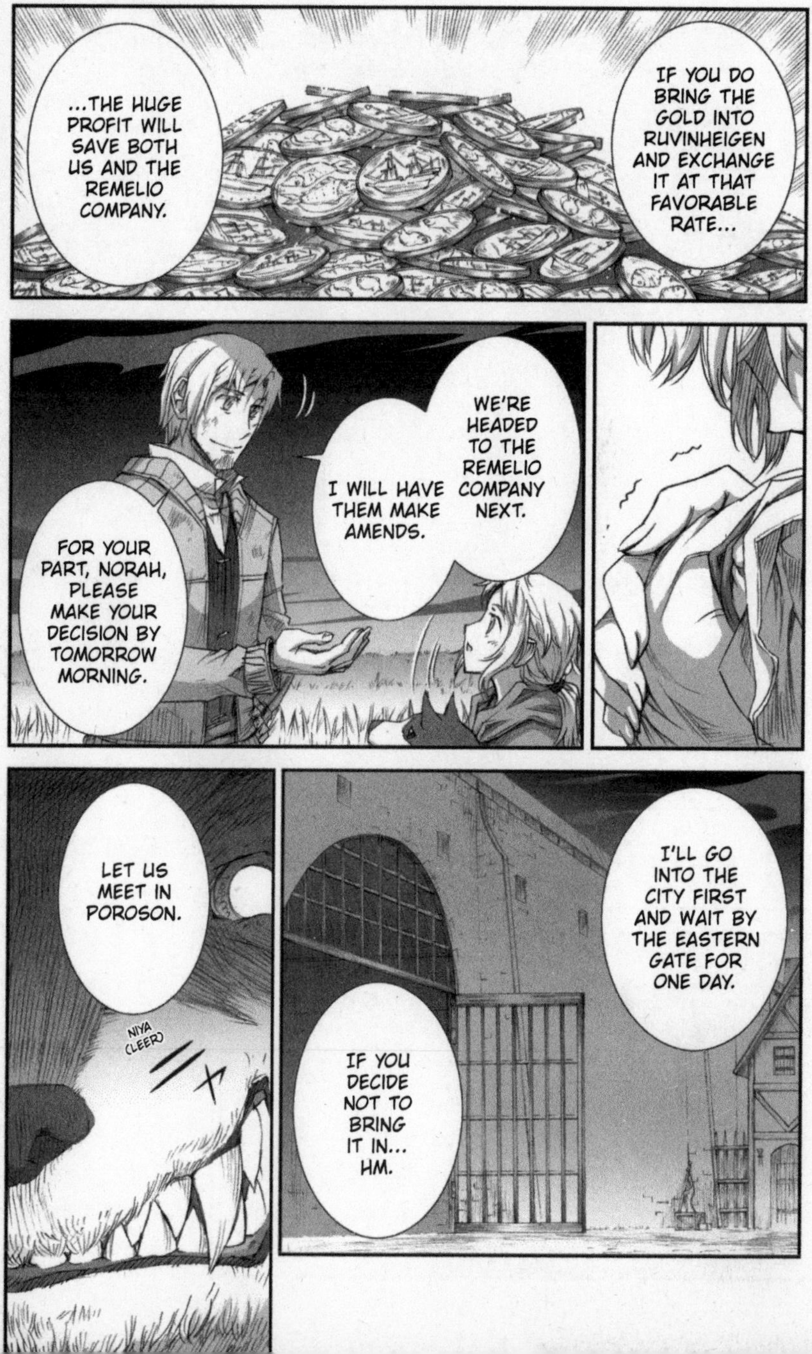
IF YOU DO BRING THE GOLD INTO RUVINHEIGEN AND EXCHANGE IT AT THAT FAVORABLE RATE...
...THE HUGE PROFIT WILL SAVE BOTH US AND THE REMELIO COMPANY.
WE'RE HEADED TO THE REMELIO COMPANY NEXT.
I WILL HAVE THEM MAKE AMENDS.
FOR YOUR PART, NORAH, PLEASE MAKE YOUR DECISION BY TOMORROW MORNING.
I'LL GO INTO THE CITY FIRST AND WAIT BY THE EASTERN GATE FOR ONE DAY.
IF YOU DECIDE NOT TO BRING IT IN... HM.
LET US MEET IN POROSON.
NIYA (LEER)

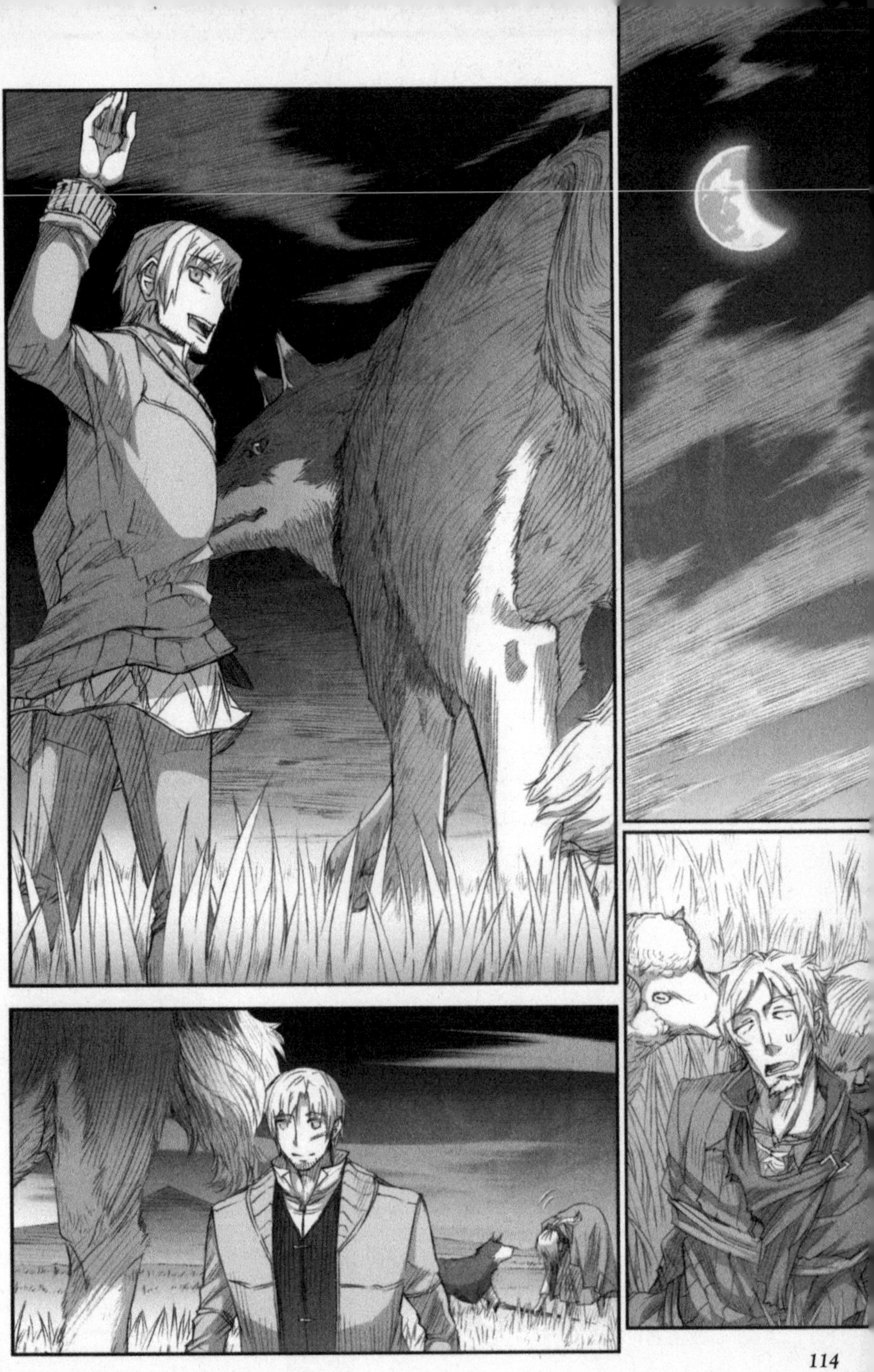

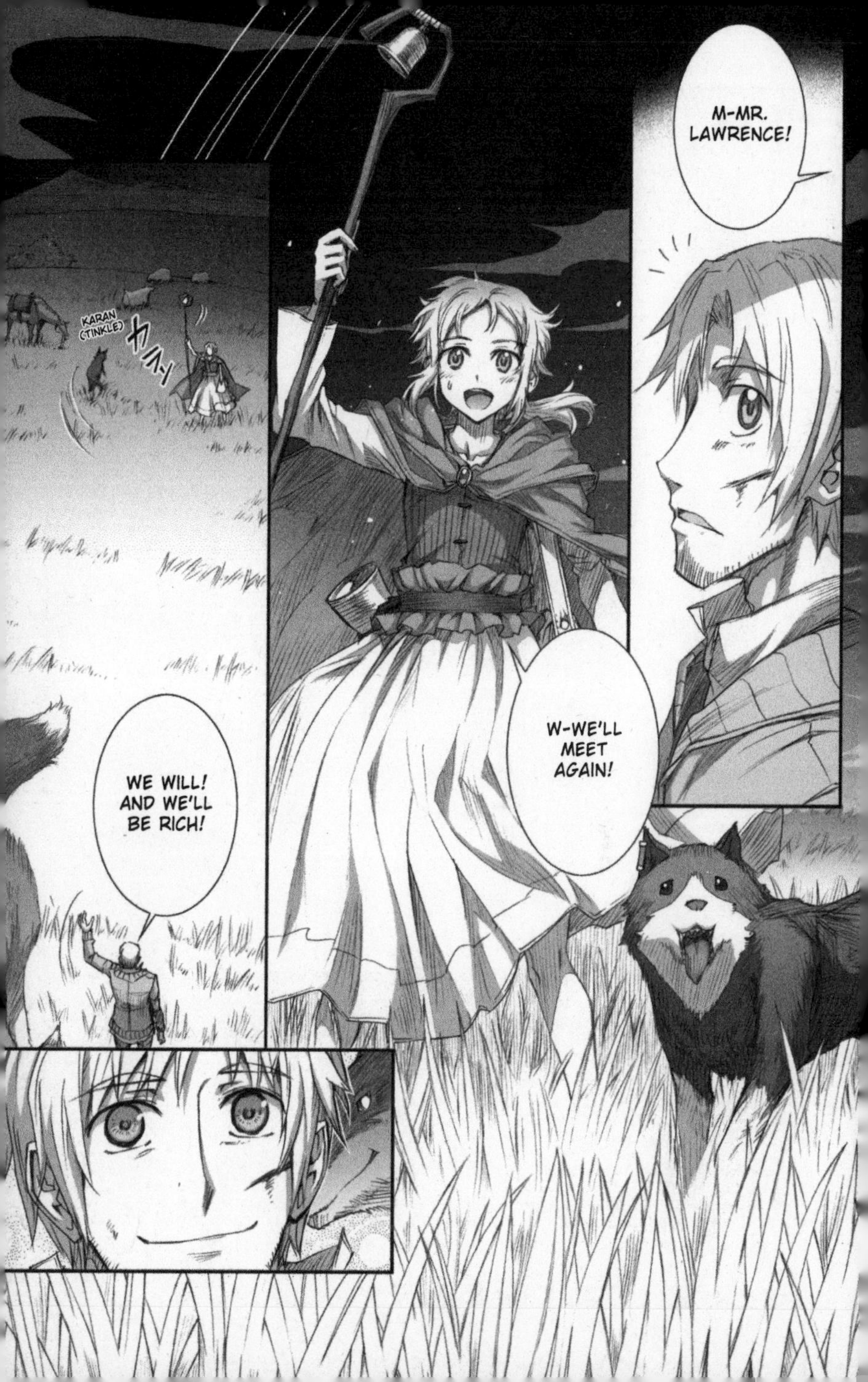
M-MR. LAWRENCE!
W-WE'LL MEET AGAIN!
KARAN (TINKLE)
WE WILL! AND WE'LL BE RICH!

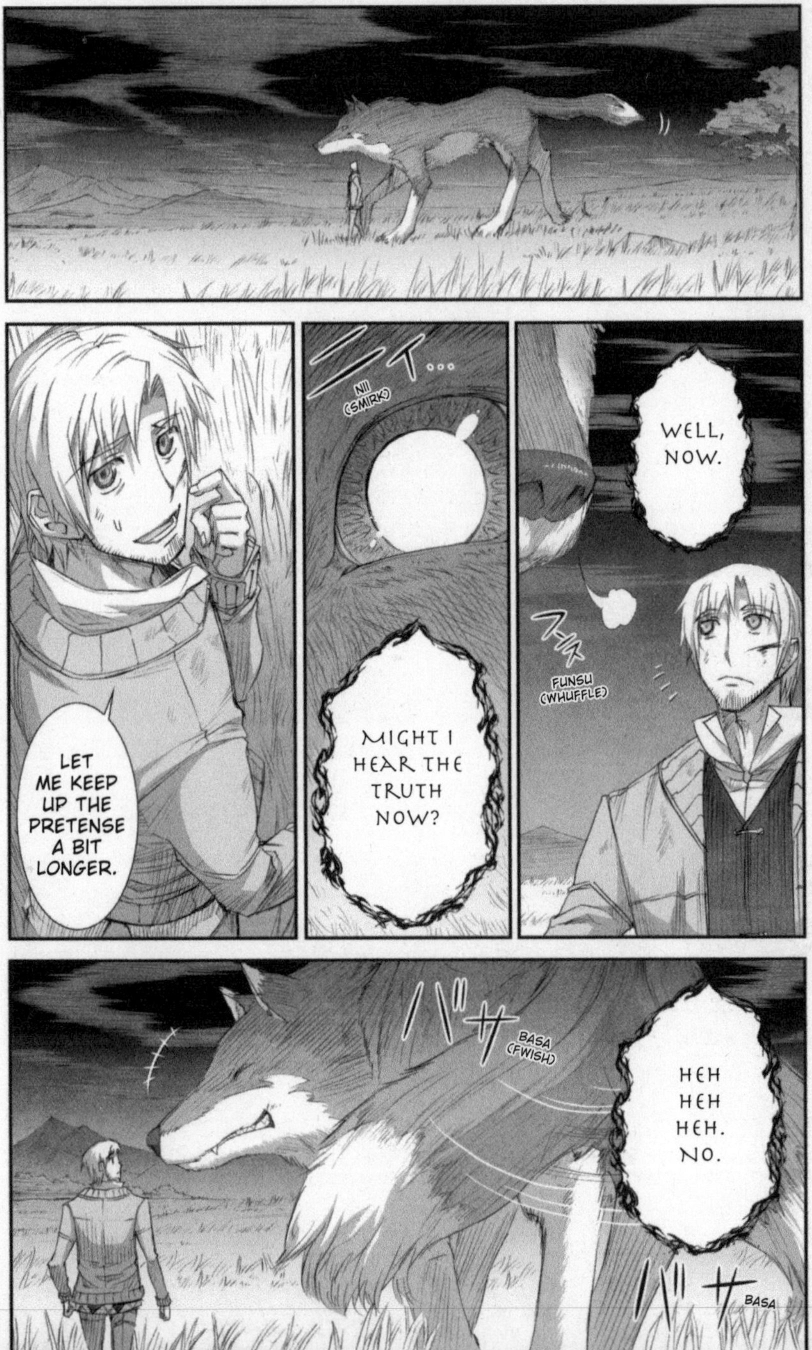
WELL, NOW.
FUNSU (WHUFFLE)
NII (SMIRK)
MIGHT I HEAR THE TRUTH NOW?
LET ME KEEP UP THE PRETENSE A BIT LONGER.
BASA (FWISH)
HEH HEH HEH. NO.
BASA

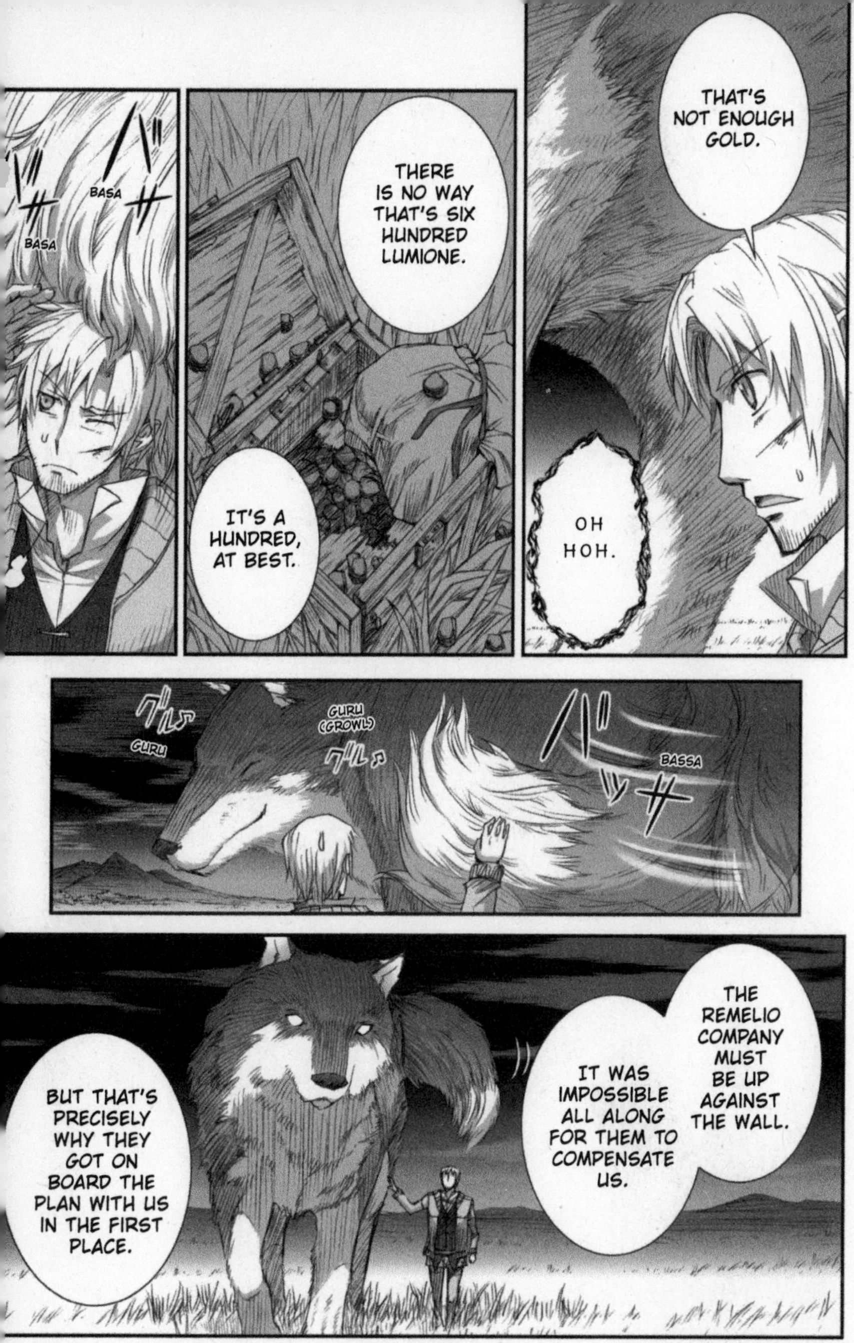
THAT'S NOT ENOUGH GOLD.
OH HOH.
THERE IS NO WAY THAT'S SIX HUNDRED LUMIONE.
IT'S A HUNDRED, AT BEST.
BASA
BASA
BASSA
GURU (GROWL)
GURU
THE REMELIO COMPANY MUST BE UP AGAINST THE WALL.
IT WAS IMPOSSIBLE ALL ALONG FOR THEM TO COMPENSATE US.
BUT THAT'S PRECISELY WHY THEY GOT ON BOARD THE PLAN WITH US IN THE FIRST PLACE.

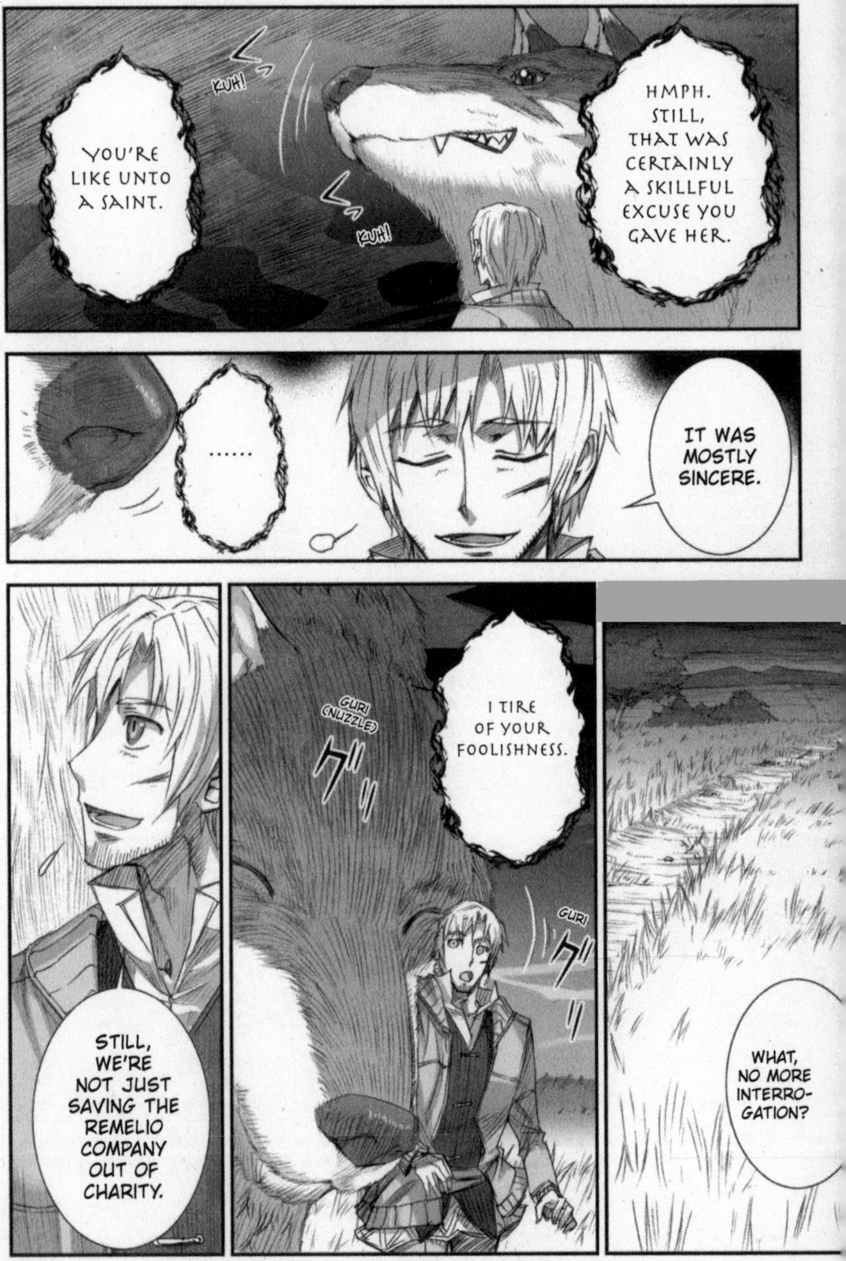
HMPH. STILL, THAT WAS CERTAINLY A SKILLFUL EXCUSE YOU GAVE HER.
KUH!
KUH!
YOU'RE LIKE UNTO A SAINT.
IT WAS MOSTLY SINCERE.
......
WHAT, NO MORE INTERRO-GATION?
I TIRE OF YOUR FOOLISHNESS.
GURI (NUZZLE)
GURI
STILL, WE'RE NOT JUST SAVING THE REMELIO COMPANY OUT OF CHARITY.

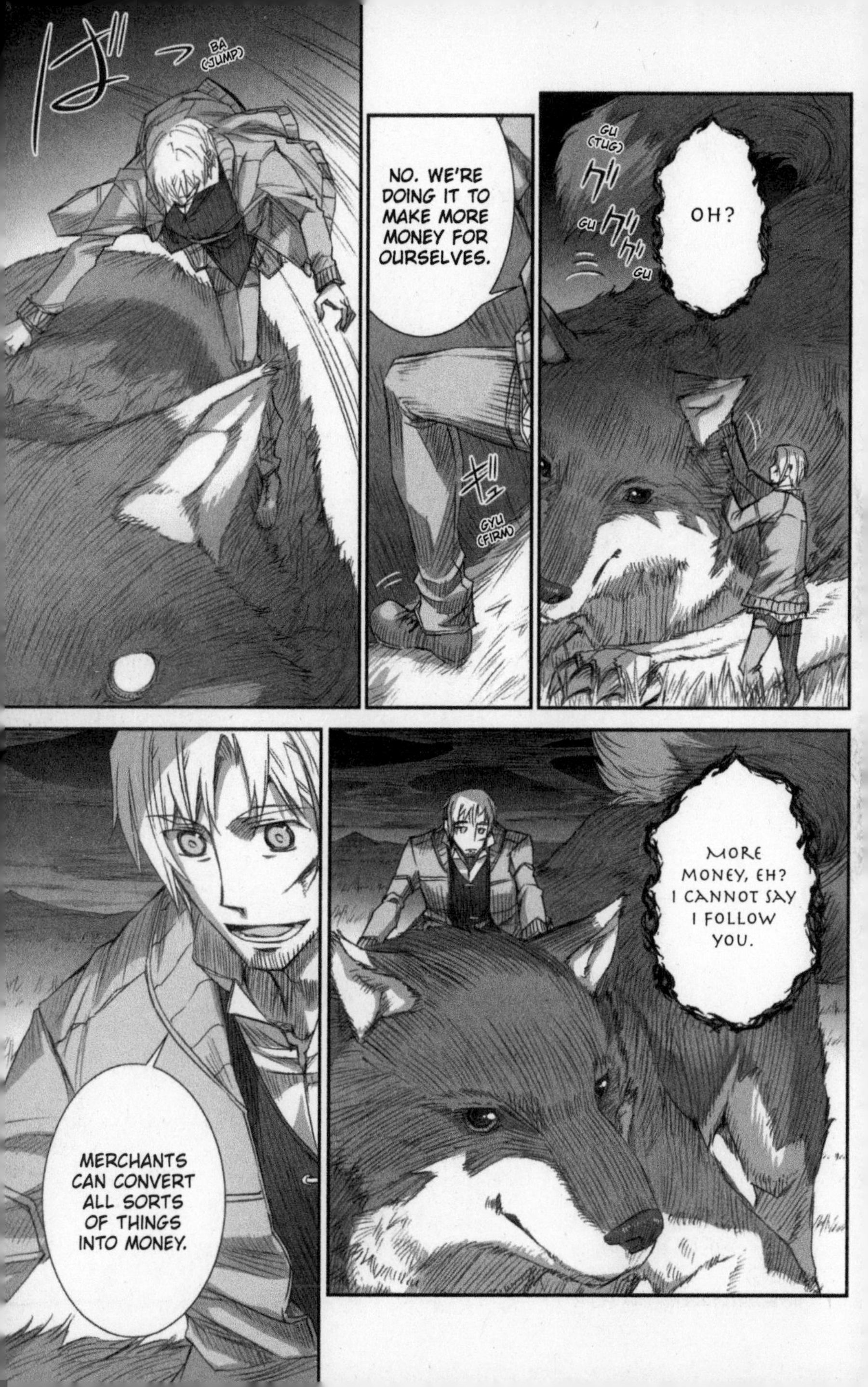
GU (TUG)
GU
GU
OH?
NO. WE'RE DOING IT TO MAKE MORE MONEY FOR OURSELVES.
ギュ
GYU (FIRM)
ばっ
BA (JUMP)
MORE MONEY, EH? I CANNOT SAY I FOLLOW YOU.
MERCHANTS CAN CONVERT ALL SORTS OF THINGS INTO MONEY.

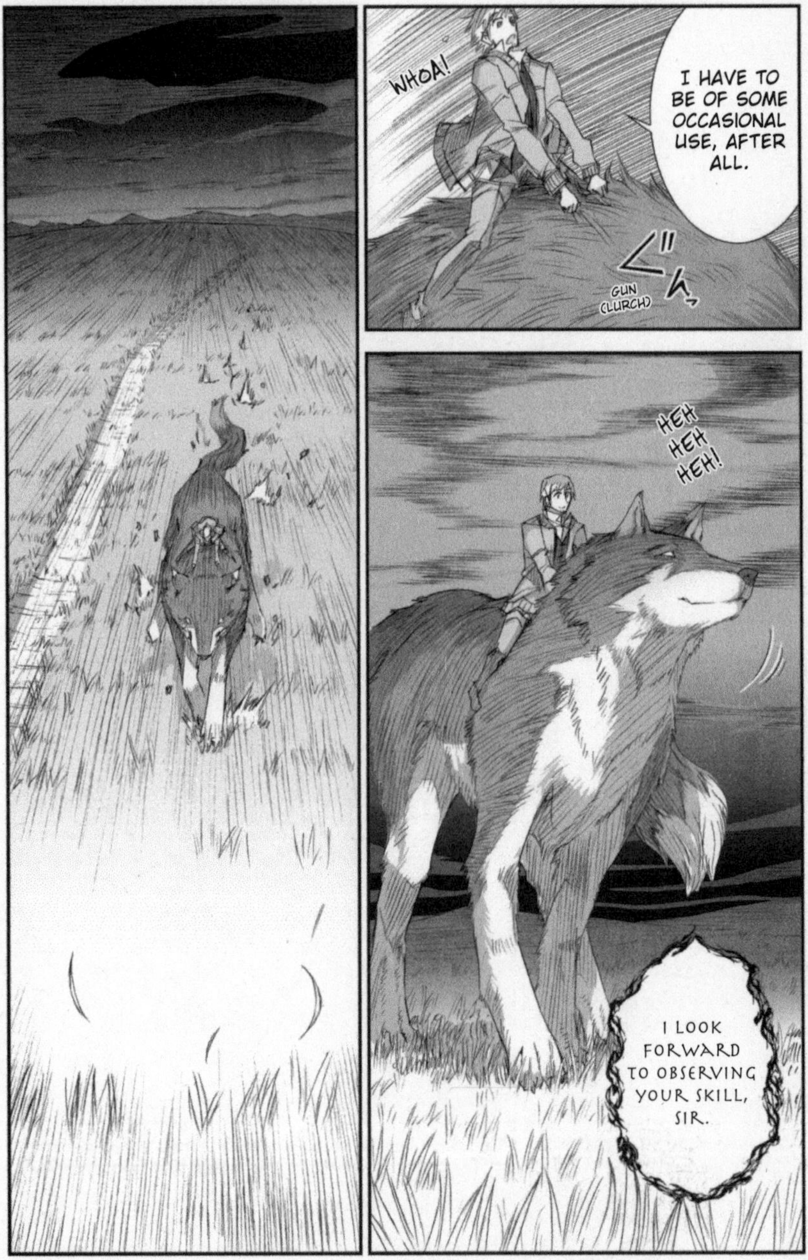
I HAVE TO BE OF SOME OCCASIONAL USE, AFTER ALL.
WHOA!
ぐんっ
GUN (LURCH)
HEH HEH HEH!
I LOOK FORWARD TO OBSERVING YOUR SKILL, SIR.

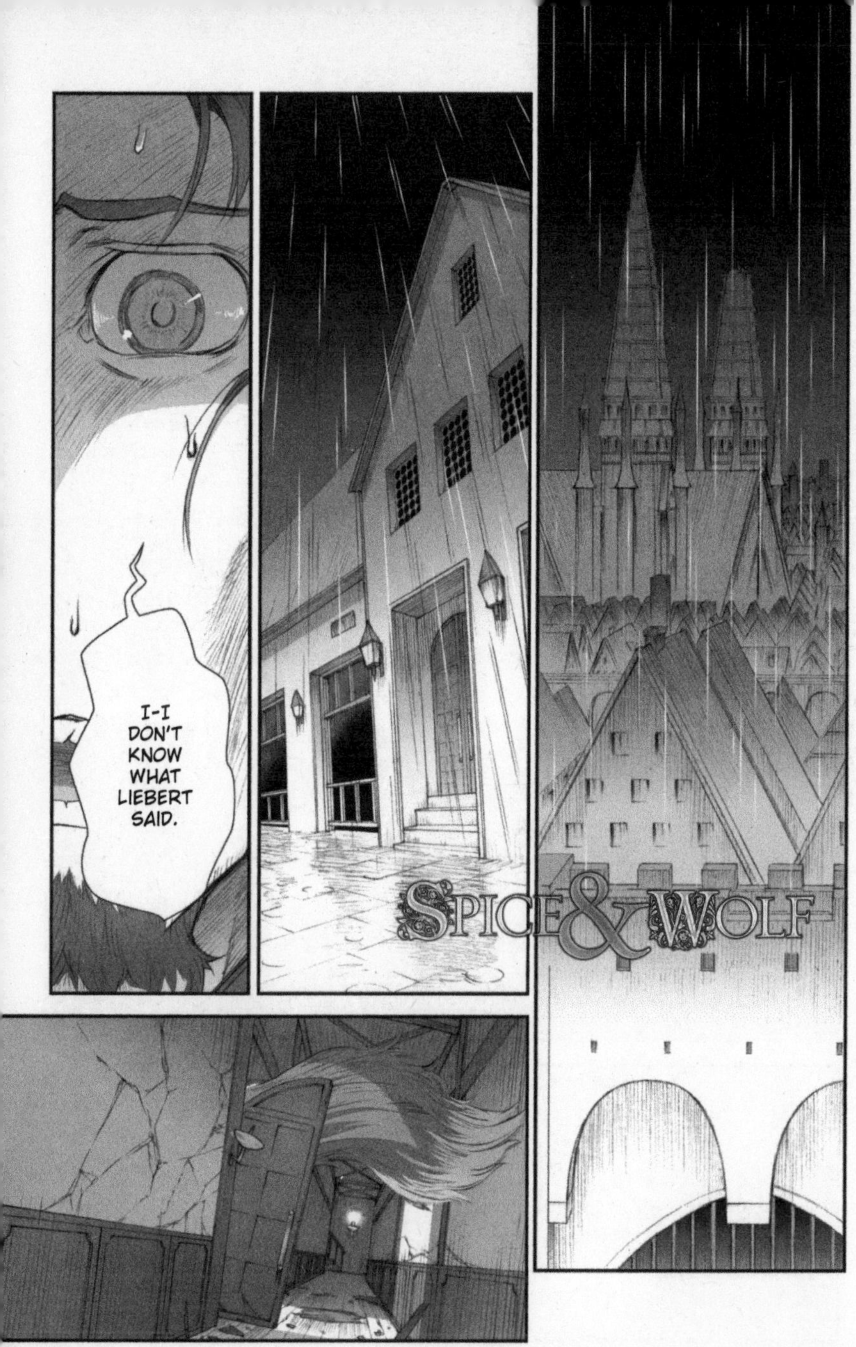
SPICE & WOLF
I-I DON'T KNOW WHAT LIEBERT SAID.

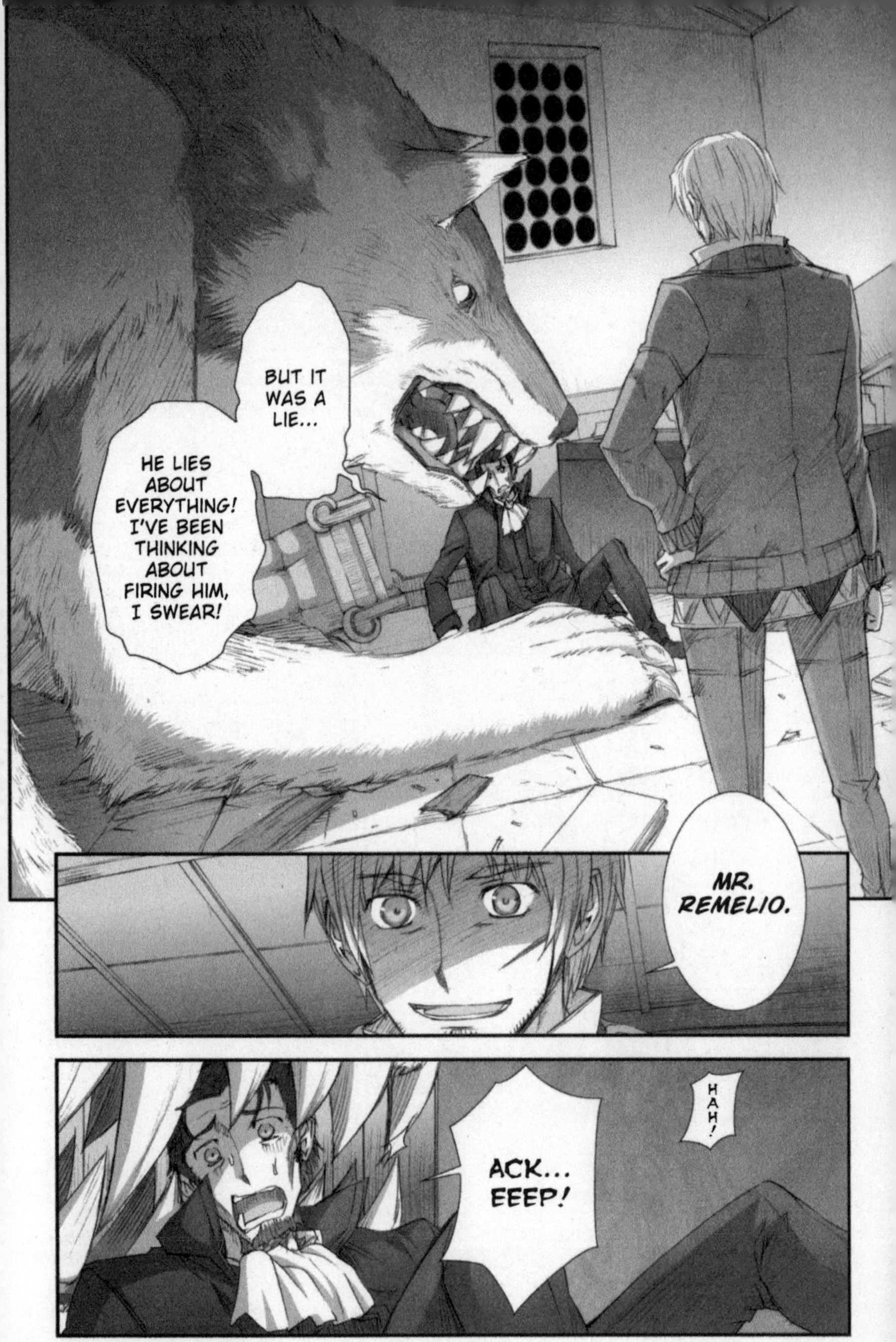
BUT IT WAS A LIE...
HE LIES ABOUT EVERYTHING! I'VE BEEN THINKING ABOUT FIRING HIM, I SWEAR!
MR. REMELIO.
HAH!
ACK... EEEP!

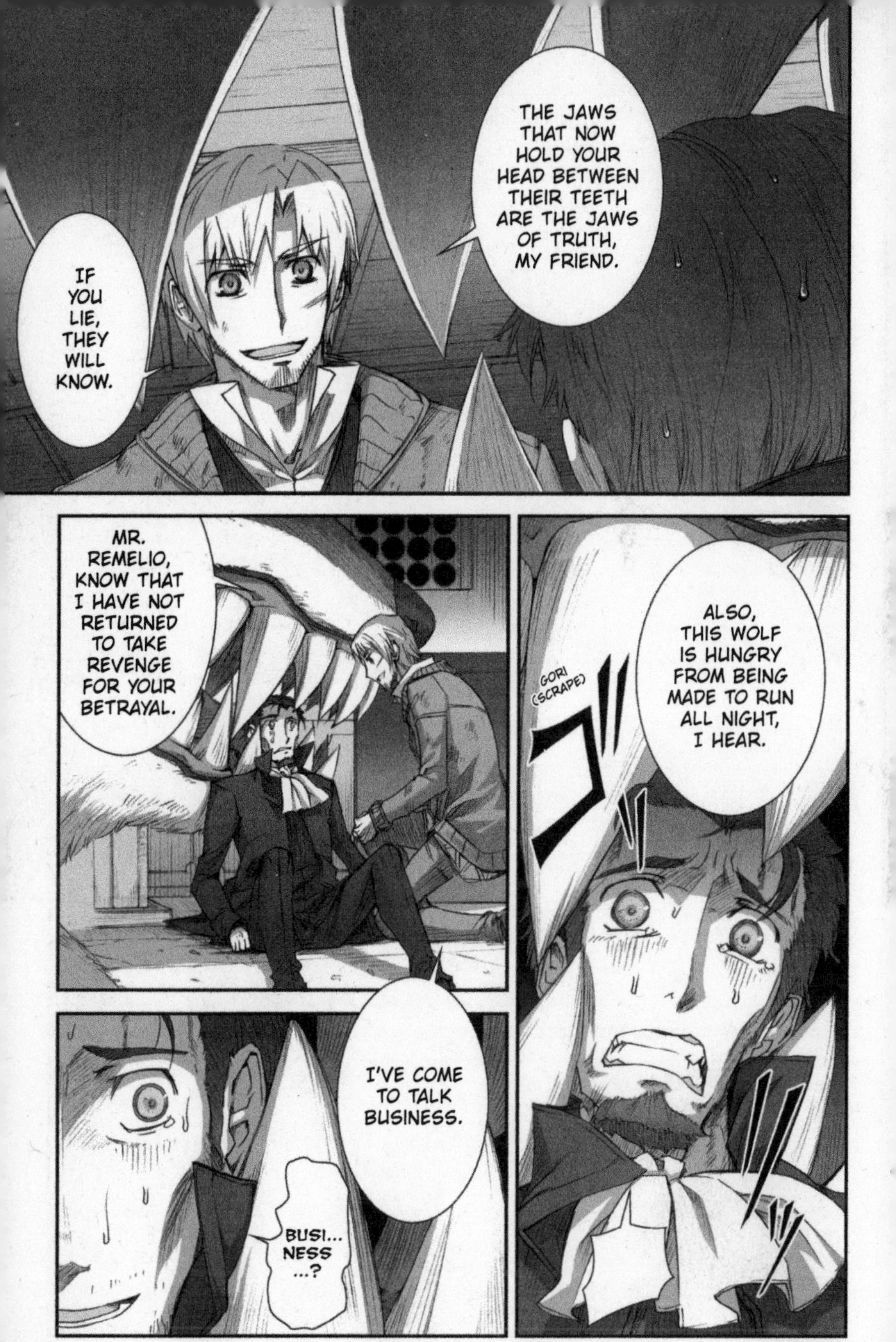
THE JAWS THAT NOW HOLD YOUR HEAD BETWEEN THEIR TEETH ARE THE JAWS OF TRUTH, MY FRIEND.
IF YOU LIE, THEY WILL KNOW.
ALSO, THIS WOLF IS HUNGRY FROM BEING MADE TO RUN ALL NIGHT, I HEAR.
GORI (SCRAPE)
MR. REMELIO, KNOW THAT I HAVE NOT RETURNED TO TAKE REVENGE FOR YOUR BETRAYAL.
I'VE COME TO TALK BUSINESS.
BUSI... NESS ...?

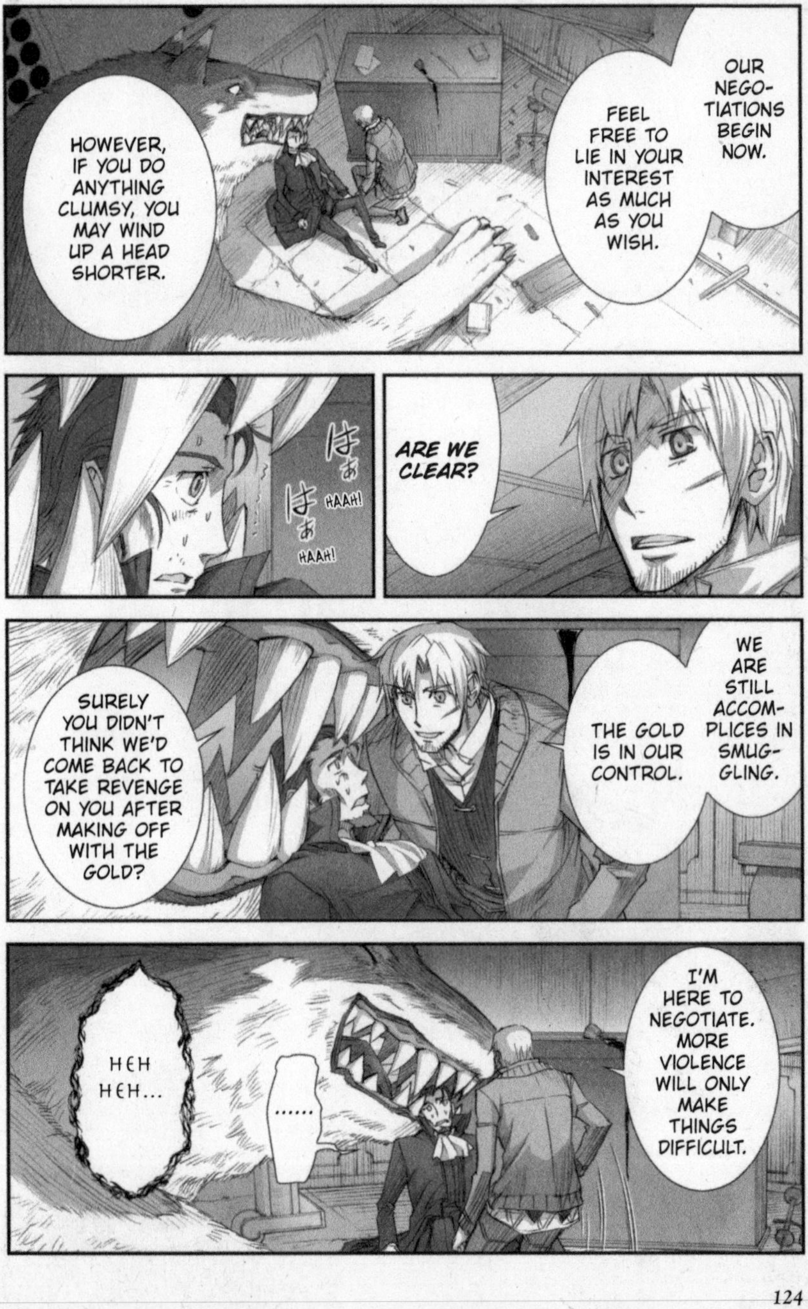
OUR NEGO-TIATIONS BEGIN NOW.
FEEL FREE TO LIE IN YOUR INTEREST AS MUCH AS YOU WISH.
HOWEVER, IF YOU DO ANYTHING CLUMSY, YOU MAY WIND UP A HEAD SHORTER.
ARE WE CLEAR?
はぁ HAAH!
はぁ HAAH!
WE ARE STILL ACCOM-PLICES IN SMUG-GLING.
THE GOLD IS IN OUR CONTROL.
SURELY YOU DIDN'T THINK WE'D COME BACK TO TAKE REVENGE ON YOU AFTER MAKING OFF WITH THE GOLD?
I'M HERE TO NEGOTIATE. MORE VIOLENCE WILL ONLY MAKE THINGS DIFFICULT.
......
HEH HEH...

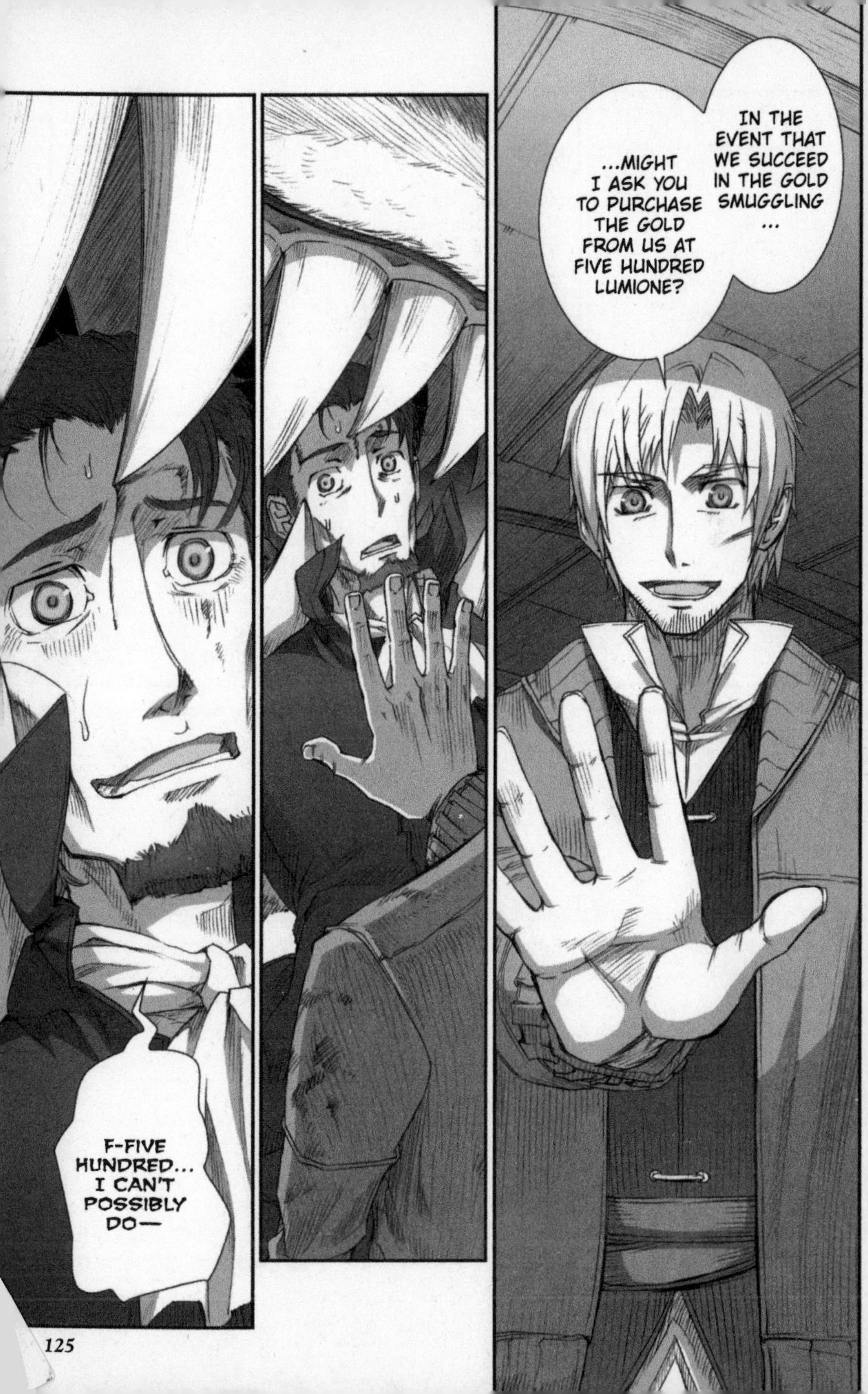
IN THE EVENT THAT WE SUCCEED IN THE GOLD SMUGGLING ...
...MIGHT I ASK YOU TO PURCHASE THE GOLD FROM US AT FIVE HUNDRED LUMIONE?
F-FIVE HUNDRED... I CAN'T POSSIBLY DO—

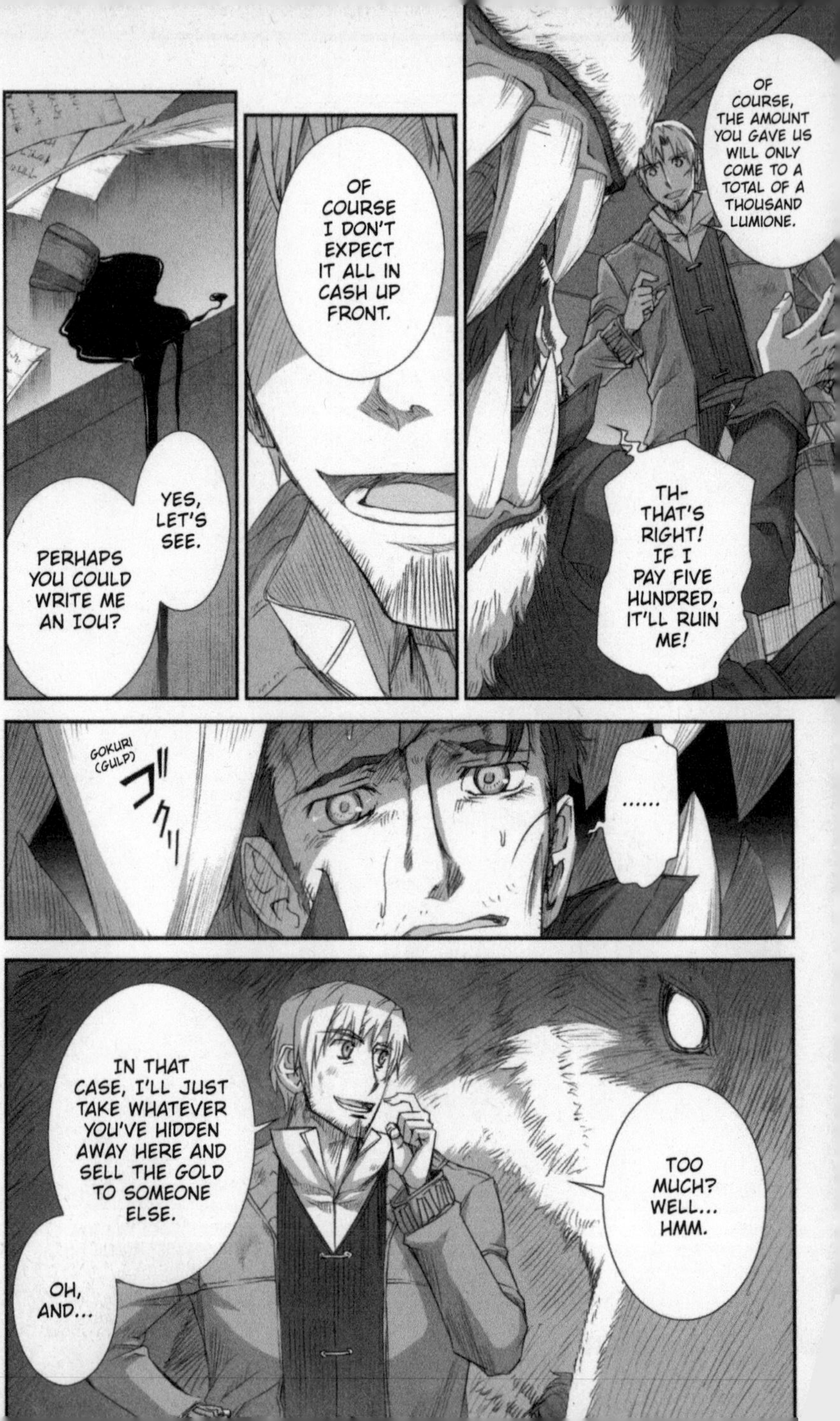
OF COURSE, THE AMOUNT YOU GAVE US WILL ONLY COME TO A TOTAL OF A THOUSAND LUMIONE.
TH-THAT'S RIGHT! IF I PAY FIVE HUNDRED, IT'LL RUIN ME!
OF COURSE I DON'T EXPECT IT ALL IN CASH UP FRONT.
YES, LET'S SEE.
PERHAPS YOU COULD WRITE ME AN IOU?
......
GOKURI (GULP)
TOO MUCH? WELL... HMM.
IN THAT CASE, I'LL JUST TAKE WHATEVER YOU'VE HIDDEN AWAY HERE AND SELL THE GOLD TO SOMEONE ELSE.
OH, AND...

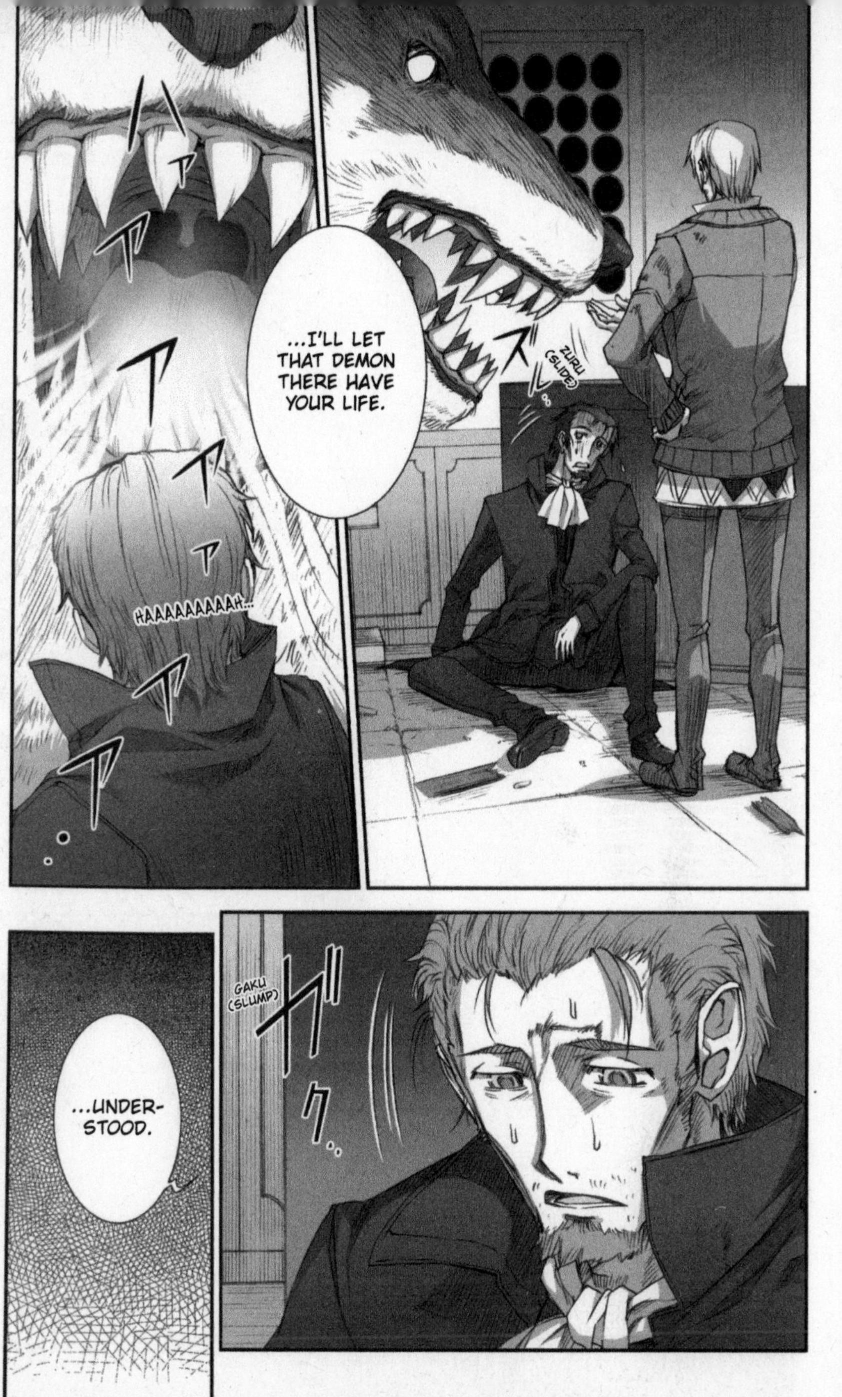
...I'LL LET THAT DEMON THERE HAVE YOUR LIFE.
ZURU (SLIDE)
HAAAAAAAAAH...
GAKU (SLUMP)
...UNDER-STOOD.

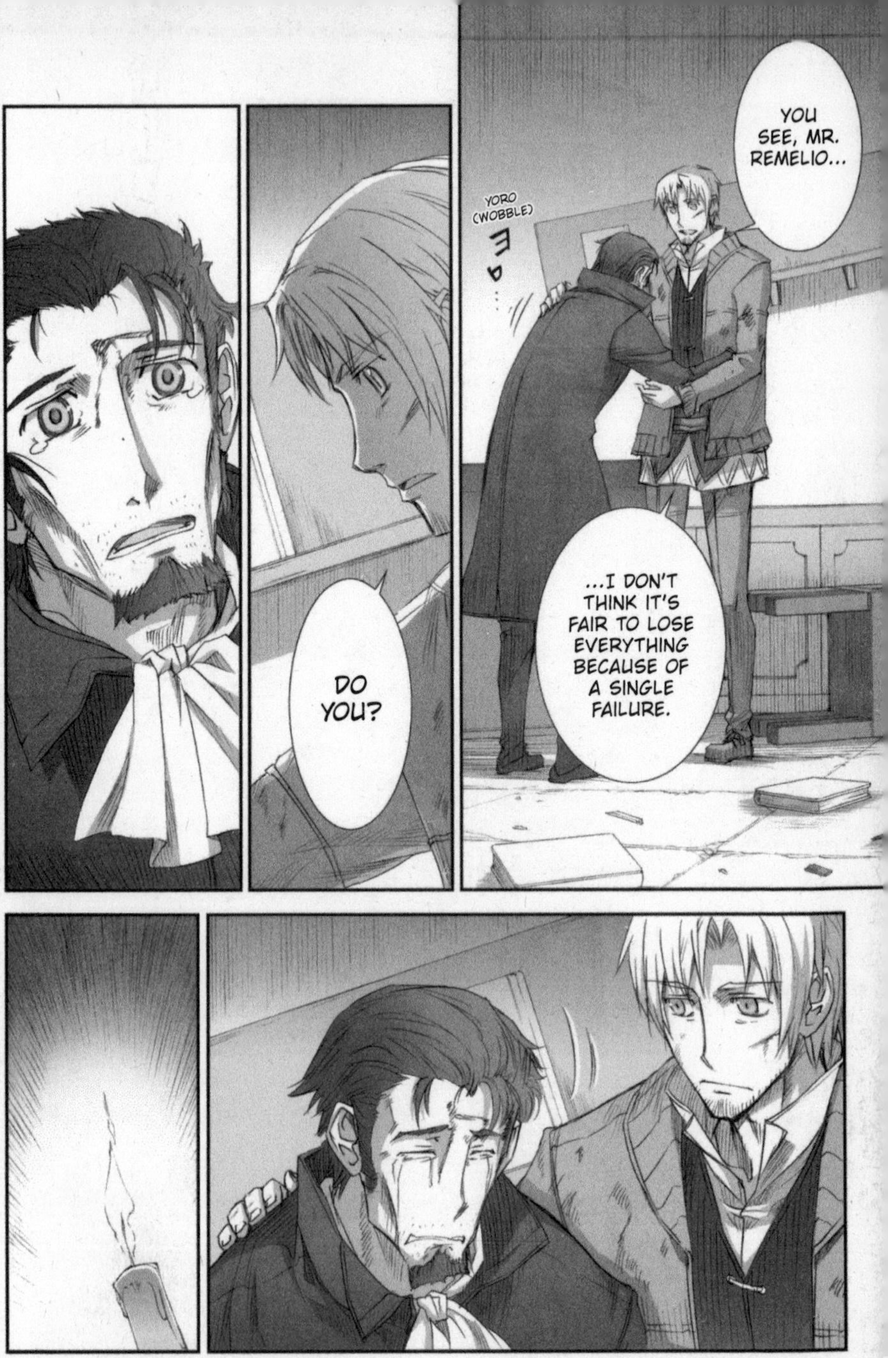
YOU SEE, MR. REMELIO...
YORO (WOBBLE)
ヨロ…
...I DON'T THINK IT'S FAIR TO LOSE EVERYTHING BECAUSE OF A SINGLE FAILURE.
DO YOU?

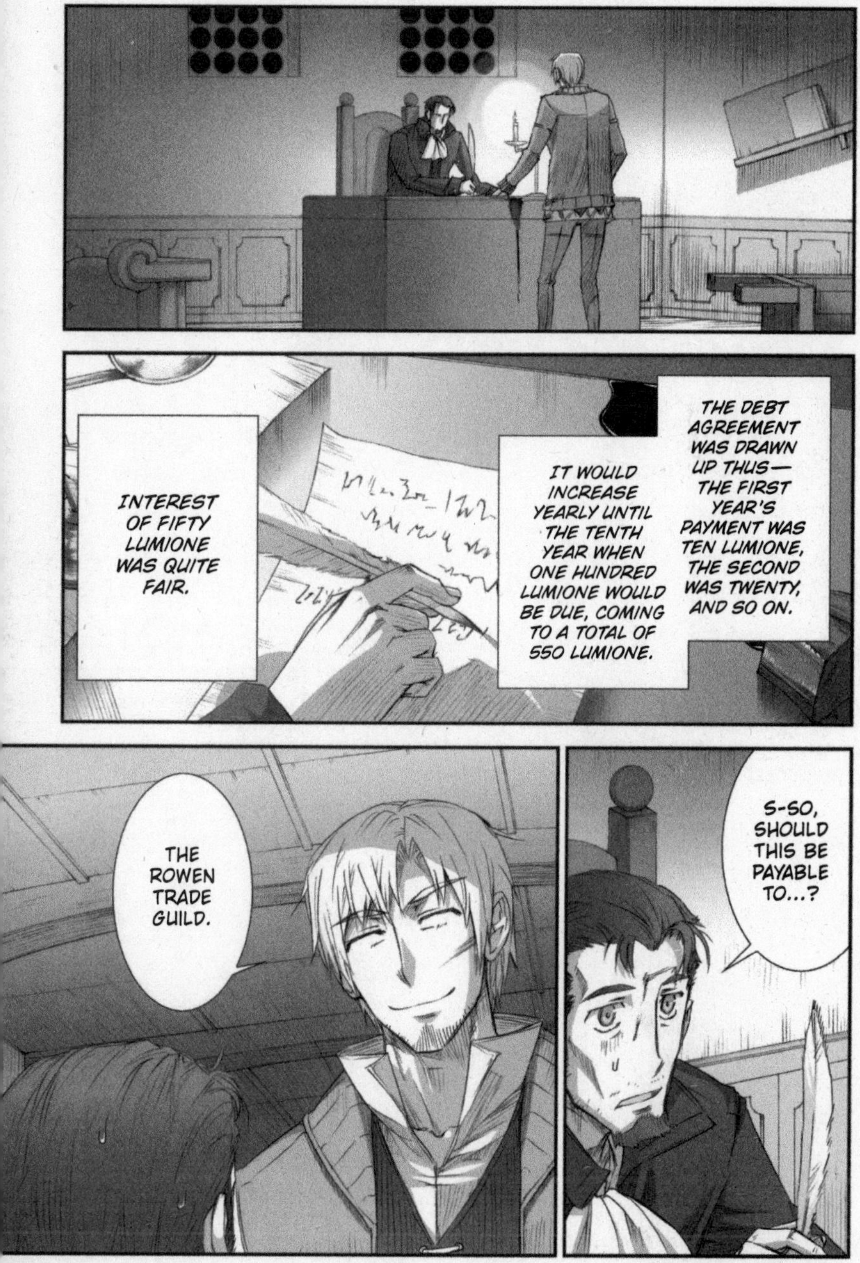
THE DEBT AGREEMENT WAS DRAWN UP THUS— THE FIRST YEAR'S PAYMENT WAS TEN LUMIONE, THE SECOND WAS TWENTY, AND SO ON.
IT WOULD INCREASE YEARLY UNTIL THE TENTH YEAR WHEN ONE HUNDRED LUMIONE WOULD BE DUE, COMING TO A TOTAL OF 550 LUMIONE.
INTEREST OF FIFTY LUMIONE WAS QUITE FAIR.
S-SO, SHOULD THIS BE PAYABLE TO...?
THE ROWEN TRADE GUILD.

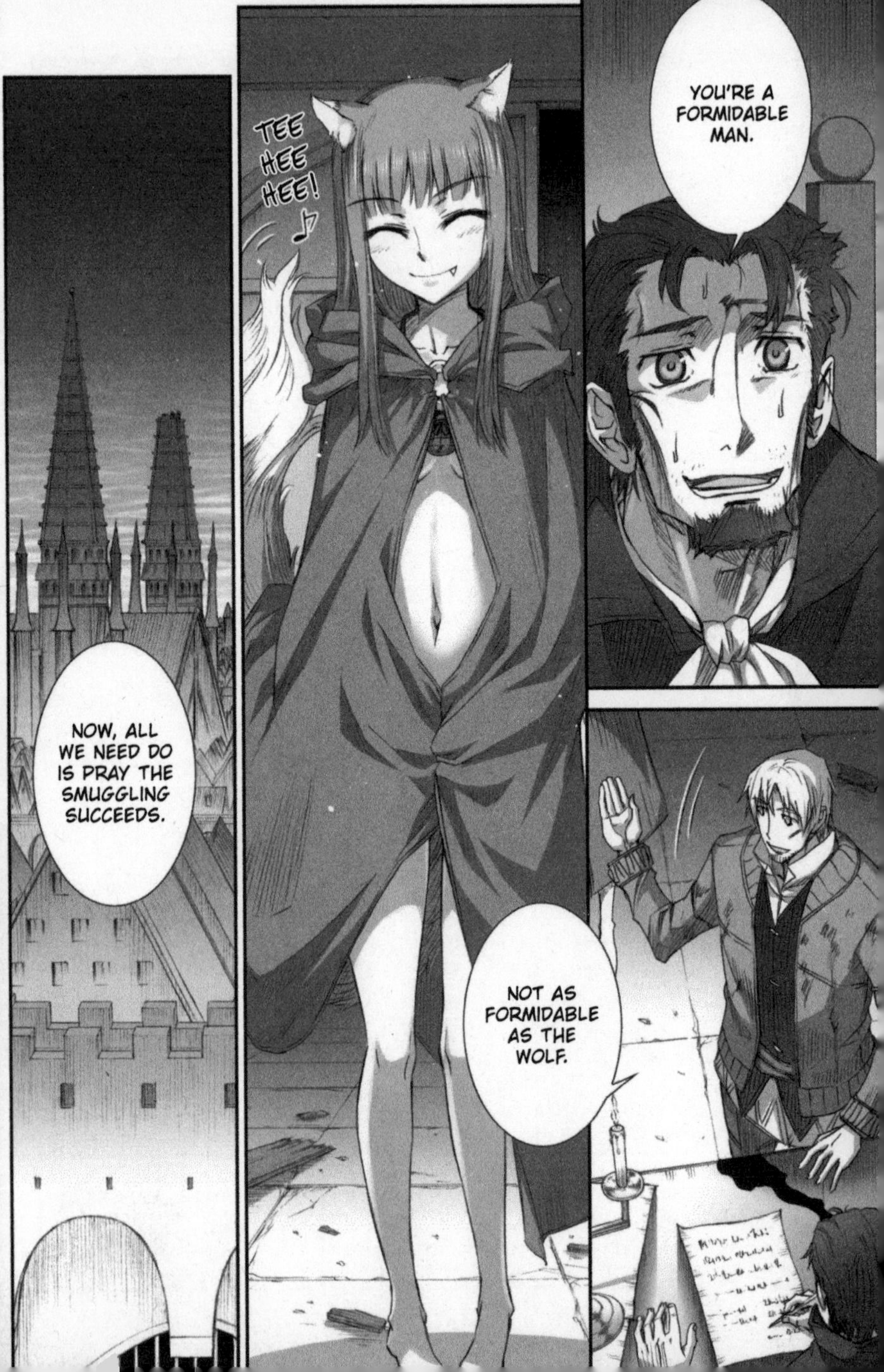
YOU'RE A FORMIDABLE MAN.
NOT AS FORMIDABLE AS THE WOLF.
TEE HEE HEE! ♪
NOW, ALL WE NEED DO IS PRAY THE SMUGGLING SUCCEEDS.

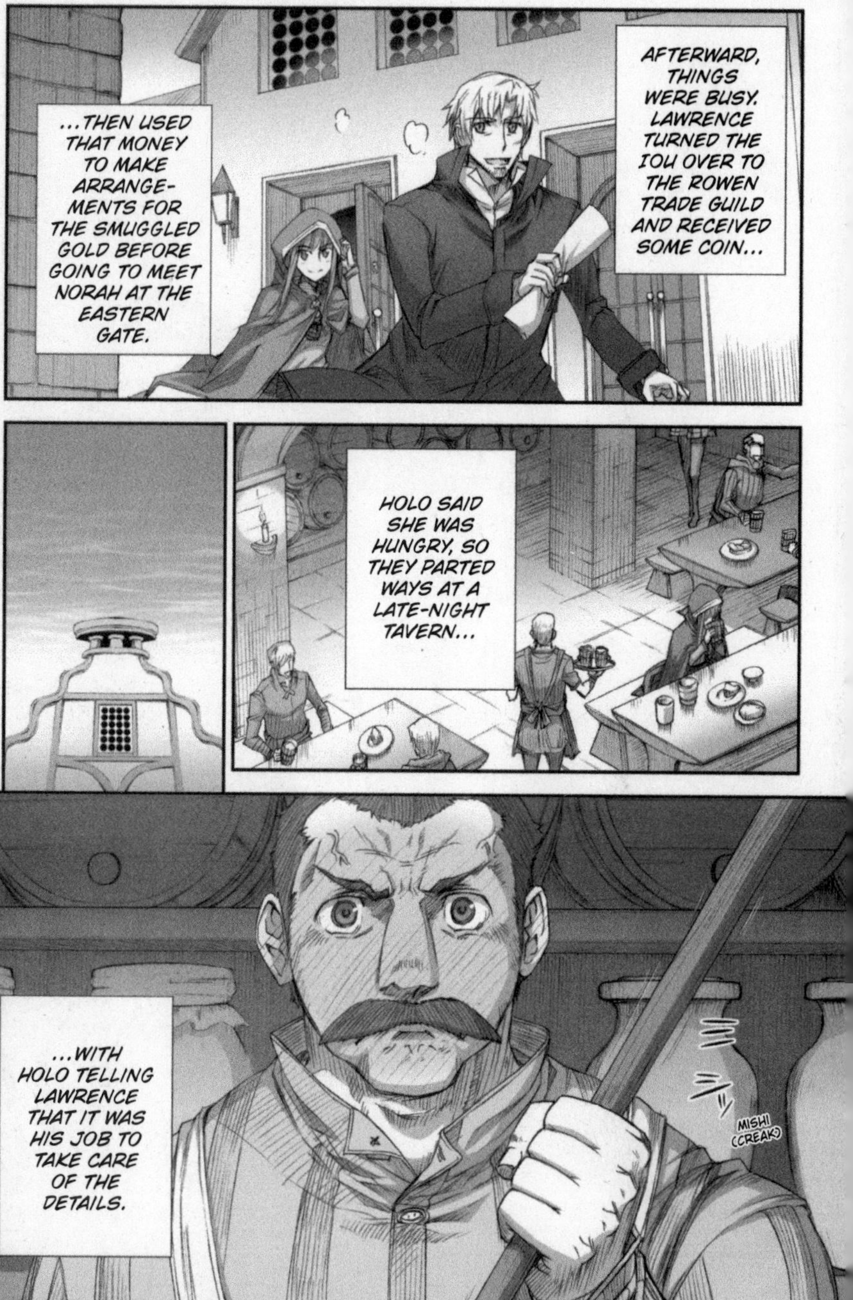
AFTERWARD, THINGS WERE BUSY. LAWRENCE TURNED THE IOU OVER TO THE ROWEN TRADE GUILD AND RECEIVED SOME COIN...
...THEN USED THAT MONEY TO MAKE ARRANGE-MENTS FOR THE SMUGGLED GOLD BEFORE GOING TO MEET NORAH AT THE EASTERN GATE.
HOLO SAID SHE WAS HUNGRY, SO THEY PARTED WAYS AT A LATE-NIGHT TAVERN...
MISHI (CREAK)
...WITH HOLO TELLING LAWRENCE THAT IT WAS HIS JOB TO TAKE CARE OF THE DETAILS.

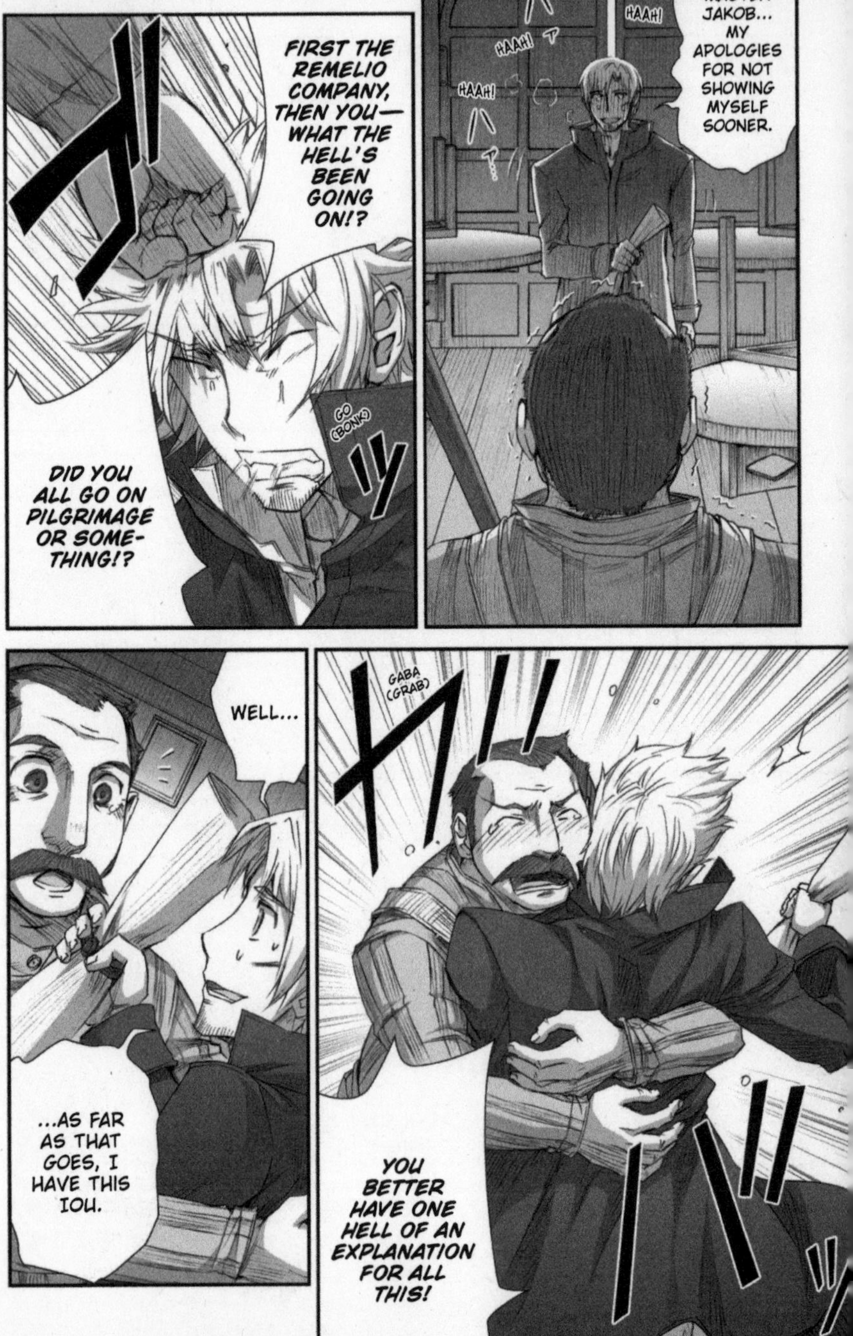
HAAH!
HAAH!
HAAH!
MASTER JAKOB... MY APOLOGIES FOR NOT SHOWING MYSELF SOONER.
FIRST THE REMELIO COMPANY, THEN YOU— WHAT THE HELL'S BEEN GOING ON!?
GO (BONK)
DID YOU ALL GO ON PILGRIMAGE OR SOME-THING!?
GABA (GRAB)
YOU BETTER HAVE ONE HELL OF AN EXPLANATION FOR ALL THIS!
WELL...
...AS FAR AS THAT GOES, I HAVE THIS IOU.

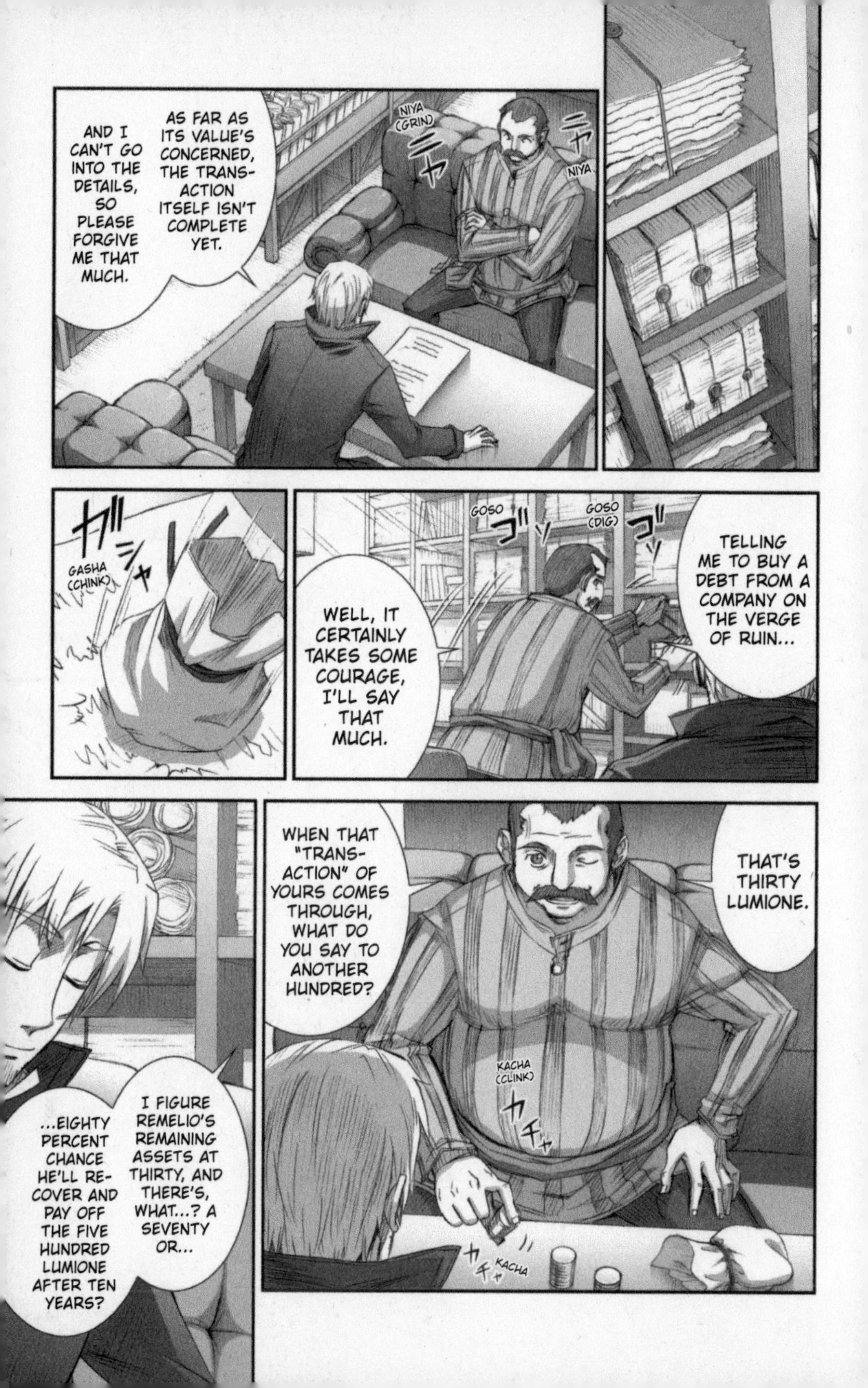
NIYA
NIYA (GRIN)
AS FAR AS ITS VALUE'S CONCERNED, THE TRANS-ACTION ITSELF ISN'T COMPLETE YET.
AND I CAN'T GO INTO THE DETAILS, SO PLEASE FORGIVE ME THAT MUCH.
TELLING ME TO BUY A DEBT FROM A COMPANY ON THE VERGE OF RUIN...
GOSO (DIG)
GOSO
WELL, IT CERTAINLY TAKES SOME COURAGE, I'LL SAY THAT MUCH.
GASHA (CHINK)
THAT'S THIRTY LUMIONE.
WHEN THAT "TRANS-ACTION" OF YOURS COMES THROUGH, WHAT DO YOU SAY TO ANOTHER HUNDRED?
KACHA (CLINK)
KACHA
I FIGURE REMELIO'S REMAINING ASSETS AT THIRTY, AND THERE'S, WHAT...? A SEVENTY OR...
...EIGHTY PERCENT CHANCE HE'LL RE-COVER AND PAY OFF THE FIVE HUNDRED LUMIONE AFTER TEN YEARS?

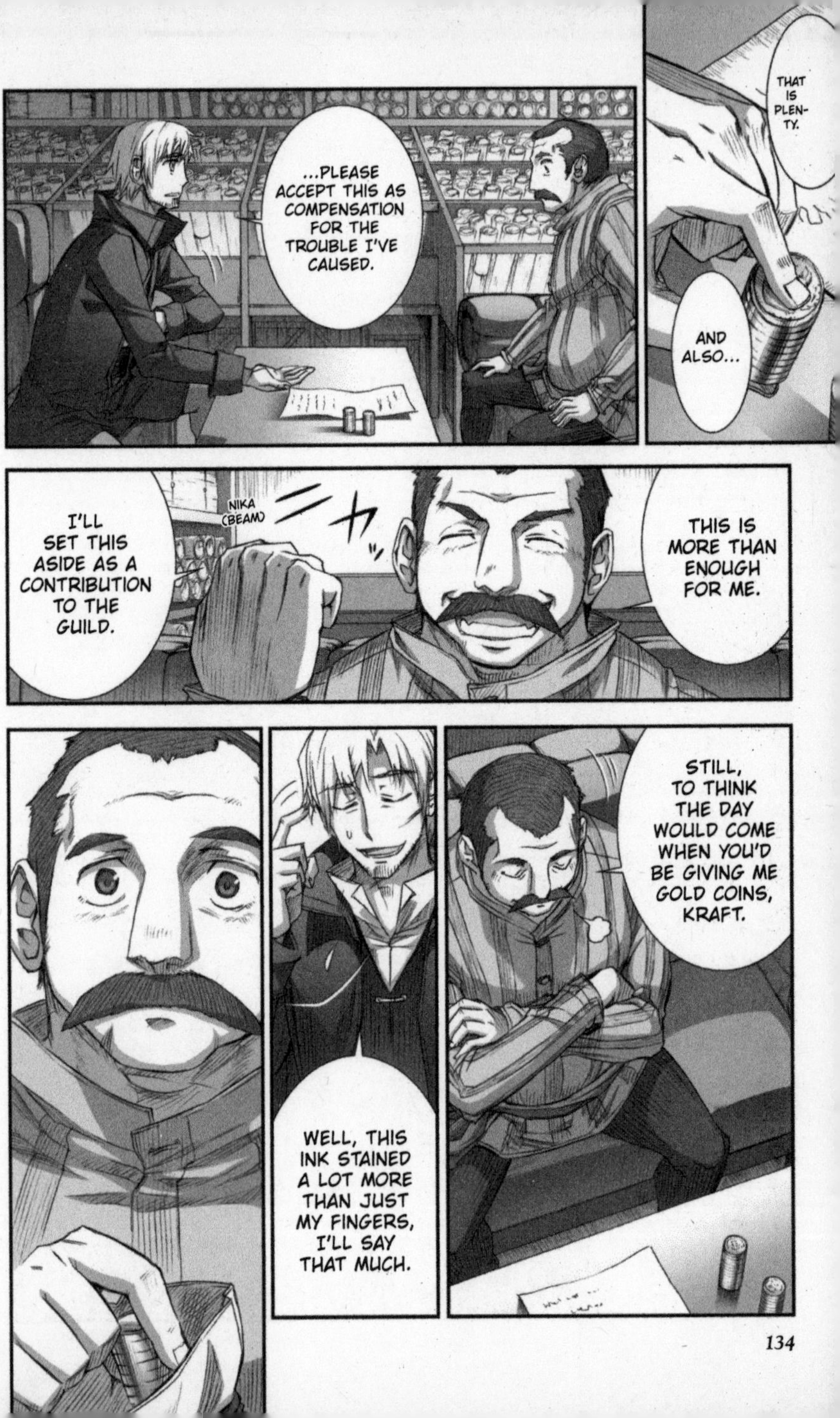
THAT IS PLENTY.
AND ALSO...
...PLEASE ACCEPT THIS AS COMPENSATION FOR THE TROUBLE I'VE CAUSED.
THIS IS MORE THAN ENOUGH FOR ME.
NIKA (BEAM)
I'LL SET THIS ASIDE AS A CONTRIBUTION TO THE GUILD.
STILL, TO THINK THE DAY WOULD COME WHEN YOU'D BE GIVING ME GOLD COINS, KRAFT.
WELL, THIS INK STAINED A LOT MORE THAN JUST MY FINGERS, I'LL SAY THAT MUCH.

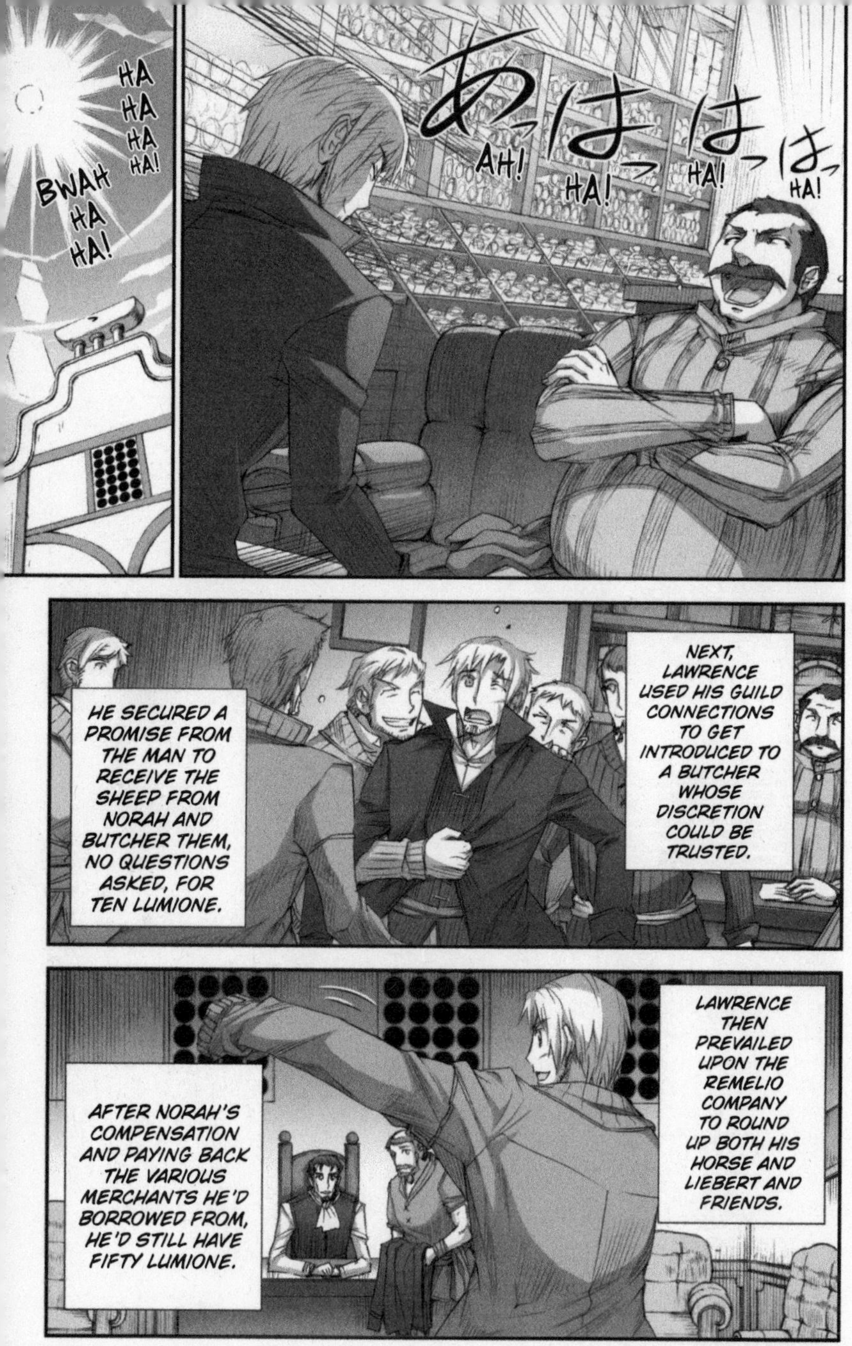
あっはっはっはっ
AH! HA! HA! HA!
HA HA HA HA!
BWAH HA HA HA!
NEXT, LAWRENCE USED HIS GUILD CONNECTIONS TO GET INTRODUCED TO A BUTCHER WHOSE DISCRETION COULD BE TRUSTED.
HE SECURED A PROMISE FROM THE MAN TO RECEIVE THE SHEEP FROM NORAH AND BUTCHER THEM, NO QUESTIONS ASKED, FOR TEN LUMIONE.
LAWRENCE THEN PREVAILED UPON THE REMELIO COMPANY TO ROUND UP BOTH HIS HORSE AND LIEBERT AND FRIENDS.
AFTER NORAH'S COMPENSATION AND PAYING BACK THE VARIOUS MERCHANTS HE'D BORROWED FROM, HE'D STILL HAVE FIFTY LUMIONE.

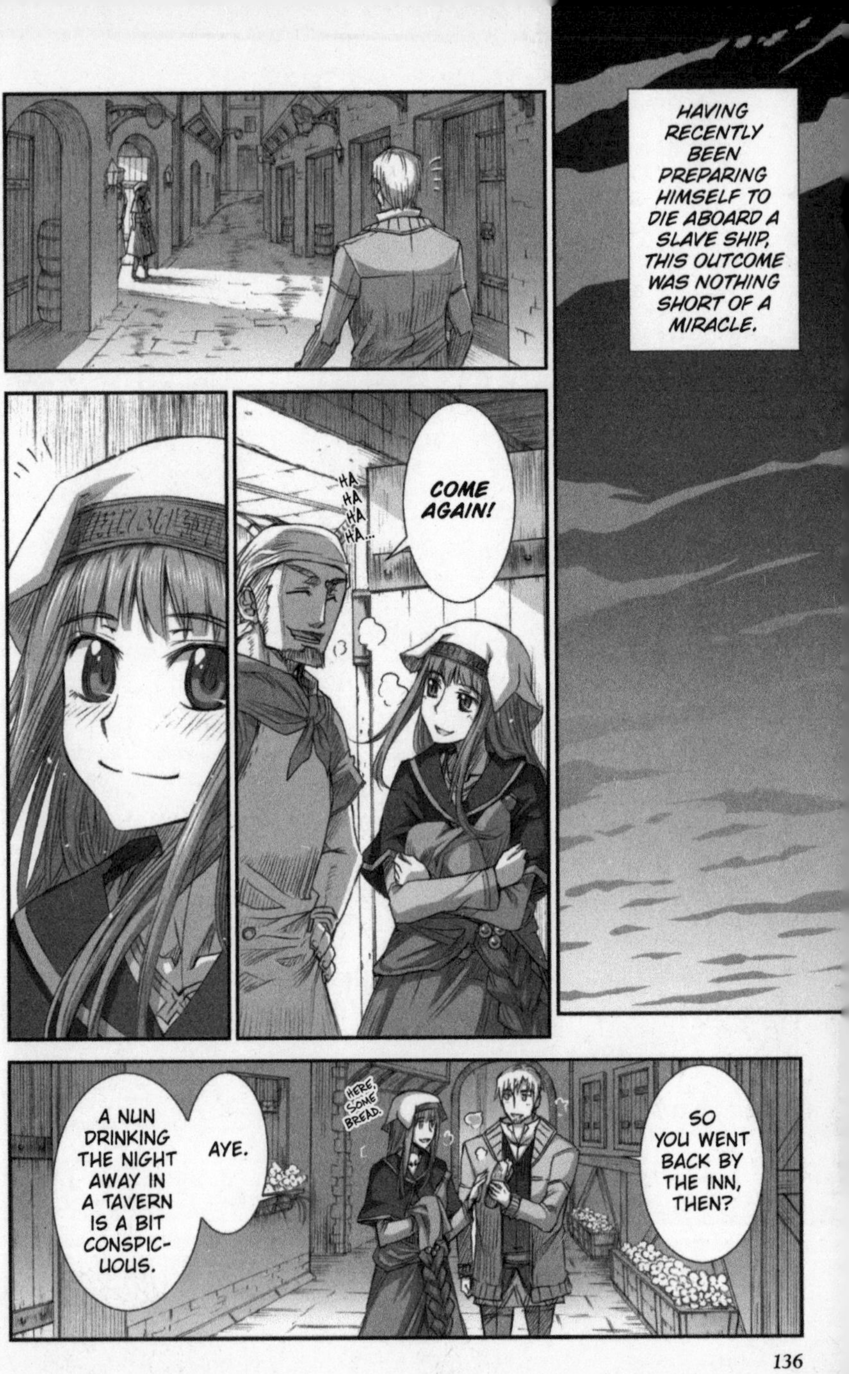
HAVING RECENTLY BEEN PREPARING HIMSELF TO DIE ABOARD A SLAVE SHIP, THIS OUTCOME WAS NOTHING SHORT OF A MIRACLE.
COME AGAIN!
HA HA HA HA...
SO YOU WENT BACK BY THE INN, THEN?
HERE, SOME BREAD.
AYE.
A NUN DRINKING THE NIGHT AWAY IN A TAVERN IS A BIT CONSPIC-UOUS.

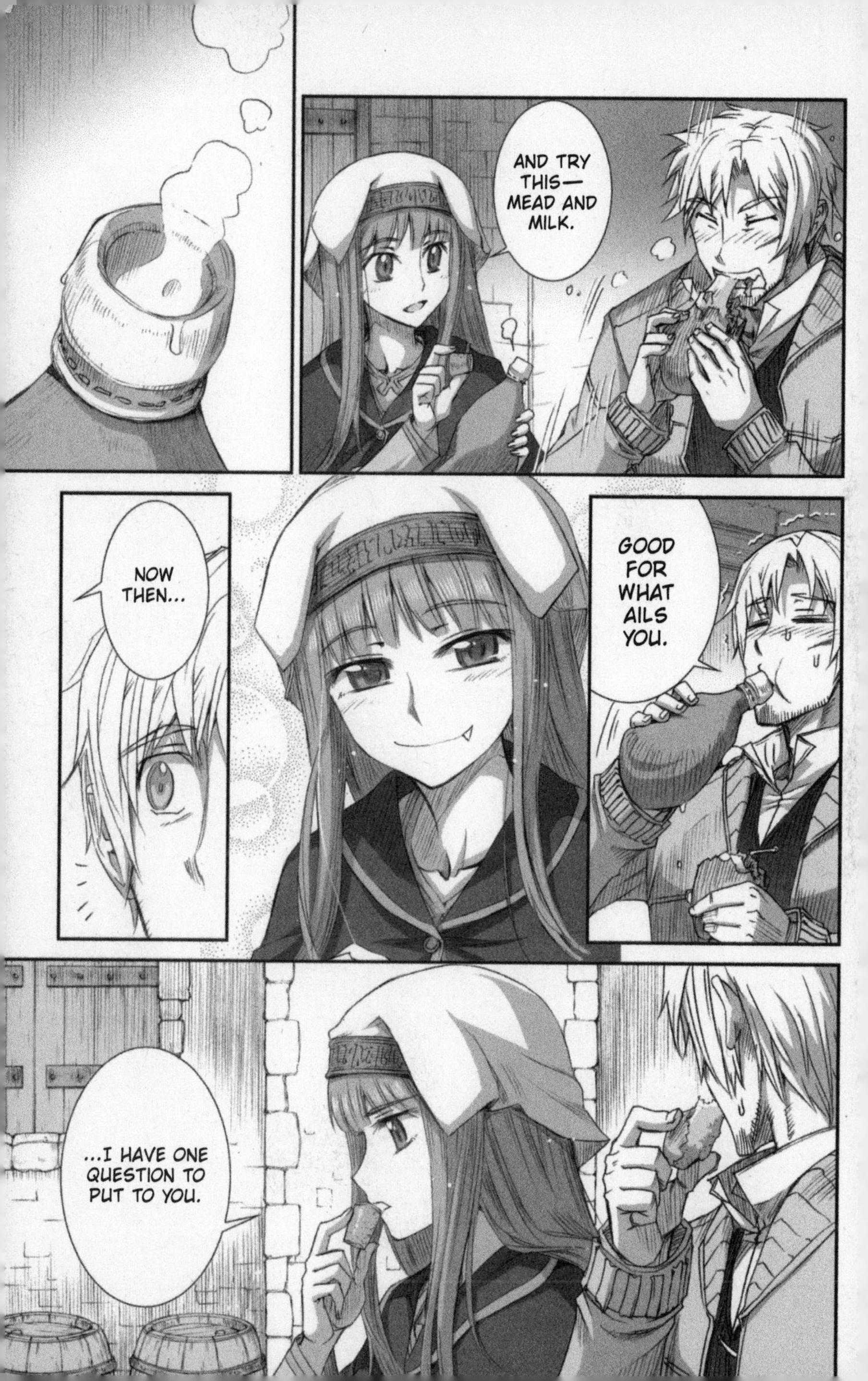
AND TRY THIS— MEAD AND MILK.
GOOD FOR WHAT AILS YOU.
NOW THEN...
...I HAVE ONE QUESTION TO PUT TO YOU.

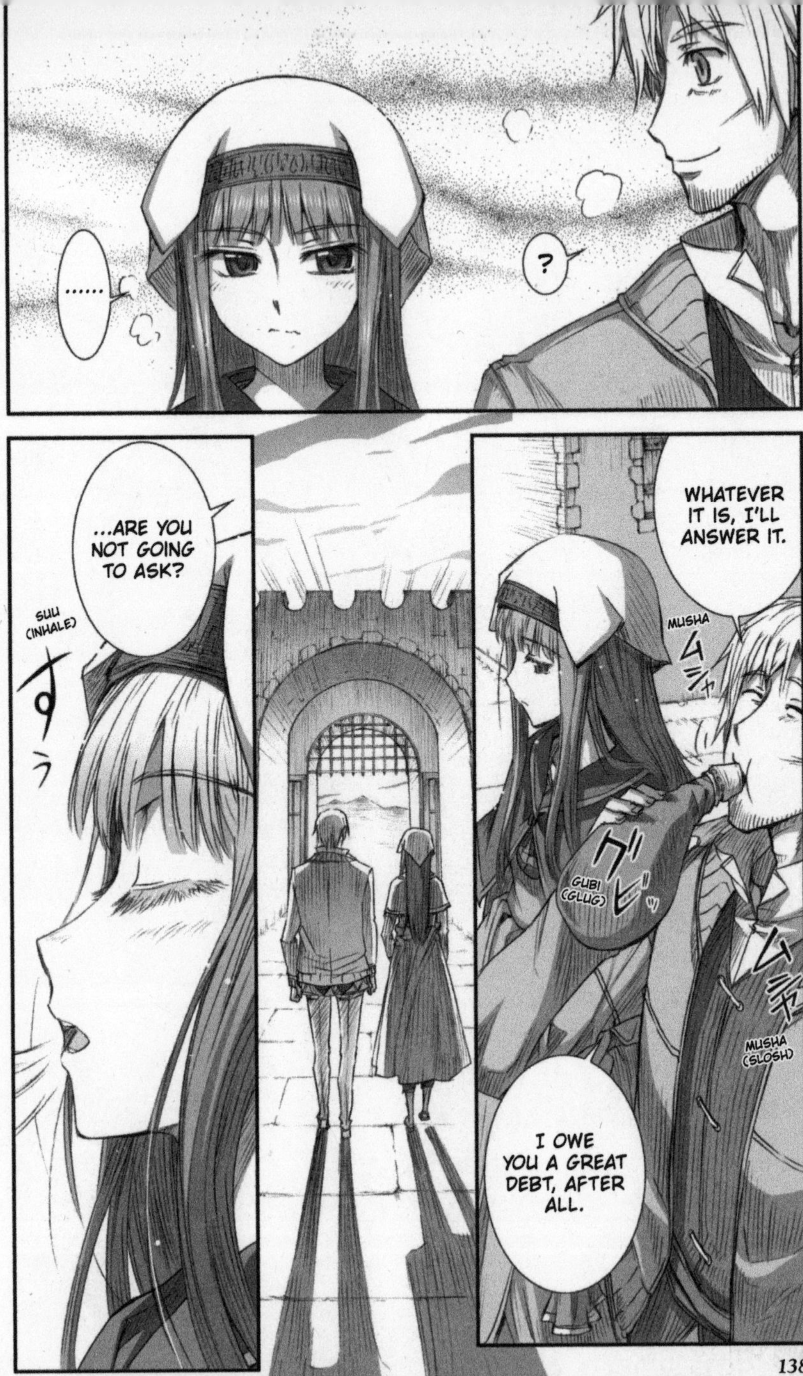
?
......
WHATEVER IT IS, I'LL ANSWER IT.
MUSHA
GUBI (GLUG)
MUSHA (SLOSH)
I OWE YOU A GREAT DEBT, AFTER ALL.
...ARE YOU NOT GOING TO ASK?
SUU (INHALE)

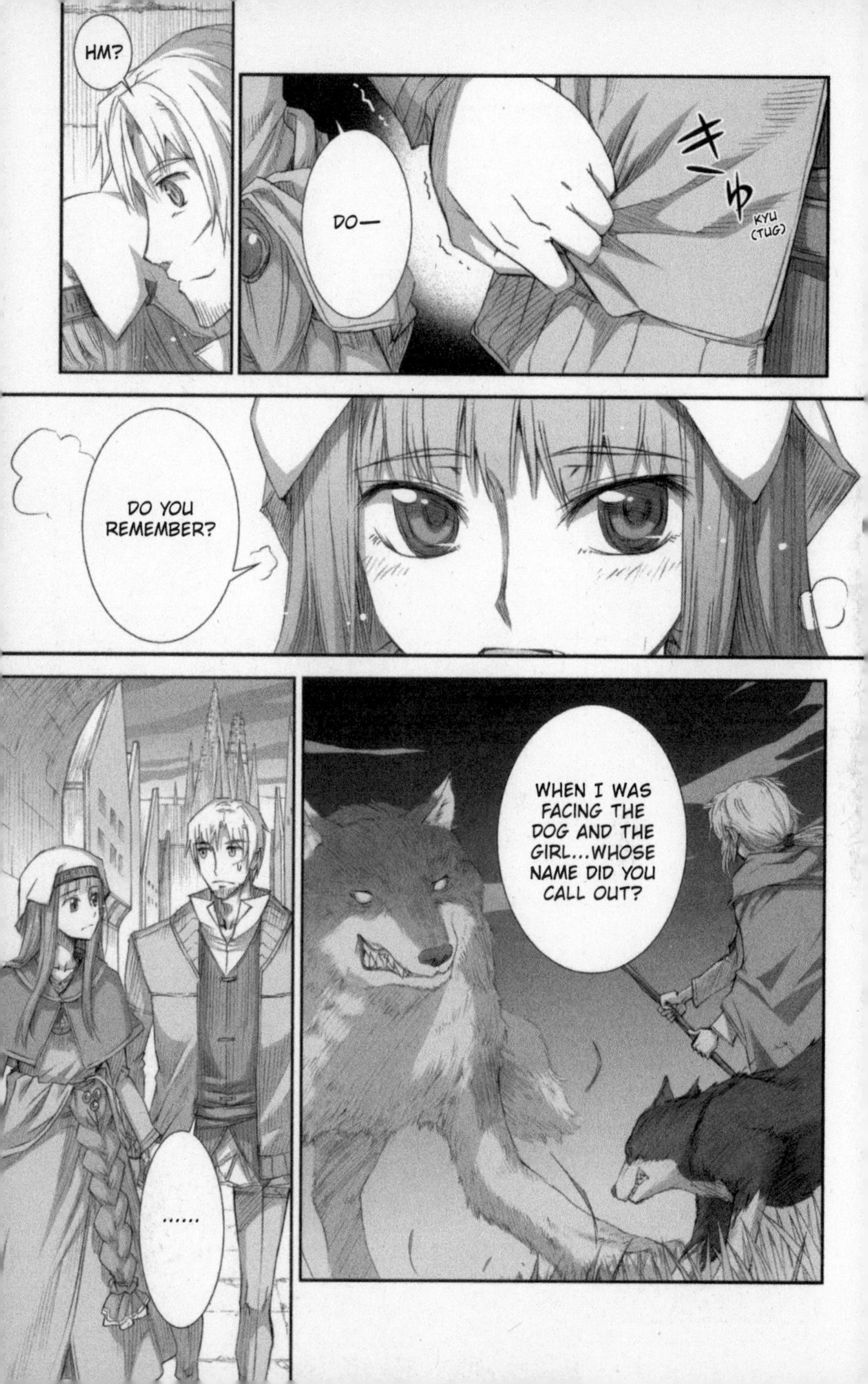
DO—
KYU (TUG)
HM?
DO YOU REMEMBER?
WHEN I WAS FACING THE DOG AND THE GIRL...WHOSE NAME DID YOU CALL OUT?
......

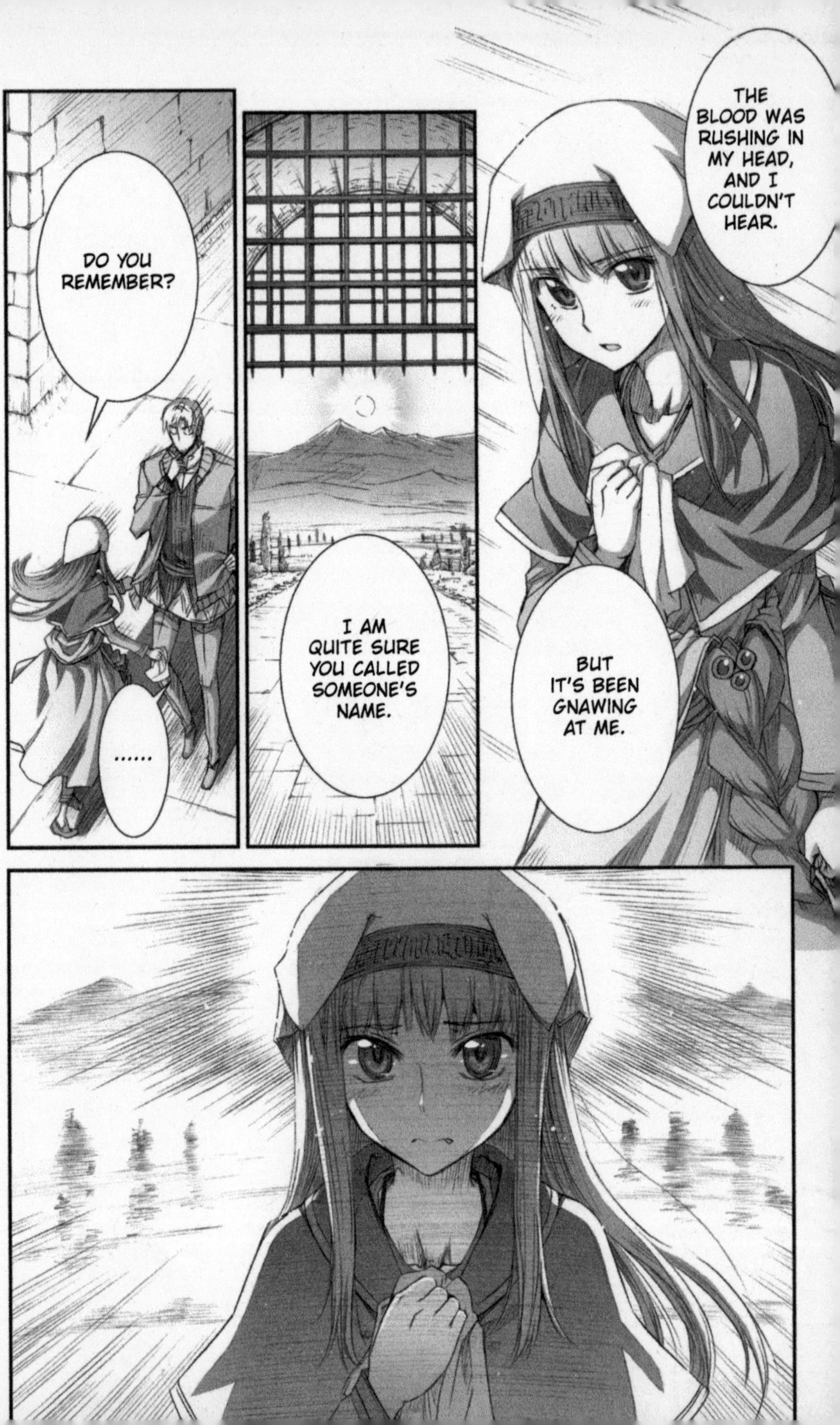
THE BLOOD WAS RUSHING IN MY HEAD, AND I COULDN'T HEAR.
BUT IT'S BEEN GNAWING AT ME.
I AM QUITE SURE YOU CALLED SOMEONE'S NAME.
DO YOU REMEMBER?
......

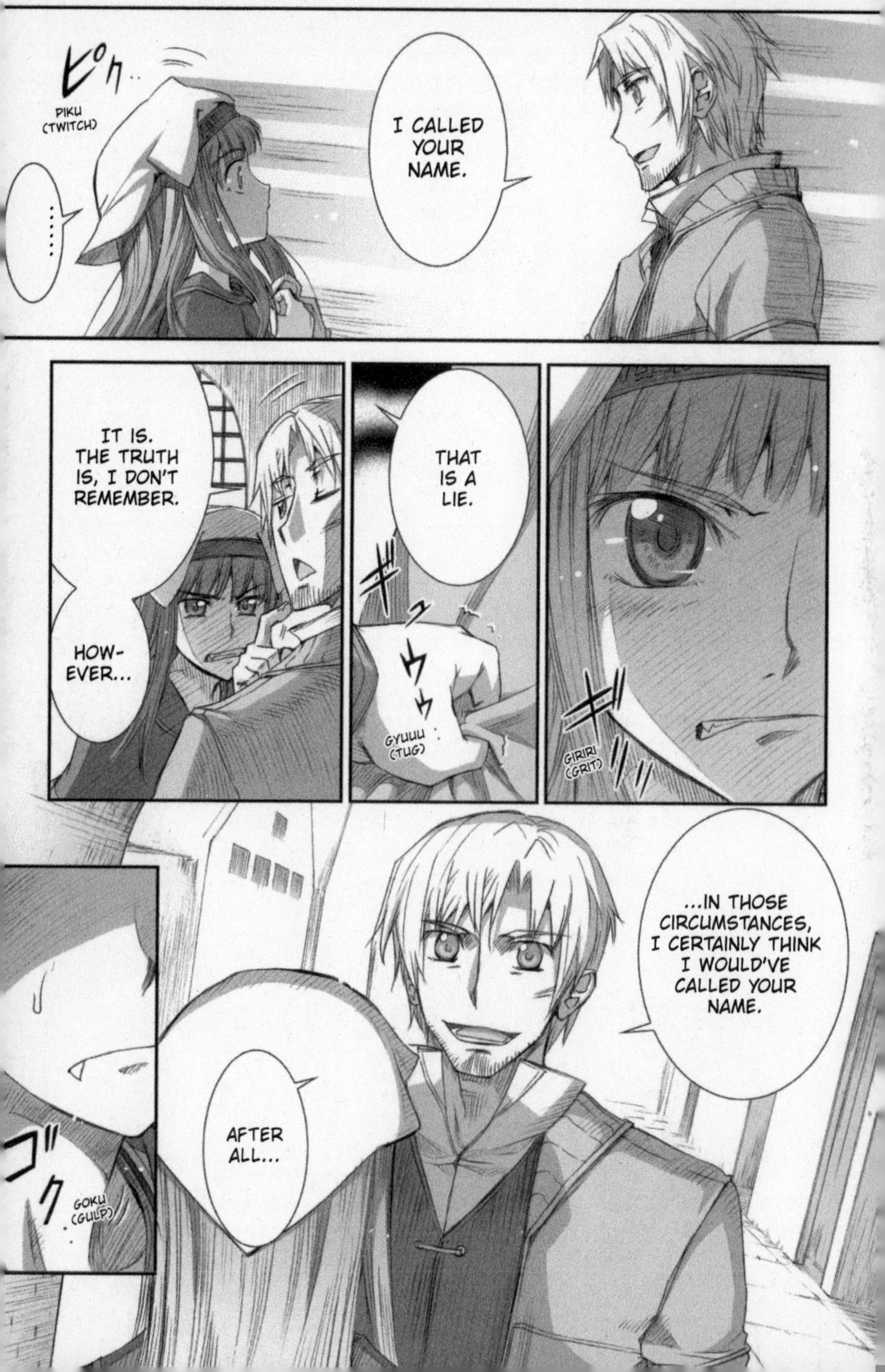
I CALLED YOUR NAME.
PIKU (TWITCH)
......
GIRIRI (GRIT)
THAT IS A LIE.
GYUUU (TUG)
IT IS. THE TRUTH IS, I DON'T REMEMBER.
HOW-EVER...
...IN THOSE CIRCUMSTANCES, I CERTAINLY THINK I WOULD'VE CALLED YOUR NAME.
AFTER ALL...
GOKU (GULP)

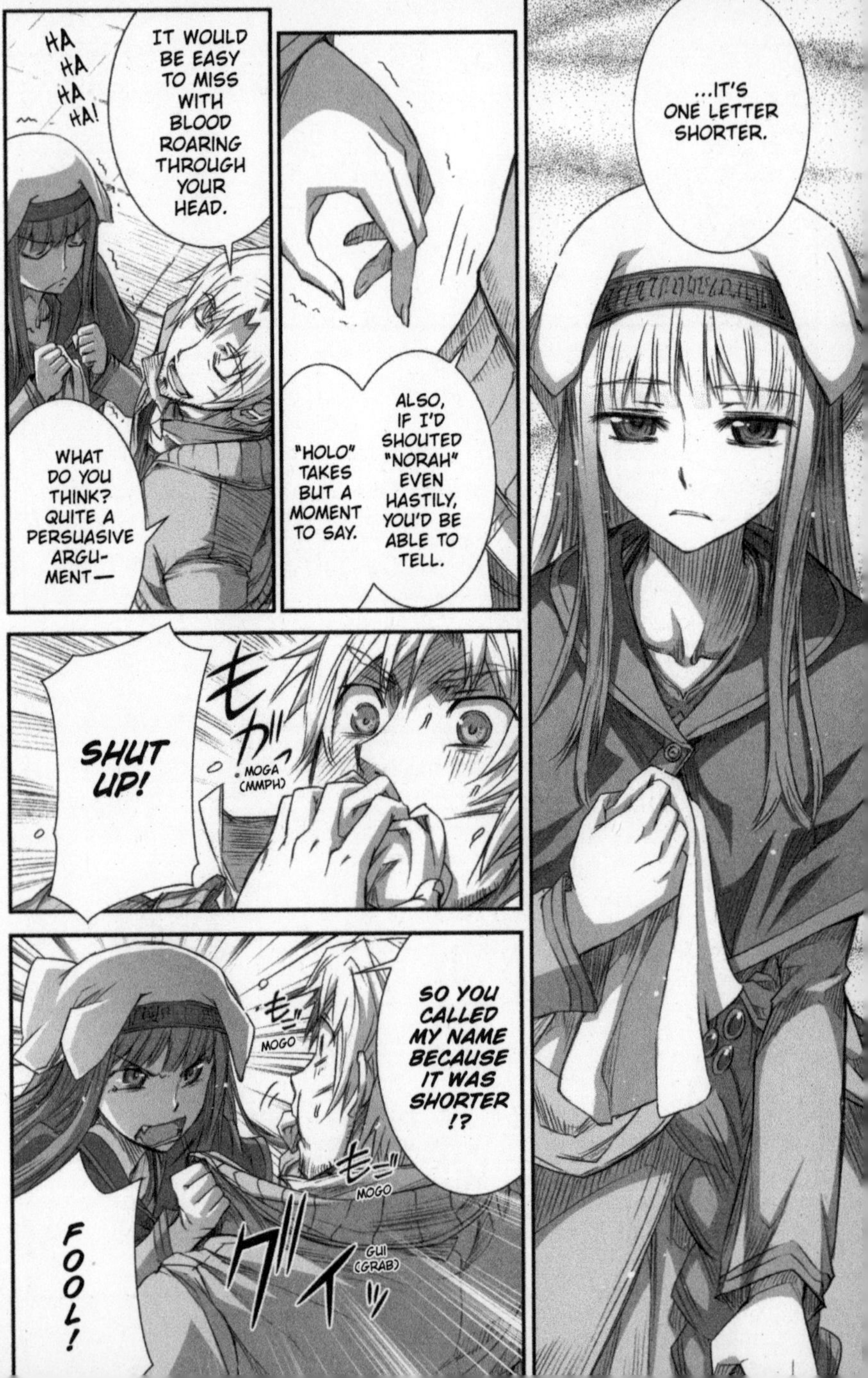
...IT'S ONE LETTER SHORTER.
ALSO, IF I'D SHOUTED "NORAH" EVEN HASTILY, YOU'D BE ABLE TO TELL.
"HOLO" TAKES BUT A MOMENT TO SAY.
IT WOULD BE EASY TO MISS WITH BLOOD ROARING THROUGH YOUR HEAD.
HA HA HA HA!
WHAT DO YOU THINK? QUITE A PERSUASIVE ARGU-MENT—
MOGA (MMPH)
SHUT UP!
SO YOU CALLED MY NAME BECAUSE IT WAS SHORTER!?
MOGO
MOGO
GUI (GRAB)
FOOL!

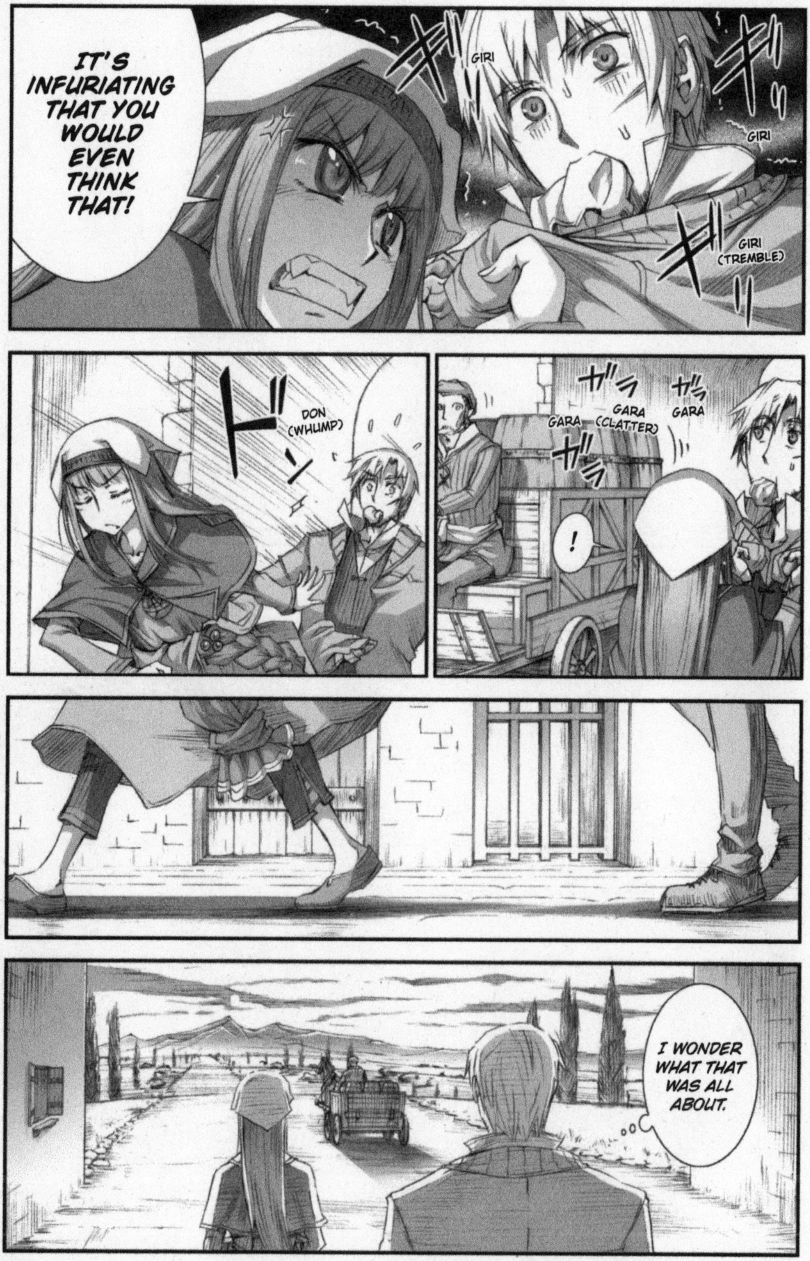
GIRI
GIRI
GIRI (TREMBLE)
IT'S INFURIATING THAT YOU WOULD EVEN THINK THAT!
GARA
GARA (CLATTER)
GARA
!
DON (WHUMP)
I WONDER WHAT THAT WAS ALL ABOUT.

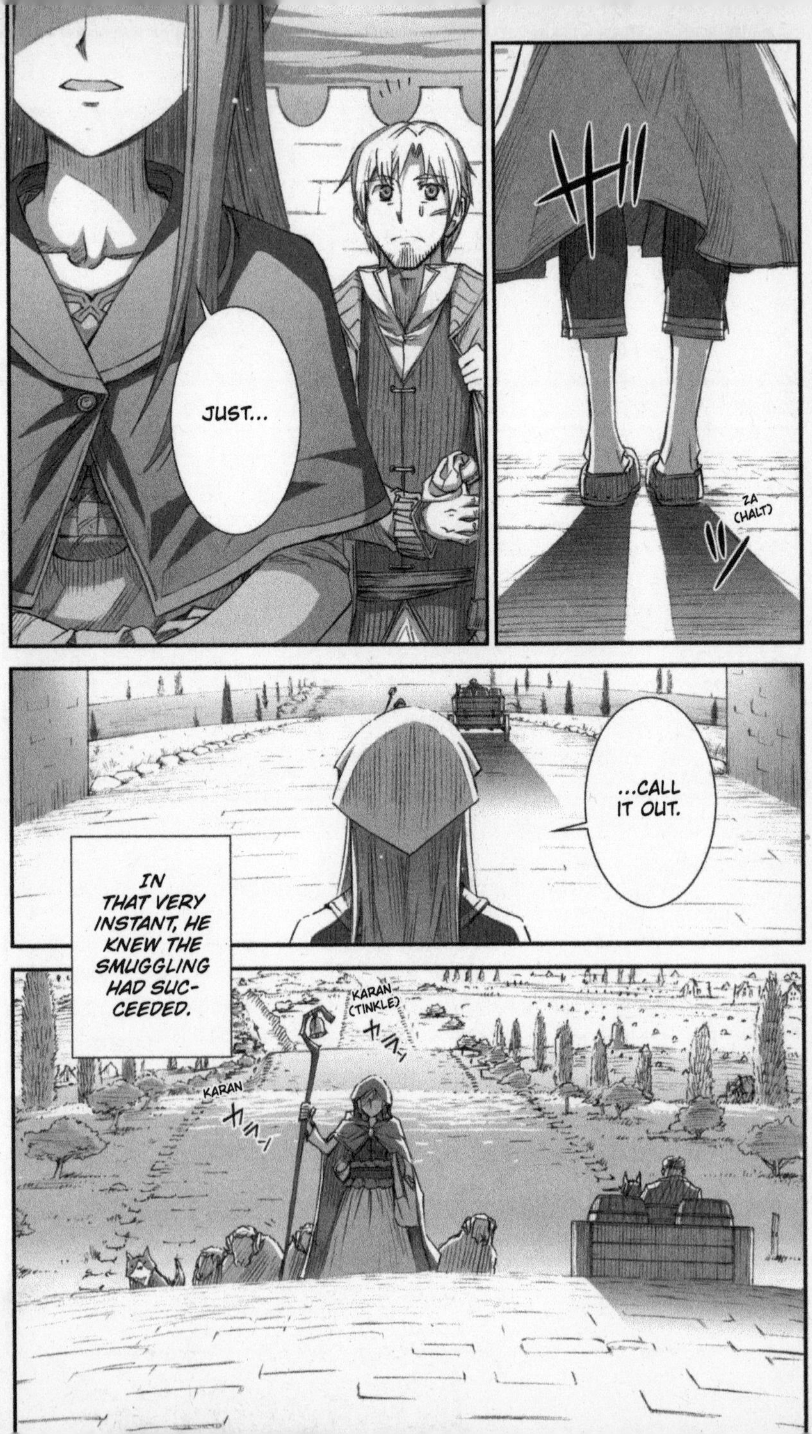
ZA (HALT)
JUST...
...CALL IT OUT.
IN THAT VERY INSTANT, HE KNEW THE SMUGGLING HAD SUC-CEEDED.
KARAN (TINKLE)
KARAN

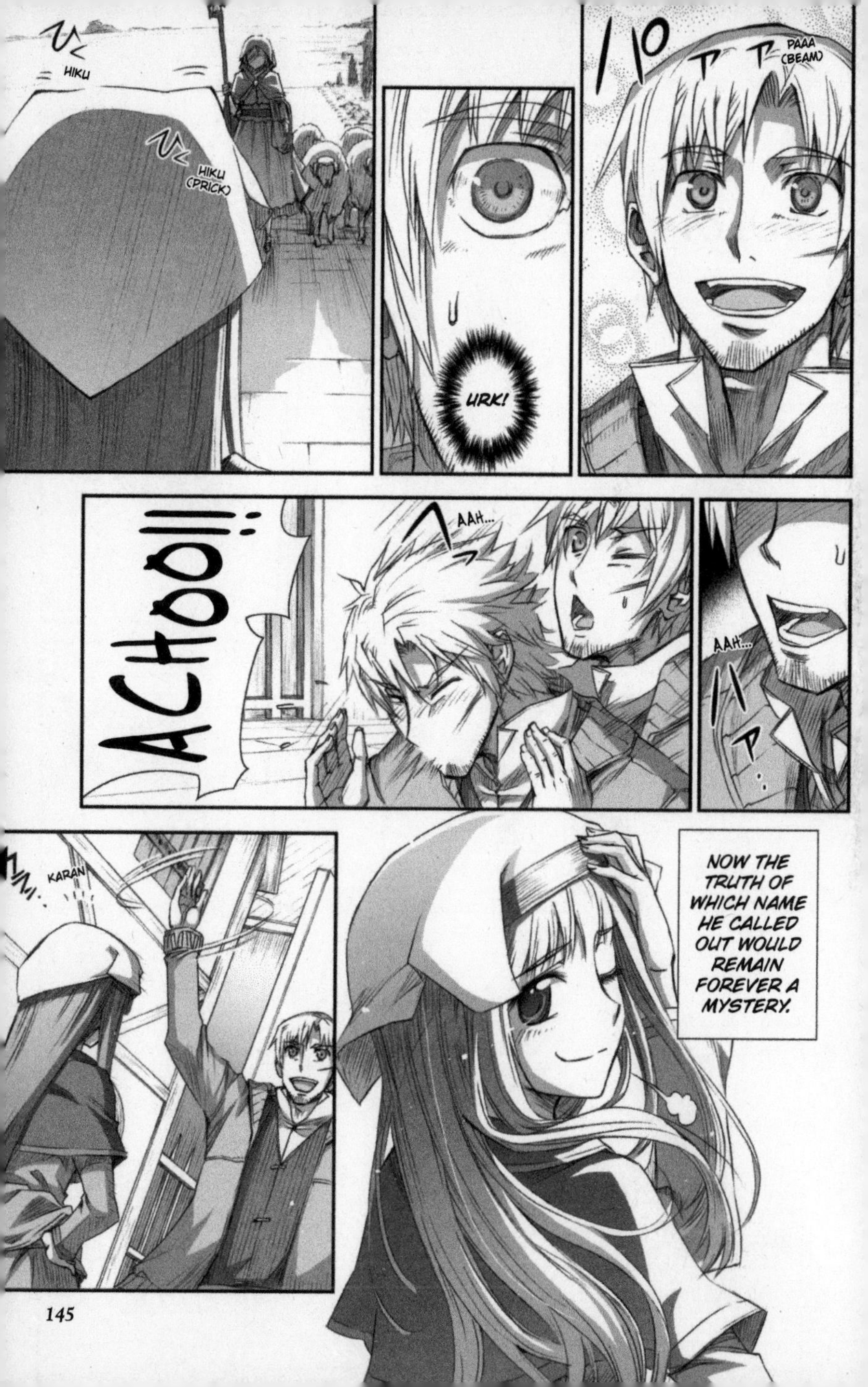

PAAA (BEAM)
URK!
HIKU
HIKU (PRICK)
AAH...
AAH...
ACHOO!!!
NOW THE TRUTH OF WHICH NAME HE CALLED OUT WOULD REMAIN FOREVER A MYSTERY.
KARAN

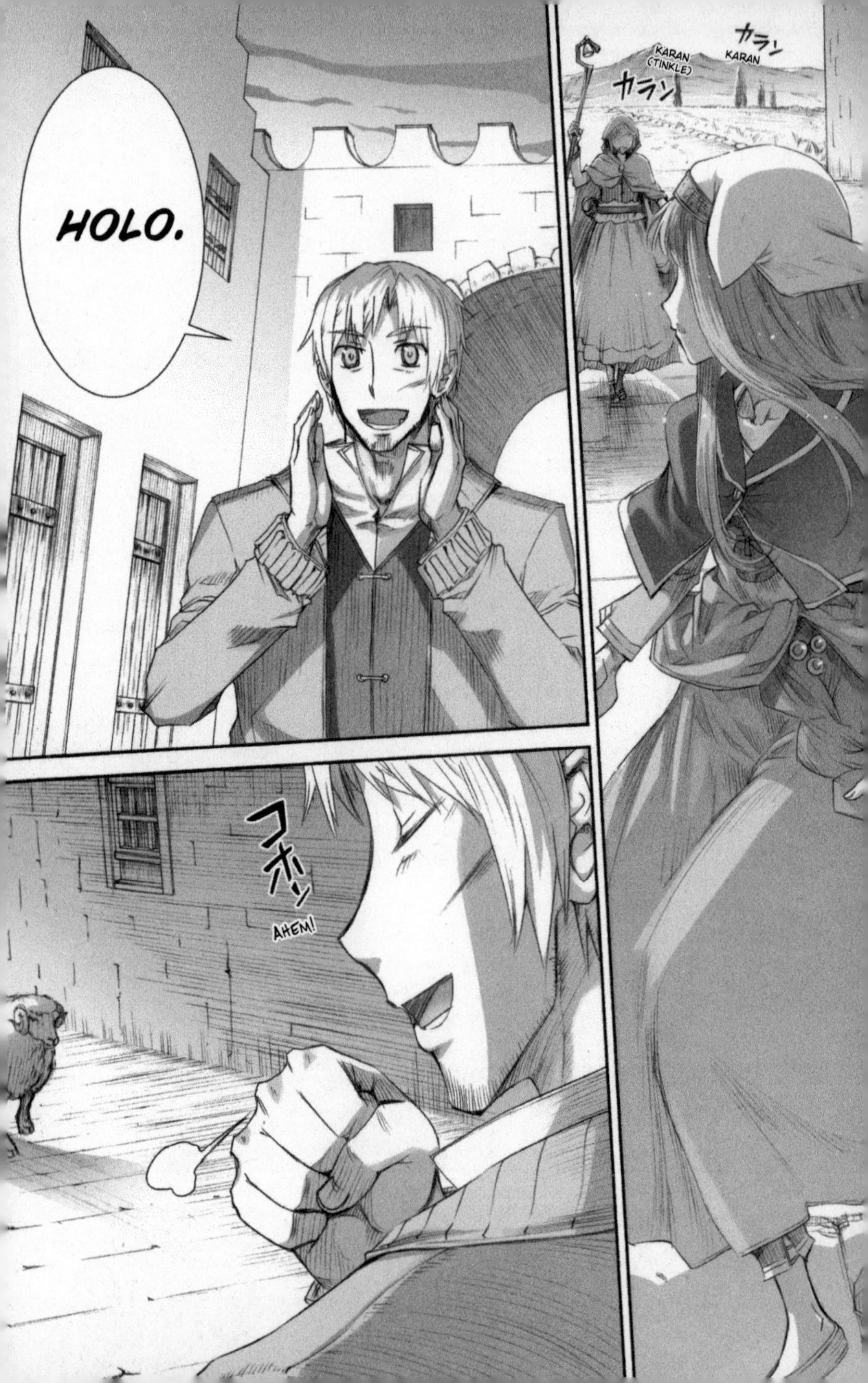
カラン
KARAN
カラン
KARAN (TINKLE)
HOLO.
コホン
AHEM!

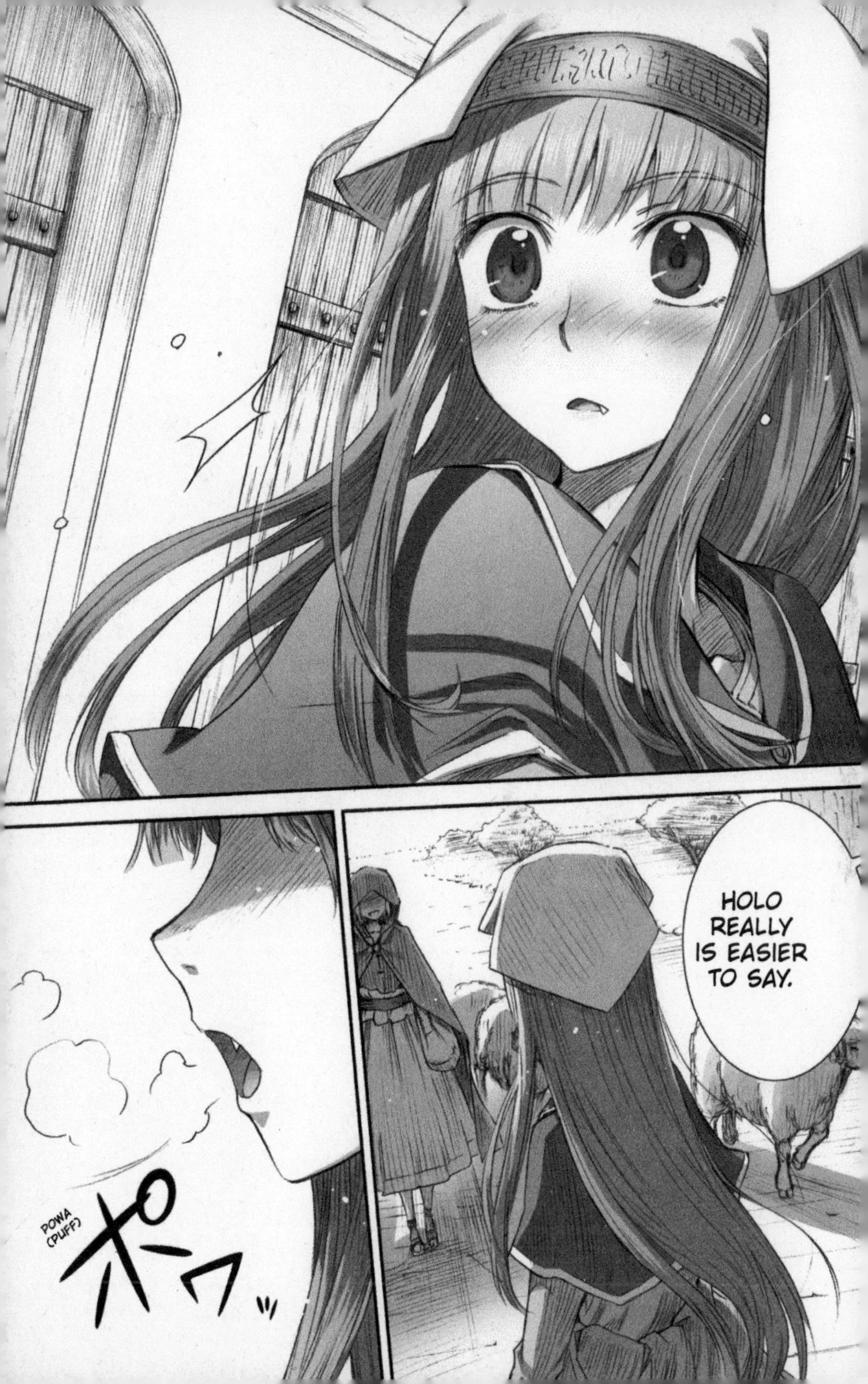
HOLO REALLY IS EASIER TO SAY.
POWA (PUFF)

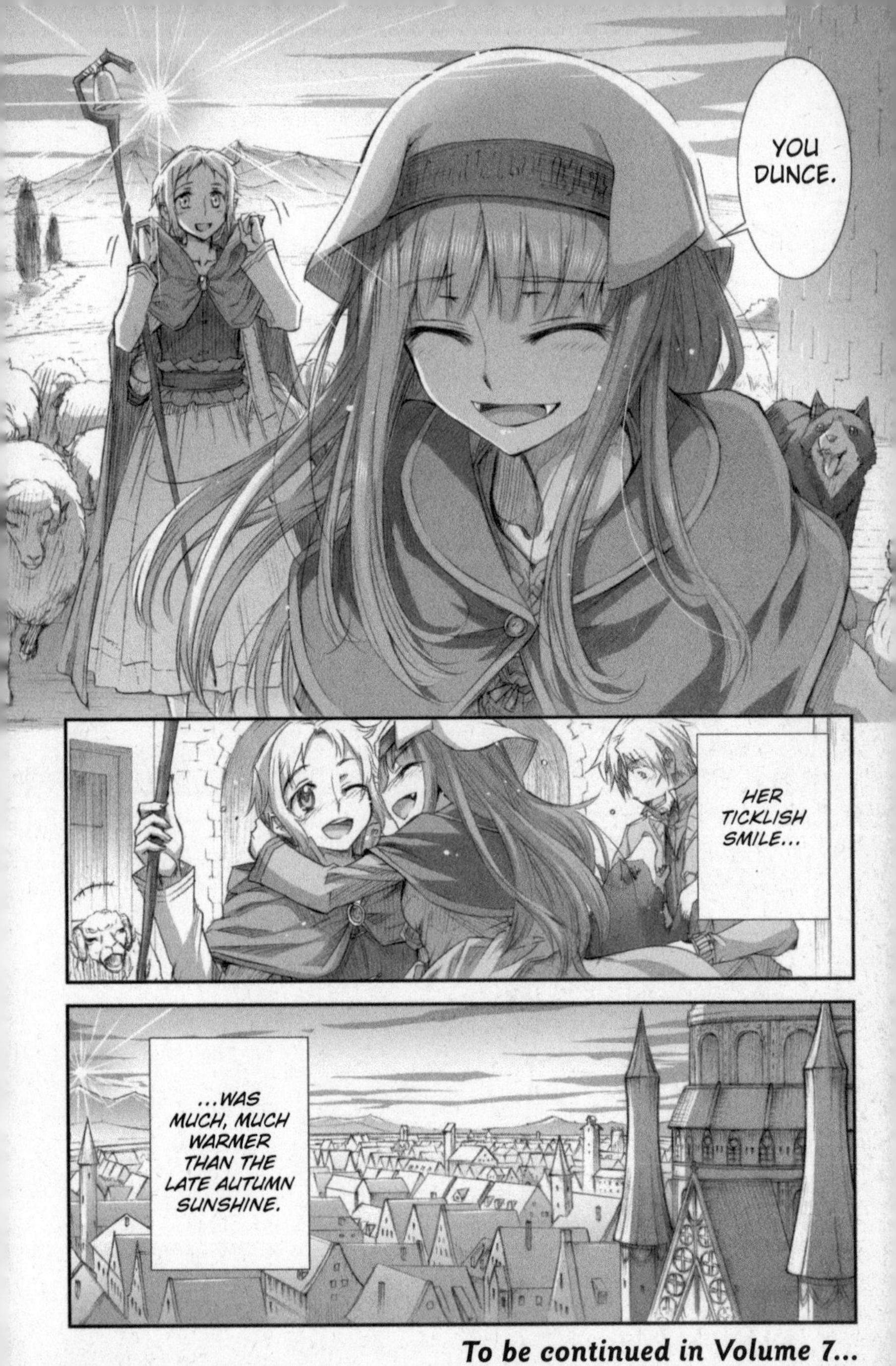
YOU DUNCE.
HER TICKLISH SMILE...
...WAS MUCH, MUCH WARMER THAN THE LATE AUTUMN SUNSHINE.

To be continued in Volume 7...

SPICE & WOLF

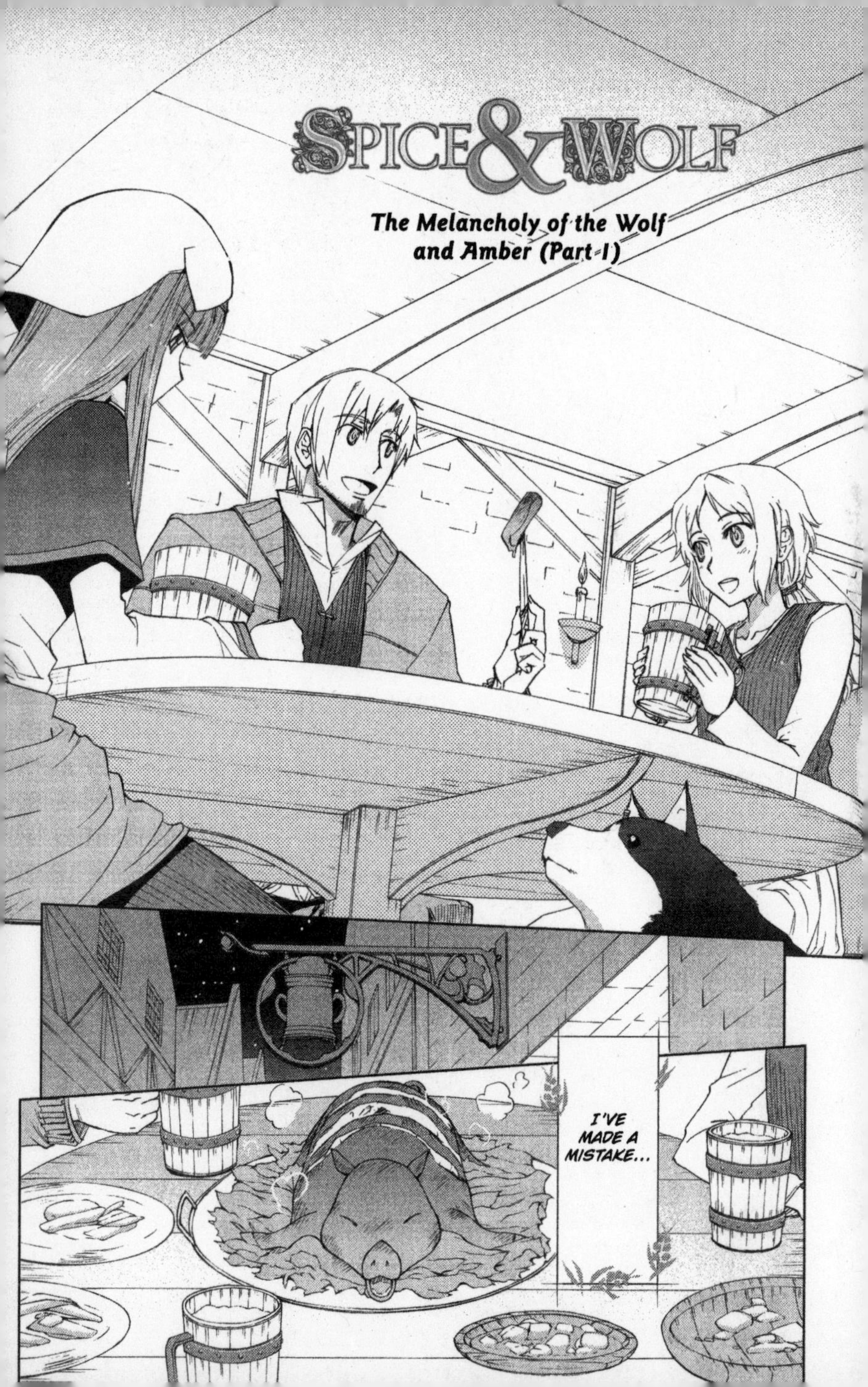
SPICE & WOLF
The Melancholy of the Wolf and Amber (Part 1)
I'VE MADE A MISTAKE...

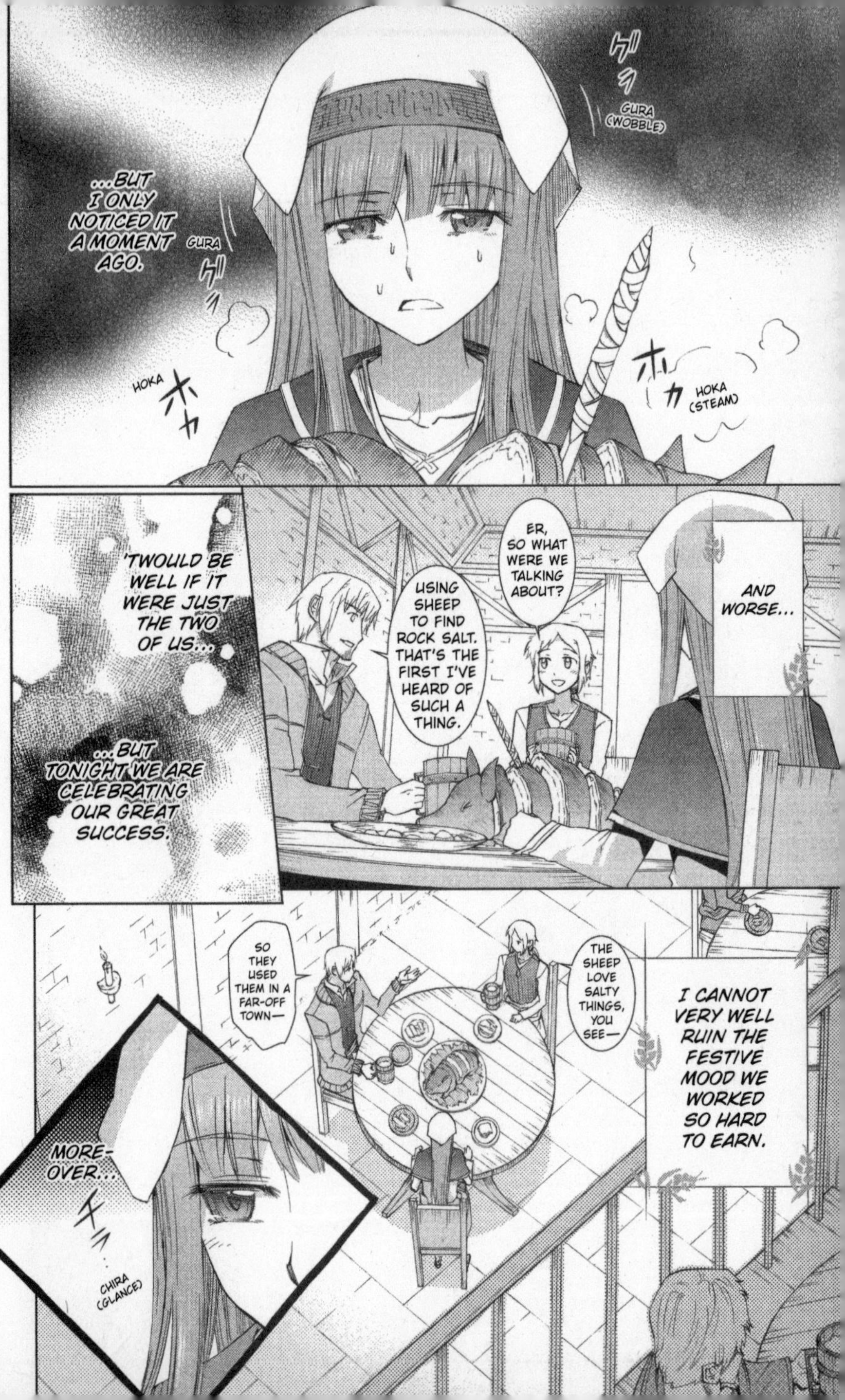
GURA (WOBBLE)
...BUT I ONLY NOTICED IT A MOMENT AGO.
GURA
HOKA (STEAM)
HOKA
AND WORSE...
ER, SO WHAT WERE WE TALKING ABOUT?
USING SHEEP TO FIND ROCK SALT. THAT'S THE FIRST I'VE HEARD OF SUCH A THING.
'TWOULD BE WELL IF IT WERE JUST THE TWO OF US...
...BUT TONIGHT WE ARE CELEBRATING OUR GREAT SUCCESS.
I CANNOT VERY WELL RUIN THE FESTIVE MOOD WE WORKED SO HARD TO EARN.
THE SHEEP LOVE SALTY THINGS, YOU SEE—
SO THEY USED THEM IN A FAR-OFF TOWN—
MORE-OVER...
CHIRA (GLANCE)

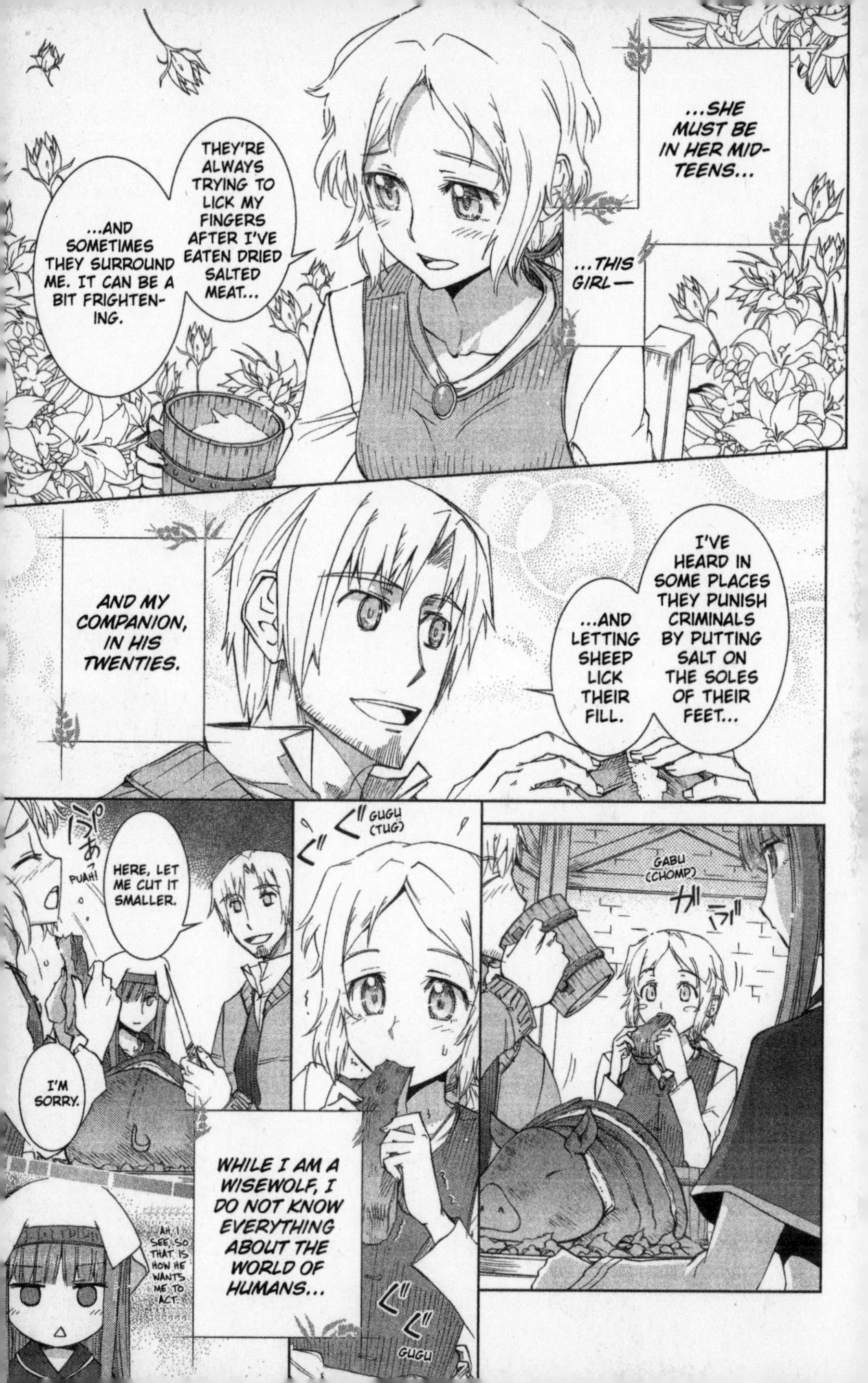
...SHE MUST BE IN HER MID-TEENS...
...THIS GIRL—
THEY'RE ALWAYS TRYING TO LICK MY FINGERS AFTER I'VE EATEN DRIED SALTED MEAT...
...AND SOMETIMES THEY SURROUND ME. IT CAN BE A BIT FRIGHTENING.
I'VE HEARD IN SOME PLACES THEY PUNISH CRIMINALS BY PUTTING SALT ON THE SOLES OF THEIR FEET...
...AND LETTING SHEEP LICK THEIR FILL.
AND MY COMPANION, IN HIS TWENTIES.
GABU (CHOMP)
GUGU (TUG)
WHILE I AM A WISEWOLF, I DO NOT KNOW EVERYTHING ABOUT THE WORLD OF HUMANS...
GUGU
PUAH!
HERE, LET ME CUT IT SMALLER.
I'M SORRY.
AH, I SEE, SO THAT IS HOW HE WANTS ME TO ACT.

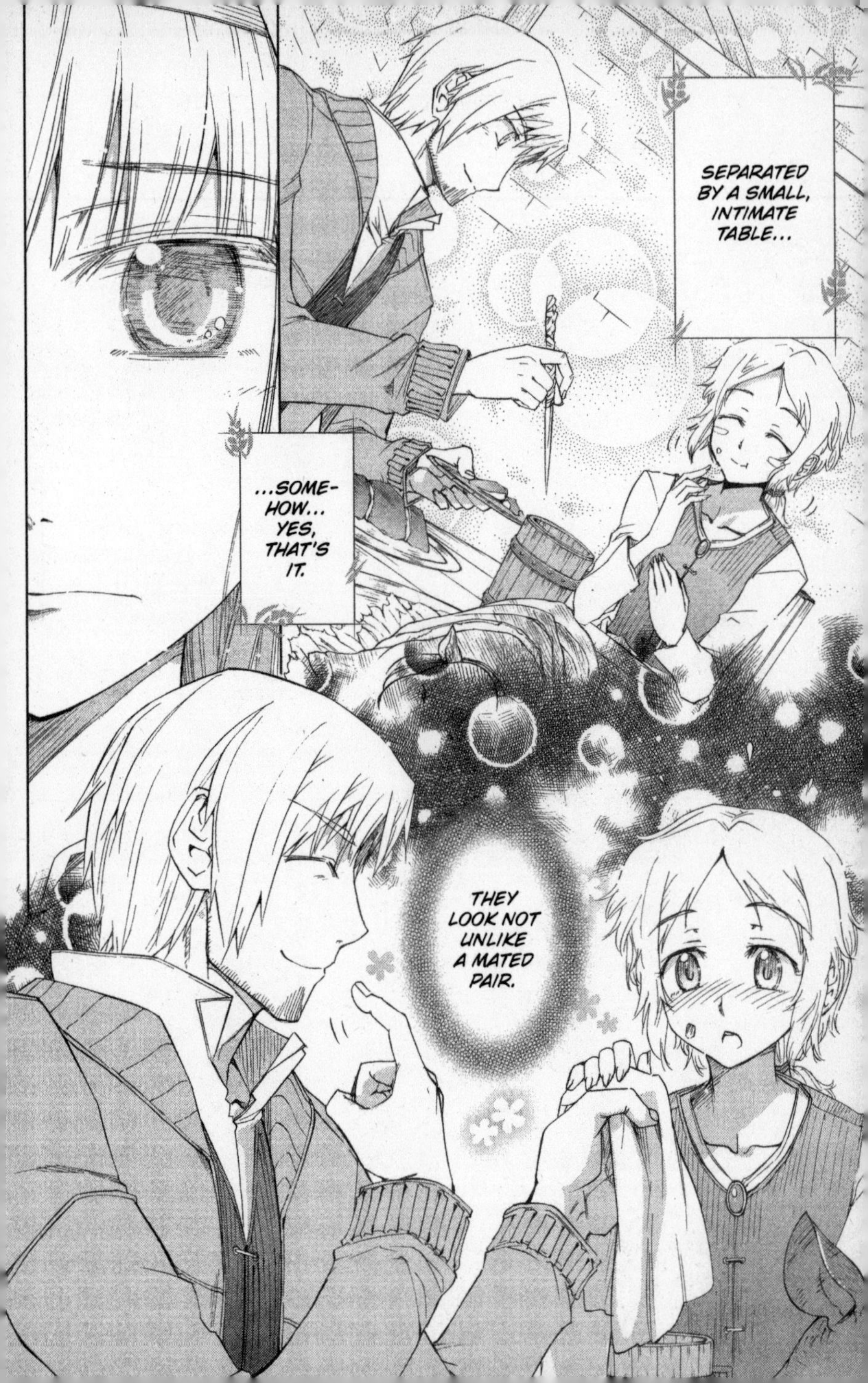
SEPARATED BY A SMALL, INTIMATE TABLE...
...SOME-HOW... YES, THAT'S IT.
THEY LOOK NOT UNLIKE A MATED PAIR.

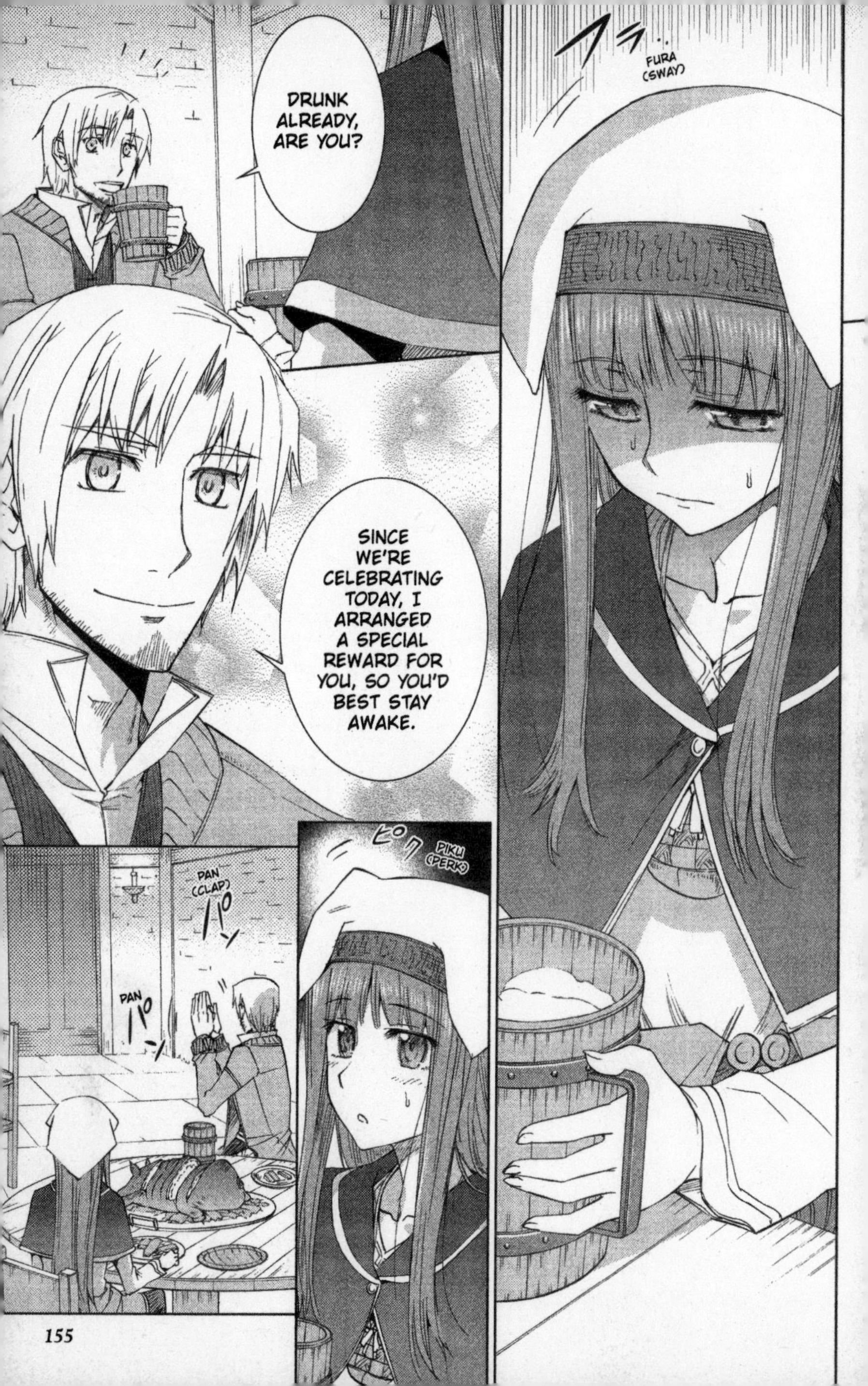
FURA (SWAY)
DRUNK ALREADY, ARE YOU?
SINCE WE'RE CELEBRATING TODAY, I ARRANGED A SPECIAL REWARD FOR YOU, SO YOU'D BEST STAY AWAKE.
PIKU (PERK)
PAN (CLAP)
PAN

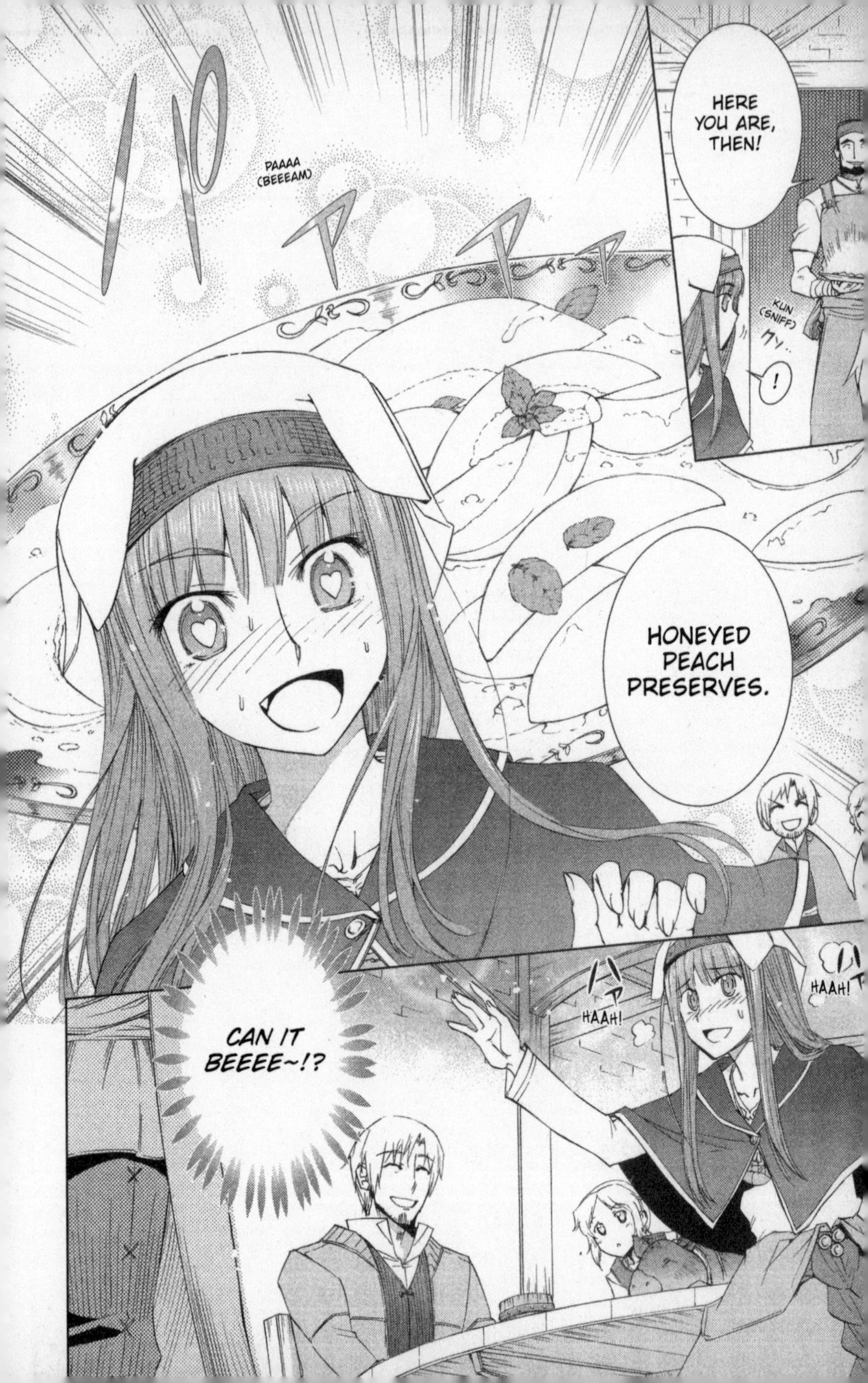
HERE YOU ARE, THEN!
KUN (SNIFF)
!
PAAAA (BEEEAM)
HONEYED PEACH PRESERVES.
HAAH!
HAAH!
CAN IT BEEEE~!?

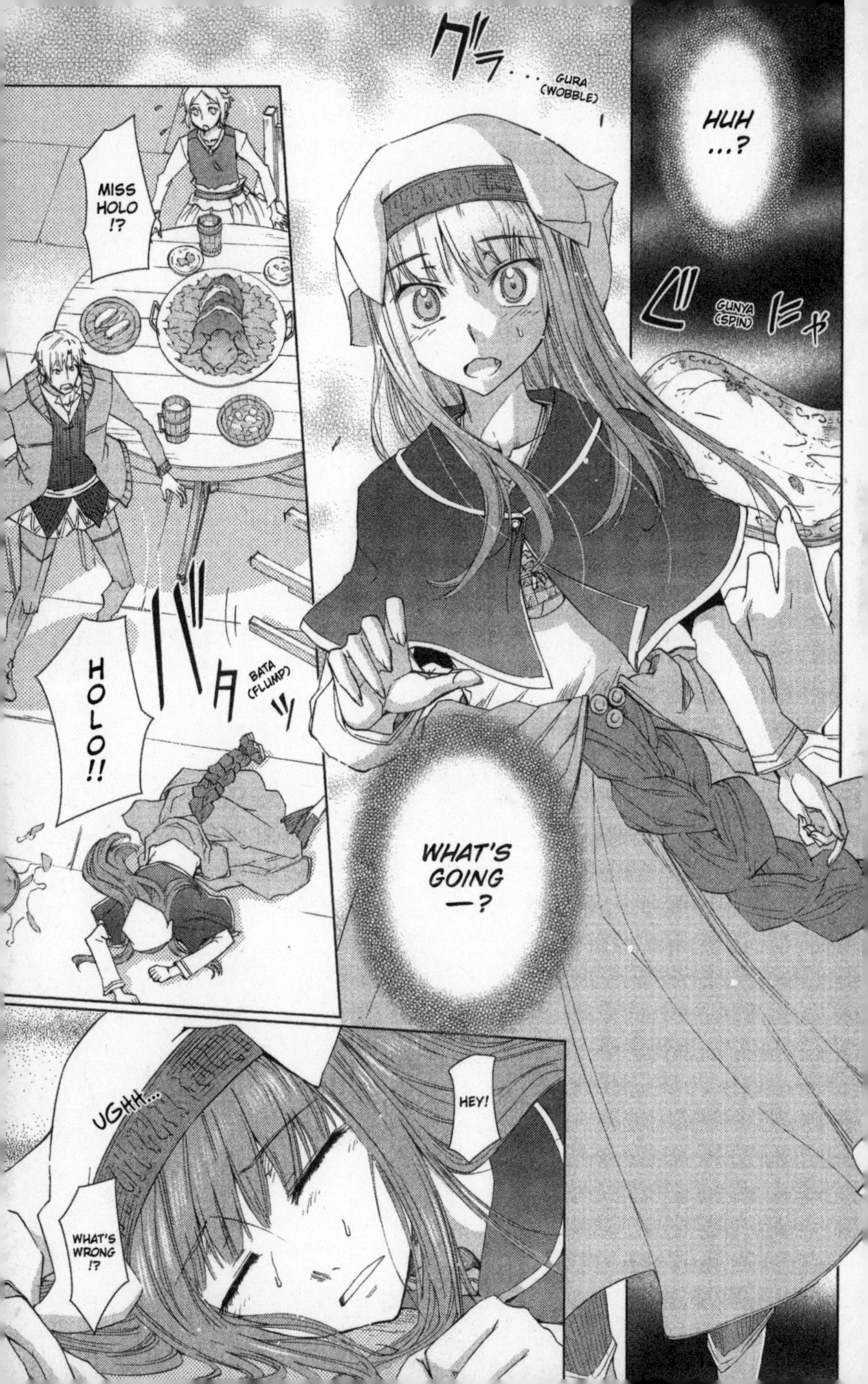
グラ
GURA (WOBBLE)
HUH ...?
ぐにゃ
GUNYA (SPIN)
WHAT'S GOING —?
MISS HOLO !?
バタッ
BATA (FLUMP)
HOLO!!
HEY!
UGHH...
WHAT'S WRONG !?

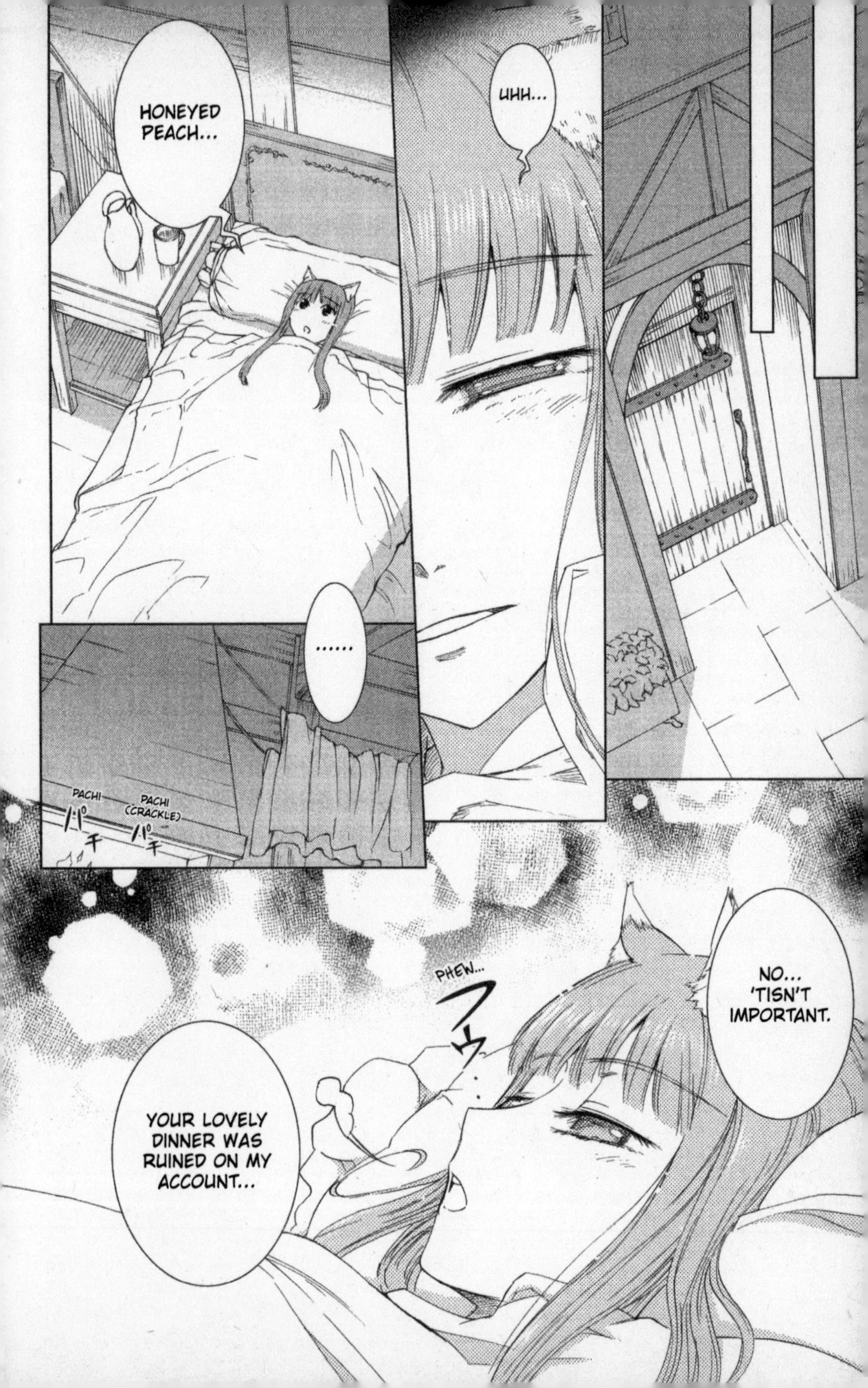
UHH...
HONEYED PEACH...
......
PACHI
PACHI (CRACKLE)
NO... 'TISN'T IMPORTANT.
PHEW...
YOUR LOVELY DINNER WAS RUINED ON MY ACCOUNT...

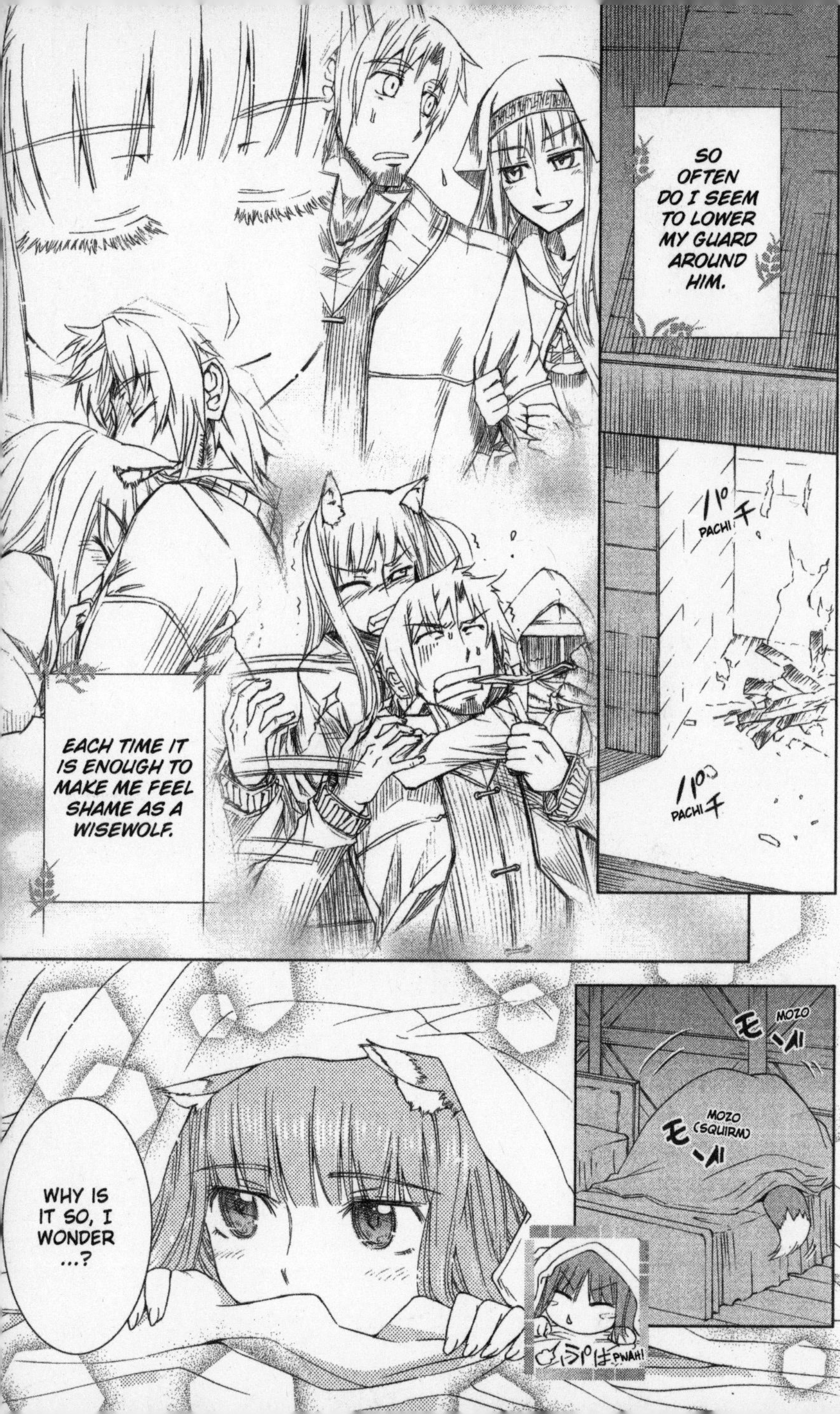
SO OFTEN DO I SEEM TO LOWER MY GUARD AROUND HIM.
パチ PACHI
パチ PACHI
EACH TIME IT IS ENOUGH TO MAKE ME FEEL SHAME AS A WISEWOLF.
モゾ MOZO
モゾ MOZO (SQUIRM)
ぷは PWAH!
WHY IS IT SO, I WONDER ...?

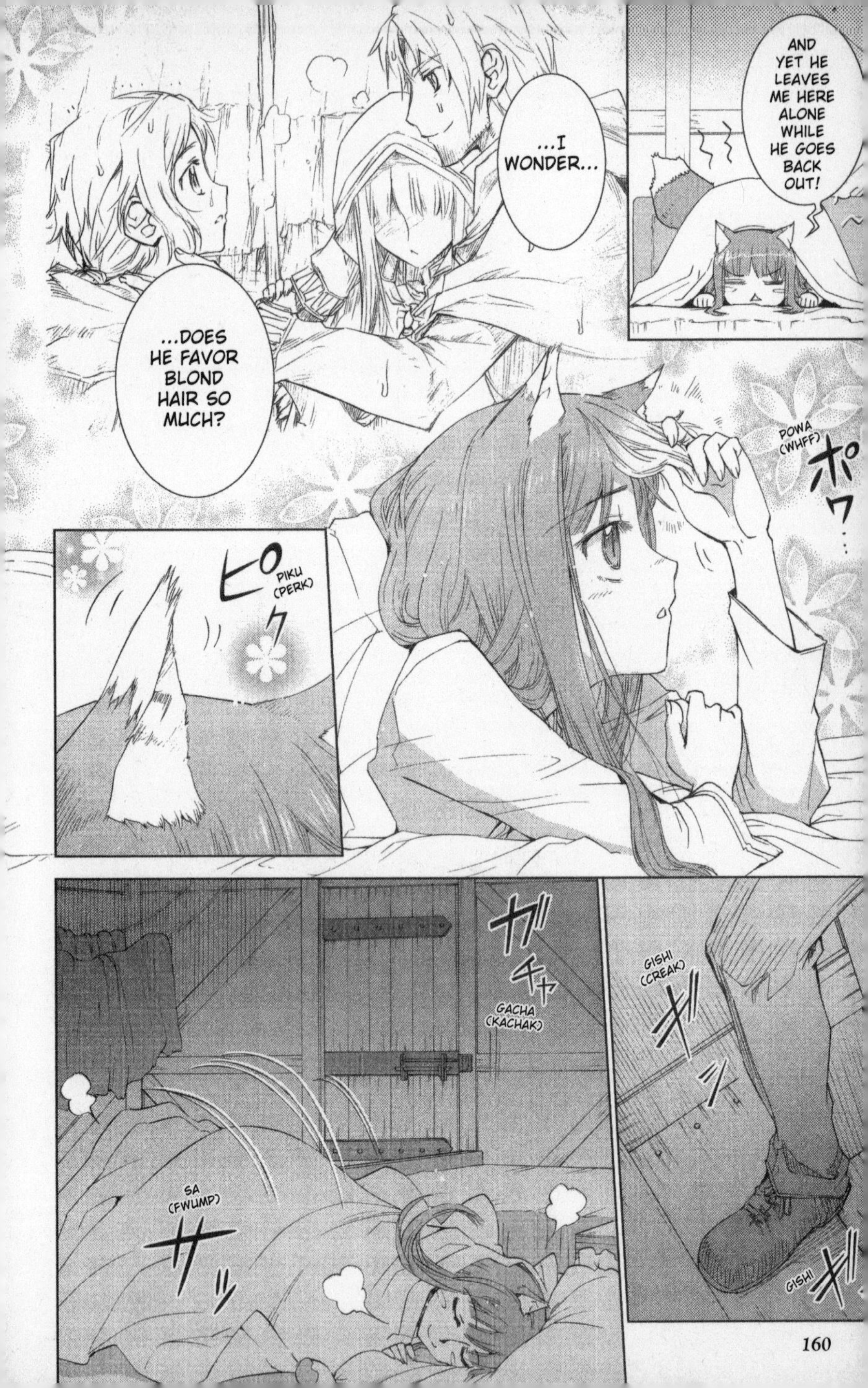
AND YET HE LEAVES ME HERE ALONE WHILE HE GOES BACK OUT!
...I WONDER...
...DOES HE FAVOR BLOND HAIR SO MUCH?
POWA (WHFF)
PIKU (PERK)
GISHI (CREAK)
GISHI
GACHA (KACHAK)
SA (FWUMP)

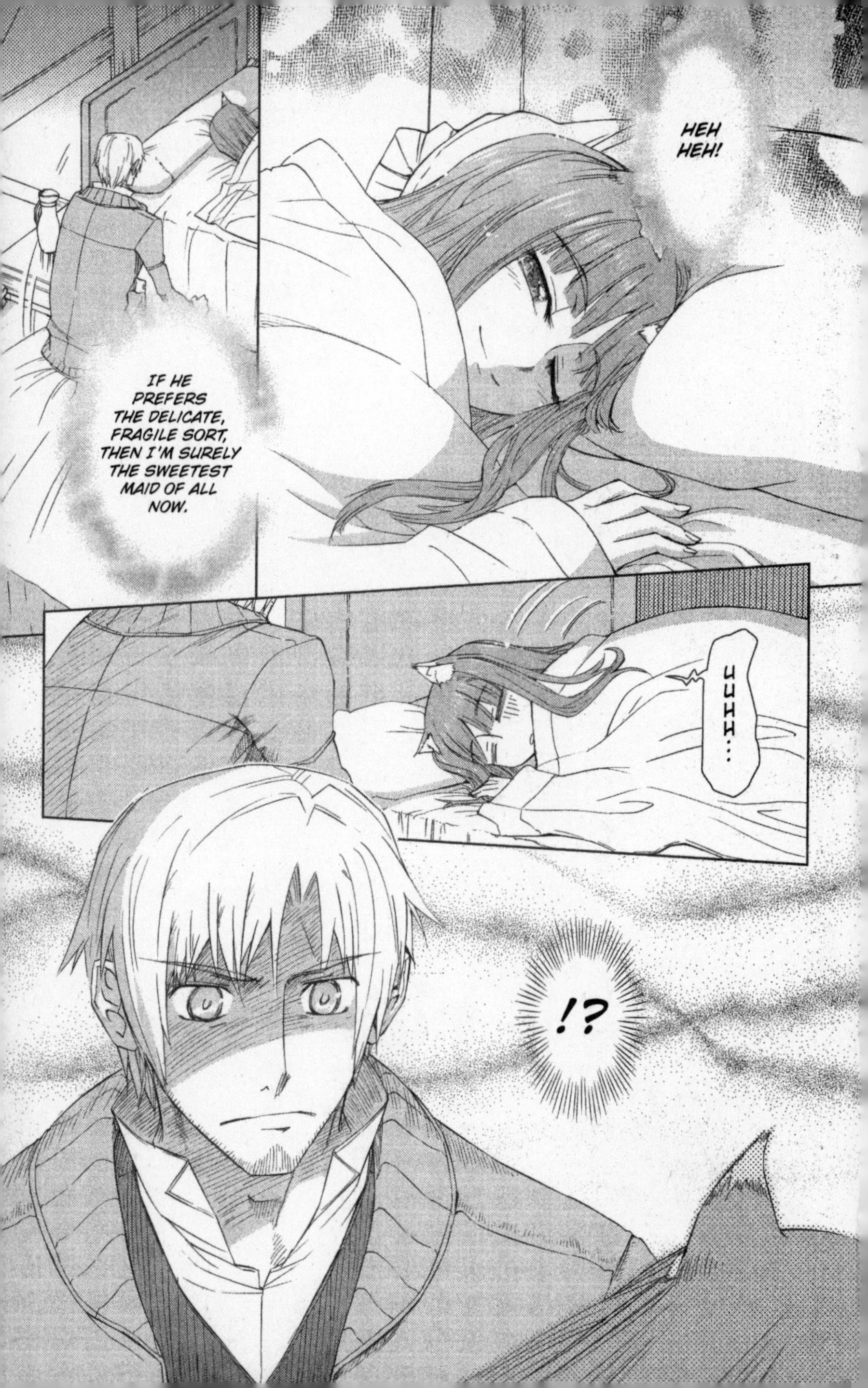
HEH HEH!
IF HE PREFERS THE DELICATE, FRAGILE SORT, THEN I'M SURELY THE SWEETEST MAID OF ALL NOW.
UUHH...
!?

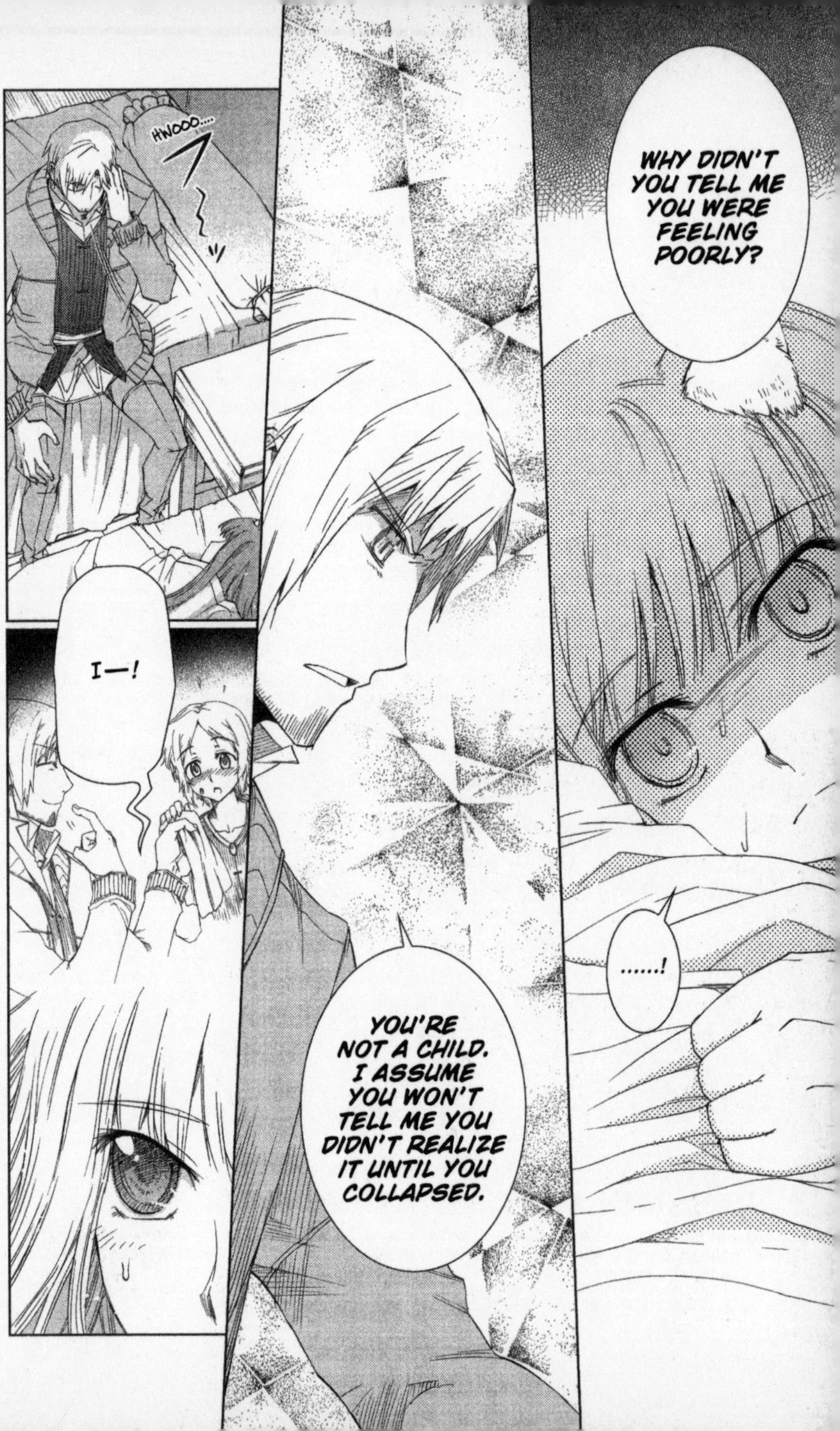
WHY DIDN'T YOU TELL ME YOU WERE FEELING POORLY?
......!
YOU'RE NOT A CHILD. I ASSUME YOU WON'T TELL ME YOU DIDN'T REALIZE IT UNTIL YOU COLLAPSED.
HWOOO...
I—!

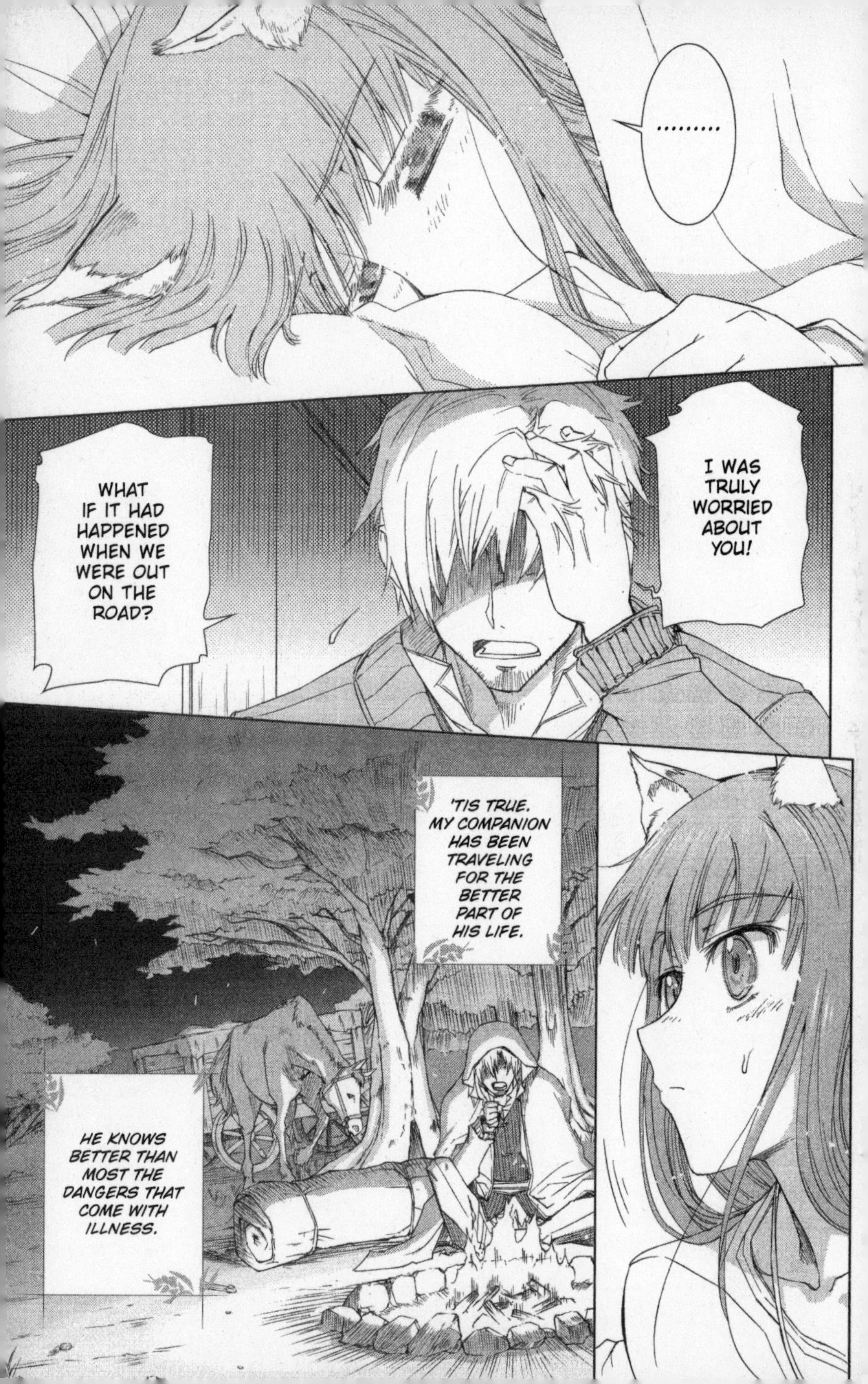
....
I WAS TRULY WORRIED ABOUT YOU!
WHAT IF IT HAD HAPPENED WHEN WE WERE OUT ON THE ROAD?
'TIS TRUE. MY COMPANION HAS BEEN TRAVELING FOR THE BETTER PART OF HIS LIFE.
HE KNOWS BETTER THAN MOST THE DANGERS THAT COME WITH ILLNESS.

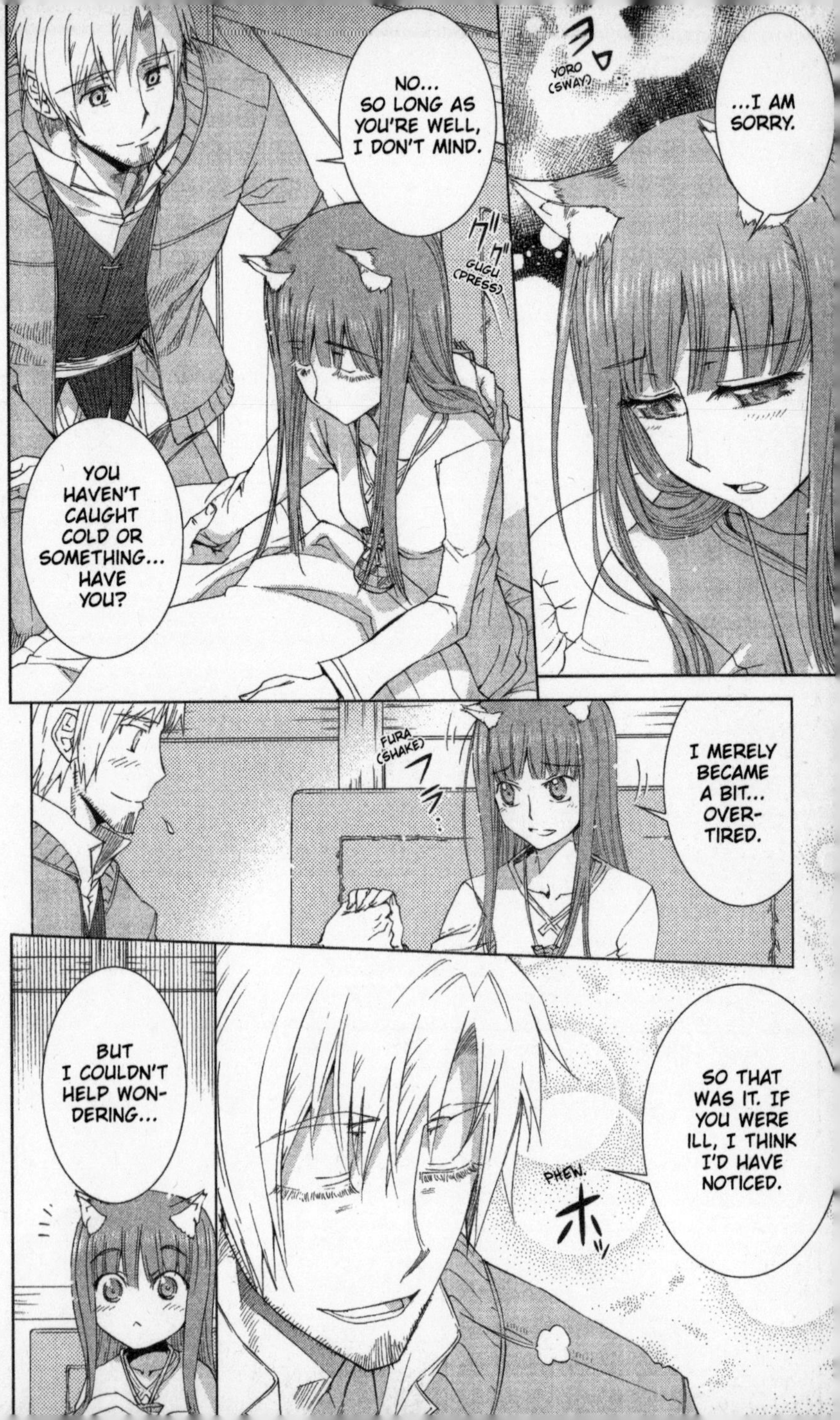
YORO (SWAY)
...I AM SORRY.
NO... SO LONG AS YOU'RE WELL, I DON'T MIND.
GUGU (PRESS)
YOU HAVEN'T CAUGHT COLD OR SOMETHING... HAVE YOU?
I MERELY BECAME A BIT... OVER-TIRED.
FURA (SHAKE)
SO THAT WAS IT. IF YOU WERE ILL, I THINK I'D HAVE NOTICED.
PHEW.
BUT I COULDN'T HELP WON-DERING...

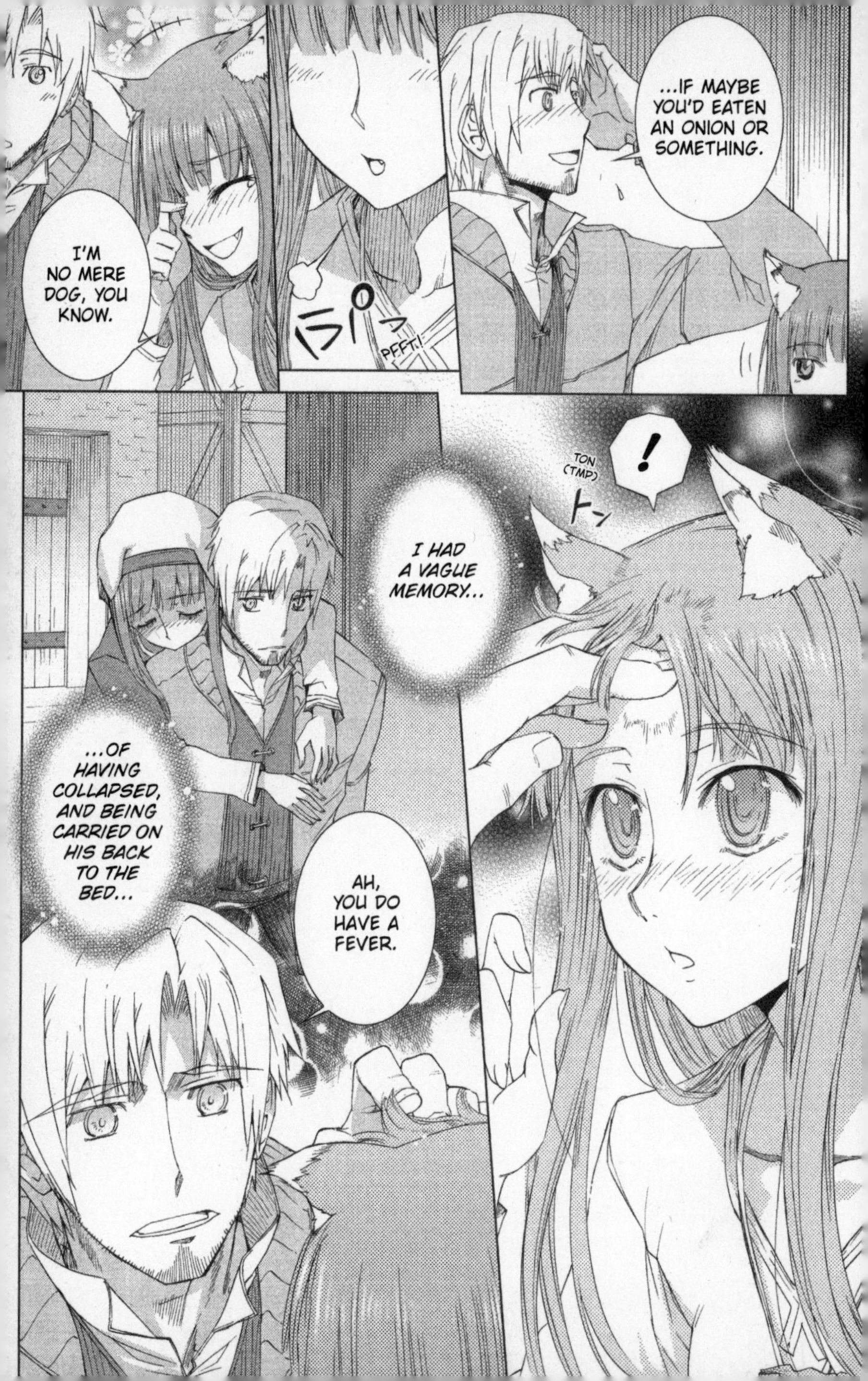
...IF MAYBE YOU'D EATEN AN ONION OR SOMETHING.
ぷっ
PFFT!
I'M NO MERE DOG, YOU KNOW.
!
トン
TON (TMP)
I HAD A VAGUE MEMORY...
...OF HAVING COLLAPSED, AND BEING CARRIED ON HIS BACK TO THE BED...
AH, YOU DO HAVE A FEVER.

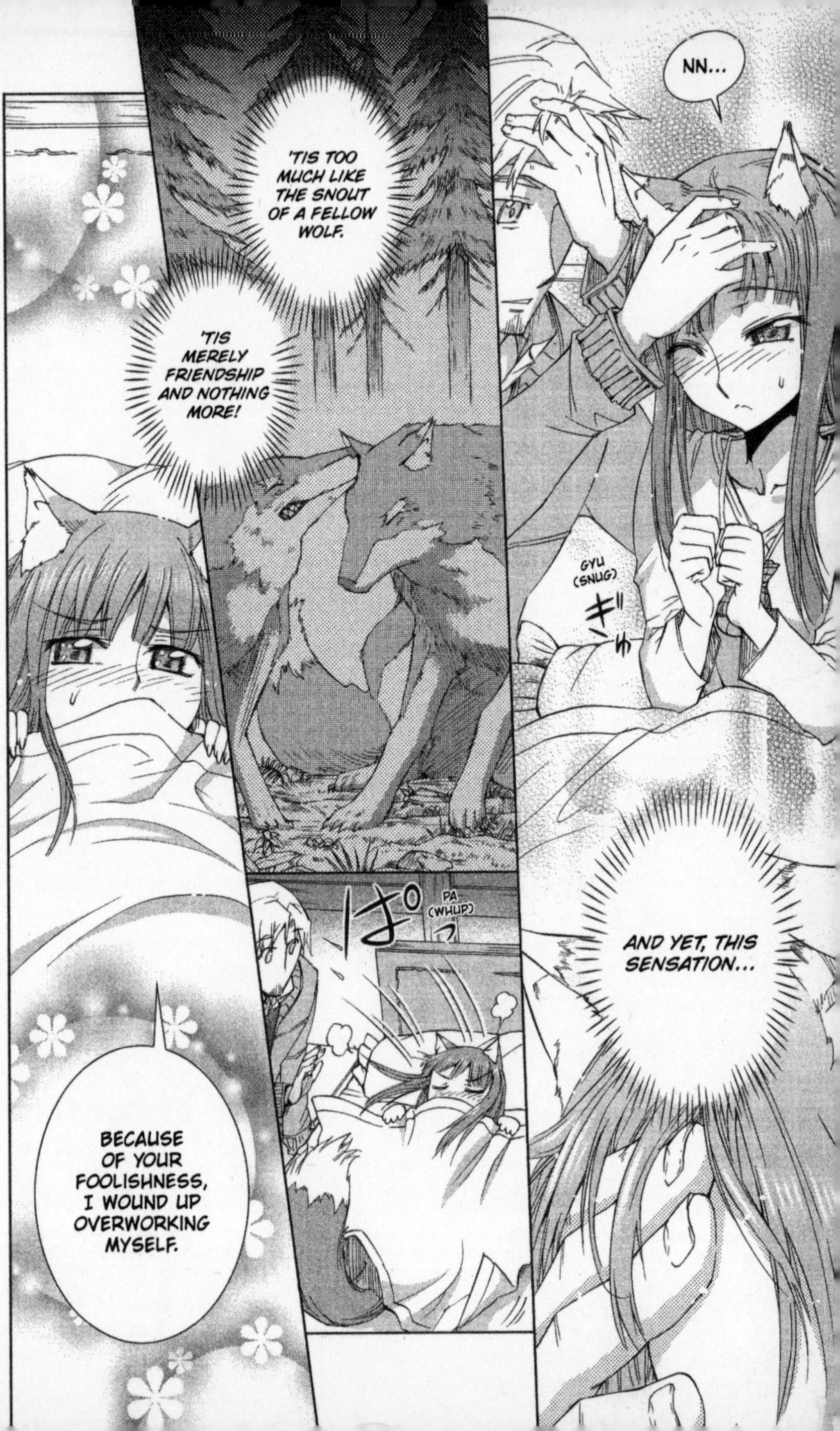
NN...
GYU (SNUG)
ぎゅ
AND YET, THIS SENSATION...
'TIS TOO MUCH LIKE THE SNOUT OF A FELLOW WOLF.
'TIS MERELY FRIENDSHIP AND NOTHING MORE!
PA (WHUP)
ぱっ
BECAUSE OF YOUR FOOLISHNESS, I WOUND UP OVERWORKING MYSELF.

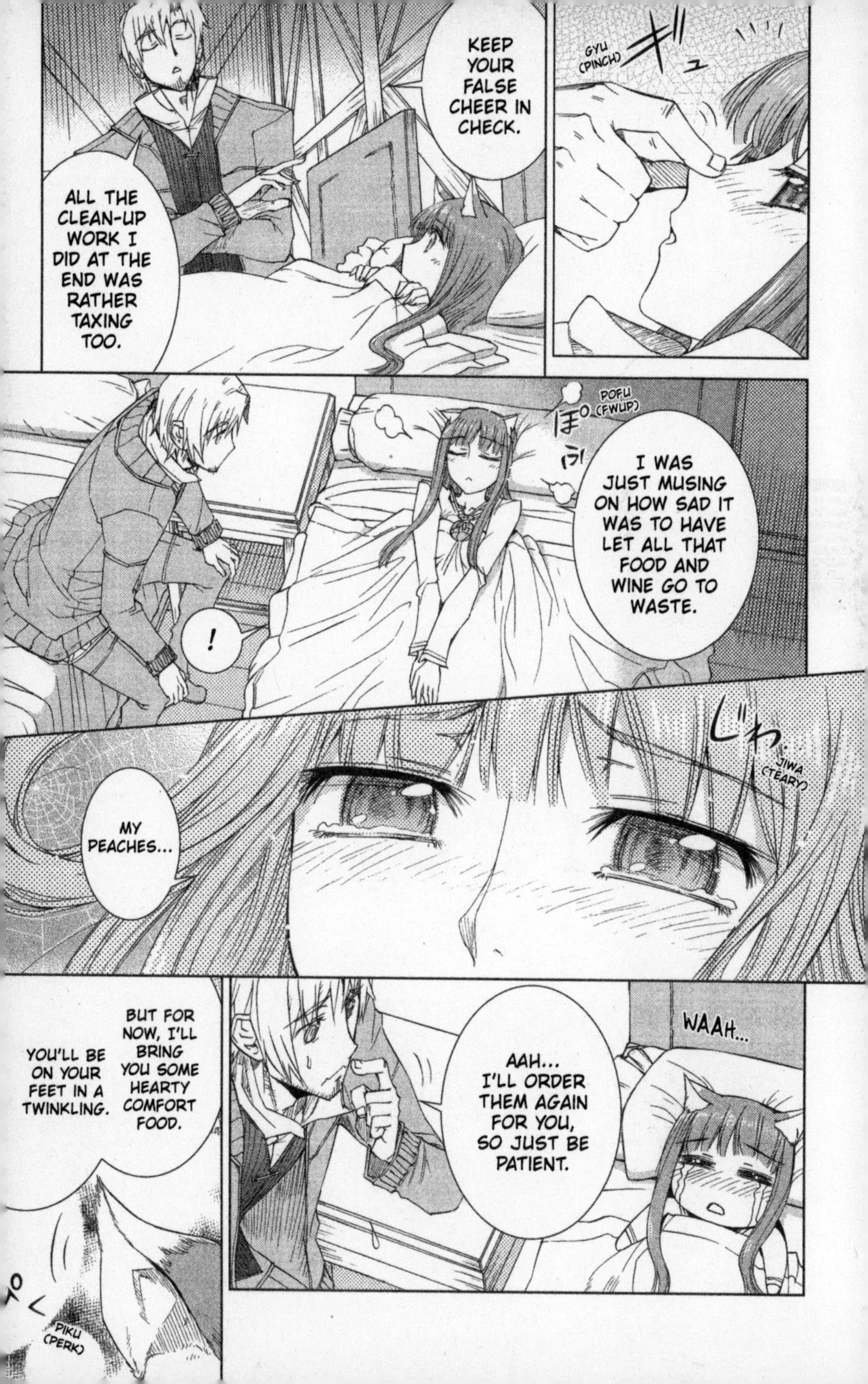

ギュ
GYU (PINCH)
KEEP YOUR FALSE CHEER IN CHECK.
ALL THE CLEAN-UP WORK I DID AT THE END WAS RATHER TAXING TOO.
ぽふ
POFU (FWUP)
I WAS JUST MUSING ON HOW SAD IT WAS TO HAVE LET ALL THAT FOOD AND WINE GO TO WASTE.
!
じわ
JIWA (TEARY)
MY PEACHES...
WAAH...
AAH... I'LL ORDER THEM AGAIN FOR YOU, SO JUST BE PATIENT.
BUT FOR NOW, I'LL BRING YOU SOME HEARTY COMFORT FOOD.
YOU'LL BE ON YOUR FEET IN A TWINKLING.
ぴくっ
PIKU (PERK)

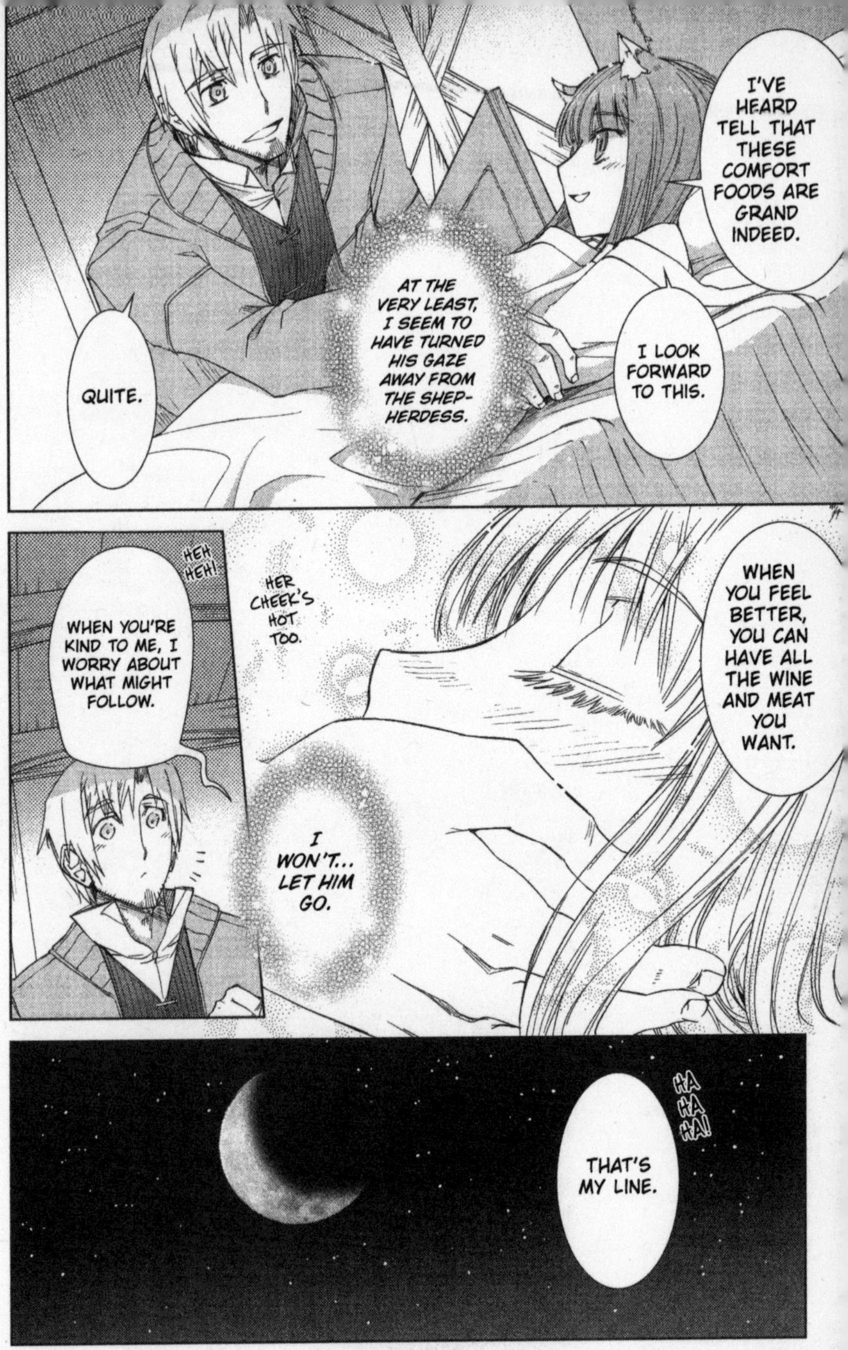
I'VE HEARD TELL THAT THESE COMFORT FOODS ARE GRAND INDEED.
I LOOK FORWARD TO THIS.
AT THE VERY LEAST, I SEEM TO HAVE TURNED HIS GAZE AWAY FROM THE SHEP-HERDESS.
QUITE.
WHEN YOU FEEL BETTER, YOU CAN HAVE ALL THE WINE AND MEAT YOU WANT.
I WON'T... LET HIM GO.
HER CHEEK'S HOT TOO.
HEH HEH!
WHEN YOU'RE KIND TO ME, I WORRY ABOUT WHAT MIGHT FOLLOW.
HA HA HA!
THAT'S MY LINE.

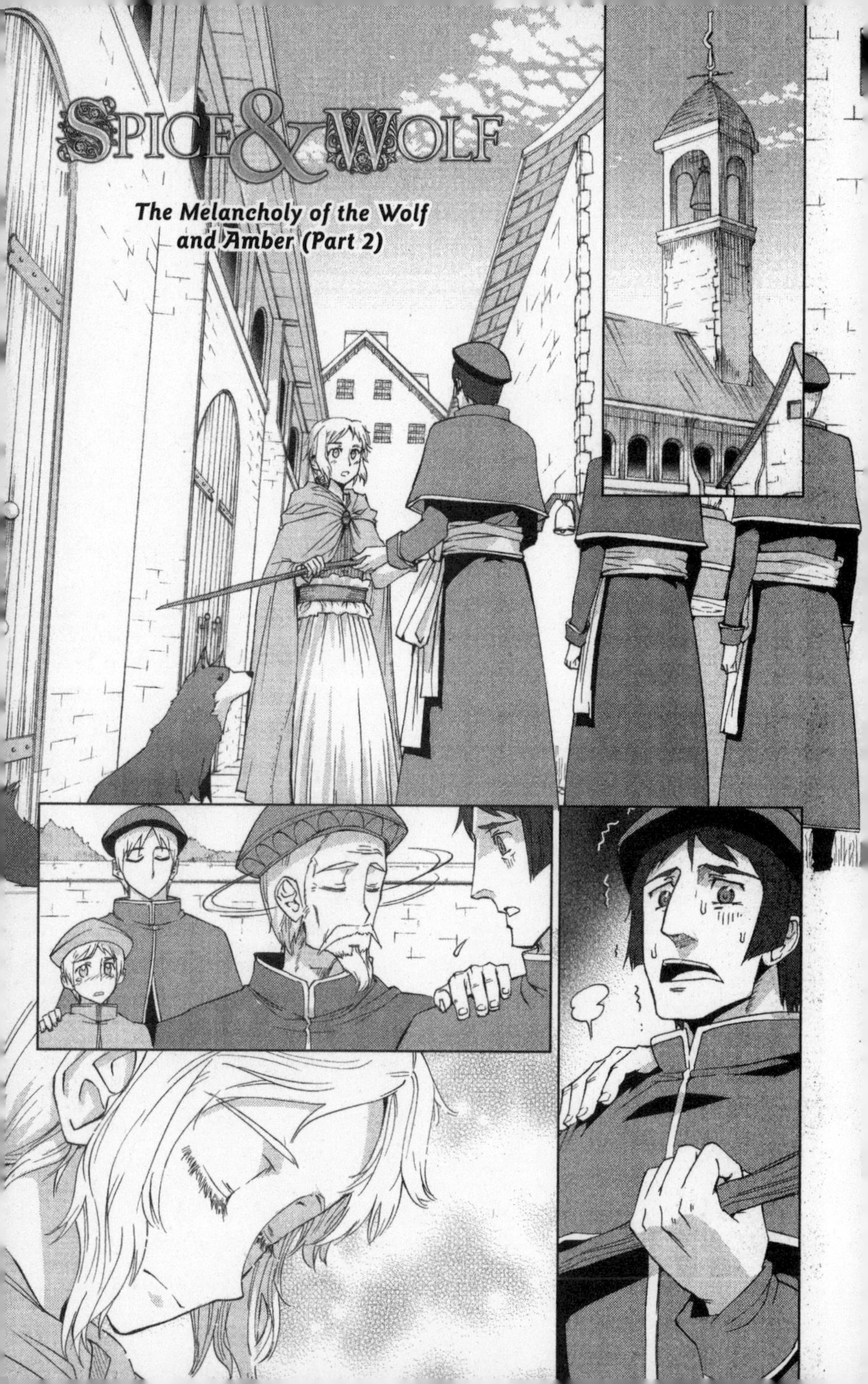
SPICE & WOLF
The Melancholy of the Wolf and Amber (Part 2)

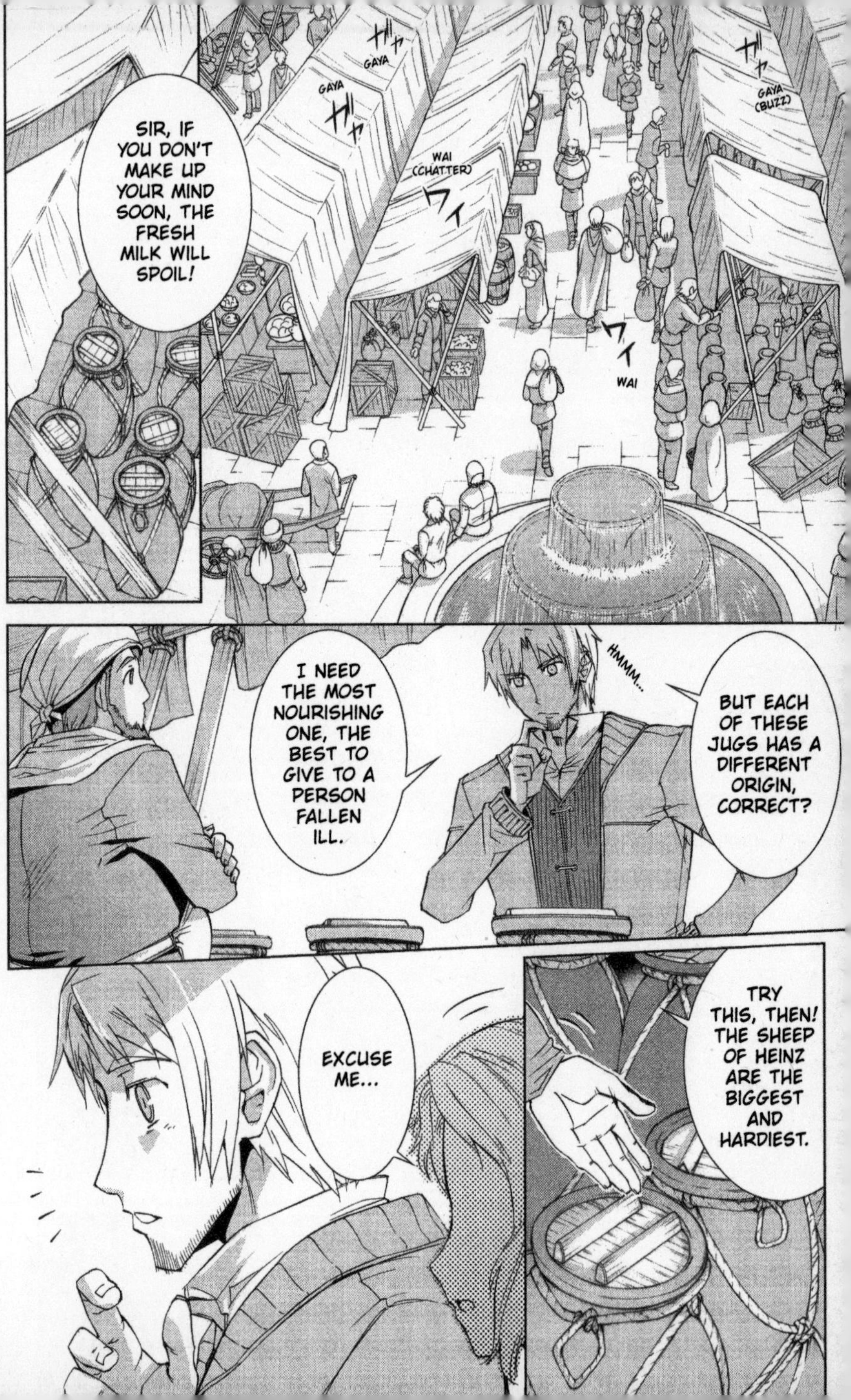

ガヤ
GAYA (BUZZ)
ガヤ
GAYA
ガヤ
GAYA
ワイ
WAI (CHATTER)
ワイ
WAI
SIR, IF YOU DON'T MAKE UP YOUR MIND SOON, THE FRESH MILK WILL SPOIL!
BUT EACH OF THESE JUGS HAS A DIFFERENT ORIGIN, CORRECT?
HMMM...
I NEED THE MOST NOURISHING ONE, THE BEST TO GIVE TO A PERSON FALLEN ILL.
TRY THIS, THEN! THE SHEEP OF HEINZ ARE THE BIGGEST AND HARDIEST.
EXCUSE ME...

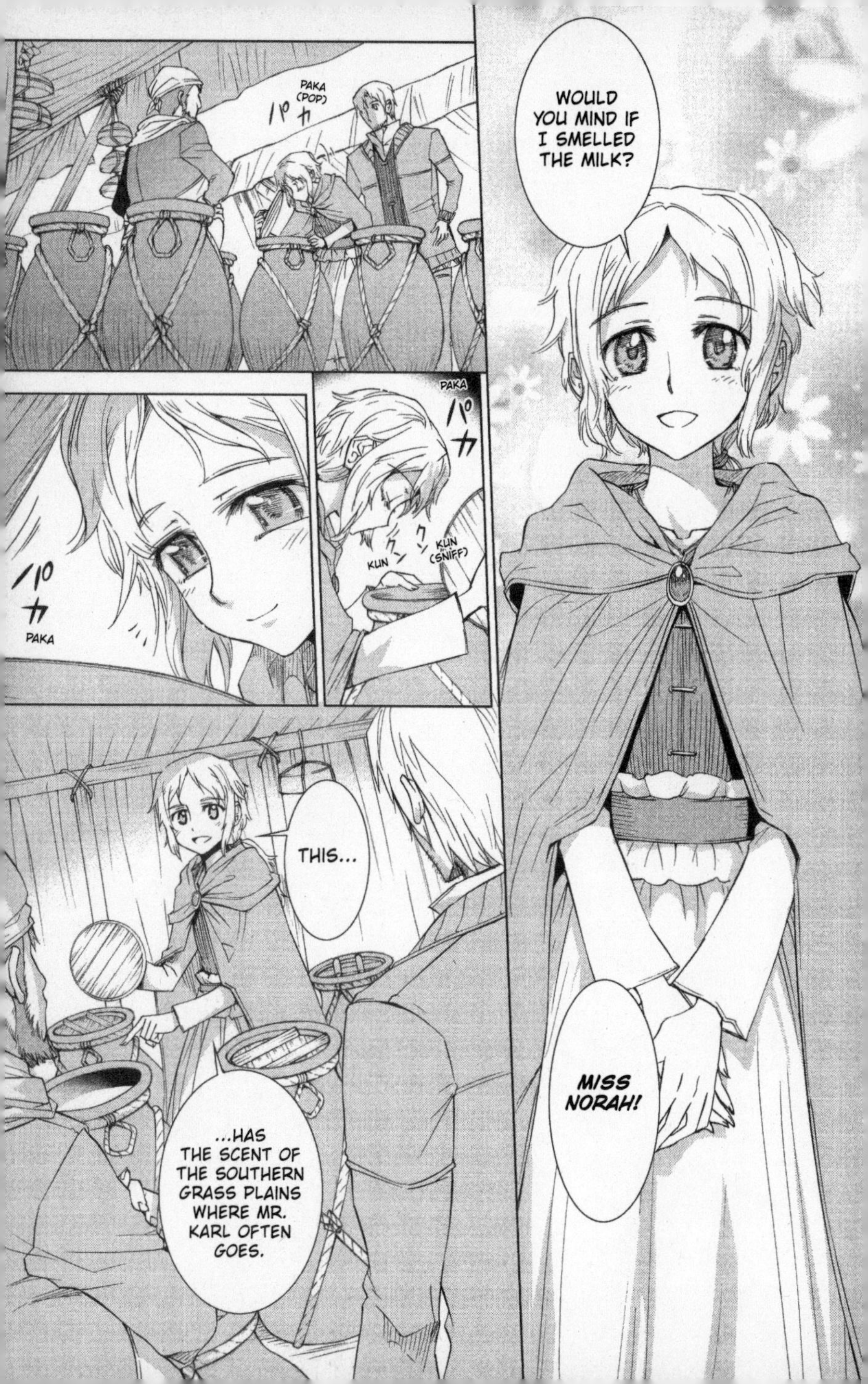
WOULD YOU MIND IF I SMELLED THE MILK?
MISS NORAH!
パカ
PAKA (POP)
パカ
PAKA
クン
KUN (SNIFF)
クン
KUN
パカ
PAKA
THIS...
...HAS THE SCENT OF THE SOUTHERN GRASS PLAINS WHERE MR. KARL OFTEN GOES.

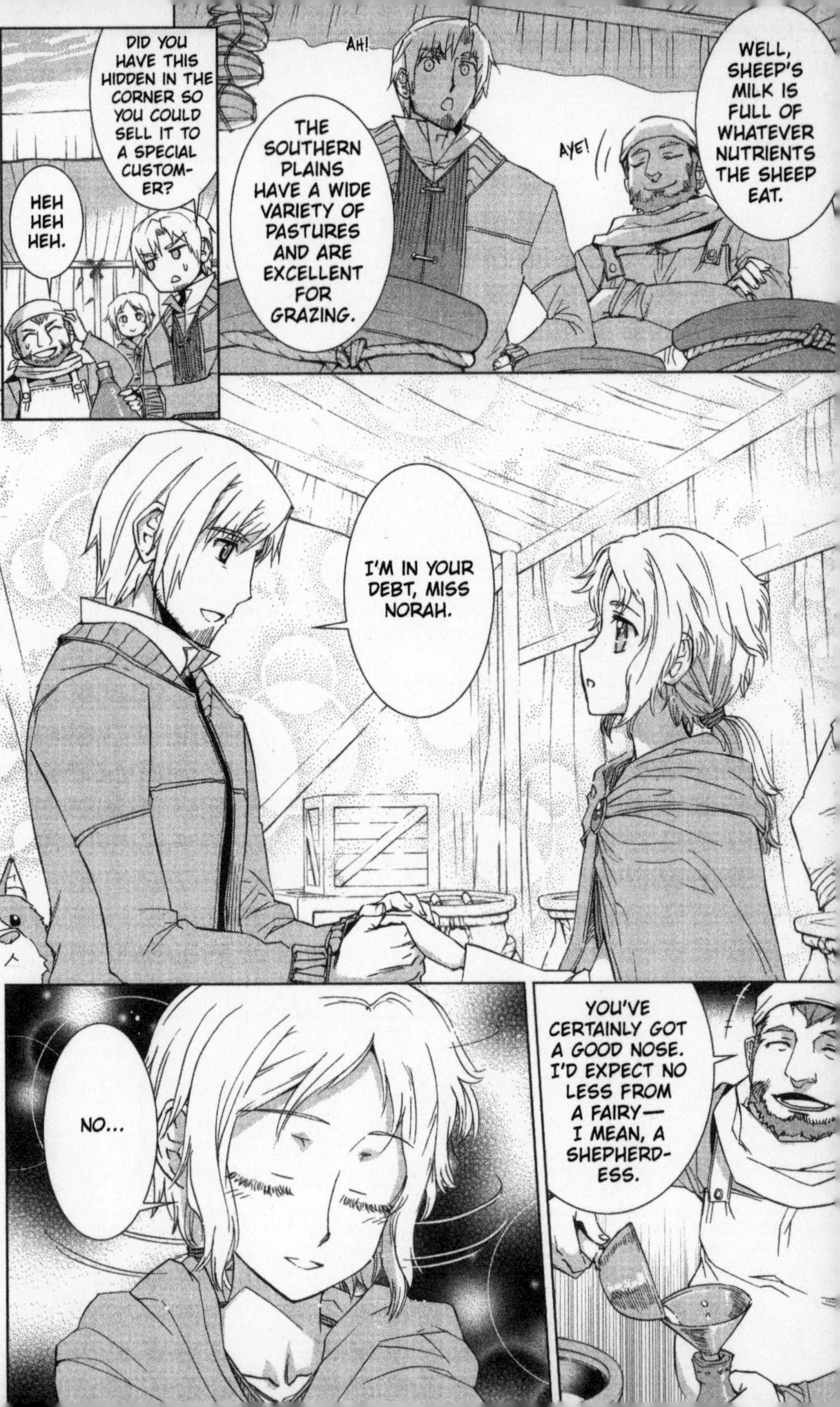
WELL, SHEEP'S MILK IS FULL OF WHATEVER NUTRIENTS THE SHEEP EAT.
AYE!
AH!
THE SOUTHERN PLAINS HAVE A WIDE VARIETY OF PASTURES AND ARE EXCELLENT FOR GRAZING.
DID YOU HAVE THIS HIDDEN IN THE CORNER SO YOU COULD SELL IT TO A SPECIAL CUSTOM-ER?
HEH HEH HEH.
I'M IN YOUR DEBT, MISS NORAH.
YOU'VE CERTAINLY GOT A GOOD NOSE. I'D EXPECT NO LESS FROM A FAIRY— I MEAN, A SHEPHERD-ESS.
NO...

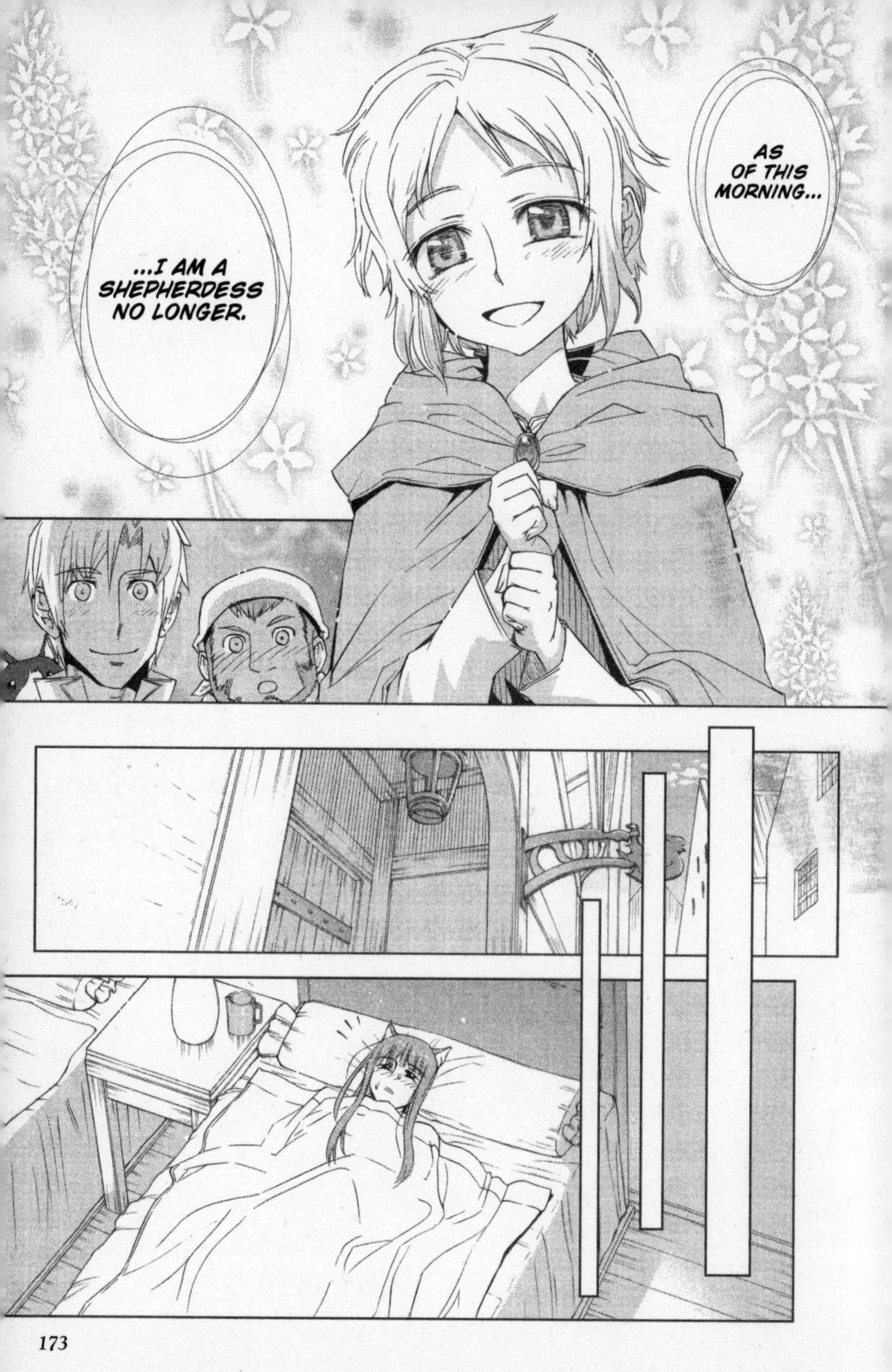
AS OF THIS MORNING...
...I AM A SHEPHERDESS NO LONGER.

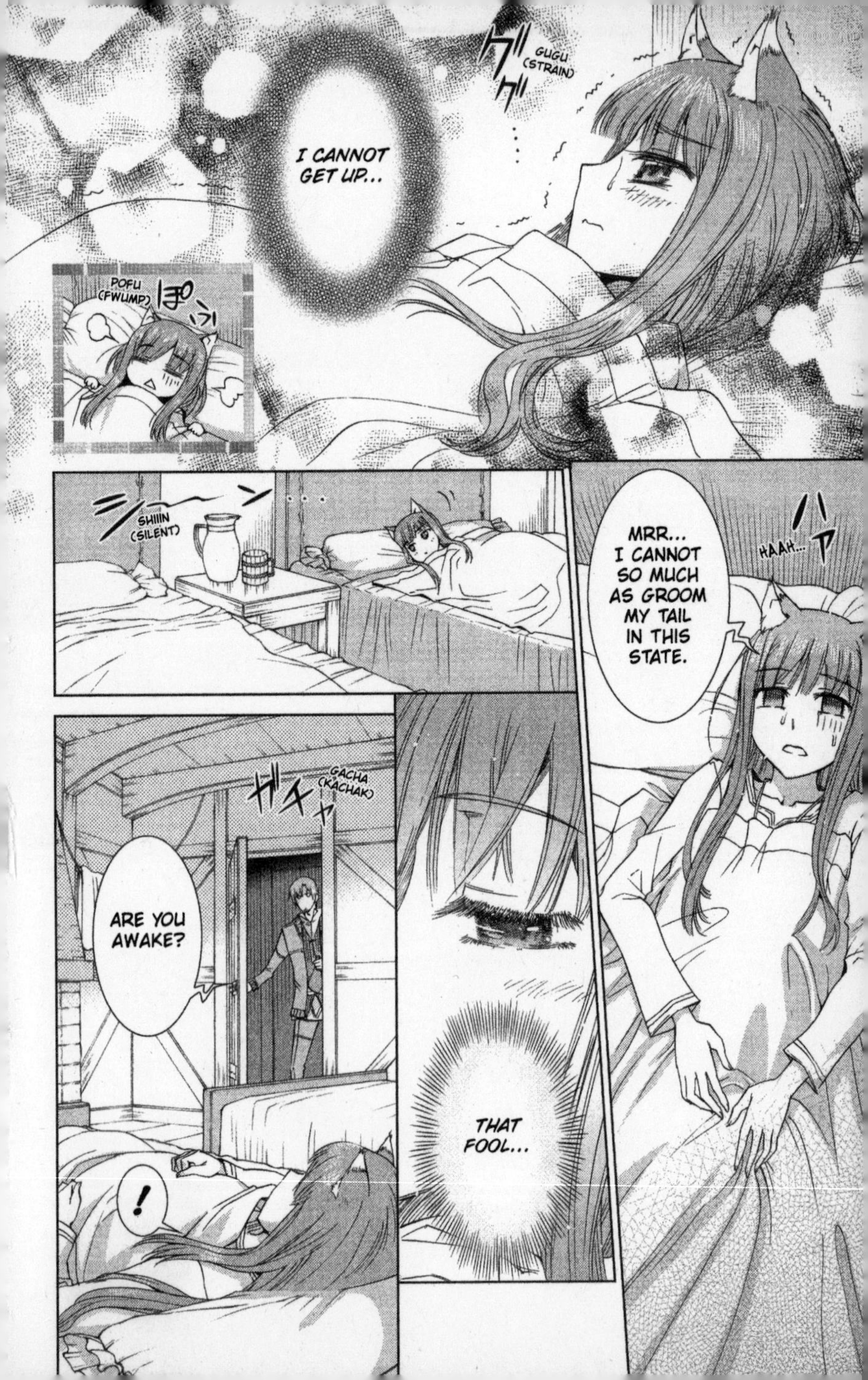
GUGU (STRAIN)
I CANNOT GET UP...
POFU (FWUMP)
MRR... I CANNOT SO MUCH AS GROOM MY TAIL IN THIS STATE.
HAAH...
SHIIIN (SILENT)
THAT FOOL...
GACHA (KACHAK)
ARE YOU AWAKE?
!

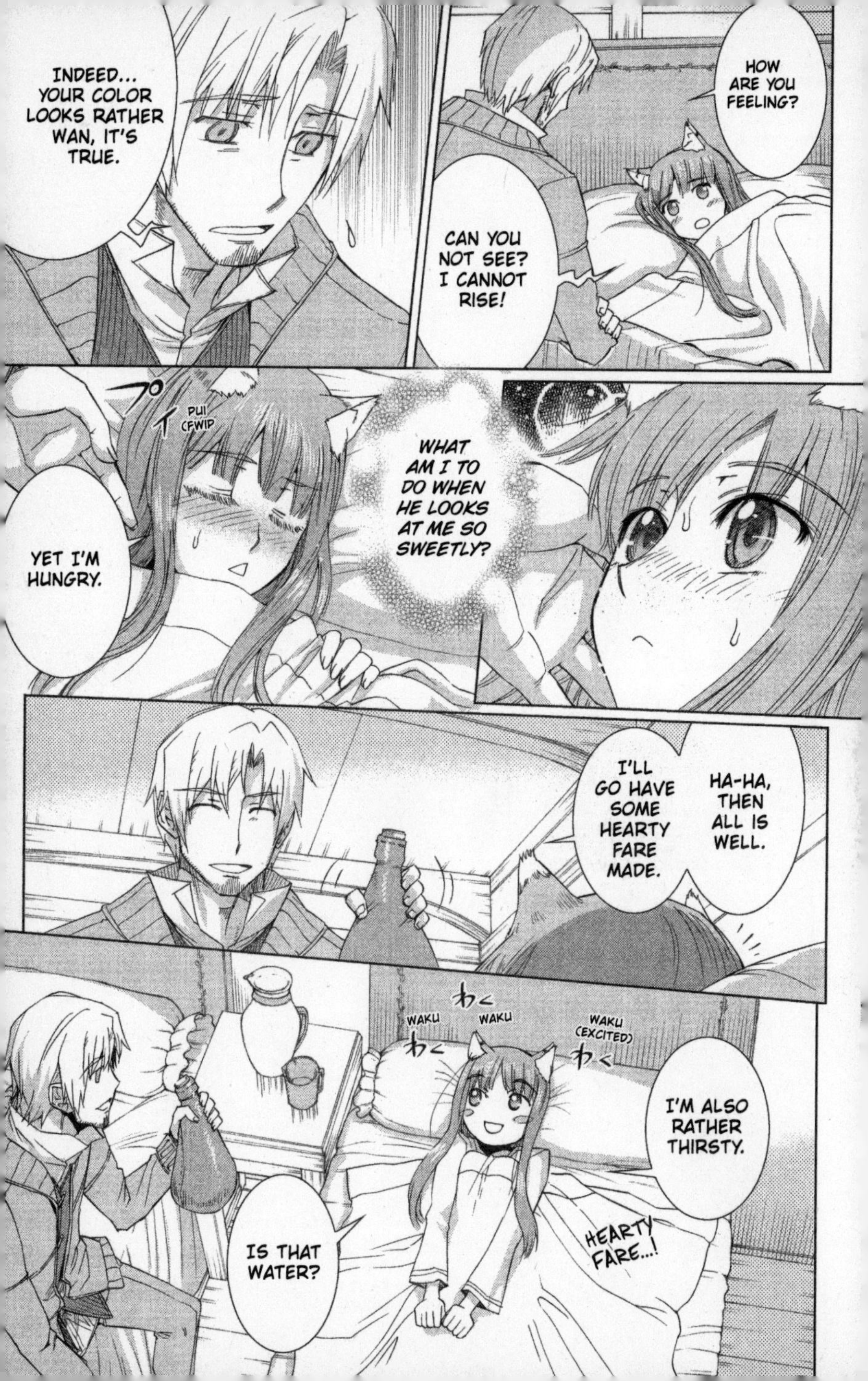
HOW ARE YOU FEELING?
CAN YOU NOT SEE? I CANNOT RISE!
INDEED... YOUR COLOR LOOKS RATHER WAN, IT'S TRUE.
WHAT AM I TO DO WHEN HE LOOKS AT ME SO SWEETLY?
PUI (FWIP
YET I'M HUNGRY.
HA-HA, THEN ALL IS WELL.
I'LL GO HAVE SOME HEARTY FARE MADE.
WAKU
WAKU
WAKU (EXCITED)
I'M ALSO RATHER THIRSTY.
HEARTY FARE...!
IS THAT WATER?

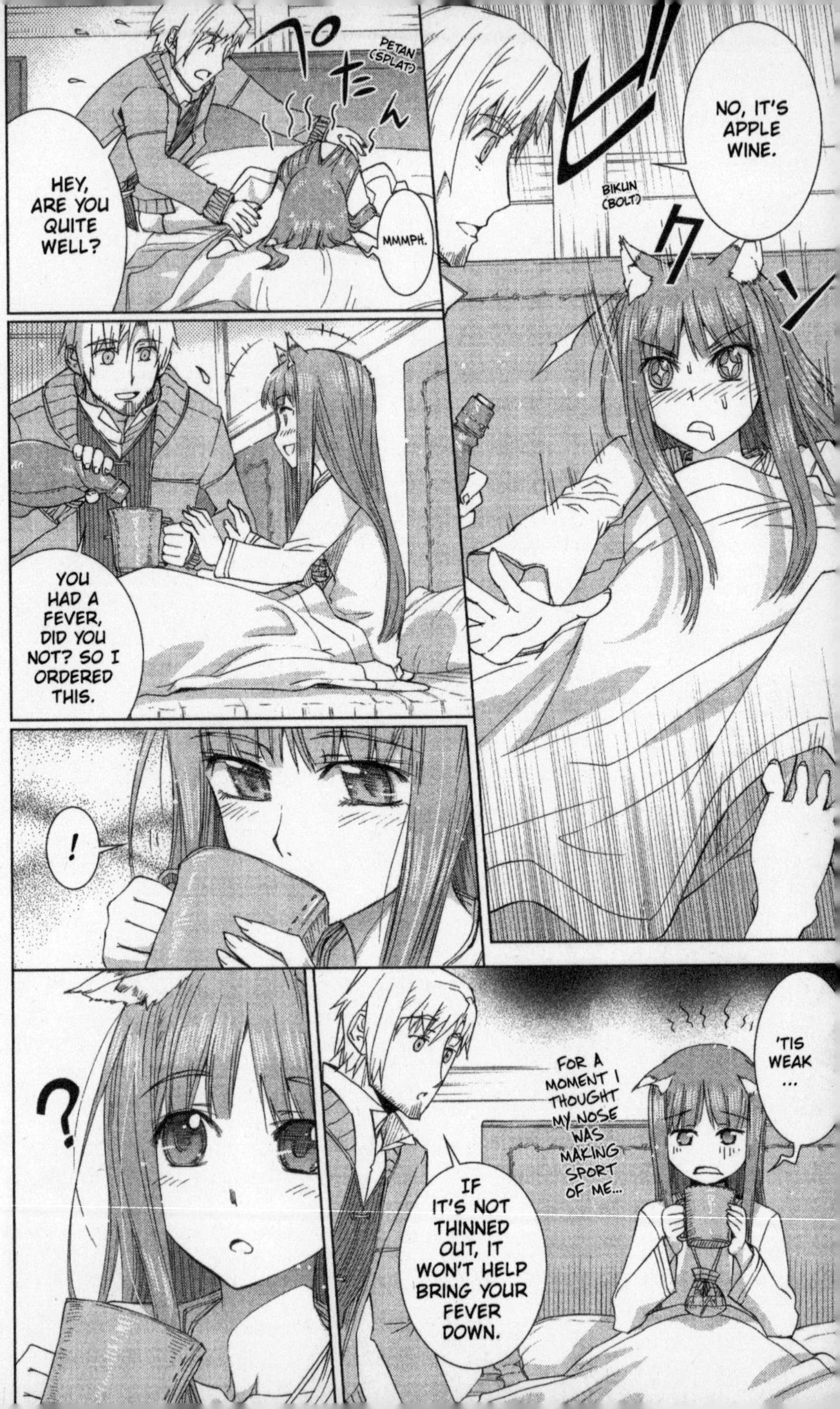

ビクン
BIKUN (BOLT)
NO, IT'S APPLE WINE.
ぺたん
PETAN (SPLAT)
MMMPH.
HEY, ARE YOU QUITE WELL?
YOU HAD A FEVER, DID YOU NOT? SO I ORDERED THIS.
!
'TIS WEAK ...
FOR A MOMENT I THOUGHT MY NOSE WAS MAKING SPORT OF ME...
IF IT'S NOT THINNED OUT, IT WON'T HELP BRING YOUR FEVER DOWN.
?

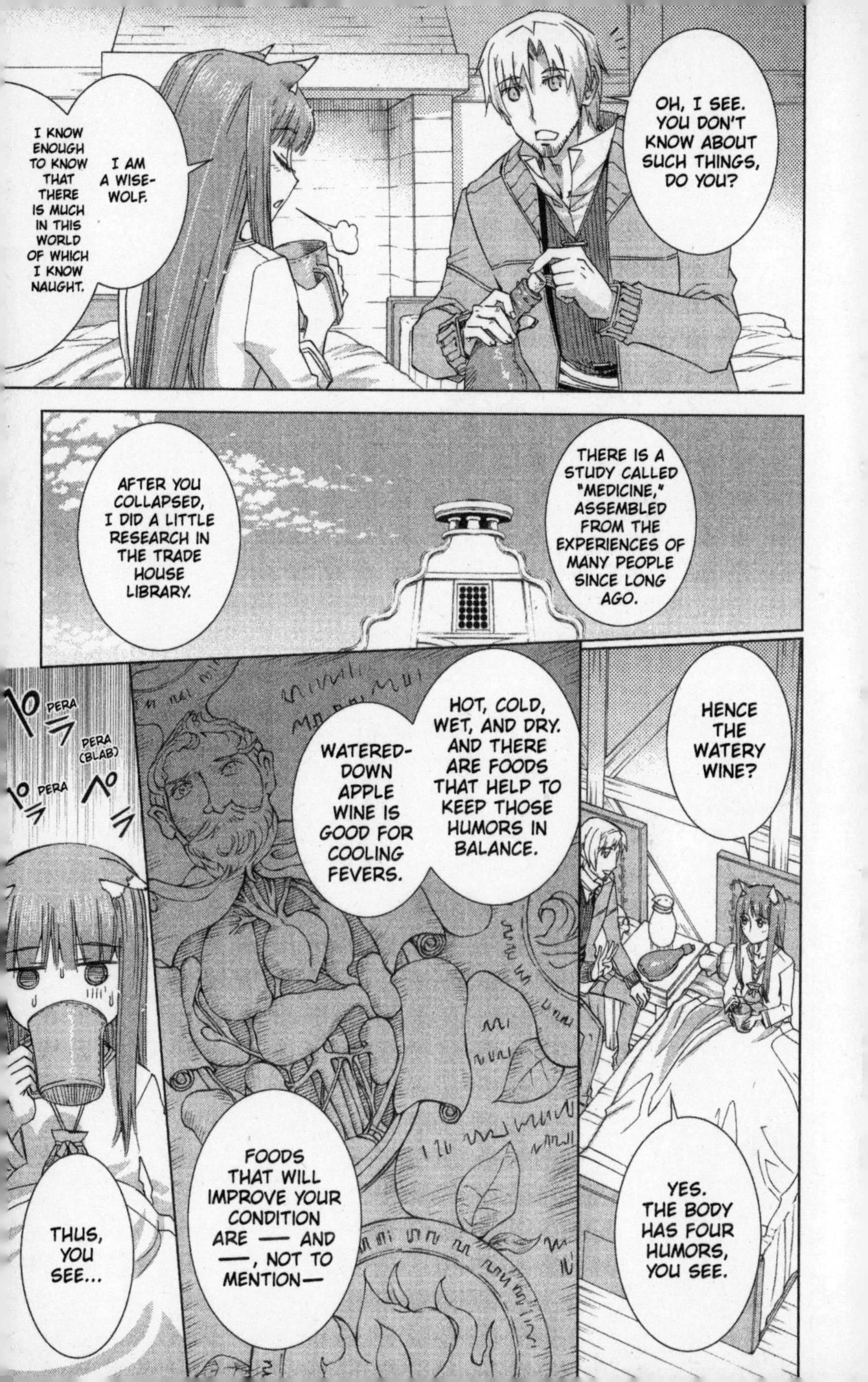
OH, I SEE. YOU DON'T KNOW ABOUT SUCH THINGS, DO YOU?
I AM A WISE-WOLF.
I KNOW ENOUGH TO KNOW THAT THERE IS MUCH IN THIS WORLD OF WHICH I KNOW NAUGHT.
THERE IS A STUDY CALLED "MEDICINE," ASSEMBLED FROM THE EXPERIENCES OF MANY PEOPLE SINCE LONG AGO.
AFTER YOU COLLAPSED, I DID A LITTLE RESEARCH IN THE TRADE HOUSE LIBRARY.
HENCE THE WATERY WINE?
YES. THE BODY HAS FOUR HUMORS, YOU SEE.
HOT, COLD, WET, AND DRY. AND THERE ARE FOODS THAT HELP TO KEEP THOSE HUMORS IN BALANCE.
WATERED-DOWN APPLE WINE IS GOOD FOR COOLING FEVERS.
FOODS THAT WILL IMPROVE YOUR CONDITION ARE — AND —, NOT TO MENTION—
PERA
PERA (BLAB)
PERA
THUS, YOU SEE...

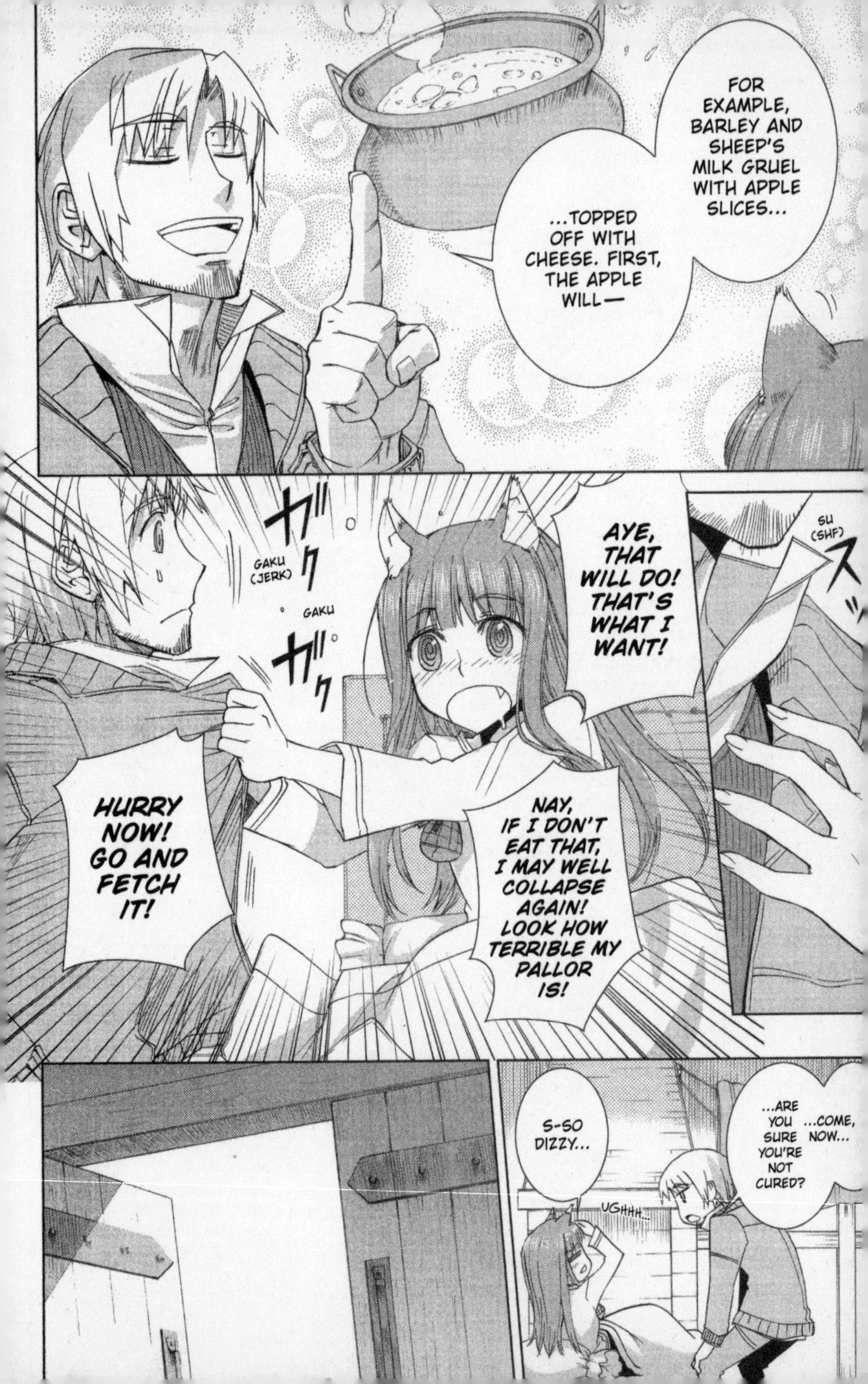
FOR EXAMPLE, BARLEY AND SHEEP'S MILK GRUEL WITH APPLE SLICES...
...TOPPED OFF WITH CHEESE. FIRST, THE APPLE WILL—
SU (SHF)
AYE, THAT WILL DO! THAT'S WHAT I WANT!
GAKU (JERK)
GAKU
NAY, IF I DON'T EAT THAT, I MAY WELL COLLAPSE AGAIN! LOOK HOW TERRIBLE MY PALLOR IS!
HURRY NOW! GO AND FETCH IT!
...COME, NOW...
...ARE YOU SURE YOU'RE NOT CURED?
S-SO DIZZY...
UGHHH...

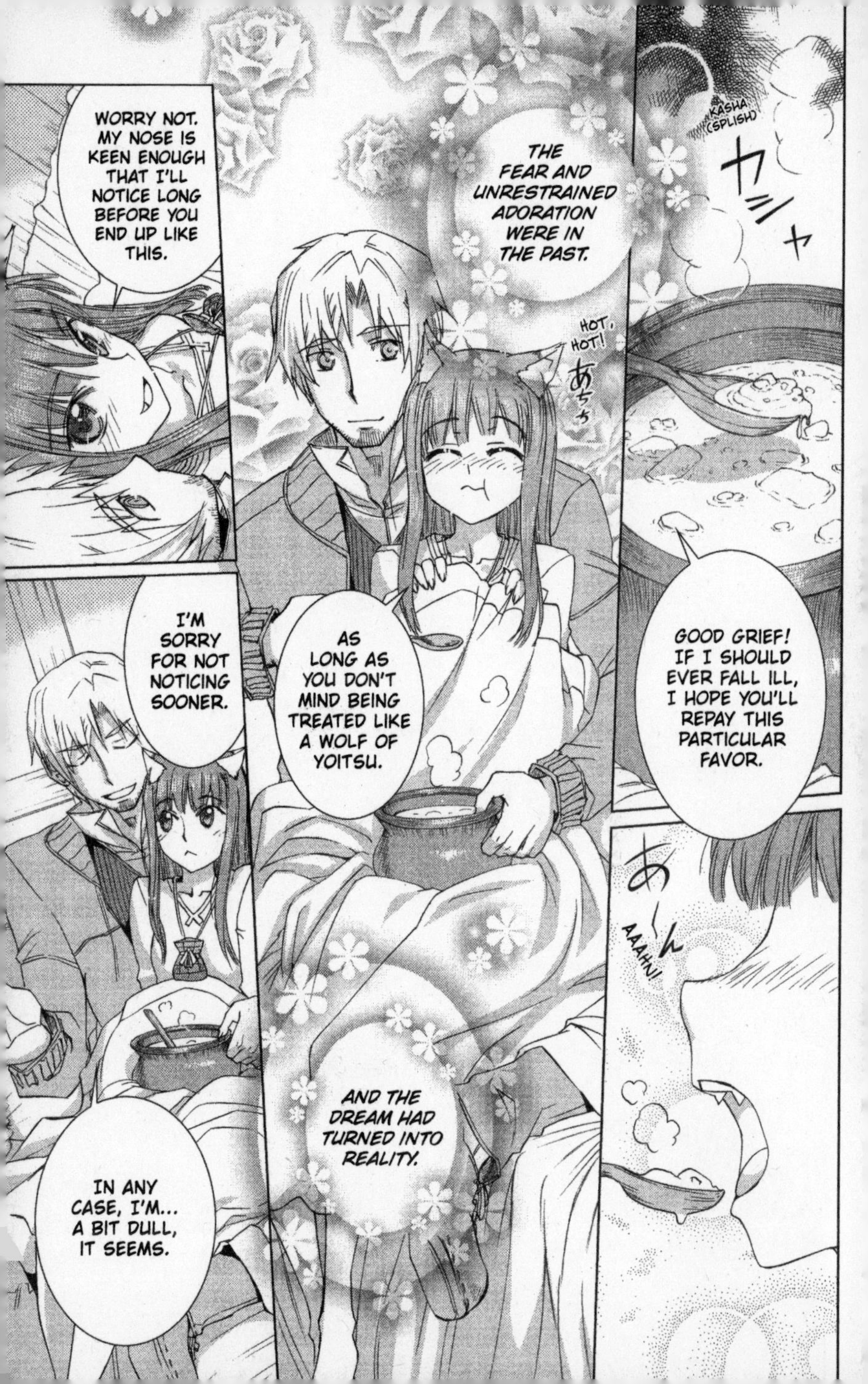
カシャ
KASHA (SPLISH)
GOOD GRIEF! IF I SHOULD EVER FALL ILL, I HOPE YOU'LL REPAY THIS PARTICULAR FAVOR.
あ～ん
AAAHN!
THE FEAR AND UNRESTRAINED ADORATION WERE IN THE PAST.
あちち
HOT, HOT!
AS LONG AS YOU DON'T MIND BEING TREATED LIKE A WOLF OF YOITSU.
AND THE DREAM HAD TURNED INTO REALITY.
WORRY NOT. MY NOSE IS KEEN ENOUGH THAT I'LL NOTICE LONG BEFORE YOU END UP LIKE THIS.
I'M SORRY FOR NOT NOTICING SOONER.
IN ANY CASE, I'M... A BIT DULL, IT SEEMS.

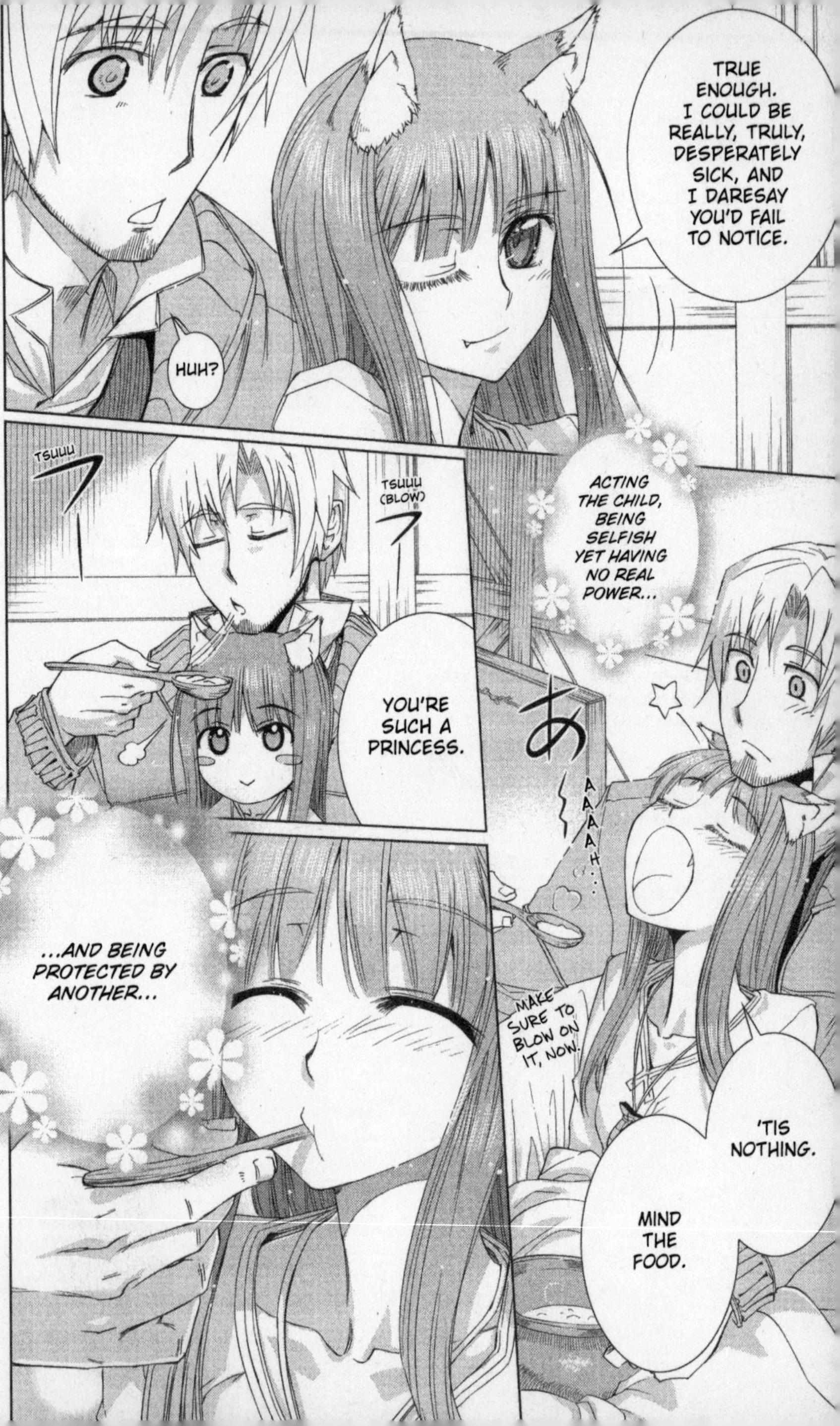
TRUE ENOUGH. I COULD BE REALLY, TRULY, DESPERATELY SICK, AND I DARESAY YOU'D FAIL TO NOTICE.
HUH?
ACTING THE CHILD, BEING SELFISH YET HAVING NO REAL POWER...
あ
AAAAH...
MAKE SURE TO BLOW ON IT, NOW.
'TIS NOTHING.
MIND THE FOOD.
TSUUU (BLOW)
TSUUU
YOU'RE SUCH A PRINCESS.
...AND BEING PROTECTED BY ANOTHER...

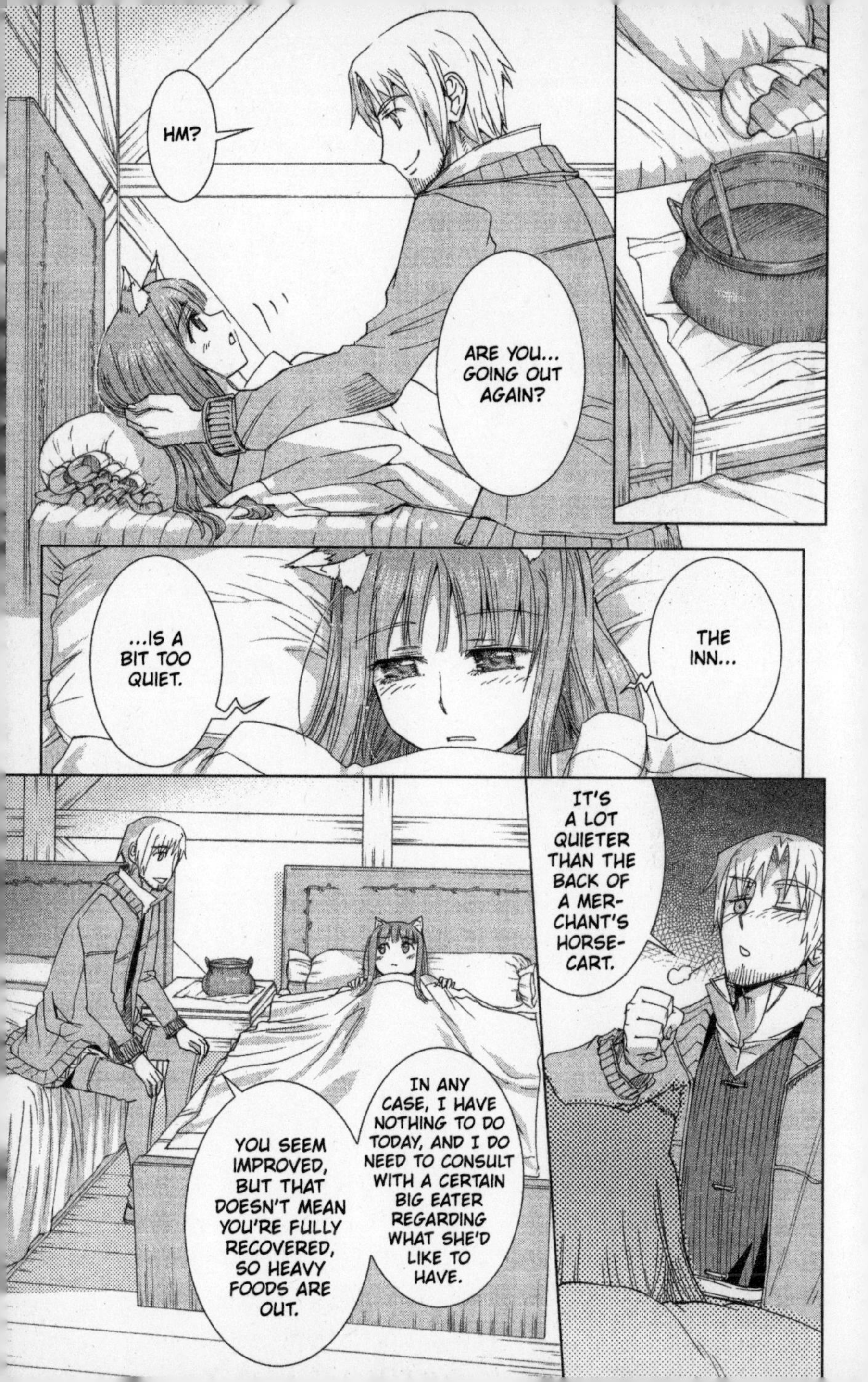
HM?
ARE YOU... GOING OUT AGAIN?
THE INN...
...IS A BIT TOO QUIET.
IT'S A LOT QUIETER THAN THE BACK OF A MER-CHANT'S HORSE-CART.
IN ANY CASE, I HAVE NOTHING TO DO TODAY, AND I DO NEED TO CONSULT WITH A CERTAIN BIG EATER REGARDING WHAT SHE'D LIKE TO HAVE.
YOU SEEM IMPROVED, BUT THAT DOESN'T MEAN YOU'RE FULLY RECOVERED, SO HEAVY FOODS ARE OUT.

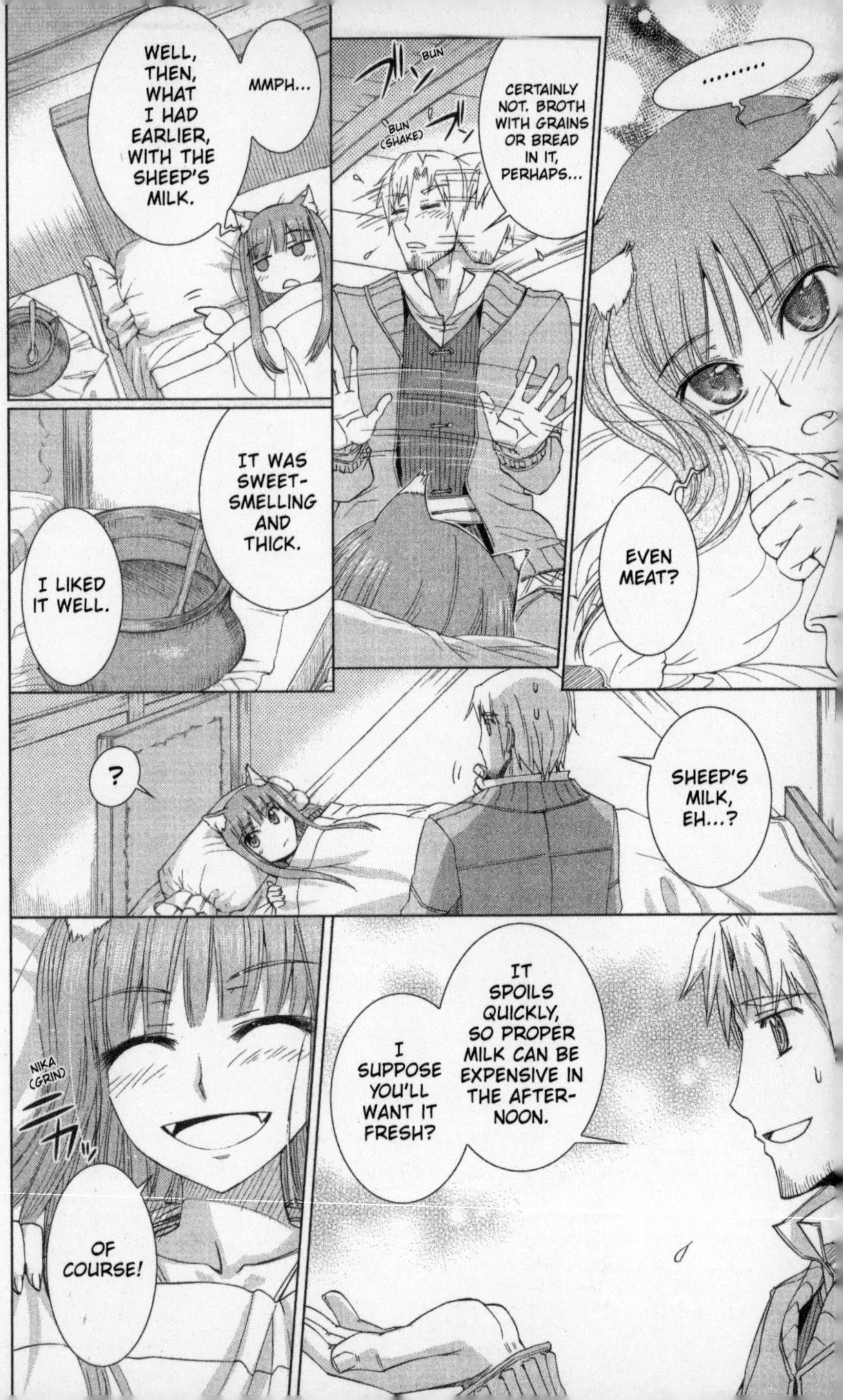
....
EVEN MEAT?
BUN
BUN (SHAKE)
CERTAINLY NOT. BROTH WITH GRAINS OR BREAD IN IT, PERHAPS...
MMPH...
WELL, THEN, WHAT I HAD EARLIER, WITH THE SHEEP'S MILK.
IT WAS SWEET-SMELLING AND THICK.
I LIKED IT WELL.
SHEEP'S MILK, EH...?
?
IT SPOILS QUICKLY, SO PROPER MILK CAN BE EXPENSIVE IN THE AFTER-NOON.
I SUPPOSE YOU'LL WANT IT FRESH?
NIKA (GRIND)
OF COURSE!

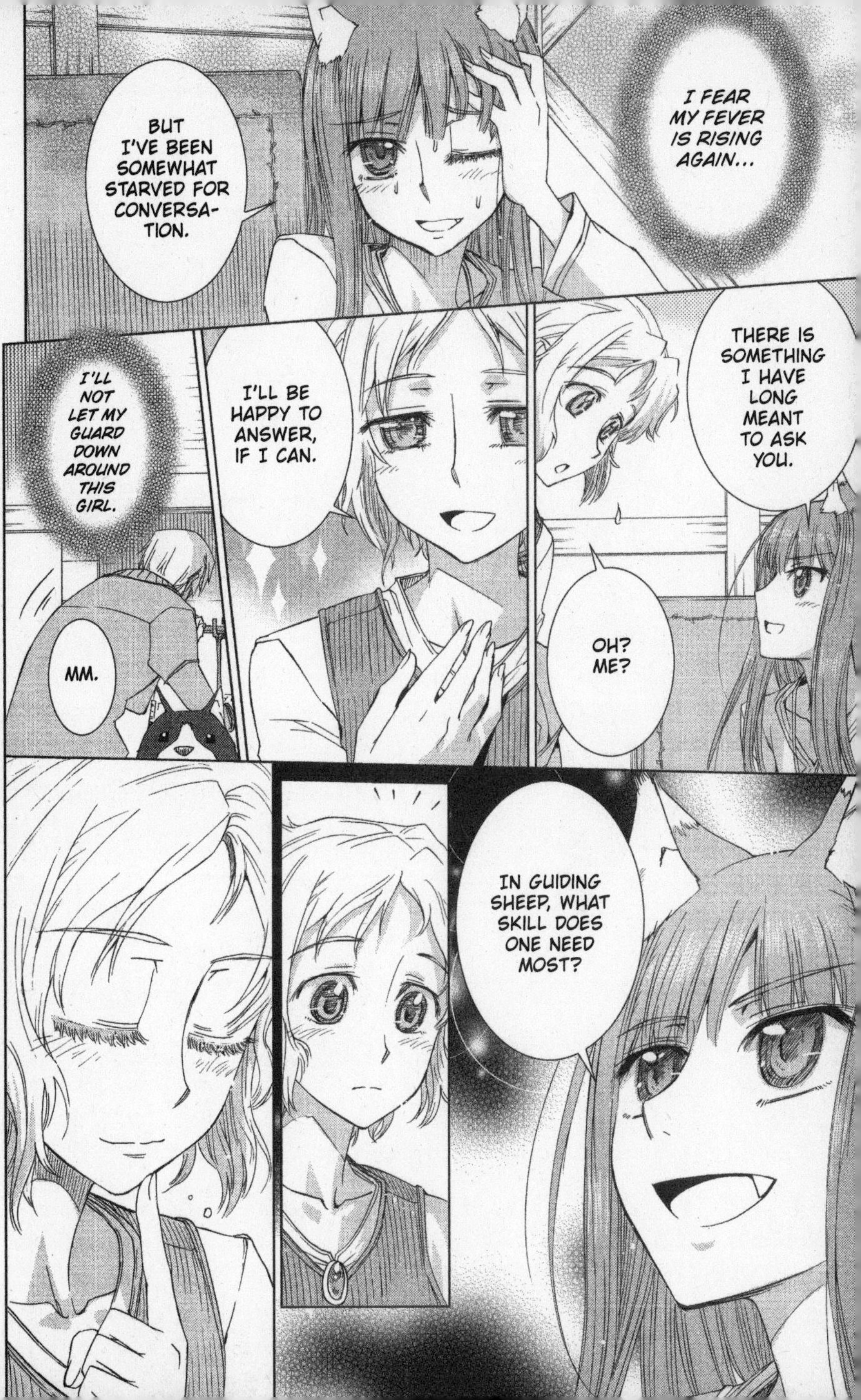
I FEAR MY FEVER IS RISING AGAIN...
BUT I'VE BEEN SOMEWHAT STARVED FOR CONVERSATION.
THERE IS SOMETHING I HAVE LONG MEANT TO ASK YOU.
OH? ME?
I'LL BE HAPPY TO ANSWER, IF I CAN.
I'LL NOT LET MY GUARD DOWN AROUND THIS GIRL.
MM.
IN GUIDING SHEEP, WHAT SKILL DOES ONE NEED MOST?

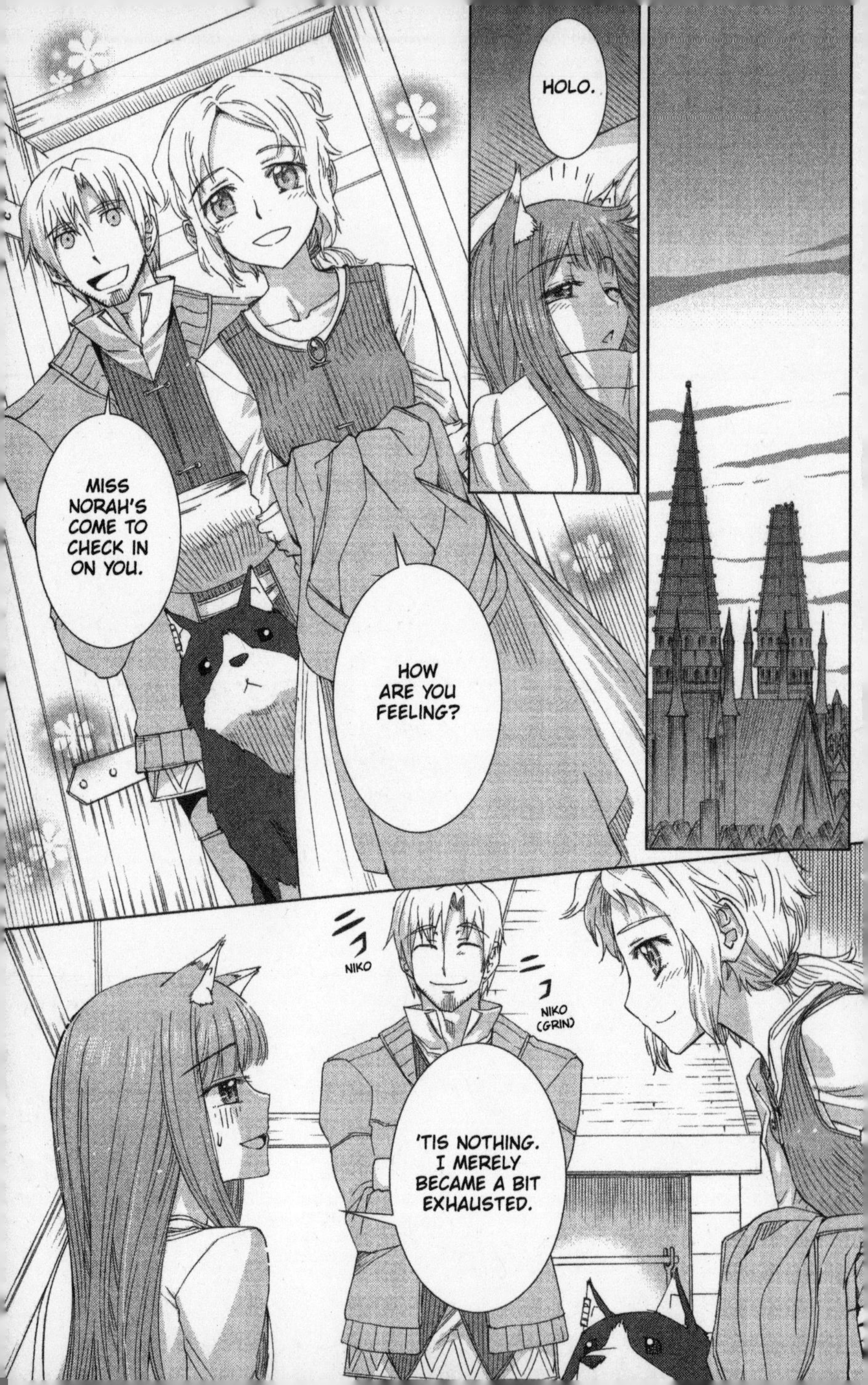
HOLO.
MISS NORAH'S COME TO CHECK IN ON YOU.
HOW ARE YOU FEELING?
NIKO (GRIN)
NIKO
'TIS NOTHING. I MERELY BECAME A BIT EXHAUSTED.

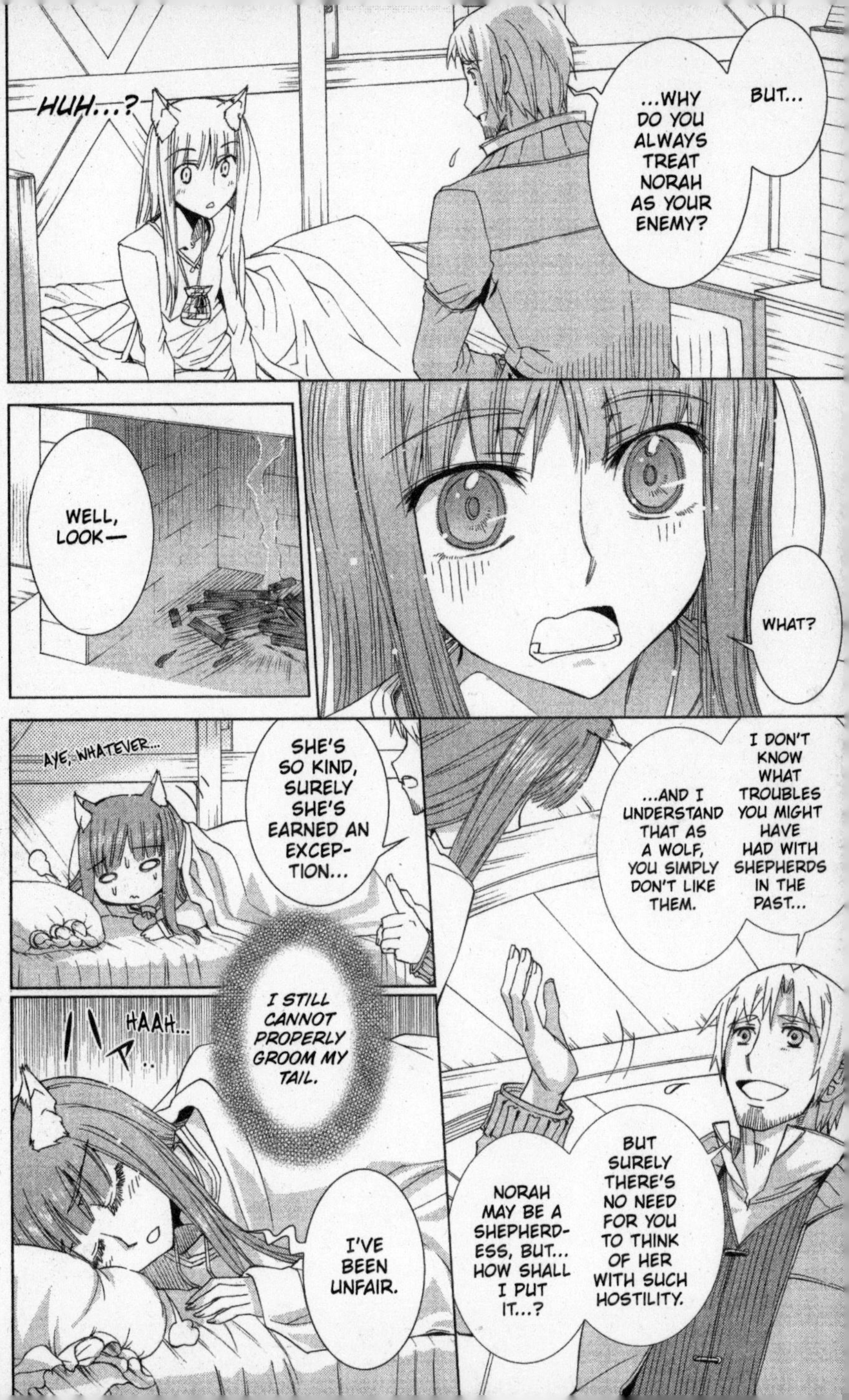
BUT...
...WHY DO YOU ALWAYS TREAT NORAH AS YOUR ENEMY?
HUH...?
WHAT?
WELL, LOOK—
I DON'T KNOW WHAT TROUBLES YOU MIGHT HAVE HAD WITH SHEPHERDS IN THE PAST...
...AND I UNDERSTAND THAT AS A WOLF, YOU SIMPLY DON'T LIKE THEM.
BUT SURELY THERE'S NO NEED FOR YOU TO THINK OF HER WITH SUCH HOSTILITY.
NORAH MAY BE A SHEPHERD-ESS, BUT... HOW SHALL I PUT IT...?
SHE'S SO KIND, SURELY SHE'S EARNED AN EXCEP-TION...
AYE, WHATEVER...
I STILL CANNOT PROPERLY GROOM MY TAIL.
HAAH...
I'VE BEEN UNFAIR.

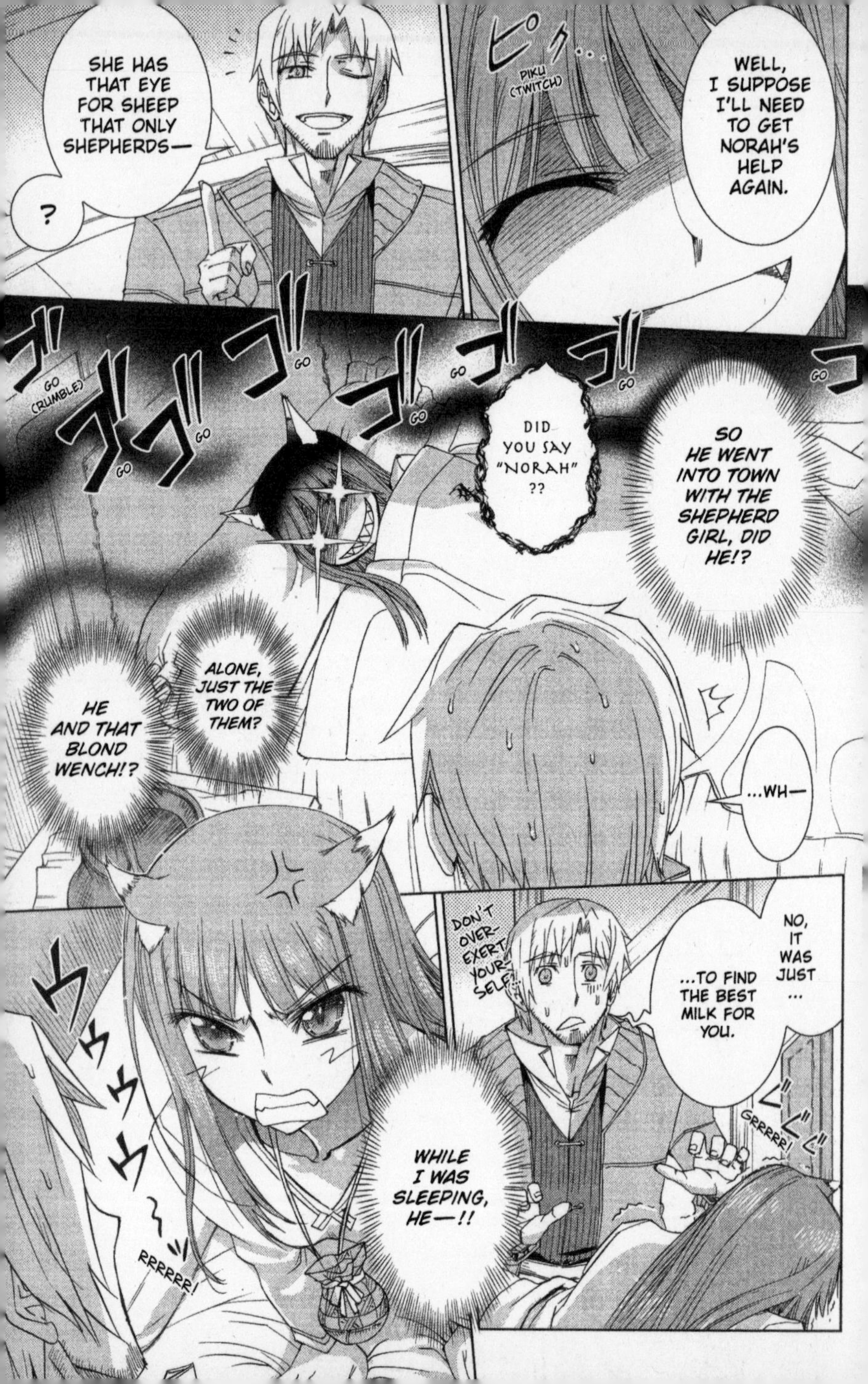
PIKU (TWITCH)
WELL, I SUPPOSE I'LL NEED TO GET NORAH'S HELP AGAIN.
SHE HAS THAT EYE FOR SHEEP THAT ONLY SHEPHERDS—
?
GO GO GO GO GO GO GO GO (RUMBLE)
SO HE WENT INTO TOWN WITH THE SHEPHERD GIRL, DID HE!?
DID YOU SAY "NORAH"??
...WH—
ALONE, JUST THE TWO OF THEM?
HE AND THAT BLOND WENCH!?
NO, IT WAS JUST ...
...TO FIND THE BEST MILK FOR YOU.
DON'T OVER-EXERT YOUR-SELF!
GRRRRR!
WHILE I WAS SLEEPING, HE—!!
RRRRRR!

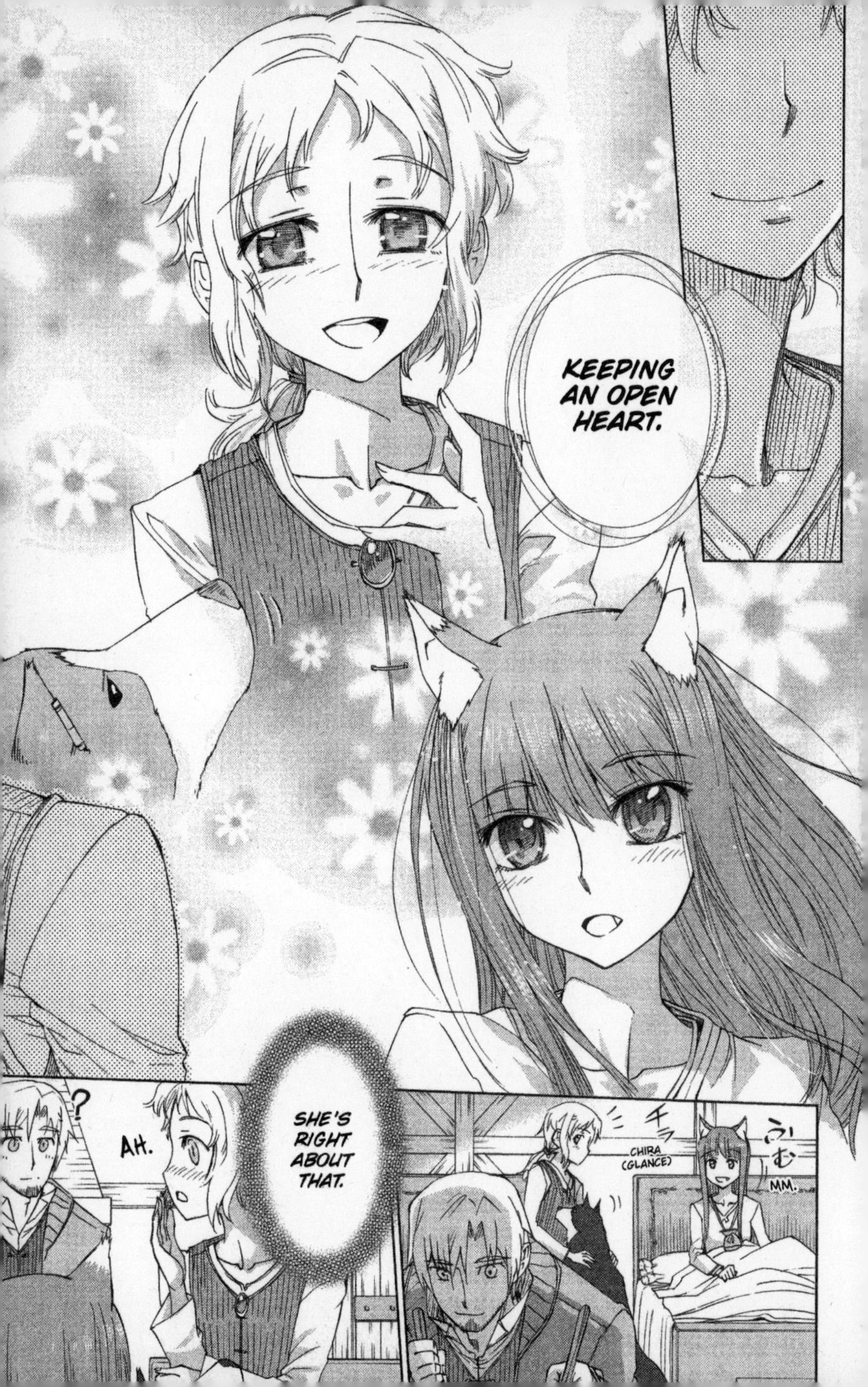
KEEPING AN OPEN HEART.
ふむ
MM.
チラ
CHIRA (GLANCE)
SHE'S RIGHT ABOUT THAT.
AH.
?

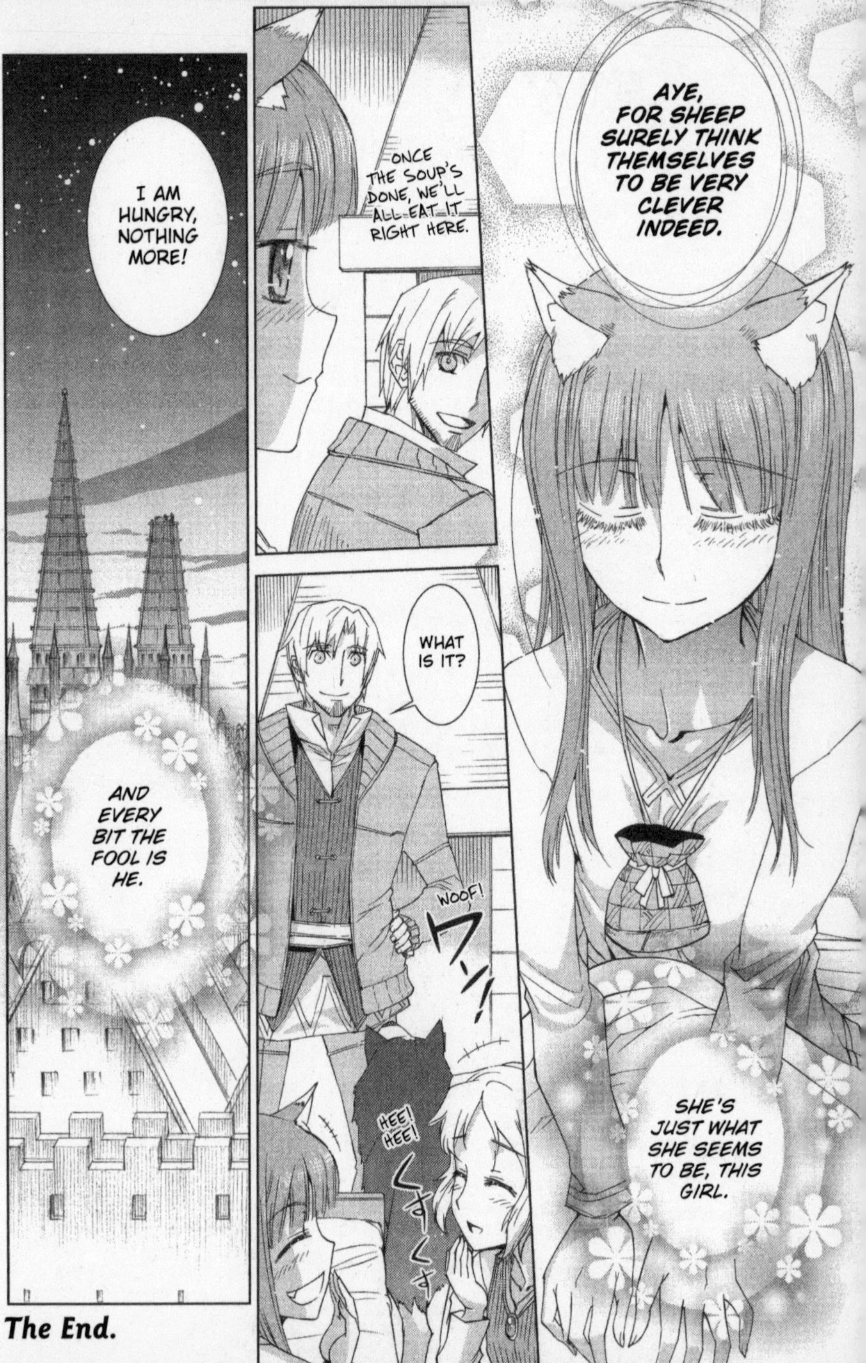
AYE, FOR SHEEP SURELY THINK THEMSELVES TO BE VERY CLEVER INDEED.
SHE'S JUST WHAT SHE SEEMS TO BE, THIS GIRL.
ONCE THE SOUP'S DONE, WE'LL ALL EAT IT RIGHT HERE.
WHAT IS IT?
WOOF!
HEE! HEE!
くすくす
I AM HUNGRY, NOTHING MORE!
AND EVERY BIT THE FOOL IS HE.

The End.

Congratulations on Volume 6!

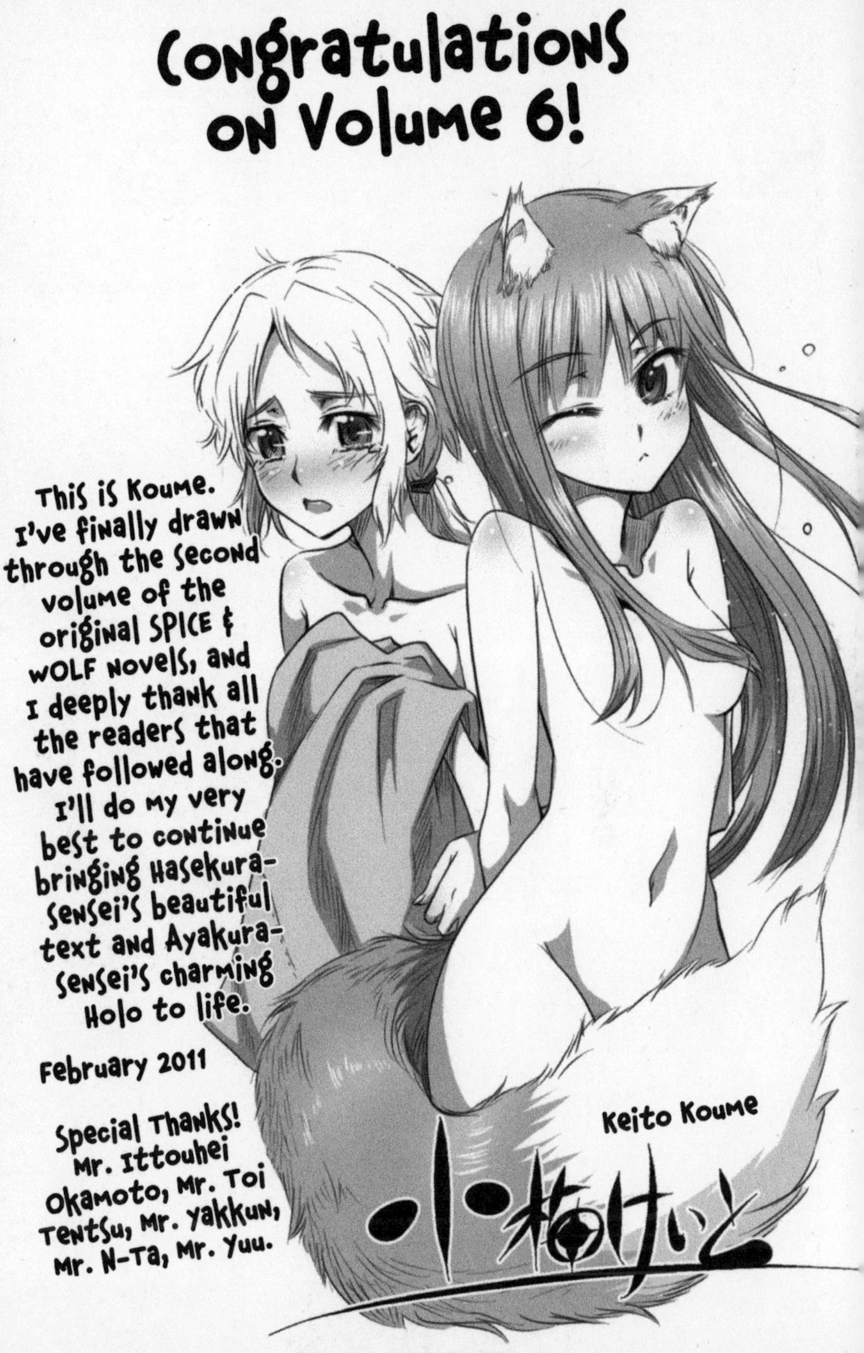
小梅けいと

This is Koume. I've finally drawn through the second volume of the original SPICE & WOLF novels, and I deeply thank all the readers that have followed along. I'll do my very best to continue bringing Hasekura-sensei's beautiful text and Ayakura-sensei's charming Holo to life.

February 2011

Keito Koume

Special Thanks!
Mr. Ittouhei Okamoto, Mr. Toi Tentsu, Mr. yakkun, Mr. N-Ta, Mr. Yuu.

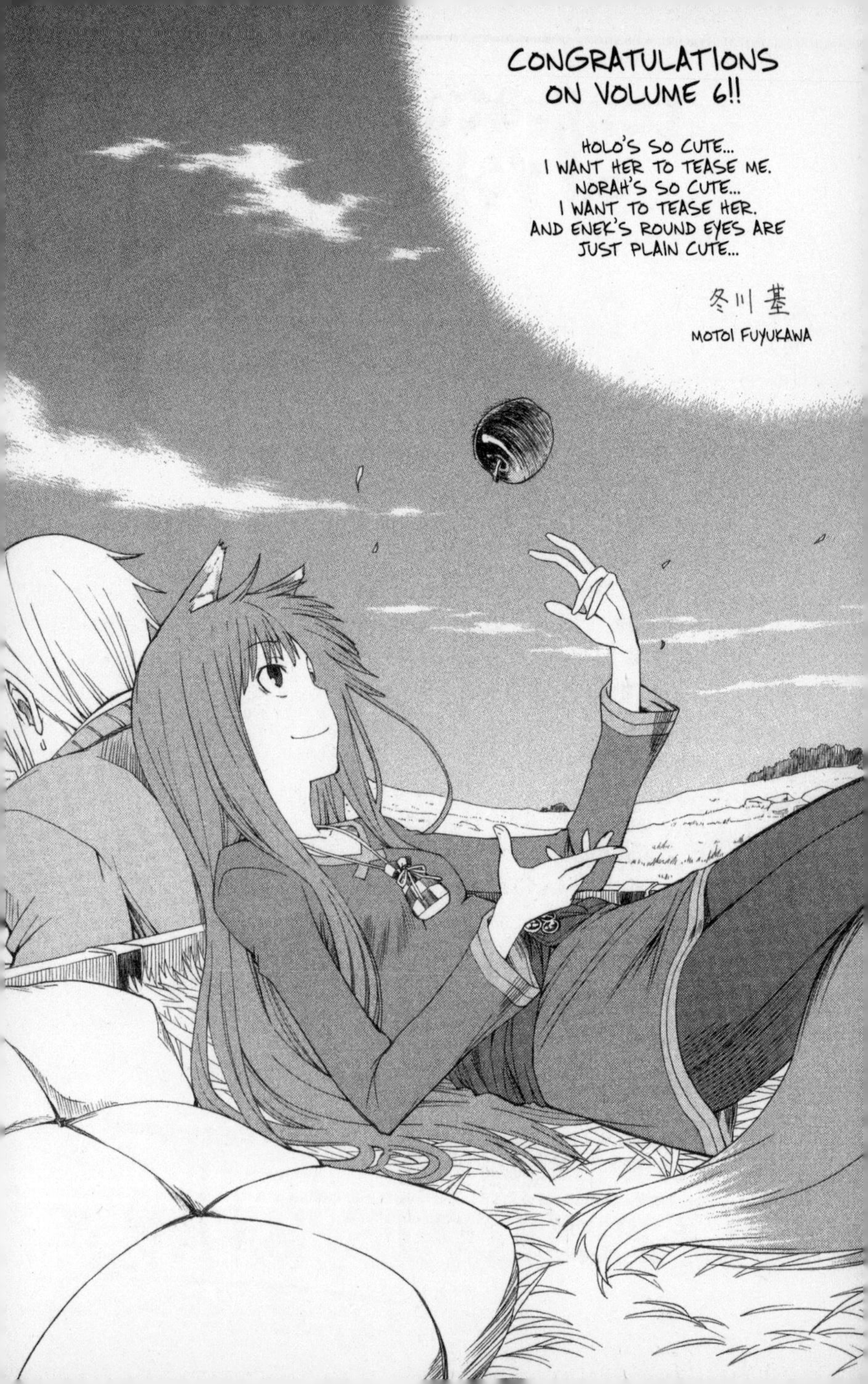
CONGRATULATIONS ON VOLUME 6!!
HOLO'S SO CUTE... I WANT HER TO TEASE ME. NORAH'S SO CUTE... I WANT TO TEASE HER. AND ENEK'S ROUND EYES ARE JUST PLAIN CUTE...
冬川基
MOTOI FUYUKAWA

SPICE & WOLF ❻

ISUNA HASEKURA
KEITO KOUME
CHARACTER DESIGN:
JYUU AYAKURA

TRANSLATION: PAUL STARR

LETTERING: TERRI DELGADO

OOKAMI TO KOUSHINRYOU VOL. 6
©ISUNA HASEKURA/KEITO KOUME 2010
EDITED BY ASCII MEDIA WORKS
FIRST PUBLISHED IN JAPAN IN 2010 BY
KADOKAWA CORPORATION, TOKYO.
ENGLISH TRANSLATION RIGHTS ARRANGED WITH
KADOKAWA CORPORATION, TOKYO,
THROUGH TUTTLE-MORI AGENCY, INC., TOKYO.

TRANSLATION © 2012 BY HACHETTE BOOK GROUP

YEN PRESS
HACHETTE BOOK GROUP
1290 AVENUE OF THE AMERICAS, NEW YORK, NY 10104

WWW.HACHETTEBOOKGROUP.COM
WWW.YENPRESS.COM

YEN PRESS IS AN IMPRINT OF HACHETTE BOOK GROUP, INC. THE YEN PRESS
NAME AND LOGO ARE TRADEMARKS OF HACHETTE BOOK GROUP, INC.

FIRST YEN PRESS EDITION: MARCH 2012

ISBN: 978-0-316-21032-4

10 9 8

BVG

PRINTED IN THE UNITED STATES OF AMERICA

Now we're up to Volume Six of the SPICE & WOLF manga that Koume-san has made into reality! As a creator and a fan, I can't wait to see what's next!

ISuna HaSekura

■ **CONGRATULATIONS ON VOLUME 6!** This volume brings us to the end of Volume 2 of the novel. The quality of the entire run has been wonderful, and I've been blown away all over again by both the Story and Koume-san's ability. I can't wait to see what comes next!

...Although I am really going to miss seeing Koume-san's Norah. I hope he puts her in some bonus material...or...something...

Jyuu Ayakura

ENEK, CAN'T YOU ASSUME HUMAN FORM TOO?

NOW SEE HERE, MISTRESS...